D1587001

Women's Suffrage in Shetland

Marsali Taylor

to dear Helen,
with love and best wishes for
the future, in God's time,
Marsali

Published by lulu.com

2010

Copyright Marsali Taylor 2010

All rights reserved.

ISBN 978-1-4461-0854-3

Women's Suffrage in Shetland

Marsali Taylor

(Above) Miss Daisy Campbell's NUWSS badge. Its actual size is 1.5cm in diameter, and it is in the red, green and white colours of the National Union of Women's Suffrage Societies.
Photograph courtesy of Douglas Smith.

Acknowledgements:

I have many people to thank for their help with the research for this book:

The National Library of Scotland, whose research week sparked all this off; Brian Smith, Blair Bruce, Mark Smith and particularly Angus Johnson of the Shetland Museum and Archives - goodness knows how many hours Angus saved me with his 'orange folder' of all the *Shetland Times* and *Shetland News* cuttings on the topic of suffrage from 1909 to 1918; David Murray, Assistant Archivist at Hocken Collections, Uare Takoa o Hakena, New Zealand; Kate Perry and Hannah Westall, College Archivists at Girton College, Cambridge, and the Mistress and Fellows of Girton College for their permission to reproduce photographs from the college collection; Nikki Brunton, archivist at the Museum of London, and the Museum of London for permission to reproduce photographs from their collection; Mari Takanayagi, archivist at the House of Commons; the Lothian Health Service Archives for the photograph of Dr Elsie Inglis; Iain Macmillan and the People's Story Museum, Edinburgh, for the photo of Chrystal Macmillan; Helen Clark, Museums of Edinburgh; Rose Piper; Moira Mackenzie, Special Collections, St Andrews; Lis Smith, Ph.D student, St Andrews; Jane Spall, Librarian at Aith JHS; Richard Durack, Archivist, Newham Heritage & Archives; Elizabeth Angus of the Shetland Family History Society; Tony Gott of Bayanne House, Yell; and all the archivists and custodians at museums which might have had our banner, or a copy of it.

Thank you to Douglas Smith and his friend John Manson, for all their help in identifying the women of the 1909 committee, one of whom was Douglas's aunt, Miss Campbell, and Douglas for more information about his mother, Jennie Campbell; Douglas Sinclair; Robert Wishart, Director of The Shetland Times Ltd, for permission to use extracts from the newspaper; Hilary Harmer, for permission to use extracts from *Lerwick during the Last Half-Century* by her grandfather, Thomas Manson; Peter Jamieson, great-nephew of Christina; John Durham, great-grandson of Harriet Leisk; Alec Sandison and Louis Mackay, great-grand nephews of Isabella Mill Sandison, and great-grandsons of Alexander Sandison; Martin Emmison, great-nephew of Ethel Moorhead; Mary Blance; Linda Riddell, for her information about the war years in Lerwick; Margaret Stuart, for her information about the Stout family; Betty Ferrie and John Smith for their information about their shared great-aunt/ great grand-aunt, Agnes Tait; Brian Williamson, through Sylvia Williamson, for the information about Brian's mother, Lottie Robertson; David Anderson, for information about Jessie Abernethy.

I would particularly like to thank Peter Jamieson, John Durham, Nikki Brunton, Hannah Westall, Louis Mackay, Douglas Smith, John Smith, Martin Emmison, John Smith, Helen Clark, Brian Williamson and Ian Tait & Jenny Murray of Shetland Museum and Archives for supplying me with the images used in this history.

Brian Smith very kindly read my first draft, and made a number of helpful suggestions and corrections.

Finally, my sincere thanks to all my family and friends who have learned more about women's suffrage than they wanted or needed to know.

This book is dedicated to my husband Philip, who has suffered in the cause of suffrage with exemplary patience.

Contents:

List of Illustrations:

Frontispiece Miss Campbell's NUWSS badge

Britain 1870:

Imagine a world where women did not have a voice. A middle- or upper-class daughter was expected to obey Mama and Papa, and focus on the important work of getting a suitable husband, with the help of some rudimentary education. Papa and his lawyers would make sure that her dowry was tied up for her – the only protection they could give, for once behind that marital door she stopped existing in civil law. Ordinary liberties of movement, of freedom from assault, of keeping her own earnings, didn't apply from wife to husband. Marital rape was not criminal, and wife-beating was accepted as normal, if it didn't go too far. Men naturally retained their own wages and took their wives' earnings. Divorce was only for a rich man to initiate, and a woman who left her home also left her belongings, her marriage settlement and her children, for a father was a child's natural guardian. If her husband wanted her back, she could be imprisoned for refusing to return.

Women were known to be hysterical, particularly at menstruation times, and the pain and danger of childbirth was felt to be sanctioned by the Bible. Women who bore a child outside wedlock were expected to name the father, but were rarely given maintenance, and as 'fallen women' generally had to resort to prostitution for an income. Women were considered responsible for straying husbands, for venereal disease, for the high rate of infant mortality.

Women were also known to be intellectually inferior. They were expected to stay in their sphere, at home; their brains were different to men's, so they could not understand politics and the importance of industry. They would not be able to organise an Empire, or send men to war. Respectable single ladies could be governesses, teachers or nurses, or they could drudge for other members of the family. Working class women slaved long hours, sewing shirts or making artificial flowers for starvation wages.

Worst of all, they had no power to change their lives. MPs were men; the voters they listened to were men. A widow could continue to run her husband's business, but although she paid his taxes, she didn't get to cast his vote. Women could not vote for town councillors; they could not volunteer to be members of a school board. They could not attend MPs' meetings of electors, for electors were male. They could not go to University. They could not study to be lawyers, and change the law in that way; they could not be doctors to try and alleviate the illnesses caused by the crowded slums of Victorian cities. They could not agitate for fresh water, dry housing, equal pay; they were not expected to agitate at all, for women making public speeches was unheard of.

The campaign for the vote was about changing all these things. It was a nationwide movement: from 1868 to 1918, women's suffrage meetings were held from Baltasound down to Land's End, in venues ranging from Manchester's Trade Hall to the open air of Lerwick's Market Cross. The shared fight cut across traditional class barriers: an Earl's sister spoke alongside middle-class teachers, fishwives from Newhaven and mill girls from Lancashire. A variety of suffrage newspapers discussed issues affecting women, and publicised Parliamentary debates. When the campaign escalated into militant action, Shetland women were directly connected with events in London: the first President of the 1909 society marched with Mrs Pankhurst, and the second was the wife of the Secretary for Scotland.

This is the story of these women who would not be silenced: who lobbied town councils, who organised fund-raising events and marched in processions, who made public speeches and sold newspapers to strangers; the women who became those first graduates; the women who forced their way into political meetings and were arrested for asking questions, then went on hunger strike to be accepted as political prisoners; the women who, when the men were sent to the trenches of World War I, took over the factories at home, and went with them abroad as nurses and ambulance drivers; the women who fought for all the freedom and legal protection that we take for granted today.

Why did women want the vote?

Journalist Frances Power Cobbe published *Why Women desire the Franchise* in 1877. It contained an eloquent appeal to legislators:

'The condition of women of the lower orders is beset with hardships; and it is for the very reason that a lady is freed from those heavy trials, that she should exert every power she possesses or can acquire, first to understand, and then, if possible, to remedy them. How these evils are to be lightened; how the burdens of the poor toilers are to be made less intolerable; how wives are to be protected from brutal husbands; how, above all, the ruin of the hapless thousands of lost ones is to be stopped: - how these things are to be done, may need more wisdom than all the men and women in England together may possess. But it is quite certain that if women had heretofore been represented in Parliament, such evils and wrongs would never have reached, unchecked, their present height, and that whenever women are at last represented, some more earnest efforts will be made to arrest them.'

This introduction was followed by the reasons why women wanted the vote:

1. Because the possession of property and the payment of rates being the admitted bases of political rights in England, it is unjust that persons who possess such property, and pay such rates, should be excluded from those rights, unless from the clearest and gravest reasons of public interest.

2. Because the denial of the franchise to qualified women entails on the community a serious loss; namely, that of the legislative influence of a numerous class, whose moral sense is commonly highly developed, and whose physical defencelessness attaches them peculiarly to the cause of justice and public order.

3. Because, under a representative Government, the interests of any non-represented class are confessedly liable to be misunderstood and neglected; ... experience demonstrates that the gravest interests of women are continually postponed by Parliament to the consideration of trifling questions concerning male electors, and, when introduced into debates, are treated by half the House rather as jests than as measures of serious importance.

4. Because, while the natural and artificial disabilities of women demand in their behalf the special aid and protection of the State, no proposal has ever been made to deal with their perils and difficulties; nor even to relieve them of the smallest portion of the burden of taxation, which they are compelled to bear without sharing the privileges attached thereto.

5. Because women, by the denial to them of the franchise, are placed at a serious disadvantage in competition for numerous offices and employments; especially women of the middle class, whose inability to vote tends extensively to deter landlords interested in politics from accepting them as tenants, even in cases where they have long conducted for their deceased male relatives the business of the farms, shops, and etc., to whose tenure they seek to succeed.

6. Because the denial of women of the direct exercise of political judgment in the typical act of citizenship, has a generally injurious influence on the minds of men as regards women, leading them to undervalue their opinions on all the graver matters of life, and to treat offences against them with levity, as committed against beings possessed only of inferior rights.

7. Because the denial of the direct exercise of their judgment has a doubly injurious effect upon the minds of women, inclining them to adopt, without conscientious inquiry the opinions which, they are warned, must be always practically inoperative; and beguiling them to exert, through tortuous and ignoble channels, the influence whose open and honest exercise has been refused.

8. Finally, we desire the franchise for women, because, while believing that men and women have different work to do in life, we still hold that, in the choice of political representatives, they have the same task to accomplish; namely, the joint election of a Senate which shall guard with equal care the rights of both sexes, and which shall embody in its laws that true Justice which shall approve itself not only to the strong, but also the weak.

1

1840 – 1873

The early movement,

a Liverpool courtship,

feminist legislation,

and the first Women's Disabilities Bills

Even earlier beginnings:

It was to be a long fight. On 31 March 1776, in Boston, Abigail Adams wrote to her husband John,

'I long to hear that you have declared an independency. And, by the way, in the new code of laws which I suppose it will be necessary for you to make, I desire you would remember the ladies and be more generous and favorable to them than your ancestors…Do not put such unlimited power into the hands of the husbands. Remember, all men would be tyrants if they could. If particular care and attention is not paid to the ladies, we are determined to foment a rebellion, and will not hold ourselves bound by any laws in which we have no voice or representation.'

In revolutionary France, women were active in politics throughout. In 1791, in response to *The Declaration of the Rights of Man*, the radical playwright Olympe de Gouges published her *Declaration of the Rights of Women,* asking for full legal equality of the sexes, wide job opportunities for women, a state alternative to the dowry system, schooling for girls and a National Assembly of Women. In 1791, Etta Palm D'Aelders established Les Amies de la Verité, a political club exclusively for women. By early 1793. women could marry without parental consent, initiate divorce, own property, name the father of an illegitimate child and secure financial compensation for seduction. However, the activities of Pauline Léon's Citoyennes Républicaines Révolutionaires led to a ban on women speaking in the Assembly, and this was followed in May 1795, after further bread riots, by a law against five or more women assembling in public. By 1804, when the Code Napoleon was established, women were back where they started.

In Britain, Mary Wollstonecraft's *A Vindication of the Rights of Women* (1792) argued for better education for women. It was widely read, although Victorian suffragists were to play down its importance because of her 'scandalous' private life.

Legally, women were only disenfranchised in Britain in 1832, by the Representation of the People Act (First Reform Act), the first act which specifically mentioned gender. It was followed by the Municipal Corporation Act of 1835, which again specified male voters.

However, what really sparked the modern movement off in Britain was the Anti-Slavery Convention of 1840. The National Portrait Gallery has a painting of this, by Benjamin Haydon, with abolitionist Thomas Clarkson in the centre, raising one hand as he speaks; behind him is a lady in a bonnet (his daughter, Mary), and down the right hand side of the painting is a row of frilled caps: Mrs John Beaumont, Lady Byron, Elizabeth Fry, Ann Knight, Amelia Opie, Elizabeth Pease, Mary Anne Rawson, Marion Kirkland Reid, Elizabeth Tredgold, and a distinguished abolitionist delegate from America, Lucretia Mott. In the audience was another American who was later to fight for women's rights, Elizabeth Cady Stanton. The American women's rights movement had already begun; Sarah Grimke was speaking publicly on women's rights, Mount Holyoke College for Women had been founded in 1837, and Mississippi had passed the first Married Women's Property Act in 1839.

Except that the ladies weren't there in the hall, as they are shown in the painting. Instead of being among the men, the women were up at a separate gallery in the back, out of sight, and the six women delegates (along with men who joined them on principle) were seated behind the bar, listening in silence; male delegates had voted that they would not be allowed to participate in the discussion. When Mott gave her address, the audience could not see her. The resolution was taken: free the slaves first, then free the women, and so the 'Transatlantic Sisterhood' was formed.

As the abolitionist movement had been begun by prominent members of the Society of Friends, so a number of the leading women in the new female emancipation movement were Quakers: Lucretia Mott in Philadelphia, Mary Wigham in Bristol; Wigham's sister Eliza, Eliza's stepdaughter Jane Smeal and Priscilla Bright McLaren in Edinburgh; Elizabeth Pease Nichol in Glasgow; Isabella Ford in Manchester. Others had Chartist links, like Jane Cobden. The women organised petitions, public meetings and rallies (demonstrating the organisational ability which women were believed not to possess); they held bazaars of sewn and handicraft items to finance pro-suffrage newspapers, and, in passing, emphasise their femininity. Speakers were invited to their meetings, including Harriet Beecher Stowe, the American author of *Uncle Tom's Cabin*.

Early publications:

The first British pamphlet demanding women's suffrage was Marion Kirkland Reid's *A Plea for Woman*, published by William Tait, Edinburgh, in 1843. It was reissued several times. Marion Kirkland Reid (1817 – 1920) had been present at the 1840 Anti-slavery Convention, and was shocked at the exclusion of the women delegates. She was also a member of the Ladies' National Association for the Repeal of the Contagious Diseases Act. *A Plea for Woman* went through the principal anti-suffrage arguments of the day, particularly 'women's influence', 'woman's sphere' and 'women's weaker intellects' and demolished each with logic and humour. Its arguments remained necessary throughout the battle for suffrage; Shetland's MP, Mr Cathcart Wason, was still using the same anti-suffrage arguments in 1909.

Harriet Taylor Mill's *The Enfranchisement of Women* (1851) gave an account of the American Women's Convention of 1850, quoted its resolutions, and argued the case for women's suffrage. Her husband, the political philosopher John Stuart Mill, aided by her daughter, Helen Taylor, developed her essay after her death in 1858, but *The Subjection of Women* was not published until 1869; Mill considered it so controversial that he deliberately delayed publication until near his own death.

During the first half of the century, a number of women had written against the male-dominated status quo, particularly with regard to a wife's non-existence in law, and her total financial dependence on her husband (the legal term for this was *couverture*). The laws as they affected women were set out in *A Brief Summary in Plain Language of the most important Laws of England concerning Women* (1854) by Barbara Leigh Smith Boudichon (1827-91). *A Brief Summary* was a clear, telling indictment of the anomalies in English law's treatment of women. It was widely read; a second edition came out in 1856, and a third in 1869.

In law, as Boudichon explained, a husband and wife were considered to be one person, and that one person was the husband; a wife had no separate legal existence. She could not sign contracts or transact any business on her own behalf. A married woman gave over all she owned to her husband, including her earnings, should financial necessity force her to work outside the home. Furthermore, the wife herself was presumed to be equally the husband's property. This was, as Boudichon pointed out, an oddity in English law, where a woman had legal existence in criminal law, but not in common law, and where ideas of justice taken as self-evident outside the home (for example that no person may use force against another, and that every person had the right to their own wages) did not exist within it.

In 1858 Boudichon was involved in the launch of *The English Woman's Journal*, the first feminist newspaper. The monthly magazine included essays, letters, poetry, practical advice and accounts of work being done; it was as much a medium of communication between the suffrage workers as a campaigning publication. It had a circulation of around 700, and ran until 1864.

Emily Davies (1830-1921) was also an editor of *The English Woman's Journal*. In 1866 she published her first book, *The Higher Education of Women*, in which she advocated a serious and systematic approach to the education of girls as rational and intelligent beings, instead of giving them a smattering of accomplishments, like singing, with the vague aim of making them 'pleasing to their husbands.'

In December 1868, Frances Power Cobbe published *Criminals, Idiots, Women and Minors: Is the Classification sound? A Discussion on the Laws concerning the Property of Married Women*. This began with an imagined being descended from 'some distant planet':

'Pardon me; I must seem to you so stupid! Why is the property of the woman who commits Murder, and the property of the woman who commits Matrimony, dealt with alike by your law?'

It continued by apparently agreeing with the main arguments for the current laws (Justice, Expediency and Sentiment). It then refuted them with actual cases, and gave witness statements from American states where the common law had been repealed.

Petitions and protest:

In 1851, the Sheffield Female Political Association presented the first British petition on female suffrage to the House of Lords. The first suffrage petition to the House of Commons was drawn up by the Kensington Society, a discussion group founded in 1865. Members included Barbara Boudichon, Emily Davies, Mary Buss, Dorothea Beale, Ann Clough, Helen Taylor and Elizabeth Garrett. Boudichon and Davies were to co-found Girton College, Cambridge; Buss founded the North London Collegiate School for Girls; Beale was the principal of Cheltenham Ladies' College, and founder of St Hilda's College, Oxford – they were the Miss Beale and Miss Buss of the old nursery rhyme. Clough founded the North of England Council for Promoting the Higher Education of Women and was later principal of Newnham College, Cambridge; Garrett was the second woman in Britain to qualify as a doctor, at St Andrews in 1862, but her matriculation was disallowed by the University Senate (the authorities didn't know that the first woman doctor, James Barry, who qualified in Edinburgh in 1812, was female). Garrett founded both the New Hospital for Women in London and, along with Sophia Jex-Blake, the London Medical School for Women. Garrett was to became Britain's first woman mayor.

The Kensington Society's petition was presented in April 1866 by Helen Taylor's stepfather, John Stuart Mill. 1,499 signatures had been collected in a fortnight. Mills was supported by Disraeli (then Chancellor of the Exchequer, under the Earl of Derby's Conservative government), who stated:

'I have always been of opinion that, if there is to be universal suffrage, women have as much right to vote as men; and, more than that—a woman having property now ought to have a vote in a country, in which she may hold manorial courts and sometimes acts as churchwarden'.

In 1867, Mill's amendment to the Representation of the People Act (Second Reform Act), replacing 'man' with 'person' was heavily defeated, and the first women's suffrage societies were formed in London, Manchester and Edinburgh.

The Kensington Society re-named itself the London Society for Women's Suffrage, and the new secretary was Elizabeth Garrett's 19 year old sister, Millicent, wife of the blind Liberal MP for Brighton, Henry Fawcett. Henry Fawcett was already a strong supporter of women's suffrage, and Millicent quickly became the London society's key organiser. In June 1867, the society split, with the Conservative members wishing to take reform at a slower pace; Clementia Taylor, wife of Peter Taylor, the Liberal MP for Leicester, formed the London National Society for Women's Suffrage, which had strong links with the societies in Edinburgh and Manchester. Millicent Fawcett joined their committee in 1868; she spoke the following year at the first pro-suffrage public meeting in London in 1869, and at a rally in Brighton in 1870.

(Right) Millicent Garrett Fawcett (1847-1929), President of the National Union of Women's Suffrage Societies, to which the Shetland WSS was affiliated. Photograph, author's collection.

In Manchester, a short-lived society had collected signatures for Mill's petition. The Manchester National Society for Women's Suffrage reformed on 11 January 1867, led by a group that included Jacob and Ursula Bright, Josephine Butler and Elizabeth Wolstenholme, later to be a driving force for feminist legislation. They were joined in February by Dr Richard Pankhurst (the future husband of Mrs Emmeline Pankhurst) and the new Secretary of the society, Lydia Becker, who was to found the *Women's Suffrage Journal* in 1870. The very first public women's suffrage meeting was held by the Manchester society in April 1868.

It was Becker who organised over 5,000 women to send in their claims as voters, and appeal against the refusal on the grounds that women had been theoretically enfranchised until the first Reform Act. In the Court of Common Pleas, on 7 and 19 November 1867, Lord Chief Justice Bovill conceded that in a few instances women had been parties to the return of members to Parliament, but proceeded to argue 'that the non-user of the right for so long a period raised a strong presumption against its having legally existed, that the legislature in 1867 used the word 'man' in order to designate expressly the male sex, as distinct from women, and that therefore Lord Brougham's Act did not apply.' The other judges concurred, and refused to hear further cases raising different points.

In spite of them, the first woman voted in Britain on 26 November 1867. A mistake in the voter's roll gave Lily Maxwell, the owner of a small shop selling kitchen-ware, her vote in the by-election. Becker drew her attention to this. The returning officer had to allow Mrs Maxwell to vote, since she was on the roll, and the others present gave her 'three cheers' as she voted for Jacob Bright. Her vote, along with those of seven other women in Manchester and three in London, was declared illegal by the Court of Common Pleas on 9 November 1868.

The President of the Edinburgh National Society for Women's Suffrage, founded on 6 November 1867, was Priscilla Bright McLaren, Jacob Bright's sister. She was the wife of Duncan McLaren, former Lord Provost of Edinburgh, and now serving as one of its two MPs. The joint secretaries were Eliza Wigham and Duncan's daughter Agnes McLaren (she was to visit Shetland in 1873, accompanying our second suffrage speaker), and the Treasurer was Elizabeth Pease Nichol. Duncan McLaren chaired the first meeting; from 1870, Louisa Stevenson took over as chair. Signatures were collected on a petition – two million of them by the end of 1868 – and Miss Burton of Edinburgh took a test case to the High Court in Edinburgh, trying, as a tax-payer, to register as a voter; the case was disallowed. The lawyer who supported Burton and other women in this attempt was John McLaren, Duncan's son. In 1870, Sarah Elizabeth Siddons Mair helped found the Edinburgh Association for the University Education of Women, and classes taught by University professors were held in Edinburgh, Glasgow and St Andrews. In that same year, Jacob Bright spoke at Scotland's first public meeting in favour of women's suffrage.

A fourth society was formed in Bristol in 1868; in 1872, it affiliated to the Central Committee of the National Society for Women's Suffrage, formed at Bright's instigation. The Liverpool committee was formed in 1871 and led by the Reverend George and Mrs Josephine Butler; it too affiliated to the Central Committee, but was to cause controversy because of its campaign to repeal the Contagious Diseases Acts. The Liverpool context is particularly important for the Shetland story, for it was here that one of the two key figures of the 1909 Shetland society grew up: Harriet Atherton, or Mrs John Leisk.

A Liverpool courtship:
Back in 1860s Shetland, a young man was making his way up in the world. John Leisk was born in 1845, in Uyea Isle, Unst; his father Joseph was a Whalsay man, and his mother, Elizabeth Sandison, was from Delting. Joseph's profession was given as Inspector of Poor. Their nine children (John was

number seven) were born in Unst. Within eleven years the young John lost almost all of his family: first his oldest brother, Thomas, whose profession is given as banker, died in 1856, when John was eleven, then his mother Elizabeth. His father Joseph moved to Lerwick immediately after, perhaps on the marriage of John's older sister Elizabeth to draper George Reid Tait of 169 Commercial Street. John's brother Joseph, next in age to John, died there in 1861; his older sister Marjory died in 1864; Joseph himself died in 1865, and John's youngest sister Anne died in 171 Commercial St in 1867 aged only 16, of phthisis (TB). Elizabeth and George Reid Tait had only one child, Sarah, soon after their marriage; Elizabeth died in 1879, and George remarried; his second son, E S Reid Tait, was to be a keen socialist as a young man, and was, with Tina Jamieson, a founder member of the Shetland Folk Society.

Reid Tait took John Leisk on as an assistant, along with Alexander Sandison, John's first cousin. In Lerwick, Leisk made friends with the son of Mr Bryan, from Liverpool, who was in charge of the Anderson Educational Institute's Elementary Department. Bryan senior became headmaster of the Upper School in 1863, and his son, James, took over the Lower Department. Both Bryans were musicians, and in their time in Shetland established brass and fife bands at the Institute. When James Bryan returned to Liverpool in the late 1860s to start his own school at 225 West Derby St, Leisk visited him there. James's wife, Mary Louisa Atherton, along with her sister Harriet, helped to teach the younger children, and that is how Leisk met his future wife.

Harriet Atherton was born in 1853. Her father, William, was variously a chemist, a house-agent and a cashier. Her mother was Harriet Goulborn. By the time young Harriet was eighteen, Liverpool had a strong suffrage society, and was also the base for Josephine Butler's fight against the Contagious Diseases Act. Butler had also been a founder member, in 1867 (not long before the Bryans returned to Liverpool) of the North of England Council for the Promotion of Higher Education for Women.

An extant letter from Harriet to John Leisk was written from Liverpool in 1871. In that year, George Reid Tait retired and Leisk and his cousin Alexander Sandison bought the business; John Leisk subsequently bought the house and gardens behind. The letter gives a touching picture of the young Harriet Leisk, involved enough with John Leisk to be permitted a regular correspondence with him (which suggests an engagement), but not sure enough of him (or too good a tactician!) to expect his visit the next time he had a holiday:

Coburg House
July 23rd 1871

Dear Mr Leisk,

I received your kind note & glad to hear that you are quite well.

You will be surprised to hear that we had a visit from Mr W Linklater of Edinburgh yesterday week, I did not see him as he only stayed a few minutes & then being a deal to do in the house after our return I was very busy at the time, he told sister he had spent a very pleasant evening with you and some other gents the Monday previous, he has promised to spend an evening with us when he next visits L'pool.

I forget whether I told you of the death of Mr Jeffries the late bankrupt or perhaps you have seen it through the mechanism of the press, he died very suddenly at breakfast. How his affairs will be settled remains for the future, there were so many people attended his funeral from curiosity & from the proceedings which have taken place.

How different was the attendance at the funeral of the late Mr Newlands, our borough engineer, who had devoted his time & talent to the improvement of the town, his remains were interred last Thursday at the Necropolis. I enclose for you a slip from the paper, the close of the ceremony is torn off but I could not get another paper.

I suppose you have a little time allowed you each year for recreation, if so I suppose you have not decided what part of the British Isles you will visit this autumn.

Harriet Atherton, aged sixteen or seventeen. Brought up in Liverpool, where there was a strong suffrage society led by Josephine Butler, she was later to become the Chairman of the 1909 Shetland Women's Suffrage Society.
Photograph courtesy of her great-grandson, John Durham.

We have had a very wet summer so far. I do hope it will be fine soon or the crops will be materially damaged, so far no harm has been done & we must hope & trust for the future.

The schools reopen tomorrow. You will be glad to hear that Mr B. has several additions also that baby B. is thriving surprisingly & takes notice of everybody & everything. [James P and Mary Louisa's daughter, Mary, was born in Liverpool in 1870.] James and Louisa wish to be kindly remembered.

I must conclude with kind regards from all & accept the same from

Yours very sincerely

Harriet Atherton

The engagement was formalised soon after, and was considered a good one; here are Harriet's brother Tom's comments, sent from Portugese West Africa:

Black Point
11th November 1872

My Dear Sister Harriet,

I was glad to receive your welcome addition to Pa's letter & I must say I was not at all surprised at the news contained therein as it was a thing, well not certain, but anticipated & I can only express my happiness in the fulfilment of such expectations.

Well sis you have done well, and I feel sure that John will endeavour to make you a good & affectionate husband & that your path thro' life may be an easy one is your brothers most earnest wish, tho' far distant.

When I hear of the date of the consummation of your Happiness I shall have a holiday all to myself, drink both your healths & enjoy myself in the African fashion by going into the bush in search of wild animals. - You will hear by my letter to what dangers we are exposed here, but with care & keeping your eyes open you can overcome them.

...

I must now close, wishing you every prosperity & happiness which a brother can wish a dear sister & asking to be remembered to John.

Believe me,

Your affectionate brother,

Tom

John and Harriet married in Liverpool two years later, in 1874, when he was 29 and she was 21. Harriet's mother visited them in Shetland in the first year of their marriage, but died shortly after. Harriet's youngest sister Sarah came to live with them after their mother's death; she was to make her home in Shetland, marrying Peter Garriock. The middle sister, Elizabeth, also married a Shetlander, Arthur Sandison. All three sisters were to be involved in the 1909 Shetland Women's Suffrage Society.

John and Harriet were to have five daughters: Ann, born in 1875, who died aged 9; Harriet (Hattie), born in 1877; Ethel Elizabeth (Bessie), born in 1879; Margaret Louisa, born in 1881; and Alice, born in 1886.

A letter from Harriet's father to 'Hatty' written just after their marriage gives some idea of how well she was loved at home, as well as of her intellectual pursuits:

... You are now settling down to home life. I often think that I can see you thus engaged, but if I were to describe my suppositions you would only smile for you see I know nothing of the geography of your house, but it is sufficient of me to know that you are happy in each other's society and have all that is requisite to make life so dear, it becomes continually brighter is our most fervent prayer! Give my kind regards to John and if need be tell his friends how grateful I am for their kind endeavours to contribute to your happiness.

All your friends here make anxious enquiries respecting you, and are pleased to learn of your welfare, and happiness, even the little ones say 'you might have waited until they were grown up.' they desire their kind love. Mrs

Williams (Park), Mrs and the Misses Leadger, Mrs Shand, Capt. & Mrs Potts, Lucy &c send their kind regards. Mow Betholt called in last evg. and was very demonstrative and will feel 'Most happy' and 'compliments' to hear from you, to know that you are happy as you so well deserve to be, when you write to him you can address to us. Uncle Robert's address is 'St James Vicarage, Ratcliff Cross, London E' You know how delighted he will be to hear from you. I have not heard from him since you left.

Ma has been much better of late, but for the past few days, she has not been too well, her back is bad, she feels weak, and tired, but I have no doubt she will be better, as she becomes reconciled to your leaving, but you know her love for her children, she would have all of you always with her, or as she expressively said the other day 'She wished that she could be at both places'.

By the way I was pleased with your essay <u>though brief</u> on Physiology, as manifested in the wise allotment of our several localities, and the adaptation of our Physical Nature thereto. I award you the Diploma of PH.D. i.e. 'Doctor-ess of Philosophy'.

Ma! sends her kindest Love to you & John she is obliged for his consideration in writing. All here are as usual and desire their best love.

> I remain
> My Dear Hatty
> your loving Father
> Wm Atherton

Ma says this is too prosy - WA

The first feminist legislation:

Suffrage societies were crucial in achieving new legislation, through lobbying MPs, holding meetings, forming committees and issuing pamphlets discussing the latest Bill from a feminist point of view. Often it was they who drew up the terms of a Bill, then persuaded an MP to sponsor it. However giving an Act a title and a date gives a misleading idea of what actually happened in Parliament. Bills were introduced by an individual MP, given a first Reading, debated, moved for a Second Reading, debated, given a Second reading or deferred for six months; after the Second Reading they could be passed to a Select Committee or a Committee of the whole House, passed to the Lords, amended, returned to the Commons, returned to the Lords and finally passed for Royal Assent, when the Act became law. An individual member's Bill could not be debated past half past twelve, and so could be blocked by a single, loquacious opponent (and they all were incredibly long winded; this was well before the ten-minute rule). Bills regularly ran out of time in one Parliamentary session, and were reintroduced in the next; the Married Women's Property Act of 1870, for example, had been debated over two previous sessions. It soon became very clear to feminists that a Bill only stood a chance if the Government was willing to support it by giving it time early in the session.

The campaigns by a mistreated wife, Caroline Norton, had resulted in a number of earlier acts improving the laws as they affected married women. The **Infant Custody Act** (1839) allowed the Court of Chancery to award mothers custody of their children under the age of seven, and access to children under sixteen. Similar provisions were made in the **Conjugal Rights (Scotland) Amendment Act** (1861)

Norton and others continued to campaign against the law of *couverture* and the proposed Marriage and Divorce Bill of 1855. The **Divorce Act** (1857) was amended under this pressure to allow a wife deserted by her husband to be treated as a *feme sole* with respect to her own property and contracts, and to allow a women to divorce her husband if adultery was aggravated by cruelty, bigamy, wilful desertion for four years or incest. However divorce in England was still the recourse only of those rich enough to afford the process, through the Divorce Court in London.

The situation was slightly different in Scotland. The only acceptable grounds for divorce were adultery or desertion, and after the Conjugal Rights (Scotland) Act of 1861, divorce was achieved through the Court of Session at a cost of £20 or £30.

The Municipal Corporations (Franchise) Act (1869), gave women in England, Ireland and Wales the right to vote in local elections on the same terms as men. At the time, the eligible women would only be unmarried women of property or widows; married women did not own property, and so did not qualify as rate-payers. The 'women' clause was introduced by Jacob Bright, and there are frequent references in later Women's Disabilities Bill debates to it having been sneaked in, late at night. The **Municipal Franchise (Scotland) Act** became effective in 1881-2.

The Married Women's Property Act (1870, amended 1874): Marriage was considered the great cornerstone of Victorian society, and the home the place that all virtue issued from. The classic picture of the bright faces around the table, with Papa at its head, Mama at its foot, was central to Victorian thought about the male-female relationship. The man, by virtue of his superior mind and strength, went out to earn money; the woman created the home and brought up the children. Although she was in charge of the household budget, she was not considered capable of dealing with finance; although she ran the household and servants, she was not credited with organisational abilities. Working out-with the home was undertaken only at a time of severe financial crisis for the family. The husband was expected to take all decisions; he commanded, and she obeyed. Many of the objections to women's suffrage came from the fear that giving women equal status with men would overturn this natural order, to the ruin of the nation.

Feminists objected to this state of marriage on the grounds that it was unjust that one rational being should have such total jurisdiction over another; that women had a right to work, and to enjoy the fruits of their labour; that it distorted the marriage bond into the relationship of master and slave, rather than a bond of affection between equals. They also pointed out that the present property laws as they affected married women bore more hardly on the poor, and were therefore inequitable, and it was the economic argument which seems finally to have swayed Parliament. If a poor wife was deserted by a husband who was able to return and take her wages, then she would be dependant on the Parish for maintenance.

The 1870 Married Women's Property Act was a chance for feminists to get married women under the normal laws of the land, as *feme sole* able to administer their own property, and no longer under *couverture*, a vital recognition for the suffrage argument; the causes were linked by both feminists and MPs. Freeing wives from *couverture* was barely considered by MPs; the Bill was drafted to protect women from predatory husbands, not to give them independence in their own right. The original Bill presented by Gurney had begun with the assertion that common law 'is unjust in principle, and presses with peculiar severity upon the poorer classes of the community,' but the amended Bill changed this to 'it is desirable to amend the law of property and contract with respect to married women.'

In practice, it gave poor women the protections that careful fathers gave their richer sisters through trusts. Its main provisions were: a married woman could retain rights in pre-marital property, but not in any ensuing legacy worth more than £200 (a rich woman could afford to ask the courts of equity to make a separate settlement; a poor woman would rarely receive so large a legacy); she could retain money deposited in a savings-bank or bonds if she had made special application to have her account so registered, and she could retain her earnings, but only from the passing of the Act.

However, the debt clauses did not allow a married woman to bear the consequences of her own actions, as an independent individual. She could sue and be sued, but only to the extent of any personal property she possessed, and she was not personally liable for a debt; she was however liable for debts she contracted as an agent of her husband. Husband and wife could not sue one another for tort (for example, suits involving duty of care). Finally, she could not make a legally binding will, even for her own property; her husband's consent to it could be rescinded at any time.

The Lords were markedly hostile to the Bill, considering it 'struck at the root of domestic happiness, introducing insubordination, equality and something more' [the Earl of Shaftesbury]. They did, however, add new responsibilities: the Poor Law Guardians could issue a maintenance order against a wife for care of her husband, and she had the same responsibility for the maintenance of her children as a widow.

One amendment by the Lords was to be revisited in 1874: the stipulation that only a wife's earnings and property settled on her in a marriage settlement were to be deemed 'for her own use', other property still becoming her husband's upon marriage. He was, however, no longer liable for debts she had contracted before marriage. This meant the wife was sufficiently a separate person to be sued for her own pre-nuptial debts, but, since her property was now her husband's, might not be able to pay. The **Amendment Act** (1874) made a husband responsible for his wife's pre-nuptial debts to the extent of assets he had received from her on marriage, and was whizzed through Parliament; 'That tradesmen – electors and fathers – should be cheated, was to Parliament intolerable.' [Arthur Arnold, MP]

The provisions of the 1870 Act and 1874 amendment did not become law in Scotland until some years later. The **Married Women's Property (Scotland) Act** (1877) protected the earnings of a wife, and the **Married Women's Policies of Assurance (Scotland) Act** (1880) permitted her to contract for a policy of assurance for her separate use. Duncan McLaren introduced the **Married Women's Property (Scotland) Act** (1881) which allowed a woman to continue ownership of all moveable property that she brought to the marriage, rather than it becoming her husband's (his *jus mariti*); he continued to administer heritable property until the Act of 1920.

The Infant Life Protection Act (1872): Through the 1860s, concern grew at the infant mortality rates. The general death rate was falling but the infant death rate remained steady at 150 births per 1000; even at the end of the century, infant deaths accounted for 25% of national deaths. This rate was even higher to infants born to an unmarried mother; in Marylebone, between 1843 and 1858, 46% of these infants died in the first 12 months. In Sheffield in the 1870s, the rate was 582 per 1,000 live births, almost five times the average for infants of married parents.

The causes were complex, but a scandalous case in 1870 focused the House of Commons' attention on baby farming. The Infant Life Protection Act enforced registration for houses where babies were taken in, and more complete recording of infants entrusted to nurses and deaths occurring under their care. The response of Elizabeth Wolstenholme, Josephine Butler and Lydia Becker was to issue a pamphlet, *Infant Mortality: its Causes and Remedies,* in which they pointed out that registration of baby farms would not help what they saw as the true causes of infant mortality: women's ignorance and poverty, male seduction and abandonment of young girls, and the difficulty unmarried mothers had in finding work which would maintain them and their children. Their suggestions for remedies included making fathers responsible for the support of their children, access to better education for women, better paid jobs, and raising the age of consent from twelve to seventeen (at that time it was a felony to seduce a girl under ten years, or an heiress under twenty-one, another case of a different law for the rich). As with the Married Women's Property Act, they felt that women were being blamed for something that was the fault of the imbalance in the country's economic system.

The **Guardianship of Infants Act** (1873) allowed mothers to petition for custody of or access to their children under sixteen under exceptional circumstances, but it ignored the principle of co-equal parental rights; fathers were still considered the child's guardian, by right of 'nature and nurture'. A mother would not automatically be the child's guardian in the event of the father's death, and did not have the right, even as a widow, to will her child's guardianship; a widow's children would still become Wards of Court. It did however show the increasing acceptance of the idea that the interests of the child should over-ride the rights of the father.

Another Act which affected women was the **Factories (Health of Women) Act** (1874). This restricted women's factory labour from not more than ten hours a day to fifty-six hours a week. **The Factories and Workshops Consolidation Act** (1878) brought all regulated industries under one statute, banned the employment of children under 10, and made enforcement the responsibility of inspectors. Home workshops and workshops where no young people or children worked remained unregulated. The newly-founded Trade Unions Council and the Women's Protective and Provident League worked to bring the hours of all workers down. Submissions to a Royal Commission in Leeds made it clear that what women feared most was that the Commons would add a ban on married women working, because of the often repeated arguments about the damage to infants' and children's health (probably a justifiable concern, given that breast-fed infants might be given totally inappropriate foods during their mother's absence). Others feared damaging the recent achievement of the Married Women's Property Bill.

A pamphlet on *Legislative Restrictions on the Industry of Women, considered from the Women's Point of View*, written by Josephine Butler, Elizabeth Wolstenholme and others, made the point that limiting the hours women could work made it harder for them to earn a living, and made them less attractive to employers; they also pointed out that 'one hour spared from paid labour at the factory, is spared in order that the mother may employ it in unpaid labour at home.' While sympathetic to the concerns over mothers nursing infants, they argued that limited hours would affect many women who were not nursing, and cause them greater poverty.

Two further Factory Acts were passed: the **1891 Act** was to prohibit employment of women for the four weeks after the birth of a child, and raise the working age of children from 10 to 11; the **1901 Act** was to raise the minimum age to 12.

The **Matrimonial Causes Act** (1878) focused on the power of husbands to mistreat their wives physically. *The Women's Suffrage Journal* published accounts of the way wives were physically abused by their husbands. Many of these were submitted by Frances Power Cobbe, who, as a journalist, attended trials. In April 1878, Cobbe published an essay called 'Wife-torture in England' which aimed to bring the frequency of violence against wives and partners to the attention of the wider public.

She began by making it clear that wife-beating was about power:

'The notion that a man's wife is his PROPERTY... is the fatal root of incalculable evil and misery. Every brutal-minded man, and many a man who in other relations of life is not brutal, entertains more or less vaguely the notion that his wife is his thing, and is ready to ask with indignation (as we read again and again in the police reports,) of any one who interferes with his treatment of her, 'May I not do what I will with my own?' It is even sometimes pleaded on behalf of poor men, that they possess nothing else but their wives, and that, consequently, it seems doubly hard to meddle with the exercise of their power in that sphere!'

She picked up the 'provocation' argument used to excuse men who had killed their wives:

'... not only is an offence against a wife condoned as of inferior guilt, but any offence of the wife against her husband is regarded as a sort of Petty Treason. . .Should she be guilty of 'nagging' or scolding, or of being a slattern, or of getting intoxicated, she finds usually a short shrift and no favour- and even humane persons talk of her offence as constituting if not a justification for her murder, yet an explanation of it. She is, in short, liable to capital punishment without judge or jury for transgressions which in the case of a man would never be punished at all, or be expiated by a fine of five shillings.'

She linked the treatment of wives with the lack of the vote:

'... Nevertheless, when we women ... are refused that privilege [of voting], and told year after year by smiling senators that we have no need whatever for it, that we form no 'class', and we may absolutely and always rely on men to prove the deepest and tenderest concern for everything which concerns the welfare of women, shall we not point to these long-neglected wrongs of our trampled sisters, and denounce that boast of the equal concern of men for women as – a falsehood?

Were women to obtain the franchise tomorrow, it is normally certain that a Bill for the protection of Wives would pass through the legislature before a Session was over.'

The essay highlighted cases such as that of George Smith, who was found 'Not Guilty' of murdering his wife by cutting her to pieces with a hatchet, as it was 'not certain she had died of the wounds.'

The Bill which ended the essay focused on protection for wives at risk of violence; specifically, that wives could obtain a Protection Order with the force of a judicial separation, that they should be given custody of their children, and that the husband should pay them maintenance. In Parliament, Lord Penzance added the proviso that the wife should not be guilty of adultery, and that the court should only issue a Protection Order if concerned about the wife's *future* safety; the current assault was not sufficient.

The Act seems to have been followed by a real fall in the instances of aggravated assault by husbands against wives, but analysis (for example in Mary Lyndon Shanley's *Feminism, Marriage and the Law in Victorian England*) suggests that this was due more to raised awareness of the issue and a change in men's behaviour than stronger action by the courts. Male judges were still reluctant to issue a separation order, even though the wife desired it. Croydon magistrates went so far as to say it was their invariable rule not to issue such decrees; they would not be party to splitting up a marriage. The Act did not give the wife the right to leave her husband, only permission to appeal to a court to be allowed to leave him. If she did leave without their permission, she was guilty of desertion, and so would forfeit her property rights and custody and maintenance claims.

In Scotland, where a judicial separation could be obtained through the Sheriff Court, there seems to have been no change in the law. The only grounds accepted were cruelty or adultery. A decree for aliment could only be obtained with a decree of judicial separation.

The first Women's Disabilities Bills, 1870 – 3:

Had it not been for the intervention of Gladstone, women might have won the vote in 1870. In that year, under Gladstone's Liberal government, Jacob Bright presented his first Women's Disabilities Bill (Bill 31), drawn up for the Manchester society by Dr Richard Pankhurst. The first reading of the bill was on 16 February 1870. The Second Reading took place on 4 May 1870, and Mr Bright spoke at length. I will quote him in full, as he goes through the principal arguments for and against women getting the vote, arguments which were to be used again and again for the next forty-eight years:

'Sir, I rise to move that the Bill for the Removal of the Political Disabilities of Women be now read a second time. If that Bill should pass into law, women will have votes in boroughs if they are householders, if their names are on the rate-books, and if they pay their rates. Women will have votes also in counties if they are householders, and if their houses are rated at £12 and upwards, or if they should be possessed of any description of property which now entitles men to vote.

The House may desire to know to what extent women would be enfranchised if this Bill became law. I have Returns of the number of women on the burgess rolls of a great many municipal towns, and I will just state one or two facts from that list. I notice that the largest proportion of women who are municipal voters is to be found in Bath, where there is 1 woman to 3.8 men. I notice that the smallest proportion is to be found in the town of Walsall. There I only find 1 woman to 22.9 men. The peculiar circumstances of these boroughs would, I have no doubt, easily explain that great difference. But I may mention two or three other towns, as showing what I believe would be about the average number of votes of women in proportion to men in the other boroughs of England. In the town of Bristol there is 1 to every 7 men; in Manchester 1 to 6; in Newcastle-on-Tyne 1 to 8; in Northampton 1 to 13; in York 1 to 7. When we last discussed in this House the question of the extension of the franchise, there was a great fear entertained by those who were within the political pale lest, by admitting those who wanted to get in, they would be swamped. I think that was the term that was then generally in vogue. Even the hon. Member for Pembroke [Thomas Meyrick, Conservative] will admit that the number of persons we propose to enfranchise by this Bill is so small that no fear need be entertained on the present occasion. The aristocratic sex—that sex in whose hands are nearly all the material privileges of life—would still be dominant in the government of the kingdom.

I advocate this claim of women to the franchise on the grounds of public justice and of practical necessity; and I may say in passing that unless I thought that this matter was one of great practical importance, I should certainly have left it in other hands. The difficulties in the way of legislation on the part of private Members in this House are so great, that no one would undertake it unless moved by a strong sense of justice. Now, it should be remembered, that Parliament does not give votes either to men or women. There are thousands of men who have no votes. There are men in every position of life—and of every degree of intelligence and education—who have no votes. Parliament applies a certain test and give votes to all those men who can submit to that test. If a man is on the rate book and pays his rates, then, though he belong to the fraternity of London thieves, though he be an habitual drunkard, or a returned convict, though he may belong to the class of those who are so ignorant that they scarcely know the name of the Sovereign who sits upon the Throne—yet, if a man be able to submit to the test, whatever his position or character may be, he is at that moment admitted to the rank of voter, and enabled to influence the proceedings of this House. It does seem a strange anomaly that this test—that this qualification— which works such magic with men, is wholly inoperative with women, and that no matter what a woman's position may be—how much property she may have—how much intelligence she may possess, she is still excluded from the franchise, though able to come and submit to every test which Parliament has established.

If there were some burdens from which they escaped which fall upon men, I might suppose that there was some kind of answer to be given to this claim. But I know of no such burden, and the only attempt of which I have ever heard to make it appear that women do not share all the burdens of men, is the attempt to show that women take no part in defending their country. It must be remembered, however, that no man is compelled to defend his country. It is a voluntary matter. We hire those who defend the country, and if women as well as men pay the taxes into the Exchequer which enable us to pay those who defend the country, that is a sufficient answer to the argument. I think Florence Nightingale could tell of the services of women who have done something even in defence of their country. The services in the hospital are almost as necessary as those which are performed in the camp; and women are always ready for that or any other kind of service.

There has always been great anxiety on the part of men to possess the franchise. From the time that I was a boy I remember associations of various kinds, differing in strength, but always laboriously at work to procure the Parliamentary vote for men. We know very well that men have sacrificed their liberty and perilled their lives in pursuit of this object. In our own generation this has been the case over and over again. Does the House suppose that these men have been misguided, that they have been following a phantom, and that that which they have desired has been of no use to them? On what ground have men always displayed this great anxiety to vote for Members of Parliament? Why, they have told us that an equal share of taxation fell upon them, and, therefore, that they ought to have some control over the expenditure of this taxation. They have told us that it was not within the power of this House either to enact a law or to repeal a law without affecting advantageously or disadvantageously the whole people of the country.

The non-electors made another statement. They said—'Your exclusion of us from the political pale is tantamount to a declaration of our moral and intellectual inferiority. It diminishes our own self-respect; it takes away from us the respect of the other portions of the community; and it necessarily makes our career in life far harder and less successful.' Is there any one of these reasons which men have so persistently urged for admission to the franchise which does not apply with equal, and even with greater, force to women? Is there a single tax which men pay which women do not pay also? Is the ability to pay on the part of men and women equal? There is not a male and female rate of taxation, but there is a male and female rate of wages and earnings. Women everywhere, with a few remarkable exceptions, are getting far less money than men; they have to work much longer for the same money; and they are even paid much less when they are doing precisely the same work. Taxation must, therefore, fall somewhat more heavily upon women than upon men. Are there any laws imposing restrictions and obligations on men—any laws of a penal character—from which women escape? No; but are there not laws of recent origin which fall with terrible harshness upon women, and which place their peace and security in peril? Are there not such laws—laws from which men wholly escape? [The Contagious Diseases Acts] These laws may be just and necessary. It is not for me to discuss them at the present moment. My hon. Friend the Member for Cambridge (Mr. W. Fowler) will give the House an opportunity of defending them in a short time; but I have a right to say that the fact that one sex legislates for another and imposes burdens upon an unrepresented portion of the people, which it does not take upon itself, forms an additional reason why women should ask for the suffrage, and strengthens the claim which I am urging at the present moment.

If it be true that men felt when they were excluded from the franchise, that it was a mark of great disrespect and injurious to their position, will not women have the same feeling? There are inferior men in every rank of life. They have no objection to degrade women and keep them in degradation. So long as Parliament legislates in this way, so long as it puts them in an inferior position politically, it gives considerable support to the course taken by the class of men to whom I have referred. At the present moment what does Parliament say to women who are occupiers and owners of property? It says to them—You are fitted to vote in local matters—in small concerns which do not greatly affect you you are entitled to have your vote; but when we come to Imperial affairs, then you are disqualified, and we refuse to admit you.

But I am told that the theoretical arguments on this subject cannot be answered; that theoretically women undoubtedly have a right to that which they claim; and the advocates of this measure are asked to deal with it practically. We are asked to show of what injustice women complain, and what changes they would propose to make in case they were admitted to political privileges? All these questions were put to the non-electors of England previous to the Reform Bill of 1867, and I believe they were not unsatisfactorily answered. But I undertake to say that the inequality of the law betwixt voters and non-voters prior to 1867, was as nothing compared with that which now exists between men and women. Allow me, then, to call attention to some of these inequalities. I am not going to say how they should be altered; but I have a right to point out that they exist, and that they have been made by that portion of society having power against that portion which has no power.

Take the law as it affects married women. I may be told that this Bill would not give the franchise to married women. That is quite true. This is a practical measure. It is only in our power to give votes to those who can submit to the tests which have been established by Parliament; but we propose to give the franchise to those who have been married and are widows, and to spinsters who are yet to be married. I contend that this would give adequate security to the whole sex. Look for a moment at the law with regard to the property of married women. According to the common law of England, a married woman, in regard to the rights of property, is in the position of the negro in the Southern States of America before the American Revolution. She cannot control her property, and she has not the possession of one farthing of her earnings. According to my view, the possession of property is necessary for education, and for the proper development of character. Be the woman ever so prudent, be the man ever so imprudent—be the woman ever so sagacious, and be the husband ever so imbecile, still he has absolute control, not only of his own but of hers. Sir, the House is agreed upon this question, and is unanimous upon the injustice of the present law. The hon. Member for Chester (Mr. Raikes) is of the same opinion as the right hon. and learned Member for Southampton (Mr. Russell Gurney).

I may, then, be asked why need women have votes, if they can obtain redress without them? It is one thing to acknowledge an evil and another to find a remedy for it. We legislate in the following order:—First, for those who can make themselves dangerous; next, for those who exercise a pressure at the polling-booth; and lastly, or not at all, for those who have no votes, and therefore no constitutional influence. The Married Women's Property Bill has three times received the sanction of this House, and it has been twice before a Select Committee; but he would be a very imprudent man who would undertake to say when it will become law, or, further, that it will become law without greater mutilations than it has yet received. But that is not the way in which the class which has the franchise is treated. Look at what has been done with regard to the working classes since the passing of the Reform Act of 1867. I have seen Members of this House sit here till daylight in order to defeat the Married Women's Property Bill, which seeks to prevent the confiscation of the property of a vast number of persons, and I have been glad to see the same hon. Members competing in this House in their desire to protect the funds of trades unionists and to protect the trades unions themselves. That is the effect of the franchise. Last Session the Government brought in a Bill to protect the funds of trades unions, and this year they propose to introduce another Bill to put these associations on a more satisfactory footing; but I am afraid it will be a long time before the Government undertake to deal with these questions which belong to a portion of society among whom the franchise does not exist.

But let us look a little further at these inequalities of the law. Look at the position of a woman who loses her husband. If he die intestate, the law protects her and gives her a certain portion of the income arising from his property, whatever that property may be; but if he choose to make a will, she is left entirely to his justice and mercy. I do not deny that the majority of widows are fairly treated in this respect; but it must be remembered that when we pass laws we do not legislate for the majority; we legislate because of the existence of that minority who possess neither justice nor mercy. I have known many cases of this sort. Take the case of a couple just entering life in one of the industrial districts of England. They begin life often with nothing but good character and intelligence. The man works at his business; the woman attends to him and to the family; and the man often becomes rich. If the law were equal, the wife would have some kind of security with regard to that wealth which she had helped to make.

As I said before, I do not propose to say what changes should be made in these matters; I merely point to an inequality, and I may remind the House that these inequalities have been made by a section of the community. It is required that a woman should receive 10 times the provocation that a man receives before she can obtain a divorce. A woman has no control over her children when they become seven years of age: the husband may part them from her when they reach that age. I know the case of a lady who was deserted by her husband when she had one child. Amidst much suffering she had to get a living for herself and her child, and when the child was seven years old, because she importuned her husband for some assistance, he threatened to take away the child, and she had to conceal both herself and her child in order to escape the danger.

I might say something also in regard to education. It is to me a very painful thing to see the difficulties which women have to contend against in order to get anything like a high education in this country. Women are charged with being frivolous; but that charge is very often made with great frivolity, and it is too often made by those who look at women through the medium of what they call society. So long as it is the custom of the country for women only to be admitted to the frivolous occupation of men, it is likely that that charge will continue to be made. Men and women may mix at the dance, the picnic, and the theatre; but when they go to the lecture room it is considered improper. However, there is a class of men growing up who consider these things, and they believe that the morality of this country will be greatly improved when the lecture rooms are opened to all. I might even go to the primary schools, in order to show what is the influence of those above upon those below. There is a great free school in Manchester—an admirable school—which takes children out of the gutter; but it only takes in the male children, and the girls are left in the streets. Surely such a thing must have a very bad influence upon those boys and girls.

I am glad that in this proposition, which I now make to the House, there is nothing of a party character, though I must say that this is the first proposition for the extension of the Parliamentary franchise which has ever been free from party conflict, and from the passions arising out of that conflict. When this proposition was made to the House in 1867, by Mr. John Stuart Mill, it received a very general support. Five of the Members of this House who supported that proposition are now Members of the present Government, and that does not exhaust the Members of the Government who are in favour of this Bill. There were also many eminent Members on the opposite side of the House who supported the proposition. The opinions of the Leader of the opposite party are, of course, no secret. I am sorry the right hon. Gentleman the Member for Buckinghamshire [Disraeli] is not now in his place, because if he had been, I think he would have supported this measure. I have an extract here from one of his published speeches, in which he says— 'In a country governed by a woman, where you allow women to form part of one of the Estates of the Realm—I allude to the Peeresses in their own right—and where they have power to hold manorial courts, and may be elected as churchwardens or overseers of the poor, I do not see, where a woman has so much to do with the Church and with the State, on what reason, if you come to right, she has not a right to vote.' But the right hon. Gentleman made a still more direct avowal of his opinions in a debate in this House in April, 1866, when he said— 'I have always been of opinion that, if there is to be universal suffrage, women have as much right to vote as men; and, more than that—a woman having property now ought to have a vote in a country, in which she may hold manorial courts and sometimes acts as churchwarden.'—[3 Hansard, clxxxiii. 99.]

But, whatever claim I may have on the support of hon. Members on that side of the House, I feel that I have a stronger claim upon the great Liberal party to which I have the honour to belong. I do not know what meaning we are accustomed to attach to that word 'Liberal' on this side of the House; but today I do not ask for liberality—I ask only for the barest justice. According to our professions on every hustings, we have certainly said that if justice does not require that every individual should have a vote, it does require that every class should be represented; and we have established it as a political axiom, that no class ever will receive legislative equality at the hands of another class. We have always said that those who are called on to obey the laws should have some voice in making the laws, and that representation should follow taxation. I have been met by this argument from some of my political friends: they have said—'Our principles do not require that we should support your Bill. We are in favour of good government; that is our only aim. We will enfranchise those who are fitted to be enfranchised; but we deny that women are fit, and we shall, therefore, oppose your Bill.'

Now, let me examine that argument for a moment. In the first place, it strikes one as not being very new. No class has ever asked to be admitted within the political pale in this or in any other country without receiving that answer; and in this country, at any rate, no class has ever been admitted to the franchise without great advantage to itself and the country. In the Southern States of America, in the Northern States to a very large extent, and in this country to a great extent also, the people were told before the American War that the negro was not fit for freedom. People never are fit for freedom or for constitutional rights until they obtain them; but now there is not a man in America who would like to go back to the terrible state of things which existed before the Civil War broke out. It was commonly said in America that the negro was not fit for the vote; but a negro population of 4,000,000 has now become enfranchised, and no one will deny that the peace and prosperity of these Southern States have been secured by that great legislative change.

I confess I am surprised when I am told that women, as a class, are unfit for the franchise; women who are the subjects of a female Sovereign, are engaged in many literary pursuits; who are at the head of educational establishments; who are managing factories and farms, and controlling thousands of businesses throughout this country! If I am told that many women are not fitted for the franchise, I am bound to admit it; but, then, the same thing may be said of many men. Anyone who says that women generally are not fitted in point of intelligence for the franchise knows very little of the agitation which has produced this Bill. There has never been an agitation more ably conducted by the various ladies who have taken part in it; and, considering the small means at the disposal of women, there never was a question which made such rapid progress in so short a space of time.

I have been told, also, that if this Bill were to pass, the Government would be handed over to the Conservative party in the very crisis of the country's fate—these are the very words I have heard used. Well, I take consolation from the fact that this country has sometimes even survived a Conservative Administration; but if there be any meaning in an argument of that kind it is this—that if the country were properly and justly represented, we should be sitting on the other side of the House. Now, I do not believe a word of it. I have paid some attention to this question, and I have considered the objections raised against the possession of the franchise by women on the ground that they would be Conservative; but I will not enter into a discussion of that point now, because I think every man will vote according to what he takes to be the justice and reason of the case, and not ask whether women are Conservative or Liberal.

I will, however, undertake to say that there would be no change in the balance of parties. There would be one great change, which would be this—from the moment women obtained the franchise, even though an election might not take place for several years to come, whenever a question affecting their interests came to the front, it would receive an amount of attention and consideration which it would not, and could not, receive now.

I have heard both in the Lobbies of this House, and in other places, many things said in opposition to this Bill, and some of the objections are very peculiar. I have been told that women are too religious; that they have too much respect for the clergy and for religious teachers in general; and that, therefore, they should be subject to political disabilities. We have had in this House some earnest discussions, to be followed by many more, on the question of education; and there is a predominant feeling in favour of giving, in some way or other, a religious education to children. I hope, if the fact of being religious is to be followed by political disabilities, that we shall not succeed too well in that task. It is true that the religious sentiment is stronger in women than in men; their path in life is a harder one, and law and custom, instead of coming in aid of their weakness, too often trample upon it and bestow their favours on the stronger sex. That being so, it is not remarkable that women, more than men, should seek consolation and strength from that Power before whom, at least, all human beings are equal.

I have also been told that women should not be political, or, in other words, that it is the duty of women to be politically ignorant. I might as well be told that grass should not be green; and, no doubt, if you sufficiently excluded air and light and moisture it would no longer be so. Women are political, and they cannot fail to be so in the circumstances in which they are placed. They are born in a free country, where public meetings are held on every variety of subjects, those meetings being open to everybody; they are born in a country where we have a daily Press which is the ablest, the most interesting, and the cheapest which the world has ever known. We were told some time ago by the right hon. Gentleman the First Minister of the Crown, that eviction notices fell like snowflakes in some parts of Ireland. The daily papers fall like snowflakes in all our houses; and if we are not to make our women political, we must shut the doors against the Press. To tell me that women should not be political is to tell me that they should have no care for the future of their children, no interest in the greatness and progress of their country. If it be true that women are not to be political, then we ought logically to take away from them the only shred of privilege which connects them with this House—the privilege of petitioning this House. Tens of thousands of women's names have been sent to this House in Petitions this year. We are supposed—[here the hon. Gentleman pointed up to the Ladies' Gallery]—not to know that there is a Gallery behind that screen; but I have noticed that it rarely happens that an hon. Gentleman comes down to make an important speech without his having some one or more of the female members of his family up in that Gallery. If women be deteriorated by political knowledge, I think the female members of the families of Members of Parliament must be in a very deplorable state indeed. I have visited them at their own homes, but I have never found that deterioration: on the contrary, I have found with larger knowledge more vivacity and interest; in short, an intellectual flavour not always to be found elsewhere.

An objection, considered to be a very great one with regard to the franchise, is, that women themselves do not care for it, and would not use it if they had it. But no one who has paid any attention to the facts of the case would raise that objection. Before the Municipal Franchise Bill gave municipal rights to women—I know this to be a fact because I made the inquiry in the neighbourhood with which I am most acquainted in Lancashire—where women had the power of local voting they used that power in the same proportion as men; and I have found that since the Bill of last year came into operation, in many municipalities they have voted in nearly an equal proportion with the men, while there are cases in which the polling of women has exceeded the polling of men. But it should be borne in mind that by passing this Bill we do not compel women to vote. There are a great many men who have no interest in politics at all, and who do not wish to vote; and unless we had organized associations to arrange the matter for them, many of them would never be upon the register at all.

Let me state what is the present position of women with regard to the power of voting in this country. They vote in all local matters; they have every parochial vote; they have votes in corporate and non-corporate towns. In the non-corporate towns and in parishes they vote under the conditions of what is known as Sturges Bourne's Act, according to the property they are rated for. Thus, a lady of property may have as many as six votes, while her servant—her gardener or her labourer—has only one. But is it not an absurdity that a woman can have six votes and her man-servant only one in local matters, while in Parliamentary elections the poor man retains his one vote, while the woman, who is in a high position and owns large property, has absolutely none. Last year's legislation appeared to me as if it should settle this question of the Parliamentary franchise for women. Without any Division in either House of Parliament, and with only one single voice raised, and that not with any earnestness, against it, women were admitted to vote in all our municipal elections. Women go up to the poll, they do not vote with the quiet of the Ballot, but they go up openly and give their votes once a year, not once in four or five years, and it must be borne in mind that these municipal elections have become as completely political as any Parliamentary election could possibly be. I do not know how or on what argument we can now say to women— 'No; you have come so far, but you shall not come any further.'

I should like to read a single sentence from the speech of Lord Cairns, made in the other House of Parliament when the Bill of last year passed, and when the Earl of Kimberley spoke on one side and Lord Cairns on the other. Lord Cairns said— As an unmarried woman could dispose of her property and deal with it, he did not see why she should not have a voice in controlling the municipal expenditure to which that property contributed? Does anyone dissent from that statement? But if it be just and right that a woman should be able to control the municipal expenditure to which her property contributes, should she not have a right to control the Parliamentary expenditure to which her property contributes? The local expenditure of the country amounts to about £20,000,000, and the Imperial expenditure to about £70,000,000; and, if justice requires that she should have the opportunity of controlling the expenditure of the smaller sum, is it not unjust to deprive her of the means of controlling the expenditure of the larger?

But we want votes for something else than merely to control the expenditure of our money. Parliament can confiscate the property of women, and it does so to a large extent. It can deal with liberty and life, and pass laws affecting the happiness of people in the remotest cottages of the land—matters of far greater importance than anything connected with expenditure. I see that an hon. Gentleman opposite has put a Notice on the Paper for opposing my Bill, by moving the Previous Question. When I first saw that Notice I asked a Member of great influence in the House what he thought of it, and he replied that it was rather a shabby way of meeting the question. I will not apply that or any other epithet of the sort to it. One remembers occasions where it was both justifiable and intelligible to take such a course as that which the hon. Gentleman proposes to adopt; and, for anything I know, that course may be quite justifiable now, but I cannot decide the point, as it is unintelligible to me. I could suggest a more manly course; and we should remember that, up to now at any rate, this House is the creation of masculine constituencies. If the proposition that I make is not founded on justice and reason, it would, I should think, be more agreeable to the feelings of hon. Members who oppose me to give a distinct 'No' to this proposition. But if, on the other hand, the claim women make upon this House be founded on justice and on reason, then let us freely concede it.

I have been told that the Government are to stand neutral on this question. Well, unfortunately it is the characteristic of all Governments to be so engrossed in attending to the wants of the powerful that they can seldom give any kind of consideration to the claims of the weak. I shall forbear quoting from the speeches of the Prime Minister; but I do remember burning periods of his in speeches which he delivered in this House and elsewhere—which did much to create enthusiasm in the country, and to place him high in the hearts of the people—that are as applicable to the case now before us as to the occasions on which they were uttered. There is, however, one thing which consoles me when I reflect upon this. There is nobody more open to conviction in this House than the First Minister of the Crown, and, when he is once convinced, there is nobody more resolute in carrying out his convictions.

One word more, and I will no longer trespass on the kindness and forbearance of the House. There is a very general movement in favour of this Bill—a movement which exists in almost every part of the three kingdoms. There have been many Petitions during the past three Sessions in favour of it. During the three short months we have already sat here this year, more than 100,000 names have come up asking us to pass this Bill. The persons who sign these Petitions only ask from a household-suffrage Parliament a Bill that will establish real household suffrage. They complain that it is not fair that a house should be passed over because a woman happens to be at the head of it. The women who are interested in the subject are only acting in the spirit of one of the noblest proverbs of our language—'God helps those who help themselves.' Is it a matter of regret to us that they should have these aspirations? Ought it not rather to be a matter of satisfaction and of pride?

That this Bill will become law no one, who has observed the character of the agitation, and who knows the love of justice of the British people, can doubt. I hope it will become law soon, for I have a desire, which will receive the sympathy of many in this House—I have a strong desire that when our children come to read the story of their country's fame, it may be written there that the British Parliament was the first great Legislative Assembly in the world which, in conferring its franchises, knew nothing of the distinctions of strong and weak, of male and female, of rich and poor. I will conclude by moving the second reading of the Bill.'

And now, some of the objections:

MR. SCOURFIELD, in rising to move the Previous Question, said... that they had no sufficient evidence that it was the wish of the women of England to have this privilege conferred upon them ... The same reason that prevented women from desiring to have these privileges conferred upon them prevented them from getting up an

28

agitation in opposition. They were bound to look not only at the express declarations contained in the form of Petitions, but also upon whatever other evidence would guide them to a conclusion as to what their real wishes were...

If [women] were to extend their political influence, they could not expect to assert so much of their social influence. If their social influence was maintained in the way it had been maintained throughout England, a considerable amount of political influence must follow; but if they fixed their minds exclusively on political things, their social influence must be weakened.

... If voting papers had been allowed, women might have recorded their votes without being under the necessity of giving personal attendance at the poll; but now they must give their votes by personal attendance, and be exposed to all the annoyances to which everyone who had taken part in a contested election knew very well that persons who engage in these matters were invariably subjected. ... He wished to see women continue in that vocation in which they were engaged, and doing all that was admirable, amiable, and delightful; but he had no wish to see them engaged in the line of the exceptional and the wonderful.

MR. W. FOWLER ... I do not think it a disability of women that they have no votes. I consider it rather a privilege, that they have no votes, because they are therefore not expected to enter into that arena in which some of us are actively engaged. ... I say that they should take care to influence their husbands and their friends to put right-minded men into this House, and then their interests would be properly looked after.

... I consider that the sphere of their influence is at home. I consider that they have a duty to perform as important, if not more important than the duties that fall to men. They have to educate their children; they have to adorn the sphere in which they live; and to perform duties with regard not merely to the rising generation but with regard to their husbands, their brothers, and all their friends which are of an importance that cannot be exaggerated.

... I want to ask hon. Members where this is to stop? It appears to me that if the argument that has been used is good, there is no reason on earth why women should not be elected Members of Parliament. There is not a single argument which has been used that does not end in that. If they have equal powers, and equal capacities, and equal rights before the law, and if, therefore, they are to have votes, and ought to enter into the political arena, where does that end? In this House. If I gave my vote for this Bill, I should feel bound to give my vote to admit them as Members of this House.

... A married woman is an existing entity, although she is married. She very often differs in toto from her husband in political matters; but, except in some cases where she has the influence described in a vulgar proverb, she is unable to influence the vote of her husband as she wishes. It may fairly be argued that she has the right to vote as much as any other woman. It is quite true that she does not pay taxes; but I dispute the proposition altogether that voting for Members to serve in this House is to be based entirely on the question whether a man pays taxes or not. When you bring in this question about women's rights, you bring in an argument far higher than that. I consider that a married woman would have a fair right to say that she was unjustly used if you admitted spinsters to have votes.

... I do not like to see women mixed up so much in all political questions. It is quite right that they should have their opinions, and that they should state their opinions and act upon them; but I do not desire to see a constant succession of women lecturers going about the country. I have shown, as I said before, my deep sympathy with the wrongs of women, and I am prepared to show it in every possible way that I can. But when I am asked to admit women to the same political privilege as men, I find that I am unable to agree to it.

MR. BERESFORD HOPE ... it is much more difficult to get Petitions from people who do not want a change than from people who do. ... They are the women who do not want to be enfranchised, and who think it is not very creditable on the part of any individuals of their sex to come forward as political speakers and political agitators, and who look on the very fact of signing their names to a Petition, not knowing what a farce sticking Petitions in the bag at the Table is, with a sort of shame as exposing their names to public notice and discussion. Therefore, I contend, women who do not want to be enfranchised will certainly not Petition, and so, to bring forward as an argument the absence of petitioning on the part of women generally is not a very conclusive mode of reasoning, while to point out that a certain number have petitioned is only to say that there is a strong body of patriotic, strong-minded, hard-headed women in the country. So much for that argument.

... enfranchise women generally, and make them a power in the country, and you will find yourselves drifting on a sea of impulsive philanthropy and sentimentalism, where you are now at anchor on the principles of political economy. With the highest respect for the female sex, I must say I doubt, if such a change as that which is now proposed takes place, whether we could discuss questions in this House or in the country with our present calmness, or, whether Parliament would retain the influence which it owes to its reputation for judicial wisdom.

SIR HERBERT CROFT said, that his fair constituents had not sent him a Petition on the subject of the Bill, whence he concluded that they did not wish him to advocate any change in the law. He should not like to see ladies exercising the franchise any more than he liked to see ladies going about ... delivering lectures on the rights of woman. He thought there was a great deal of truth in what their old friend Punch had recently said, that those who want woman's rights also want woman's charms. His own constituents were fair, graceful, and feminine; therefore they did not want a vote, and they had not sent him one single Petition on this subject, and, therefore, he should vote against the Bill.

124 MPs voted for a Second Reading of the Bill, a majority of 33. The MP for Orkney and Shetland, Frederick Dundas (Liberal), is not among the 'No' names, but may not have been present on that occasion. The Bill was therefore read a second time, and committed to a Select Committee of fifteen MPs, led by the Attorney General, and with power to send for persons, papers and records. The Bill then went to the Order for Committee, on 12 May 1870, where again MPs debated whether it should be put forward to Committee. This time, the Prime Minister, Gladstone, rose to speak in the debate:

'... A very important element in the consideration is, whether there is a practical necessity for the interference of the Government, or whether the Government are convinced that the matter is one on which the House is perfectly competent to act for itself. That undoubtedly is a matter that may very naturally influence their conduct; and I may say for most of my Colleagues as well as for myself, that we were both surprised and disappointed at the result of the debate on Wednesday last. [The vote moving the Bill to Committee] We do not attempt to limit the freedom of anyone either in the official body or elsewhere; but, undoubtedly, there is a prevailing opinion, which I, for one, strongly entertain in common with all those who are sitting near me, that it would be a very great mistake to proceed with this Bill. My hon. Friend the Member for Fife (Sir Robert Anstruther) has made a most gallant and chivalric defence of the opinions which he entertains. But I cannot say that his argument weighed with me. He said that he regarded the turbulent proceedings at elections as likely to be abolished by the Bill which has been introduced by my noble Friend the Postmaster General; but in answer to that I may say that we had better wait until that Bill has become law, and those happy results have been achieved, before we venture to assume as a fact such a transformation in the elections of this country. My hon. Friend says that the property held by women requires to be represented, yet if that be so that argument does not apply to the principle on which this Bill is founded, because the Bill excludes all married women from the benefit—or the evil as it may be—to be derived from the franchise. But even if women are as competent as men to exercise the franchise—if it is a function equally suitable for them, why do you not recognize in married women that which you recognize in joint proprietorship, in joint ownership, in joint trade, in joint tenancy, and allow both a man and his wife to vote in respect of property which is sufficiently valuable to qualify them?

Again, if it be true that the property of women ought to be represented, the ingenuity of the legislators of other countries has discovered a mode of attaining that end without its being open to the objection which attaches to this measure. In Italy widows and single women who are possessed of a property qualification are authorized to exercise the franchise, but only through the medium of a relative whom they appoint for the purpose. These, however, are particular points in the question; and the real matter at issue is much broader, for the question really is whether there is a necessity, nay, even, whether there is a desire or a demand for this measure. I must say I cannot recognize either the one or the other which would justify such an unsettling not to say uprooting, of the old landmarks of society, which are far deeper than any of those political distinctions which separate Gentlemen now on these Benches from those on the other. I am not aware of any such case, while I think that the practical matters that we have in hand are amply sufficient for our energies and our best attention. At nearly 2 o'clock in the morning I will not attempt to go into the general arguments, but I have listened to the debate with interest, and I am perfectly content to give my adhesion not only to the proposal, but also to the declaration and the reasoning of my right hon. Friend the Member for Kilmarnock, and I shall therefore cheerfully follow him into the Lobby.'

In spite of a final speech from Jacob Bright, the Bill was put off for a further six months, by 220 votes to 94; Hansard doesn't give a list of voters.

Jacob Bright reintroduced the Bill for a Second Reading on 3 May 1871. In his opening speech, he stressed the country-wide support for women's suffrage:

'...The great towns had recently decided in favour of household suffrage for men; and they had now decided, not with entire unanimity, but with a remarkable approach to it, in favour of this Bill for giving household suffrage throughout the country without any distinction of sex. Edinburgh and Birmingham, Manchester and Bristol, Leeds and Brighton, Oldham and Sheffield, Halifax and Bolton had given an undivided vote in favour of the Bill. ... during this Session there had been presented to Parliament in favour of the Bill 420 Petitions, to which 150,000 signatures were attached; and 150 meetings ... had been held in support of it in the United Kingdom, but mainly in Scotland and England. It was said that the franchise would be a curse to women; but it might be assumed that women were the best judges of that; and there had recently been presented to the Prime Minister a Memorial in support of the Bill, signed by women, and headed by the names of Florence Nightingale, Harriet Martineau, Miss Carpenter, and several ladies of title.'

He went on to give examples of the inequality in the law between men and women, and commented on the way the Married Women's Property Act had finally been framed:

'It passed that House and reached the other Chamber, where the voice of justice was not always heard unless its demands were in harmony with the supposed interests of those who assembled there. What was done with it? The Peers destroyed the Bill and created another. ... That Bill came back with the principle knocked out of it—a thing of shreds and patches, very good for the lawyers, but very difficult for anyone else to understand; and to this hour confiscation of property at marriage was the law for women in this country.'

Other Bills affecting women were also citied: the Deceased Wife's Sister Bill and the Infant Life Preservation Bill. Women had commented on these in the *Women's Suffrage Journal*:

' ... That journal, conducted by a woman, was as ably conducted as any journal in the kingdom, and more than any other paper represented the suffrage associations of the country. Women, however, were not satisfied with that sort of irregular representation in this House. What they said was that if their opinions were of any value, if their condition was to be studied at all, they ought to express their views by the constitutional method—through the polling-booth, precisely as men did.'

He touched on the education of women, where Sophia Jex-Blake and others had just been refused their medical degree:

'At Edinburgh University some half-dozen women of great ability, high character, and industry desired to become qualified as medical practitioners—not seeking emoluments and honours, but simply the education which such institutions were supposed to give; but nobody came down to that House for their relief; no great party was set in Motion; the Government was silent while half-a-dozen women were heroically fighting their own battle against a high-class trade union in that city.'

He finished:

'Last year, the Government being neutral on this question, the House passed the second reading of the Bill by a large majority, and then there came over the scene a remarkable change, which he never could understand; but there was a panic, and in a state of panic men always saw that which did not exist. There was set to work machinery which more than once he had seen employed to upset just decisions; and on that occasion this result was achieved. ... Last year the Home Secretary did not conceal, but rather attempted to avow, that if he had been left unfettered he would have voted for it; the Solicitor General voted for the Bill, and had spoken warmly in its favour before his constituency; the Solicitor General for Ireland voted for it; and the Secretary of the Poor Law Board was a supporter of it; the Secretary to the Admiralty voted for Mr. Mill's Resolution in favour of the enfranchisement of women. There were other Members of the Government who had never availed themselves of any opportunity of voting against the Bill. The Attorney General had not done so; the Vice President of the Council, who had admitted women to the membership of school boards, would hardly be likely to do so; the Under Secretary at the Home

Office, and the Secretary to the Treasury, had not voted against it; and, without inferring that all these were in favour of the Bill, he must conclude that there was something favourably suspicious in the fact that they had not voted against it. The great principle of the Liberal party was that taxation and representation should go together; and with so many Members of the Government favourable to the Bill, and others not hostile to it, it would not be a very unlikely thing that they should on this occasion leave this an open question, and allow the House to dispose of it free from their influence. [Mr. GLADSTONE: Hear, hear!] He rejoiced that the Prime Minister would co-operate with them so far as to allow the House to dispose of the question according to its own view. Parliament had made the home the political unit, do not let it maintain disabilities in those homes bereft of the father, and where the support to be derived from the presence of men was not to be found.'

As with the Order for Committee, the main opponent was Mr Bouverie, MP for Kilmarnock, who gave a rather entrancing picture of women's life if they were given the vote:

'... mixing up women in contested elections would be to contaminate the sex—that sex which we were bound to keep in respect, and whose modesty and purity we were especially bound to hold in reverence. ... Politics would be forced upon them—they would be driven to the poll whether they liked it or not—their lives would be made a burden to them during a contested election; and there was no woman who would not be assailed, bothered, annoyed, and persecuted to give her vote. ... At the last municipal election it was his duty to preside at one of the booths in Ardwick, and he must say that more unseemly sights took place on that occasion than he ever witnessed at any previous election, either municipal or Parliamentary. Women in a state of semi-drunkenness were hustled into public houses by men in the same state; and he made up his mind then that before the Parliamentary franchise was extended to women they ought to have the Ballot. ... He would ask whether any gentleman present would like to see his wife, daughter, or sister taking part in the disgraceful scenes which were witnessed at the last municipal election. Staggering women, supported by staggering men—not their husbands—were seen going up to vote, both sexes boisterous and obscene in their language.'

Then he blamed America:

'...This was not a new idea, nor a notion originating in this country. The issue now raised sprung up in a country which was fertile in strange notions and ideas—the United States of America—those States which were often extolled by his hon. Friend and those who acted with him as furnishing an example of everything wise and expedient in political life. Now, what had our practical kinsmen on the other side of the Atlantic done in reference to this question? Why, the Legislatures of several of the States, and even Congress itself, had repudiated the notion of woman suffrage, and the American women themselves had also repudiated it. Would the House allow him to read an extract from a letter of the New York correspondent of a daily newspaper in this country?— I am afraid it must be confessed that the Woman Suffrage Movement in the United States is pretty well 'played out.' It has become unmistakably evident of late that the women of the country do not want the suffrage.'

Mr Bouverie also emphasised that this was indeed the 'thin end of the wedge':
'... if we conceded electoral power to women, how could we refuse them a share in legislative power, in judicial power, in administrative power? All the great branches of political power—the legislative, the administrative, the judicial, and the electoral—must be equally conceded. This was a state of things which the House ought seriously to contemplate if it intended to pass the Bill.'

Mr Gladstone spoke at length, neatly suggesting support for the principle but not for this Bill. While disclaiming any influence from the Government,

'...it is neither desirable nor advantageous that the Government should make a rule of interfering, as a Government, in the discussion of every measure at its earliest stages',
he made his own misgivings about the Bill very clear:

'... the Bill, indeed, is somewhat remarkable in one point of view — namely, that it avoids any statement of the reasons for the change which it proposes to make in the law. ... my hon. Friend has altogether dispensed with a Preamble, as though unwilling to commit himself to a limited purpose in the changes he wishes to bring about.' He agrees that women should not take part in elections: 'I am inclined to say that the personal attendance and intervention of women in election proceedings, even apart from any suspicion of the wider objects of many of the promoters of the present movement, would be a practical evil not only of the gravest, but even of an intolerable character.'

He brought up the spectre of universal female suffrage:

'I am not quite sure that my hon. Friend, in excluding married women from the operation of his Bill, has adopted a perfectly consistent course. It is clear that married women, if they possess the qualification, ought not to be excluded from any privilege conferred upon single women ... we have done wisely, on the whole, in giving both the franchise and the right of sitting on the school boards to women. Now we are asked to go further, and we have to consider whether the same principle that has been applied to parochial and municipal elections shall, or shall not be extended to Parliamentary elections also.' He also suggests the numbers of eligible women may be greater than Bright suggests: 'The number of absolutely dependent women is decreasing from year to year, while the number of self-depending women, especially in the great towns of the country, is rapidly increasing. ... If it be true that there is a progressive increase in the number of self-dependent women, that is a very serious fact, because these women are assuming the burdens which belong to men; and I agree with the hon. Member for Manchester that, when they are called upon to assume those burdens, and to undertake the responsibility of providing for their own subsistence, they approach the task under greater difficulties than attach to their more powerful competitors in the battle of life.

Now, Sir, I cannot help thinking that ... there are various important particulars in which women obtain much less than justice under the social arrangements of our life. ... I scarcely ever see in the hands of a woman an employment that ought more naturally to be in the hands of a man; but I constantly see in the hands of a man employment which might be more beneficially and economically in the hands of a woman.

... the case of farms. The not unnatural disposition of landowners is to see their farms in the hands of those who, sympathizing ... with his landlord, can give effect to that sympathy by voting at the poll, and I believe to some extent in the competition for that particular employment, women suffer in a very definite manner in consequence of their disqualification to vote. I go somewhat further than this, and say that ... where the peculiar relation of men and women are concerned, ... the English law does women much less than justice, and great mischief, misery, and scandal result from that state of things.

... Although, therefore, I am unable to give a vote for a Bill with respect to which there is no promise of modification, if we cannot adopt it in its present form, ... if it should hereafter be found possible to arrive at a safe and well-adjusted alteration of the law as to political power, the man who shall attain that object, and who shall see his purpose carried onward to its legitimate consequences in a more just arrangement of the provisions of other laws bearing upon the condition and welfare of women, will, in my opinion, be a real benefactor to his country.'

The debate continued with a number of speakers. This time the majority for reading the Bill in six months time, rather than now, was smaller: 220 to 151, with F Dundas voting with Jacob Bright to read it now.

The Bill was presented for a Second Reading again on 1 May 1872. In his opening speech, Bright emphasised the growing support the Bill had in the country; in his closing speech, he dismissed the bugbear of married women voting. 222 MPs voted to defer the Bill for six months, a majority of 79, with F Dundas now among them.

The last presentation of Jacob Bright's Bill was on 30 April 1873. In his opening speech, he emphasised the security of the new Ballot Box:

'We were told that there was great turbulence on the day of election, and that there were scenes of such a disreputable character that no right-minded man would desire a woman to partake in them. The Ballot has now been tried in the largest as well as the smallest of the constituencies. ... it has succeeded in securing peace and order at the poll. I believe no one will deny that a woman can now go to the polling booth and return from it with far greater ease than she experiences in making her way out of a theatre or a concert-room.'

The Bill was again deferred for six months, but with a smaller majority of 67. Hansard does not give a list of voters, so we do not know how Shetland's new MP, Mr Samuel Laing, voted. Jacob Bright lost his seat in the 1874 election, and his Bill was not presented again; the next suffrage Bill was to be Fowler's Bill of 1874.

Lerwick as it would have looked in the 1870s. Photographed by G W Wilson; courtesy of Shetland Museum and Archives [NE08699]

2

1872 – 1874

The first Shetland Women's Suffrage Societies

Lerwick, 1872. Imagine you're in a boat, off the Victoria Pier, looking at the shore. The new Anderson Institute, the Widows' Homes, the buildings along the sea front, punctuated by little beaches between lodberries, have hardly changed, except that the lodberries all have their pulleys swinging from poles, and the doors are open to let the constant flurry of flit boats and bomshuits unload their cargo. The Tolbooth looks as it now does again; after it, a beach and James Greig's house where the Post Office now stands, then a new pier extending fifteen yards into Bressay sound. Today is Tuesday; the steamer came yesterday, and the ten packet boats, *Lady Alice, Matilda, Rattlesnake* and *Sylph, William Tell, Elizabeth, Alabama, Imogen, Nelson* and *Star of the West*, are loading up with goods and passengers for other parts of Shetland. These embark precariously in flit boats from the slips on the north and south sides of the pier. The packets will return on Friday with news, goods and mail.

The skyline's different too; the Town Hall is yet to be built, as are the Gilbert Bain Hospital, the Central and Old Infant Schools, the Territorial Drill Hall, the Post Office, the Grand Hotel, the Rechabite Hall, St Ringan's Church, St Clement's Church Hall, St Margaret's Church and the Union Bank. The Hillhead's just a road, with no houses alongside it yet; there's only crofting land and the imposing shape of Hayfield House beyond Burgh Road.

If you land at the pier, the buildings of Commercial Street are pretty much the same, although with different names on the shop fronts. It's crowded with people, though, and there are open sewers still running down some of the lanes, although the town now has tap water in the houses, and better sanitation. Houses and town are lit by the new gas lamps. Some of the ladies are fashionable in colourful taffeta dresses with a flattened front and elaborate draperies behind, and a small, tilted hat pinned firmly to their pile of plaited or curled hair. In this small Lerwick, these middle-class women all know each other. The women of the Lanes are in full woollen skirts, with shawls thrown over their heads. The better-off men wear black suits; the poorer wear any combination of warm jacket, waistcoat and trousers they have. There's a swarm of small children busy at the waterfront and in the lanes, because schools are only for those who can afford them.

Lerwick's a thriving town, about to embark on huge expansion. The new town below the Hillhead, Victoria Pier, a second water scheme, the direct telegram cable, and, most importantly, the great herring boom, are all about to begin. For the poor, the lively, bustling waterfront never sleeps; for the gentry, evenings are filled with church soirees, choral practices, Good Templar meetings or just dining with friends. The population rose by 500 in the last decade, to 3,655.

Things are different in the country. There, it's a life of unremitting work, coaxing crops out of ground that's been subdivided and subdivided among too many families, just so the laird can have crew for his haaf boats. The famines of the 1840s are a vivid memory; to qualify for meal, men and women of good character were employed to lay the first roads the length and breadth of the islands. Some of the lairds have already begun to talk of clearing their tenants for sheep. Many country families have come to Lerwick, and are managing to survive in a room in the lanes; others have already taken ship for New Zealand, on one of the free passages advertised in the county's new paper. In this decade, a quarter of Shetland's population will emigrate.

The first *Zetland Times* appeared on Monday 17 June 1872, and was very different from our modern paper. It consisted of four pages – one large sheet folded in half. The front page was given over to boxed advertising, including names which will appear in the suffrage story: Leisk and Sandison, successors to George Reid Tait, and Hector Morrison Bookseller Stationer & Bookbinder. Page 2 was halved vertically. The advertisements continued on the left hand side:

'Wanted IMMEDIATELY for the Burgh of LERWICK, an ACTIVE, STEADY MARRIED MAN, not exceeding 40 years of age, to discharge the duties of SUPERINTENDANT of POLICE, SANITARY

INSPECTOR &c. A person of experience in TOWN IMPROVEMENTS and management of WATER WORKS preferred.'

On the right hand side were literary or political essays: the 'Norse literature' column, 'Remarks on the state of religion... in Shetland about the turn of last century', and the political editorial. Page 3 had letters to the editor, a column of poetry, and the markets; page 4 had general news and a serial story entitled 'Dangers of the Deep: A tale of the American War.' The general news was a series of short paragraphs, and on 19 August 1872 I found the first mention of the suffrage movement, interspersed among Reader's Digest style funny stories (later these became an 'Amusing and Instructive' column) and adverts beginning 'If there are any Ladies who have not yet tried Glenfield Starch ...':

'Miss Olive Logan, an advocate of the female suffrage movement, is preparing a protest against the 'free love principle' which it is the aim of certain men and women to engraft upon the women's movement, under the title of 'Get thee behind me, Satan'.'

School boards 1872 - 3:

The *Zetland Times* agreed that one of the most important Bills of the parlimentary session of 1872 was the Scotch Education Bill. On Monday 26 August 1872 there was a full account of its provisions, which included the creation and election of school boards to be decided by a vote of male and female rate-payers. A later news section gave a detailed description of the contents of the bill, by which the 'transition of whole school system of this country from its old connection with the Established Church to the new popular management will have been accomplished' [*ZT* 17 March 1873].

Women could now stand for school boards. In Manchester in 1870, Lydia Becker was the first woman in the country to be elected, five days before Emily Davies and Elizabeth Garrett in London. Garrett was returned with more votes than any other candidate. In that year, they were the only ones; by 1875 there were 17 women members in England and Wales, in 1880, 71, and the numbers rose steadily thereafter to 270 women members in 1900. [Figures taken from *The March of the Women* by Martin Pugh] An English Education Act of 1902 removed women's elegibility to stand for school boards, although they could still be co-opted, and were; the number doubled to 594 in 1905.

The first Scottish woman to take up the challenge was Flora Stevenson, in Edinburgh, 1872. She proved so successful that she remained on the board for over thirty years, ending up as chair, and in 1902 an Edinburgh primary school was named after her. There were also women on School Boards in Glasgow, but none in Dundee until the early 1890s, and none in Perthshire or the Highlands [*The Schooling of Victorian Girls in working-class Scotland,* Jane McDermid, Woburn Education Series, p 110]. The only Scottish figures I can find are from much later (after the 1903 Act making women unable to be elected, but able to be co-opted), in answer to a question in the House of Commons question. There were 972 School Boards in Scotland in 1907, with 5,680 members; a total of 76 women sat on 63 individual Boards.

The *Zetland Times* was having no truck with such practices. The editorial of 26 August 1872 began promisingly:

'But we have no fears for the future. We anticipate nothing but the most satisfactory results from the great measure which has now become law... especially will every voter, male or female, desire to learn the whole bearings of a law so important as the new Education Act...'

Alas for women, it ended by saying the voter must ask himself:

'Who are likely to be the most intelligent, the most judicious, the most liberal minded men to whom I shall entrust the control of the secular education of my children and my neighbour's. And having made up his mind on that point, let him go and vote for the men of whom he approves.' [*ZT* 26 August 1872]

The *Zetland Times* gave the account of one Lerwick public meeting in full. It was led by Sheriff Mure, who explained the provisions of the act:

'the electors are all persons, females as well as males, who are of lawful age, whose names are entered on the Valuation Roll as owners or occupiers of land or houses of the annual value of £4 and upward...'

There was no mention of women standing:

'..I trust that gentlemen will be selected who will fearlessly do their duty under the act ...'

There was also a detailed explanation of how to vote, by placing your cross - women had not done this before. [*ZT* 31 March 1873]

However, two ladies did stand for the School Board of the United Parishes of Bressay, Burra and Quarff, and were elected on 25 April 1873: Miss Cameron Mouat of Bressay and Miss Webster, Manse, Quarff.

Margaret Ann Cameron Mouat, b 1816, was the sister of Major Cameron of Garth. Her father, Captain William Cameron [Mouat], seems to have been genuinely dedicated to the welfare of his tenants. When he died in 1855, Miss Mouat ran all the estates for her mother until the arrival of her brother Major Thomas Cameron, in 1862 -3. The Major, however, was not interested in the estates and installed an unscrupulous factor, John Walker. At first Walker's depredations were confined to the Delting and Unst estates. When Mrs Cameron died in 1871, Walker turned his attention to the tenants

on Bressay, people Miss Cameron Mouat knew, and the following year she bought the Bressay estate from her brother. Her first act was to buy Walker out of his tenancy of Maryfield, paying over the odds, in spite of her reputation for stinginess, just to be rid of him. He was also involved with the school boards, so her presence on this one was perhaps part of the same campaign to limit his influence. It didn't work; he stayed on after she left, or perhaps that was why she left. There were no more evictions from Bressay during her tenure, and she also began a substantial house-building programme, including a fishing village at Ham. She donated a stained-glass window and a bell to the new Town Hall, and re-landscaped and planted the gardens at Gardie House. She died in 1900 at Tingwall Manse; her niece May McCulloch Baynes was the minister's wife.

(Above) Margaret Cameron Mowat as an old lady. Photograph courtesy of the Gardie Trust.

Miss Clementina Mary Webster b 1835, was the daughter of the Reverend Alexander Webster, minister first in Burra, then in Quarff; her mother was Mary Scott of Scalloway, previously married to a cousin, John Scott of Melby. Mr Webster was born in Old Deer, Aberdeen, and Clementina died there in 1885.

A suggestion was made of nominating 'two ladies [for the Lerwick board] ... but as they and ministers would be out of place during the Board's first term of office, I will refrain'. No ladies were nominated in Nesting, Lerwick, Sandsting, Walls, Delting, Unst, North Yell, Mid and South Yell or Tingwall.

However, the ladies did not sit on the Bressay, Burra and Quarff School Board for very long. The last meeting Miss Cameron Mouat attended was on 3 December 1875; Miss Webster's last meeting was on 25 April, 1876, which simply set the election day for a new board. The new Board, elected on 1

May 1876, was Major Cameron, Rev Hamilton, J Kirkland Galloway and John Walker, with Lewis F U Garriock as a co-opted member.

After such an early start with the school boards, Shetland was not to have a woman serving on one for almost forty years: Christina Jamieson was the next, serving on the Lerwick School Board from 1911, and on the County Committee of Secondary Education from 1915.

Women did serve as Compulsory Attendance Officers; perhaps it was seen as more suitable that they should visit potentially sick children. A good attendance in school was important, as if the roll numbers were not kept up, the school lost its grant. *Manson's Shetland Almanac*, which began in 1892, gives us their names. In Lerwick, Miss Mary Mackay was the 'Officer' from before 1892 to 1898, initially with George Mackay, probably her father, Police Superintendant George Mackay, who died in December 1891, just as the *Almanac* would have been going to print. She was replaced in 1899 by Misses Annie Manson and Bella Gair, who served until 1902. Ann Manson was the Matron of the Widows' Homes at this time, and her mother and sister lived with her there. The Bayanne Shetland geneaology website has an Isabella Bruce Gear (her grandfather was a Gair of Eswick, Nesting), who married a sawyer, William Williamson, in 1903.

After 1902, the Lerwick Officers were male.

Sandsting and Aithsting also had a woman Officer, Miss Mary Jessie Abernethy, of Braewick, Aith, who served for many years from 1901, along with John Ridland of Sandsting. She was born in 1872, the oldest daughter of Thomas Abernethy, of the Haa, Braewick, Aith, and Mary Garriock of Innersand, Sandsting. Thomas' father was Mitchel Abernethy, a sheriff's officer, and so a powerful person in the area; it might have been through his influence that she got the post. She was twenty-nine when her truancy officer career began, and she did her rounds on a bicycle, wearing a huge Edwardian hat. She was exceptionally tall, over six feet, and so was known as 'Lang Jessie'. When she came into a house she made a grand entrance, leaving all the doors wide open behind her. She was very clever, a keen reader, and given to sharp, witty remarks - for example, an eccentrically dressed visitor asked her, 'Don't you ever want to get away and see all the sights?' Jessie gave her a withering look and retorted, 'No, I wait till the sight comes to me.' Children locally were afraid of her, and she had many a set-to with their mothers, to the extent that one mother, when her son cut his foot and could not walk from Aith to Clousta, carried him to Clousta on her back to show his foot to the schoolmaster, and demand that he kept Lang Jessie away.

In her later years, Jessie suffered from chronic asthma ('You could hear her before you saw her,' commented David Anderson of the Ayres, who had childhood memories of her). Three of her brothers emigrated, and she lost her remaining family between 1905 and 1918: first her brother Peter, aged 29, then her only sister Louisa, aged 24, both from TB, then, in three years, her father, her brother Thomas, and her mother. From then she lived as a recluse among piles of books, letting few people through her door. A concerned neighbour asked about what she ate, and was told that the night before she had received a new book, and had become so absorbed in it that she had let the kettle boil dry and the fire go out, 'So I went to bed without supper.'

There are a number of photographs of Jessie Abernethy in the Shetland Museum, taken by Edmund Fraser, the laird of Vementry in the first years of the twentieth century.

Mary Jessie Abernethy, of the Old Haa, Braewick, Aith, who served as one of the two Compulsory Attendance Officers for Aithsting from 1901. When the two Lerwick CAOs stepped down in 1902, she was the only woman official in Shetland until the appointment of two women registrars in 1908. Photograph by Edmund Fraser of Vementry, July 1901, courtesy of the Shetland Museum and Archives [EF00074]

The Contagious Diseases Act and the 1872 by-election:

The repeal of the Contagious Diseases Act was an important feminist and religious cause of the 1870s. The Contagious Diseases Acts of 1864, 1867 and 1869 gave plain-clothes policemen the right to arrest women suspected of being prostitutes and force them to undergo medical inspection and treatment. Naturally, since it was only the women who were examined and treated (they could be interned in locked hospitals, initially for three months, later for up to a year), this had little effect on venereal disease in the army, but it could be used as a weapon of intimidation against any woman suspected of being a prostitute, and there were accusations of police misuse of power. Men were not examined, as it was considered degrading. Feminists were outraged by the double standard that allowed men to divorce women for adultery, but permitted married men to patronise prostitutes; John Stuart Mill went as far as to say that a woman should be allowed to divorce a man who knowingly infected her with venereal disease. Moralists were horrified at the idea that 'vice' (ie adultery and fornication) was seen as a 'necessity' for men, and saw the Contagious Diseases Acts as enshrining this vice in law; hence the number of clergymen campaigning against it. The best known campaigner against these acts was Josephine Butler, in Liverpool, but Edinburgh was one of the named Garrison Towns where this act could be applied, and the President of the Edinburgh WSS, Priscilla Bright McLaren, was a member of the Executive Committee for the Repeal of the Contagious Diseases Acts. Later anti-suffragists would refer in horrified tones to the 'unwomanly language' of the pamphlets against the Acts.

Jacob Bright gave one example of this Act in practice, asking in the House of Commons whether 'an English woman of the name of Elizabeth Holt is now or has recently been a prisoner in Maidstone Gaol because she declined to subject her person to the fortnightly inspection of a surgeon; and, whether her refusal or the refusal of any other woman to submit to this outrage would be followed by repeated periods of imprisonment so as to amount practically to perpetual incarceration?'

Mr Bruce replied that

'According to the law on this subject, under section 28 of the Act of 1866, any woman subjected by order of the justices to examinations by a surgeon, and refusing so to submit herself, was liable to imprisonment, with or without hard labour, in the case of the first offence, for a term not exceeding one month, and for a second offence three months. In the case of this woman, who lived in Woolwich, she attended fourteen examinations, and was sent to the hospital five times suffering from disease. In January last, after repeated warnings, she neglected to attend the periodical examinations; she was summoned, and sentenced to fourteen days' imprisonment. [Hansard, HC Deb 10 March 1870]

Bright addressed the House again in the debate to repeal the Contagious Diseases Act on 20 July 1870:

'Sir, the hon. Member for Ayr (Mr. Craufurd) may be unaware of the fact that in the present Session of Parliament some 700 or 800 Petitions, signed by nearly 500,000 persons, have been presented to this House, asking for a repeal of the Acts which are now under discussion. ... [These Acts] have been brought forward either late at night or late in the Session, and every effort has been made to stifle discussion. ... [The House of Lords] passed these odious Acts entirely without debate. The Press joined this great conspiracy of silence. ... there are great London newspapers which have opened their columns freely to the supporters of these Acts, and which reject answers from, the most competent persons. ... The Association for extending these Acts has been doing all in its power ... to frighten the public into accepting this legislation. I am supported in this view by the most eminent authorities. ... We are told that these Acts are required in the interest of innocent wives and children. This seems to me like asking the Chancellor of the Exchequer to spend the people's money in order that British husbands may commit adultery with impunity. I could give the highest authorities to prove that inherited disease, even among the lowest and least protected class of the London poor, is small. ... Sir William Jenner says he never knew a case go beyond one generation. ... From 1860 to 1865, a period during which these Acts were not in force, there was a remarkable decrease of disease at the military stations. From 1865 to 1868, when the Acts were generally in force, there was no diminution of disease. ... in scarcely any of the stations, under the Acts, has there been any falling back. ... The House is aware that the Act professes to be directed against common prostitutes. ... a definition in the Police Act ... implies women who are seen soliciting in the street. The operations of those who carry out the Contagious Diseases Acts are limited by no such definition. Poor men's houses are entered, women suspected of incontinence, but who are in no sense common prostitutes, are forced into this vile slavery. ... It is the most indefensible piece of class legislation of which I have any knowledge. How are these Acts carried out? Their victims are not brought into Court and fairly judged. There is a provision by which they can be made to sign what is called a voluntary submission. Women frightened by the police are induced to sign their names or put their crosses to a paper of the meaning of which they know nothing. ... Among the regulations issued by the War Office, on the 1st December, 1869, is the following:— Should any woman object to sign, she is to be informed of the penal consequences attending such refusal, and the advantages of a voluntary submission are to be pointed out to her. Now, Sir, there are no penal consequences attending such refusal. A woman who refuses to sign can only be summoned before the Bench, where she has the opportunity of showing that she is not a common prostitute.'

Then, Sir, we have the examining house. I will not undertake to describe that disgraceful institution, but will leave it to the imagination of those who now hear me. I will simply say that women who are young, women who are not young, those who are hardened in vice and those who are barely past its threshold, are driven up to this examining house, herded like cattle in a pen, waiting for the ordeal which a Parliament, representing only men, has prepared for their victims. There is a clause in the Act of 1869, I believe it is the 3rd clause, which exhibits in the extremest way the injustice and indecency of this system. I will refrain from any further reference to it, and I am glad to be told that the authors of the Act are themselves ashamed of it, and would be more at ease if it had no existence.'

The debate continued with a number of Army surgeons giving statistics reinforcing their opinions that the Acts do help control disease among their barracks:

'Venereal affections, which are little more than half the number returned for 1868, notably diminished during the period the troops were quartered at Aldershot, the existence of a Lock Hospital being conducive to that result.' [Medical Officer, 35th Regiment].

Statistics were given to show that it had reduced the number of registered prostitutes in each town. The Bill ran out of debate time, and seems not to have been re-debated in that year.

On 21 Oct 1872, the *Zetland Times* began to focus on the forthcoming by-election following the death of Mr Dundas:

'the only gentleman who has offered himself is Mr Samuel Laing, late MP for the Northern Burghs ... who is a native of Orkney.'

Laing, born in 1812, had been the MP for Wick from 1852 to 1857, from 1859-60, when he served as Financial Secretary to the Treasury, and from 1865 – 1868. He gave his own electorial address on 11 November, and in subsequent issues until 30 December:

'My opinions on politics remain unchanged since I served under Lord Palmerston.'

Ireland was then an important issue:

'...the honour of Great Britain requires we should pursue a firm Protestant policy.'

The election became a contested one; Laing was challenged by Sir Peter Tait, who grew up in Lerwick. Women's suffrage was not mentioned in either candidate's manifesto, but the Contagious Diseases Act was an issue. In the report of Mr Laing's meeting in Scalloway:

'Rev Mr Macfarlane, addressing the chairman, said there was a subject on which he wished to know if Mr Laing was prepared to give his support for its abolition, he referred to the Contagious Diseases Act.

Mr Laing in reply stated that the subject was a very delicate one; and as the Home Secretary was collecting information on it, he would give the subject his best consideration.

Mr Macfarlane, again rose, and said he regretted that Mr Laing did not see his way clear to give his support for its total repeal. Were its provisions adopted in Lerwick, it would be dangerous for any respectable girls to walk the streets for fear of having their characters ruined. There was some noise during Mr Macfarlane's speech, so we were prevented from hearing all that he said.' [*ZT* 18 November 1872]

The report of Sir Peter Tait's election address suggested that the 'noise' was approval of Rev Macfarlane's stance:

'Since his [Sir Peter's] arrival in Orkney his attention had been drawn to the Contagious Diseases Act, which he had thought must have been smuggled through Parliament. As a husband and a father he would support its total repeal and abolition (Loud cheers).'

At the end of the meeting, Rev Macfarlane made a lengthy speech in which he expressed his previous doubts about Sir Peter's candidature, and his new resolution to 'render [him] all the aid and lend him all the influence I can command.' [*ZT* 2 December 1872]

A letter signed by A CHURCHMAN on Mr Laing's opposition to repealing the Acts called it 'an act that is atrociously opposed by the Statute Book of God' and appealed to the ministers of Protestant churches to unite against the 'legalizing of prostitution'. [*ZT* 2 December 1872]

By 9 December Sir Peter Tait's committee for promoting his return took up two columns of the front page; it included the Rev Macfarlane, Mr John Robertson (Bailie Robertson) and Mr John Leisk, Merchant, Commercial Street. He was billed by his committee as 'the True Liberal Candidate ... a staunch adherent of the Gladstone government, and a friend of progressive reform.' The *Zetland Times* editorial was also strongly behind him (due to bribery, according to Thomas Manson in *Lerwick in the Last Half-Century*, p 23-5, which gives a most entertaining account of the whole campaign) and threw Mr Laing's mistakes in his face: ' the Turkish Loan transaction, the Cave of Adalbum, his voting for Professor Fawcett's motion to throw the expenses of Members of Parliament on the poor rates ..' There were several letters about this last.

However, Mr Laing won by a narrow majority – 25 votes. The Editorial of 27 January 1873 was not impressed: 'he has been elected our representative by mere accident' and persisted in calling him our '*interim* MP.' Again, there was no mention of women's suffrage in the Queen's Speech for 1873; the burning issue was University Education in Ireland. Gladstone's government was to be defeated on this by three votes, leading to his temporary resignation in March.

Samuel Laing was to prove a friend to the women's suffrage cause, voting for all the Women's Disability Bills presented in his twelve years as an MP for Orkney and Shetland.

Mr Laing must have taken his constituents' views on board, for on 3 July of the following year he also voted with the minority in favour of hearing the Second Reading of the Bill repealing the Contagious Diseases act. The Second Reading was put back by 250 votes to 158; it was heard in November 1874. Speaking against the Bill (to repeal the Acts) Mr Hardy said

'his official experience showed him the good they had done. He concluded with an indignant and sensible protest against the literature with which the ladies of the agitation, having every good intention no doubt, had disgraced and were corrupting the country.'

The bill was rejected by 308 votes to 116. An Act of 1883 removed the need for examination, and the 1886 Act repealed the previous acts entirely.

On 9 June 1873, in the general news, there was another suffrage item:

'Miss Jane E Taylor has been presented by a number of friends in acknowledgement of her efforts on behalf of women's suffrage, with a piece of jewellery and a purse of 150 guineas.'

Taylour was at that moment preparing her autumn tour of Scotland, which was, this time, to include Shetland.

Jessie Craigen, August, 1873:

There is a belief that the women's suffrage movement was predominantly middle-class. This is an over-simplification; middle-class respectability was emphasised by the women, but working-class women like Sarah Reddish, a Lancashire mill-girl and trade unionist, were also involved during this early period. Shetland's first speaker was another triumphant exception. Jessie Hannah Craigen was born in 1834 or 1835, and was described by a friend as 'the restless daughter of a Highland seafaring father and an Italian actress mother.' She was brought up in the theatre, but as a young woman felt religious scruples, and began giving lectures on the temperance movement and the suffrage movement, often in the open air, to working class crowds on the local green, or at the factory gate. A description from 1879 says she would hire a bell-ringer to attract attention. She travelled throughout the country, staying in lodgings, speaking and organising petitions, and accompanied only by her dog, Tiny. She was a passionate and electrifying speaker with a powerful voice (her theatrical training), but not 'ladylike' ('outlandish appearance' was a description used on several occasions, with 'massive features' and a deep voice), and so in part an embarrassment to some suffrage workers, who feared she would confirm popular beliefs that suffragists were man-like eccentrics. Lydia Becker, however, was hugely impressed by her ability to move a crowd. This public speaking landed her in gaol on at least one occasion during the 1870s – the first suffrage woman to be imprisoned. During the late 1870s she became involved in the Irish struggle for Home Rule, along with her friend Helen Taylor (J S Mill's step-daughter). In 1879, she was employed to speak to women workers before the Manchester by-election, and Priscilla Bright McLaren asked her to speak at the public meetings of 1880 and 1882. In 1883, she caused controversy among suffragists over her defence of married women's right to vote. Later, she would be involved in setting up a women's union among the jute workers of Dundee and another in Aberdeen. She died in 1899.

Here in Shetland she gave three lectures for the temperance cause, followed by one on the suffrage movement.

'MISS JESSIE CRAIGEN delivered the first of a series of Popular Lectures, under the auspices of the Lerwick Good Templars in the Congregational Chapel on the evening of Friday last - her subject being 'The History of the Drinking system, and the struggles against it.' Bailie Robertson presided, and there was a pretty fair attendance. The lecture, as we have been informed, was treated in an able and comprehensive manner, although it is said some of her remarks savoured too much of 'shop'. We understand the series is to be continued on Monday and Tuesday evenings first.' [*ZT,* 4 August 1873]

'WOMEN'S RIGHTS: On Wednesday evening last, Miss Jessie Craigen concluded her series of lectures here. Mr William Duncan occupied the chair, and in a few appropriate words introduced the lecturess to the meeting. Miss Craigen then entered into the subject, and occupied two hours in pointing out the rights and wrongs of her sex. Some of her remarks against the male sex were very sarcastic. At the close it was moved that a petition signed by the chairman in favour of women's rights, be forwarded to Parliament.' [*ZT,* 11 August 1873]

The memorandum was received by the House of Commons on 23 March, 1874:

'LERWICK in public meeting assembled; William Duncan, Chairman (*Mr Laing*) ... 1 signature.'

William Duncan was born in 1820 in Noness, Sandwick, and married Barbara Johnson in Lerwick in 1846. Their first child was born in Aberdeen, the next three in Banff, the fifth and sixth in Edinburgh and the seventh and eighth at Garths, Nesting, in 1858 and 1859. He returned to Lerwick, according to Thomas Manson, about 1867, and set up his grocer shop in Commercial St with the help of two of his sons, William and David.

'Though he took no prominent part in public affairs, he was greatly interested in temperance matters. He was a pillar among the Good Templars, and was closely associated with the inauguration of that body in the town and throughout the islands. Mr Duncan was an excellent platform speaker, and his incisive and telling speeches at public functions of the Order were always listened to with respect.' [*Lerwick during the Last Half-Century* by Thomas Manson p 49]

Jane Taylour and Agnes McLaren, September 1873:

Shetland's second speaker, Miss Jane Taylour of Belmont, Stranraer, was a much more acceptable face of women's suffrage. She was the Honorary Secretary of the Galloway branch of the National Society for Women's Suffrage, apparently of independent means, and undaunted by travel. By April 1871 she had addressed 41 public meetings, all of them presided over by men of the establishment: chief magistrates, sheriffs and church ministers. She was described as 'chaste and elegant, her voice distinct and agreeable, and her manner attractive and graceful.' A photograph shows her as fair-haired, with a broad brow and a frowning, determined expression.

Taylour was accompanied by Miss Agnes McLaren, joint secretary of the Edinburgh Ladies' Emancipation Society, and a remarkable lady in her own right. The daughter of Duncan McLaren's second wife, who died when Agnes was only three, she was born in 1837, so was now in her mid thirties. As a young woman she had helped with Dr Guthrie's 'Ragged Schools' for children of the poor, both teaching and fund-raising. Surprisingly, in view of their support of Sophia Jex-Blake, both Duncan and Priscilla McLaren were opposed to Agnes's wish to study medicine. McLaren was the tenth British woman to qualify as a doctor; she began training at the University of Montpellier in 1876, then, to permit her to practise in Scotland and England, passed the examinations at the Royal College of Dublin. After that she practised in Cannes. In 1877 she was a member of the governing council of the London Medical School for Women, and in 1882, the Royal College of Dublin made her a Fellow.

In 1898, aged 61, she converted to the Catholic Church, and wrote to the Pope and other dignitaries in support of the anti-vice work still being done by Josephine Butler. She had an interest in missionary work, and established a small chapel and lodging for missionaries at her retirement home in Antibes. From one of these missionaries she learned of the system of purdah, and that Indian women were not permitted to see male doctors. Horrified by the un-necessary suffering and deaths of mother and child, she founded the Medical Mission Committee in London, who financed St Catherine's Hospital in Rawalpindi. It was opened in 1909. The first doctor put in charge felt unequal to the task and so, at the age of seventy-three, Dr McLaren travelled out there herself. After petitioning the Pope five times to try and persuade him to lift the ban on missionary nuns practising as midwives, she asked the Medical Mission Commission to sponsor one pupil's medical training at Cork University on condition the pupil went to Rawalpindi for five years. She was corresponding in French with her successor, Anna Dengel, when she died in April 1913. The *British Medical Journal* said, in her obituary:

'She was a woman of strong individuality and character, and was known to a large circle of philanthropic workers of many nations, many kindreds and many creeds. She has died at an advanced age, though somewhat unexpectedly, and will be missed by many.' (*BMJ* April 26, 1913)

Taylour and McLaren had visited Orkney in October 1871, speaking at Kirkwall and Stromness, and backed on the platform by local church ministers. Now, on 12th September 1873, they spoke in the Lecture Hall, Mounthooly Street, Lerwick, at a meeting chaired by Bailie Robertson. The meeting was fully reported in the next *Zetland Times*, including a detailed account of Taylour's speech:

Jane E Taylour from Stranraer, Secretary of the Galloway WSS, who gave a lecture in Lerwick in September 1873.
Photograph reproduced by kind permission of the Mistress and Fellows of Girton College, Cambridge.

'[Miss Taylour] said they had come there to give reasons why they desired changes in electoral representation, and why they should grant a political status to women. She went on to speak of the origins of the movement, and stated that it had assumed a public aspect when the late John Stuart Mill introduced it into the house of Commons; but it did not succeed. However the ladies themselves had taken up the question, and the speaker had no doubt that by labour and perseverance they would obtain these rights which were at present denied them.

They (the ladies) firstly, claimed the right to the electoral suffrage as it is consistent and logical; secondly, as taxes can only be levied by a Parliament, elected by the tax-payers, they held that it was unconstitutional to impose a barrier on [tax-paying] women; and thirdly, she went on to show that a great many of her sex were self-supporting. Miss Taylour then went on to notice many of the objections urged against giving women the right to vote, but as the limited space at our command prevents us from giving more than an epitome of what she said, we do not deem it necessary to mention any of them, as most of them have already appeared in print. Among other rights of which the female sex were deprived she cited Christ's Hospital, which was founded for boys and girls alike, but while 1100 boys were in attendance, there were only 25 females in it, who were being brought up as general servants. Some opponents of women suffrage had said that men should receive better education than women, but she doubted this assertion; and stated that often husbands had to look to their wives for aid and guidance. The present were stirring times, and the men would require the aid and sound reason of women to guide them aright. There would not have been so many black pages of history if women had not been ignored. Women (she said) had the first moulding of the lives of our statesmen; although their opinions were perhaps afterwards either enlarged or modified. Miss Taylour next defined what politics meant, and stated that the management of a household was, though on a small scale, similar to the management of a nation. Man had arrogated to himself the divine right to rule the world; although it must be confessed women was sent to be a co-worker with him in his larger as well as his smaller affairs. Miss Taylour, in grandiloquent terms, sketched the rise and progess of woman from the barbarous ages, when she was merely the slave of man, until the light of Christianity dawned and set her free, and now she had come to claim her right. The ladies did not want to subvert the Constitution, but to help on the world's reform. She also referred to some of the objections that had been raised against women taking an active part in elections and appearing personally at the polling booths; but said that that objection had no foot to stand upon, seeing women were allowed to attend balls, fancy bazaars, and places of amusement. She concluded by appealing to the men to help them in obtaining their right. Miss Taylour was applauded frequently during her address.

After Bailie Robertson's vote of thanks, the meeting was addressed by Rev A MacFarlane, proposing the first resolution of the meeting: 'That as taxation is the basis of representation in this country, it is unjust in principle to make sex a ground of disqualification; therefore this meeting authorises the chairman to sign a petition in favour of Mr Jacob Bright's Bill, 'To remove the Electoral Disabilities of Women' [due, in theory, to be presented again in November] and to forward the same to both Houses of Parliament at the proper time, as well as a memorial to the county member.' The motion was seconded in a speech by Dr Cowie.

The Rev Mr Dobson proposed the second resolution of the meeting: 'That a committee be appointed to promote the cause of women's suffrage in Shetland; and the committee to consist of Rev Andrew Macfarlane, Mrs Macfarlane, Rev Robert Walker, AM, Robert Cowie Esq, AM, MD, Mrs Cowie, Miss Ogilvie, Miss Spence, John Robertson Esq, Mrs Robertson, Mr Morrison, Rev J K Dobson; with power to add to their number.

Miss McLaren closed the meeting with 'a vote of thanks to Bailie Robertson, at the same time sketching the rise and progress of the women's suffrage movement, and concluded by trusting the committee now formed would aid them in their endeavours to obtain what they considered their rights.' [*ZT* 15 September 1873]

The memorandum sent after this meeting was received by the House of Commons on 20 April, 1874: 'Inhabitants of LERWICK in public meeting assembled; John Robertson, Chairman ... 1 signature.' It was presumably sent directly, rather than through Mr Laing.

Agnes McLaren, the daughter of Duncan McLaren, and stepdaughter of Priscilla Bright McLaren. She was the first joint Secretary of the Edinburgh WSS, and came with Jane Taylour to lecture in Shetland in September, 1873. Later, she qualified as one of Britain's first women doctors.

Photograph reproduced by kind permission of the Mistress and Fellows of Girton College, Cambridge.

Taylour and McLaren didn't get on so well in their next venue: the same issue of the *Zetland Times* had:

'UNGALLANT THURSO ... the show of hands went against her.' However, the visitors had the last word: ' ... Miss McLaren commented that Thurso are 'very far back in this movement indeed. ... In Shetland they had two ladies members of school boards.' [*ZT* 6 October 1873]

The Lerwick Women's Suffrage committee:

Looking more closely at the members of that first committee gives a fascinating and rather chilling snapshot of mid-Victorian families at the upper end of Shetland social life. Forget the idea of Papa and Mama surrounded by their dozen children. Here is a list of infant deaths, and of the four married couples, three include a step-parent. No contraception; the first child is generally born a year after the marriage. More shocking to me, because more unexpected, was the number of child and teenage deaths. There was a shortage of men, and too many girls, so we see the realities of the marriage market, with Mr Walker's girls of twenty marrying men in their late thirties. From 1871 to 1884, *a quarter* of Shetland's population emigrated, and that's in these records: New Zealand, Australia, Canada. You can see, too, the small network of people that made up 'Lerwick society' – names and relationships are criss-crossing all over the place.

One name conspicuous by its absence was that of the Reverend Alexander Saunders, minister of the 'Muckle Kirk', and involved in many other public committees. In Shetland it does seem to have been the ministers of other denominations who led the suffrage movement, and so far as it can be deduced by marriage records and *Zetland Times* reports of church activities, the lay people were either of Mr MacFarlane's or Mr Walker's congregation; only Miss Spence was a member of the Muckle Kirk. This could be because the non-conformist congregations were more active in the temperance movement. Major Cameron, who was active in a number of committees of the time, was not involved either; that too is typical of the pattern south, where few 'aristocrats' were suffrage workers. Otherwise, there was a good representation of Lerwick 'gentry': four ministers, a doctor, the civic powers through Bailie Robertson, the new merchants like Hector Morrison, and the older merchant families like the Spence, Ogilvy and Hay familes all represented through connections.

Of the eleven committee members, only five were women, three of them wives of male committee members, and the other two, Miss Ogilvie and Miss Spence, were single women. Again, this was typical; women who were active suffragists against their husband's wishes (for example, the later Scottish suffragette Dr Dorothea Chalmers Smith) seem to have been unusual.

Bailie Robertson, who chaired the meeting, and **Mrs Robertson**:

There were two John Robertsons very active in the affairs of Lerwick at this time, uncle and nephew, and I've done my best to distinguish between them. In general, the uncle is called Bailie Robertson, or John Robertson senior, and where neither of these is used I've taken the man in question to be John Robertson junior. Bailie Robertson was born in 1810. His father seems to have been a teacher in Lunnasting. He was a merchant and fish-curer, first at the North Ness, then he moved to 3 Queen's Lane, 'The Trance', between Quendale House and Bain's Court; his store was at the south end of Bain's Beach. He was the owner of the smack *Vigilant* built by Laurence Arcus. His first wife, Margaret Burgess, was from Dunrossness. They married when both were 22, and had one daughter, Margaret, who died aged 16, in 1849, and possibly two others who died as infants. Margaret senior died of phthisis (TB) in the month of their 30th wedding anniversary. He married again three years later. His second wife, Ann Fordyce, was born in 1827, and came from Unst. Her father was a merchant seaman, and she'd been a neighbour of the Robertsons both at North Ness and in Queen's Lane. Their son John (Dr John Fordyce Robertson) was born in 1866, and their daughter, another Margaret, a year later; she died aged only 12, in 1879.

His services to the town included financing public works. In the late sixties, according to Thomas Manson, Morrison's pier

'was considerably extended and made a public pier, chiefly through the efforts of the late Bailie Robertson, ... who was then agent for the North of Scotland Company. Mr Robertson collected subscriptions for the purpose, but the amount received was not sufficient, and I believe he was out of pocket over the transaction.' [*LLHC*, p 128]

Bailie Robertson was a member of Mr Macfarlane's church, and generally chaired their missionary meetings, large events with a number of clergy present, and a missionary speaker (the format of the suffrage meetings seems to be based on these). He was chairman of the Parochial Board of 1870, and a member of the first Lerwick School Board; he was also a Town Councillor, a Police Commissioner, and Chief Magistrate of the Burgh from 1874. He took a leading part, along with John Leisk, in carrying through the new Harbour Works. He died in 1892, and as a mark of the esteem in which he was held the Town Council attended his funeral as a body.

Reverend Andrew Macfarlane and his wife **Janet:**

Mr Macfarlane (born in 1816) was the senior minister of the United Presbyterian Church, St Ringan's, and lived at Brough Road, Lerwick. At this point he was in his late fifties. He was originally from North Berwick. Mr Macfarlane had been appointed to Shetland in the 1850s – his third child, Margaret, was born here in 1856. He had had three children by his first marriage, to Christina Wright, but his only son Andrew, born in 1848, had died young. He was interested in education for all classes: in 1855, soon after his arrival in Shetland, he appealed for young people to teach reading and writing to some of the many children who were unable to find a place in the Parochial School. The men who volunteered formed the Lerwick Instruction Society, under the secretaryship of Arthur Laurenson, and taught from 8 – 10pm, Monday to Friday. It was for pupils not attending day school, and whose parents were unable to afford school fees. Later, they were joined by eighteen 'young lady teachers' to instruct 106 younger children during the day [*Centenary of the A E I, Lerwick*]. There was apparently criticism of the ladies' involvement by a local clergyman in the *John o Groats Journal,* 25 September 1860. Mr Macfarlane was also one of five Superintendants of the Sunday Schools for Lerwick.

Thomas Manson called St Ringan's church a vigorous one, and spoke of Mr Macfarlane as

'an able preacher of the old school, a man who held strong views on religion, on public and family life, and his position as minister, and fearlessly expressed them...Naturally, everyone did not see eye to eye with him on all points, even in his own congregation; but no one doubted his sincerity.' [*LLHC, p 200, p 288*]

In 1862, his first wife Christina died of hepatitis, and his oldest daughter, Ann, died of peritonitis aged 21 three years later. The following year, 1866, he and Janet Johnston married; they had no children. They were the first couple to occupy the newly-built Manse. Since he was resident in Lerwick, and she was down in North Berwick, and, at nine years his junior, too young to be a childhood sweetheart, one wonders if she was chosen as 'suitable' by his mother, or was the younger sister of a school friend. In 1881 he married his daughter Margaret to teacher Frederick Adie, of Delting, who was a teacher in Lerwick. Margaret and Frederick had five children between 1882 and 1889, who all died in infancy; after that, they seem to have emigrated to Canada, and perhaps Janet went with them, for she disappears from the records after 1881. Mr Macfarlane was still minister here in 1881, but resigned in 1882. His death, in 1886, was registered in Glasgow.

Robert Cowie Esq, MA, MD, Mrs Cowie:

Robert Cowie was a native Shetlander, born in Lerwick in 1842, and taking his MD in Edinburgh, and his MA in Aberdeen. His father, John, was also a highly respected doctor, who died in 1866; his mother was aunt to Mrs Walker's first husband. Robert succeeded his father in the Lerwick practice. His wife Janet was from Aberdeen, and was born in 1846; she was a widow of 24 when she married him in 1869, having been married at only sixteen, in Aberdeen, to George Gray. Robert was a member of the Parochial Board in 1870, and mentioned as the convener of the new cemetery board in 19 June 1873; he was also the honorary surgeon of the Zetland Rifle Volunteers. Thomas Manson described him as

'a big, strong, active man ... besides being an enthusiast in his profession and a hard-working practitioner, [he] found time to write a history of Shetland [*Shetland and its inhabitants*], which was first published in 1871 ... an excellent and reliable guide to the islands.' [*LLHC*, p 284]

He and Janet lived in the house built by Mr Greig of Sandsound, on the site now occupied by the Post Office. They had four daughters: Mary, born in 1870, Margaret, who died young, and posthumous twins Elizabeth and Roberta, born on 29 May 1874, within a month of their father's death. Robert died of peritonitis on 1 May 1874, aged only 32, after an illness of 26 hours:

'The Kirk session [hereby record] their deep sorrow at the loss of one of the most devoted and active members of the congregation, and one to whom they looked with much expectation of good work in the eldership to which he had been elected' only the night before [*LLHC* p 283].

Baby Elizabeth died in August 1874, but Mary and Roberta went to Edinburgh with their mother, who was aged only 28.

His obituary in the *Zetland Times* ended:

'Dr Cowie held several important public appointments. He was medical officer to more than one Parochial Board, the Prison Board of Shetland, the Northern Lighthouse Board, beside being Admiralty Surgeon at this port, in which last capacity his duties, as connected with the numberous force of Royal Naval Reserve were very important. We believe he was just about bringing out a new edition of his book on Shetland, which has met with much public favour. Much sympathy is felt by all classes with Mrs Cowie, in this trying bereavement which has befallen her and her children.' [*ZT* 4 May 1874]

Miss Ogilvie:

The 1871 Census lists only two unmarried Miss Oglivies of sufficient standing (ie of independent income), both elderly, and both Shetlanders. One was Jessie Ogilvie, of 2 Commercial St, Lerwick, born in 1802 in Lerwick, and the other was Mary Ogilvie, born in 1802 in Dunrossness, and living at the Old Manse. She gave her profession as retired governess. Jessie Ogilvie had Miss Spence as her companion at 3 Tait's Place in the 1861 Census, which makes her more likely to be the Miss Ogilvie on the committee.

Miss Jessie Ogilvie was the youngest child, and second daughter, of Thomas Ogilvy and Andrina Malcolmson; Thomas was the brother of Charles Ogilvy of Seafield. He died when Jessie was nineteen. Her oldest brother, Thomas, was a Lieutenant RN, and his wife Sarah was born in Martinique; their first children were born in Liverpool, but they lived in Lerwick from 1835. He died in Burma in 1848, leaving Sarah in Lerwick with five children in their late teens. Her second brother, James, died in New Orleans in that same year.

The 1841 census shows Jessie living at Tait's Pier. In 1851 she was at Mariner's Court; in 1861, at 3, Tait's Place, with Miss Spence as her companion, and one servant, Margaret Mouat; in 1871, at lodgings at 2 Commercial St, as a householder with two servants, Margaret Dalziel, Table Maid, and Margaret Mouat, Domestic Servant. In 1881, she was at 1 Commercial St, with one servant, Jane Linklater. She died in 1881.

Reverend Robert Walker, MA:

Mr Walker, of the Parsonage, Lerwick, was born at Marykirk in 1823, and was the first Rector of St Magnus Episcopal Church, Lerwick; he was also Chaplain to the Morton Lodge of Freemasons. He taught in what was known as 'Walker's School', now the St Magnus Church Hall, but then a school for 80 pupils, open to all denominations. He was one of the examiners of the first class of the Anderson Institute in 1861. His wife was Emma Heriot Buchan, a widow who had gone with her Shetland husband, James Greig of Westhall, to Australia, soon after their marriage in 1854 (he was son of James Greig, Procurator Fiscal, who built the house where the Post Office now stands). Their first daughter, Emma, was born in Australia in 1855, and their second, Louisa, was born in Lerwick in 1857. James died in Australia in 1859. Emma married Robert Walker in 1864, and they had three children: Mary, born in 1865, Christina, born in 1866 and Ann, born in 1868, who died at only two days old. In 1869, Emma Walker was involved in a court case against a woman who had claimed to be the wife of a seaman from Yell, and imposed on her to the extent of 4d and a glass of wine.

In 1873, Mr Walker would be fifty, and his wife forty-five – a similar age to Mr and Mrs Macfarlane. Mrs Walker was to die in 1876, 'at the Parsonage, Lerwick, suddenly, on the morning of 14th inst' [*ZT*, 18 November 1876], leaving Robert with four girls aged 20, 19, 11 and 10. The two older girls both married soon after. Louisa married Robert Muir in Lerwick in 1877. She was 20, he was 31. He was Inspector of Schools in Shetland from 1873 to the late 1890s; John Graham's book *A Vehement Thirst after Knowledge* describes the complaints Peter Williamson made about his behaviour at Gulberwick School (p 149-151). There is a link to the second Shetland WSS here; Muir was a friend of Robert Jamieson, and stayed with the family on his visits to Sandness.

Emma junior married Dr Francis Skae in 1878; she was 23, he was 39. Dr Skae had come to Shetland in 1871, and became medical officer for Delting Parish and Northmavine in 1875. In 1877 he was the medical officer for the Burgh of Lerwick, and for Bressay. He was the surgeon to Lerwick gaol, MO for the Northern Lighthouses, and for the Combination Poor House and Hospital. The Skaes lived at 26 Church Lane, Lerwick, and were still resident in Lerwick in 1891, when Francis died. Emma died in 1896, in a railway accident in Scotland.

Robert's older daughter, Mary, was sent off to school after her mother's death. In 1881, aged fifteen, she was at St Mary's School, Edinburgh, so perhaps she was exceptionally musical. A concert given in August 1881 by the Lerwick Choral Society, along with the organist of St Mary's Cathedral, T H Cullinson, was hosted in St Magnus by Mr Walker. Mary married twice, to a minister both times, the Reverend William Charteris Duncan of Wick, then the Reverend William Claxton, Snelland Rectory, Lincolnshire.

The youngest girl, Christina, married Alexander Cunningham Hay, merchant, grandson of William Hay of Hayfield House, fourth son of Charles Hay the banker, and seemingly the only member of that family of ten who was to return to Shetland. He was 48, she was 27. Alexander's grandmother was Margaret Ogilvy, aunt to Miss Spence who was also on the committee. The Hays lived at The Cottage, King Harald Street, and had one son, born in 1894.

Mr Walker remained at St Magnus until his death in January 1896.

Rev. Robert Walker

Photograph reproduced by kind permission of Douglas Sinclair and the Shetland Museum and Archives.

Miss Spence:

Miss Elizabeth Spence, born in 1821, was described shortly after her death as 'the last member of an old family, and a lady held in the highest esteem by all' [Jas M Crawford's *The Parish of Lerwick, 1701 – 1901*]. Her father, Balfour Spence, was an Unst man, but seems to have moved to Lerwick as a young man ; her mother, Charlotte Ogilvy, was a daughter of Charles Ogilvy senior of Seafield, chief magistrate of Lerwick for many years, banker, merchant and half of the Hay and Ogilvy partnership which is now Hay & Co. It's not strictly true that she was the last of an old family; she had an older half-brother, Aneas Spence, born in 1808 in Lerwick, and living in Midhouse, Dalsetter, North Yell with his family.

Miss Spence's story is a record of loss. She was probably not aware of her older sister Barbara who died as an infant before she was born, but when she was only six, her mother died, and her baby brother Thomas died a year after that. Her father died in 1843, when she was twenty-two, and her second brother, William, died at sea three years later. Her oldest brother, James Ross, was a ship's chandler and shipping agent for the Netherlands, Hanseatic Consul and later for the German Empire. He was resident, in 1851, at 1 Spence Court, which was built by him, and was a well-known figure in the town; Thomas Manson described him at length in *LLHC,* p 11-12. He died at sea off Sumburgh in 1870. The youngest brother, Charles, died unmarried the following year.

Miss Spence gave her profession as Governess. In 1851 she was listed as a visitor to Andrew Hay, retired India Merchant, his wife Joan Mary and Joan's mother, Martha Nicolson. Martha was also a Spence from Unst, very remotely related to Elizabeth (fourth cousins) and Joan was only two years younger than Elizabeth, so she was perhaps a cousin who was close in friendship, if not a close cousin by blood. In 1861 she was at 3, Tait's Place, as a companion to Jessie Ogilvie, her mother's first cousin. She's not on the 1871 census, and so must have been off Shetland. At the time of this suffrage meeting she had just become a lady of independent means, through the death of her brothers. The 1881 census had her living in Spence's Court, Lerwick, on 'income from dividends'. In the 1890s, she donated a stained glass window to St Columba's church in memory of her family; the window illustrates Matthew xi 28, 'Come to me, all you who labour and are heavy burdened, and I will give you rest.' The figure of Christ is taken from a classical sculpture by Thorvaldsen in Copenhagen. The inscription below reads: 'To the glory of God and in loving memory of Balfour Spence his wife Charlotte Ogilvy and their sons James Ross Charles Ogilvy William Edward Parry and Thomas John.'

Miss Spence died at 85 Commercial St in 1901. She bequeathed gifts to several Church and charitable schemes, and left £50 for distribution among the poor.

John Robertson Esq, Mrs Robertson:

John Robertson junior ('Young John o the Trance') was the son of Bailie Robertson's oldest brother Robert, also a merchant in Lerwick, and his wife Helen Leask. Young John was the third of a family of eleven. He was born in 1826, and was the only surviving son. His oldest sister Jessie died aged 16 when John was only three; his younger brother Robert died, aged 6, when John was 8; a second Robert died aged 7 in 1842, when John was 16; the next child, William, died aged 9 six years later. His sister Mary, born in 1832, married Peter Garriock in 1850 and remained in Lerwick. His father died in 1855, leaving John with his mother, his younger sisters Eliza, Martha, Barbara and Janet (Jessie), and possibly his older sister Helen all living at 3, then 2, Victoria Wharf. Eliza and Martha were still there at the 1871 census; Barbara and Janet had gone to Liverpool and were both at 28 Carter Street, Toxteth. Barbara had married a seaman, Andrew Dalziel, in 1866, but had returned to Victoria Wharf for her daughter Jessie's birth in 1868. Andrew Dalziel died sometime 'after 1871', and Barbara returned to the family home; Jessie was brought up there, and married John William Laurenson in 1892. There is less information on Janet, and no date is given for her marriage to John Dalziel, perhaps Andrew's younger brother; their daughter Florence Emily was born in 1883. Florence married Mitchell Umphray Williamson in St Ringan's church and had four children, all born in King Harald Street. Janet is registered as having died there.

Thomas Manson spoke very highly of John Robertson:

'... a man of mark in the community of Lerwick. A member of the Town Council and Parochial Board and of the Harbour Trust, for a long period, he was a regular attender at all the meetings of these bodies, and one whose opinions were listened to with respect ... One of the original members of the County Council which came into being in 1890, he continued to represent Lerwick Central till his death, and ... was elected Vice-Convener. A man of cultured tastes, as well as possessing excellent business abilities, Mr Robertson wielded considerable influence on public affairs throughout his long life.' [*LLHC*, p 18 – 19].

He had served on the Council for 42 years by the time of his death in 1905.

However 'Young John' wasn't married, and his mother was dead by the time of the meeting, so perhaps he was escorting his aunt, Bailie Robertson's wife Ann, perhaps Mrs Robertson is a misprint for Miss Robertson, one of his sisters, or perhaps this John Robertson is in fact Bailie Robertson's name repeated. As a 'Spirits Merchant and Grocer' young John was maybe not too active in temperance affairs!

Mr Morrison:

Hector Morrison was born in 1829 in Sutherland, and was a Bookseller and Stationer. According to Thomas Manson,

'Beginning business in the shop now tenanted by Mr T L Bruce ... Mr Morrison gradually and steadily built up a large connection in town and country (which he regularly visited) until his business was the first of its kind in town. Along with ... Mr Wm Duncan and others, he was instrumental in forming the Good Templar Lodges in Lerwick and throughout the island; and during his long life he continued to evince the keenest interest in the Order, and did everything that lay in his power to further its cause. A shrewd, capable man, while giving his business his first attention, he was also warmly interested in public affairs, but more particularly in temperance matters.' [*LLHC* p 30]

He was also a member of the Parochial Board. His oldest son, William, drowned aged only 15, in 1870; his second son, George, was a missionary on Foula for many years; his daughters Mary, Elizabeth and Margaret were all teachers. Donald R Morrison was the 'son' of the business, a member of the Lodge and one of the Reverend A Campbell's elders. Both men were on the Parochial Board. Mrs Morrison was mentioned as singing in the choir on Jubilee Day in 1887.

Mr Morrison's daughters were later to be active in the 1909 Shetland Women's Suffrage Society.

Rev J E Dobson:

The Congregational Manse was built in 1873, and Rev Dobson was the first to live there:

'a tall, dark-complexioned gentleman, full of life and energy' *(LLHC)*.

He left Shetland in 1875:

'We regret to have to announce that Mr Dobson, who has been ailing for some time past, has been advised by his medical attendants to remove from the variable climate of Shetland ...' [*ST,* 11 Jan 1875].

His farewell address was given in full on 15 February, and there was news of him after that, in a parish in Wilton, then settling in Gainsborough.

Activities of the Lerwick Women's Suffrage Committee:

The newly founded Lerwick committee was reported on 29 September 1873 as having had

'several meetings. A convener and secretary have been elected, and active measures are being taken to give effect to the resolutions adopted at the meeting.' [*ZT* 29 September 1873]

This was followed, on 6 October, by a column-length article on women's suffrage in the editorial position. It was a closely argued essay, giving the argument clearly while at the same time allaying fears of women taking over:

'The principle is distinct, and the object is simple, notwithstanding the many efforts which have been made to create an aversion to the one and a prejudice against the other...women do not want to be ministers of religion, MPs, professors of universities, partisans of political parties ... but to secure for women who rent houses and own property the privilege of voting for Members of Parliament ... there should be no taxation without representation.'

The writer pointed out the incongruity of being able to vote for school boards and 'in all matters connected with our poor-law system', and finished that argument triumphantly:

'Either, therefore, let our women, possessed of the requisite qualification, have the full enjoyment of the right of representation to its full extent, or let them be denuded of the privileges they presently enjoy, and deprive them of all civil right at once.... the sooner the present anomolous case of the law be altered the better, and let women be treated as intelligent and responsible beings.'

A last reassurance:

'...We have no idea of women forgetting their proper sphere of action or ignoring their proper duties ... should they be entrusted with the Parliamentary Franchise.'

The essay ended with a call for constituents to cast their vote for

'such candidates as will not fail to support that measure which [will] secure for women their power to record their votes at the Parliamentary Office.' [*ZT* 6 October 1873]

The essay was unsigned. The clarity of the prose sounds like Jane Taylour's speech, but it seems more likely that one of the committee would have written it, probably the secretary, Miss Spence; not Mr Macfarlane, from the style of the speech reported as by him, at Sir Peter Tait's meeting.

The *Zetland Times* also published the Lerwick suffrage committee's letter to Mr Laing:

Sir: - At a well-attended public meeting, which was held here on the 12th curt, it was unanimously resolved to memorialize you, as our county Member, on the subject of Women's Suffrage, and to request you to support Mr Jacob Bright's Bill, 'To remove the Electoral Disabilities of Women'. But, as the Committee appointed to carry that resolution into effect have been led to understand that, with the majority of Scotch members, you are disposed to favour the passing of the measure, they have resolved through their Convener and Secretary, to request your attention to the subject.

In adopting this resolution, the Committee were anxious to ascertain how far your views coincided with their own, and that, if possible, to avoid all further agitation of the question, in so far as you are personally concerned.

It would, therefore, be esteemed a great favour by the Committee if you would be so kind as to indicate your opinion on the question, and the line of procedure you may be disposed to follow regarding it.

In the hope that you will favourably entertain our request, give us your assurance of cordial co-operation in the good and just cause, and save us the necessity of stirring the constituency, and getting up a formal memorial to you, we indicate the wish generally entertained on the important question now raised, as the resolutions adopted at the public meetings in this place and Scalloway require. We are, Sir,

Your obedient servants
Andrew Macfarlane, Convener
E Spence, Secretary   [*ZT* 20 October 1873]

Mr Laing's reply, published in the same edition of the *Zetland Times*, was neatly uncommitted:

'I have no objection in principle to women exercising the right of voting in respect of property which would give the Suffrage if held by men ... I would however like to see the measure in a practical shape, and see the course taken on it by such men as Mr Gladstone, Mr John Bright and others, who have taken the lead in recent measures of Parliamentary Reform, before I give any positive pledge as to my vote on the subject .' [*ZT* 20 October 1873]

He was however to consistently vote for women's suffrage bills in the House.

There is an intriguing but unconfirmed suggestion that the Lerwick society had a banner embroidered for them by Mrs Mary Garriock, sister to 'Young' John Robertson. The idea came from Angus Johnson of the archives, who thought he had seen a bill for it, but so far we haven't managed to locate it. Mary's husband Peter Garriock, born in 1827, was the son of R S Garriock of Scottshall, ship owner, land owner and commission agent. She and her husband Peter had eleven children. The fourth, Peter, born in 1858, was to marry Sarah Charlotte (Lottie) Atherton, from Liverpool, in 1885 at 171 Commercial St, Lerwick - Harriet's little sister.

The Scalloway meeting:

Miss Taylour and Miss McLaren also spoke in the Congregational Chapel, Scalloway on 13th September 1873. The meeting sparked off this letter in the *Zetland Times*:

'The following memorandum agreed upon at a meeting of the inhabitants of Scalloway, and signed by the chairman of said meeting, L F U Garriock, Esq, has been forwarded to Mr Laing, MP:

That the exclusion of women, otherwise legally qualified, for voting in the election of Members of Parliament is injurious to those excluded, contrary to the principle of just representation, and to that of the laws now in force regulating the election of municipal, parochial and other representative bodies.

That the recognition by the legislature of the fitness of women for the responsible office of members of a school board [ie the powers granted by the 1870 Education Act of voting for and serving on such bodies], renders anomalous the maintenence of the disability which excludes them from voting in the election of Members of Parliament.

That the legislature in preserving and restoring the ancient rights of women in local government and in conferring on them the new franchise created by the Education Act, has pursued a course in regard to the civil and political status of women of which the removal of the remaining electoral disability is the natural and consistent conclusion.

That the interests of women suffer greatly from the operation of this disability, inasmuch as the denial of representative government to women makes it possible to maintain laws depriving them of property, educational and personal rights, which could not be withheld from any section of the community which had the protection of the suffrage.

Your Memorialists therefore pray that you will give your support to the Bill to be introduced next session by Mr Jacob Bright to remove the Electoral Disabilities of Women.' [*ZT* 27 October 1873]

Lewis Francis Umphrey Garriock

Mr Garriock of Berry and Burwick, the chairman of that meeting, was born in 1825. He was a general merchant and fish curer. His father was from Reawick; his mother seems to have owned the shop there, a legacy perhaps from her first husband, Lewis Francis Cumming Umphray, who was also from Reawick. Unusually, Lewis was given his name as well as that of his own father, James Garriock. Lewis's wife Evangeline Young was from Dundee, and they married in September 1872; their first child was born in Dingwall in August 1873, and their subsequent children were born in Dundee. However presumably Garriock travelled up and down, as he's mentioned again in the *Zetland Times* of 22 May 1875:

'A protest by the inhabitants of Scalloway' against Mr L F U Garriock, JP and Mr William Harcus, Merchant ... they had ... agreed to appropriate for their personal use that plot ... having been used by the public for keeping their BOATS and PEAT STACKS since time immemorial ...'

In 1876 he gave £400 towards the creation of the Victoria Pier – only John Robertson gave more (£600). He was also at the opening of the Town Hall in 1883; he was one of the donors of the fireplaces.

The Tingwall Parish and Burra Isle Committee:

A new suffrage committee was listed in the same *Zetland Times*:

'WOMEN'S SUFFRAGE: We hear that the friends of this movement are acting vigorously in Tingwall Parish. The following list forms the Committee for Tingwall Parish and Burra Isle: - Rev James Craig, UF Manse, Burra Isle; Rev Mr Farnell, Wesleyan Minister, Scalloway; Mr Moncrieff, Scalloway; Mr Gifford Laurenson, Scalloway; Rev Mr Macdonald, FC Manse, Weisdale; Miss Macdonald; Mrs Irvine, Strom Bridge, Whiteness; Miss Moncrieff, Scalloway, Secretary. [*ZT* 27 Oct 1873]

Rev James Craig, born 1837, minister of the United Presbyterian church, Burra, unmarried.
Rev Mr Farnell – he spoke at the end of the Good Templar Soiree of Jan 1875 (at length), mentioning then that this was his second year in Shetland.
Mr Moncrieff: possibly Mr Laurence Moncrieff, Bank or Bake House, Scalloway, born in 1829, Baker and grocer. His wife Ann, born in 1834, was the daughter of Robert Scott, a Scalloway Baptist missionary and sailmaker, and at this point they had five children. They must have emigrated to Canada in the following year, for their sixth child was there born in November 1874. Laurence Moncrieff had three sisters, Jean, b 1825, Helen b 1834, and Margaret, b 1842. Helen and Margaret are listed as Dressmakers and Milliners, 42 Commercial St, Lerwick, in the 1871 and 1881 Census; I can't find any trace of Jean. One of them was perhaps **Miss Moncrieff.**
Mr Gifford Laurenson, born in 1828 on Bressay, occupation given as Mason. He married Margaret Tait in 1854, and moved to Westerhoull, Scalloway, where his seven children were born. Unusually, all survived. The family emigrated to New Zealand on *Soukar* on 22 Aug 1874.
Rev Mr Alexander Macdonald, Free Church Manse, Weisdale, born in 1826, Dunkeld. He was unmarried in 1871 and 1881. **Miss Macdonald** was his sister Christina, born in 1842, 'housekeeper'; she married Magnus Robertson of Delting in 1882. Their father was dead, and their mother staying with them too – she died in June 1877. One of the witnesses to Christina's wedding was Mary P MacDonald, perhaps Alexander's wife.
Mrs Williamina Margaret Irvine, Strombridge, Whiteness, born in 1827. The census listed her as a 'farmer's wife', but like the other committee members, she was professional class. Her father was a Shetlander and a surgeon, Dr Arthur Craigie, practising in Leith at the time of her birth, but afterwards at Brow, Dunrossness; her mother, who was living with them at this point, was a minister's daughter. Her husband, Magnus Irvine of Voe, Dunrossness, was listed as farmer, landed proprieter, and they had three children. Their eldest daughter, Mary, had died in 1870 aged 20, and the others, Arthur, born in 1851, and Susan, born in 1864, were still living.

The 1874 election and 1874 suffrage petitions:

On 9 February 1874, the re-named *Shetland Times* gave notice of the dissolution of Parliament 'on Friday afternoon'. This meant another election: 'the Orkney papers are highly pleased that Mr Laing is not to be opposed.' [*ST* 9 Feb 1874]

That same edition reported the quarterly elections of the Good Templars of Ultima Thule Lodge, and it's interesting to notice three women among the twelve officials elected: Janet Arcus, Jane N Tait and Helen Stanley. Similarly, the Star of the North Lodge had six women among its thirteen officers, including Mrs H Morrison and Mary Morrison [*ST*, 4 May 1874]. There was a touch of sarcasm in the *Shetland Times*'s comments on the officials for the Choral Union, which was short of directors, leaving them one under complement:

'We believe it was suggested that the ladies should not be entirely excluded from the directorate, seeing they are as much interested in the welfare of the society as the gentlement, and may have difficulties to contend with which the gentlemen fail to realise in due measure; beside it would seem to be quite as gallant to allow them a representation, notwithstanding we live at present under a Tory government. The suggestion, however, was carefully put 'on one side' ... [*ST* 20 May 1874].

Although uncontested, Mr Laing still held a public meeting and was supported by some Suffrage committee members:

'Mr Laing was accompanied on the platform by Bailie Robertson, Mr Cameron, Dr Cowie, George Reid Tait and Charles Robertson. Major Cameron took the chair.' [*ST* 16 Feb 1874]. There were no awkward questions this time. As expected, the victory went to Disraeli, and the *Shetland Times* of 2 March 1874 gave a list of the Cabinet members in the new Conservative government.

The suffrage cause was not, however, being neglected:

'WOMEN'S SUFFRAGE

We understand that an opportunity will be afforded this week to the inhabitants of our town, to help forward the movement for Women's suffrage. A petition in its favour will be submitted for signature, and as its object is simply to secure the right of voting for Members of Parliament to women who possess the requisite qualifications, we have no doubt that it will be well received by all classes, and numerously signed both by men and women.' [*ST* 6 April 1874]

'WOMEN'S SUFFRAGE

The petition in favour of the extension of the Parliamentary Suffrage, to women possessing the requisite qualifications, was despatched by last mail. It was signed by 727 of our population, and is entrusted to our member, Mr Laing, for presentation to the House of Commons. That a petition for such an object, and so numerously signed, after very short notice, should leave us, says not a little for the intelligence and liberty of our community.' [*ST* 20 April 1874]

'In the House of Commons, on Tuesday last, Mr Laing M P presented petitions from the inhabitants of Lerwick, and from several parishes in the islands, in favour of women's suffrage.' [*ST* 25 May 1874]

The petition was presented by Mr Laing, along with one from Tingwall, with 155 signatures, and several from Orkney, on 12 May 1874; the official record of the Lerwick one only allows 726 signatures. In that year, 1,404 petitions with 430,343 signatures were received by the House of Commons. Fourteen of these petitions came from Town Councils, but Lerwick doesn't seem to have been among them. As a memorandum from a meeting or body signed by the chairman counted as only one signature, this shows a very large body of support for women's suffrage across the country. Of negative interest: the House of Commons archivist, Ms Mari Takanayagi, very kindly looked up other names for me in the index of petitions for 1874, and didn't find Aithsting, Baltasound, Cullivoe, Delting, Dunrossness, Northmavine,

Scalloway, Unst, Walls or Yell, suggesting that there was no petition, and so probably no suffrage activity, outside the central area of Shetland.

(Above) The record of Shetland's first petition, presented after Jessie Craigen's meeting, and the record of the 1874 petition from Lerwick, with 726 signatures (left).
Photographs courtesy of Mari Takanayagi, Archivist at the Parliamentary Archives.

The 1874 Disabilities Bill:

The 1874 Disabilities Bill was presented by Willam Forsyth QC, Conservative MP for Marylebone. He added a clause saying that no married woman would be entitled to vote in a parliamentary election, and this was to split the feminists. Lydia Becker and the National Society for Women's Suffrage decided to support the Bill on the grounds that allowing widows and spinsters the vote could be the thin edge of the wedge; Richard Pankhurst, Jacob and Ursula Bright, Elizabeth Wolstenholme, Josephine Butler and others argued it reinforced the legal split between married women and others. This disagreement over principle and strategy would later lead to the formation of the Women's Franchise League, in protest against the national suffrage societies fighting for suffrage only for those women not under *couverture*.

The Electoral Disabilites of Women Bill was withdrawn in July 1874 session, and re-presented by Mr Forsyth in April 1875. Again, he emphasised it was not for married women:

'I rise to move the second reading of this Bill. It is extremely short, consisting of only a single clause. Its object is to enable women who are not under the coverture of marriage, if they are rated householders in boroughs, or possessed of sufficient property qualifications in counties, to vote at the election of Members of Parliament. I say, emphatically, 'women not under the disability of coverture,' for I am strongly opposed to the claim of married women to vote at Parliamentary Elections, and there is nothing in the present Bill which will enable them to do so. ... As regards the growth of public opinion in favour of the measure, I assert fearlessly that there has been no question introduced by a private Member which has in so short a time made so rapid a progress. ... This is shown by the number of Petitions for the Bill, which increased from 75, with 50,000 signatures, in 1858, to 1,404, with more than 430,000 signatures, in 1874. Between the years 1869 and 1873, exactly four Petitions were presented against the Bill, and these proceeded from Scotch municipal burghs, where women have no votes at all. This year no fewer than 30 town councils in Scotland have petitioned in its favour, and not one against it.'

He proceeded to a powerful speech, and the debate which followed was seriously argued, but again, there was a 'no' vote for reading the Bill, by a majority of 87, and the Second Reading was deferred by six months. One of the voters for reading the Bill now was Samuel Laing.

The next reading of a Women's Disabilities Bill was in June 1877 – this was a different Bill (Bill 17), which did not exclude married women. It was sponsored by Jacob Bright, Sir Robert Anstruther, Russell Gurney and Mr Stansfeld. It was again talked out, in what suffragist Helen Blackburn described as 'a scene of disorder ... a painful afternoon' and the 1878 attempt, led by Mr Courtney, MP for Liskeard, failed to secure a Second reading. In his opening speech he mentioned the recent death of Russell Gurney, a strong supporter of women's causes. Samuel Laing voted with Courtney and Bright for reading the Bill now.

3

The 1870s to 1890s

Further education for women

Gradually, the Universities were becoming open to women. In 1867 the University of London had been given powers to hold special examinations for women, and the following year plans were drawn up to grant them certificates. The University of London was the first in the country to admit women to its degree courses, in 1878. Among those graduating was Sophia Bryant, the first woman Doctor of Science, and from 1895 the Headmistress of London North Collegiate School. Her pupils there included Dr Marie Stopes, Stevie Smith and Eleanor Graham, who founded the 'Puffin' imprint. Dr Bryant wrote books on mathematics, education, psychology, Irish history and moral philosophy. She was an advocate of Home Rule for Ireland, President of the Hampstead Suffrage Society, and, according to tradition, the first woman to own and ride a bicycle. Another graduate was Louise Creighton, social activist, novelist and biographer. She was the first President of the Union of Women Workers, who did mostly voluntary work in the social sector; it's now known as the National Council of Women of Great Britain.

The Edinburgh Association for the University Education of Women had been founded in 1867, with strong support from David Masson, Professor of Rhetoric and English Literature at Edinburgh University, and other tutors. Masson was a friend of John Stuart Mill, and his daughters Flora and Rosaline were both involved in the women's suffrage movement. Professor Masson offered the first degree-level arts courses in 1868, and gradually the scope was widened to include science subjects. In 1874 a university certificate was offered in arts subjects, and from 1877 the association's classes were listed in the Edinburgh University calendar. However, women students could not yet graduate.

In 1869, Sophia Jex-Blake and six others had been given permission to attend lectures at the Edinburgh Medical School. They passed their examinations, but the University would not qualify them as doctors, and so they took the University to Court. In 1873, the Court of Session ruled in favour of the University, that they could not be given degrees, and, further, that they should not have been admitted in the first place. Jex-Blake went to London and helped Elizabeth Garrett Anderson to establish the London School of Medicine for Women. She took her medical degree in Berne in 1877, and returned to Edinburgh as the city's first woman doctor in the following year. There she started up a clinic for poor women and children.

The first women to sit a degree exam in Cambridge were noticed by the *Shetland Times*. The 'College for Women' was established by Emily Davies and Barbara Boudichon, and opened at Benslow House, Hitchin, on 16 October 1869. In 1872, the College bought the site of Girton College, Cambridge, and an Association was formed to build and run a College for the higher Education of women, and to take steps to place that college in connection with the University of Cambridge, in particular to gain admission for the students to sit examinations for degrees at the University. Tutors and students moved to the new buildings in October 1873; also in 1873, the college received the donation of a portion of the library of Mary Somerville, mathematician, astronomer and popular science writer (the word scientist was coined for her in an 1834 review of her book *On the Connexion of the Sciences*).

'Two of the lady students at Girton College, near Cambridge, have attained, in an examination for which they offered themselves at Cambridge, a certificate of proficiency equal to that of a first-class in the subjects which they took up. I am told that one of these ladies lives at Bristol and that the other comes from Manchester. What a delight this would have been to Mary Somerville, who lent to this college her library, or the greater part of it, and who, if she had been a student there now-a-days, would most surely have come out equal not to a mere 'first class' but to a 'Senior Wranglership'! ['Gossip of the Clubs from our London correspondent', *ST* 29 June 1874]

In fact the London correspondent was late with the gossip: the 'Girton Pioneers' had taken their Cambridge Tripos examinations in the Lent Term, 1873. Sarah Woodhead, who took the Mathematical Tripos, was from Manchester; Rachel Cook and Louisa Lumsden took the Classical Tripos. Two would have been placed in Class II, one in Class III, but they do not appear on the official class lists.

A song, 'The Girton Pioneers', to the tune of 'The British Grenadiers', was written by several students at Hitchin in 1873 – according to Kate Perry, College Archivist at Girton, 'it's still sung with great gusto after the College Feast!':

Some talk of Senior Wranglers,
And some of Double Firsts,
And truly of their species
These are not the worst;
But of all the Cambridge heroes
There's none that can compare
With Woodhead, Cook and Lumsden,
The Girton Pioneers.

Whenever we go forward
A hard exam to try,
Their memory goes before us
To raise our courage high.
They made old Cambridge wonder;
Then let us give three cheers
For Woodhead, Cook and Lumsden,
The Girton Pioneers.

And when the goal is won, girls,
And women get degrees,
We'll cry, 'Long live the three, girls,
Who showed the way to these!
Who showed the way we follow,
Who knew no doubts or fears,
Our Woodhead, Cook and Lumsden,
The Girton Pioneers!'

The let us fill a tea-cup
And drink a health to those
Who studied well and played well,
As everybody knows,
May we fulfil the promise
Of Girton's earliest years,
Of Woodhead, Cook and Lumsden,
The Girton Pioneers!

'The First Five': these women were the first students at Girton College in October 1869. Back, left to right, Townsend, Woodhead and Gibson; seated, left to right, Cook and Lumsden. Cook didn't start until the Lent term, January1870, due to ill health. A sixth student, Anna Lloyd began in October 1869, but left in the Michaelmas Term of 1870, due to 'the pressure of family claims' [College Register] Woodhead, Cook and Lumsden were the 'Girton Pioneers'; Lumsden later became Warden at the first Women's College in St Andrews. Photograph reproduced by kind permission of the Mistress and Fellows of Girton College, Cambridge.

The debate for the Universities (Scotland) Degrees to Women Bill (Bill 6), 3 March 1875 gives an idea of what women were up against. It was introduced for a Second Reading by William Cowper-Temple, MP for Hampshire South. He went through the legal authority the University had to confer degrees, the women's appeal to the Court of Law, with decision given in the their favour, and its overturning by the Court of Session, on the grounds that the University did not have the power without special legislation. His amendment proposed to make it 'in the power of the authorities of the Universities, if they should think fit, according to their discretion ... to extend the benefits of the Universities beyond the male students to female students.' After stressing the number of Professors in favour of admitting female students, and the classes already established by the Edinburgh Ladies University Education Association, he comes to the difficulty:

'...The Petition of the Senatus was adopted by a majority of medical Professors, the majority of the non-medical men being in favour of University education for women. ... The opposition to be encountered was not against the admission of women to a higher intellectual culture, but to their admission into medical practice; and this opposition came from the medical profession. Amongst the pleas of objection was a warning against the association of the sexes in the same classes. But there was no prospect of the two sexes being taught together in the classes of anatomy and surgery. ... Objections were urged; against the capacity and competence of women for the medical art. ... The four ladies who were practising in London and provincial towns had plenty of patients, and cured as high a proportion as other practitioners. ... There were numberless cases of young women who shrunk from applying for advice at the commencement of a disorder or in small ailments, who yet would at once have recourse to a competent practitioner of their own sex if they were allowed to do so. ... The experience of Girton College, and of Merton College, Cambridge, proved that women could pass examinations equally with men, when equally taught. ... The feeling of Edinburgh had declared itself so strongly in favour of extending the benefits of University education to women, that money had been amply contributed for every purpose for which it had hitherto been required; the Town Council had petitioned in their favour; ... By opening the door for competent women to become medical practitioners—an honourable profession for which nature had fitted them—they would remove an obstacle at present in the path of many young women who were anxious to earn their own livelihood, and who did not desire any longer to burden their families. It would occupy other young women who, although not absolutely obliged to take up a profession, yet were anxious to rise out of a life of uselessness and frivolity to one of practical work in curing disease. 16,000 women last Session had petitioned Parliament to allow them to be treated medically by their own sex. Surely that was a want to which some attention might be paid.'

Seconding him, Mr Forsyth too gave the case of the Edinburgh medical students:

'In 1869, five ladies entered a University in Scotland. They went through their examinations, and had every reason to believe that they would be admitted to take their degrees. But some time afterwards 'a change came o'er the spirit of their dream,' for a resolution was come to which practically stopped them from taking their degrees. An appeal was made to a Court of Law which supported the views of the University authorities. The ladies felt, however, that it was a great hardship that they should be prevented from taking a degree by an accidental barrier arising out of the construction of an Act of Parliament. Aberdeen and St. Andrews might be in favour of the admission of women. Edinburgh and Glasgow might be opposed to it. Was it not a hard thing that those Universities which were willing to make arrangements should be debarred from doing so, simply because Edinburgh and Glasgow objected? ... there was a general and growing opinion throughout the community that women who desired to have scientific education ought to have the way open to them, and ought to be encouraged rather than discouraged in their honourable pursuit. He might rest his case in favour of the measure on the fact that this was an enabling Bill, and not a compulsory one. It left things as they were, and merely took away an artificial barrier. If the authorities of the Universities did not wish to admit ladies, they need not do so; but the Bill gave the authorities power to admit them if they thought fit.

Although the Bill, if passed, would open the University examinations generally to female students, permitting them to take all degrees—and he was quite prepared to go that length—he believed they would confine themselves almost exclusively to the study of medicine. ... Take the case of Mrs. Garret Anderson and Miss Blackwell, whose names had been put on the register, and who had a large and extensive practice. It was surely a narrow and bigoted view to take of any question like the present that England and Scotland should refrain from taking a forward movement, until they had received an example and an impetus from foreign countries. In reference to the argument of sex, he said that women constituted the majority of the population, and that in many diseases they shrank from the attendance of a male doctor. In that view, who were more fitting attendants on women than women themselves, if they were properly qualified? The object of the Bill was to enable them to get the best education the Universities could supply with regard to medicine to enable them to practise. ... ... If women of education could earn a livelihood in an honourable and useful career, he thought it was a cruel injustice that that career should not be open to them. For those reasons he would vote most assuredly for the second reading of the Bill.'

And the opposition:

Mr Beresford Hope: 'Why had his right hon. Friend entered into a local squabble? What did his right hon. Friend care particularly about Scotland? Scotland was a very active, intellectual, money-making, and picturesque, not to say patriotic, portion of the United Kingdom; but yet it was hardly fair, under the pretext of a Scotch grievance, that an attempt should be made to snatch a precedent from Parliament on a matter in which the whole of the United Kingdom was concerned... It was really an instalment of the question of women's grievances. ... His right hon. Friend could not conceal from himself... that the question really was, whether women should graduate in every branch of art and science, and follow any profession. The grievance was not only that ladies had not been able to practise as doctors of medicine. It was equally a grievance that they should not be barristers or attornies-at-law, and he supposed his right hon. Friend would quite as logically complain that they could not be able to deliver an occasional sermon in Westminster Abbey. ... Why should not the ambition of those women who desired to do good to their fellow creatures in some branch of this healing art develop their unrivalled speciality in the art of nursing? The duty of prescribing and dictating the course of treatment had, by instinct and common sense, fallen to the share of the men. The carrying out of their orders, the watching and tending of a patient, were admirably suited to the gentle patient temperament of the female sex. Let them follow the example of Florence Nightingale and Mary Stanley, women whose names were household words in the history of the art of healing. Was it not better to be a nurse like one of those noble women than to make one of those she-doctors elbowing their way in the world with a masculine activity? He strongly objected to the Bill, with its slippery enabling faculties, when it was really a pistol put to the head of the Scotch Universities.'

Mr Noel: 'He would yield to no man in his [belief] in the higher education of women, and in his anxiety to promote such an education as would give their intellectual faculties the greatest scope possible, so as to qualify them for any post for which they might be fitted. He even went further, and said he agreed with much that had fallen from the hon. Members, who believed that women might be perfectly fitted for the profession of medicine, and for many other professions. ... [However] Evidence had been advanced during the debate to show that in the judgment of those who had the best right to form an opinion on the subject—namely, the large majority of the teachers in the Universities concerned—such a Bill as this, if carried, would be injurious to the Universities.'

The Lord Advocate quoted '... one of the Scotch Judges, who was one of the minority in favour of the ladies. He said he felt it to be his duty to state his decided opinion that the promiscuous attendance of men and women in mixed classes, with concomitant participation in the administration of medical exposition, was a thing so unbecoming and so antagonistic to the delicacy of the female sex, that the law and constitution of the University, which was bound to seek to promote the advancement of morality as well as learning, could not sanction or accept such a proposition.'

The Second reading was put off for 6 months; women were not to be granted the right to go to University in Scotland until 1889. Mr Laing does not seem to have been present at the debate.

University education was going too far for many people. The *Shetland Times* of 20 July 1874 had what proved to be the opening shot in a seemingly popular campaign for 'Female Industrial Training'. The correspondent urged a return to teaching girls domestic tasks, instead of fripperies like music, and raising the status of the housewife:

'When household work is acknowledged to be the most honourable of women's calling; when faithful service is admitted to be noble and admirable; when the 'lady' shall once again be known as the mistress and skilled administrator of her yard, kitchen, pantry and larder; when ignorance of a woman's true work shall be held to be not admirable but despicable in a lady - then the common people who like to follow their betters will be more ready to set store by such domestic arts as we are now insisting on.'

A MEMBER OF A SCHOOL BOARD [*ST* 20 July 1874]

The following week's letters page had 'Household' agreeing that:

... 'girls who were thus instructed ... would take such an interest and *pride* in houses, and all connected therewith, that their husbands would not have the expense ... of 'raking the street' simply because they are not made comfortable at home.'

Poor things, being forced to go to the pub. Today, I'm sure 'Household' would be blaming rising divorce and crime rates on working wives.

'Household' admits that higher social classes will want other accomplishments:

'but with all due respect to 'young ladies', I trust even *they* will not be above taking *domestic* accomplishments in addition to others ...' [*ST* 27 July 1874]

On 28 September 1874 there was an 'advertisement relating to the establishment of a school prize fund for the better training of girls in domestic matters.'

SHETLAND GIRLS' INDUSTRIAL TRAINING SCHOOL PRIZE FUND

With the view of encouraging in the Public Schools of Shetland the industrial and domestic training of girls – especially in the necessary branches of Plain Sewing, Mending, Darning, and other useful household arts – it is proposed to raise by Subscription a small fund out of which could be provided, at the annual examinations of the schools, Prizes for proficiency in such things; and also, when required, the materials for sewing lessons to the poorer children in the country districts who might not be able to furnish these for themselves.

It is hoped that this proposal may meet the approval of all Shetlanders at home and abroad, who may have the good of their native land at heart, and who, by kindly co-operating with even small subscriptions, may afford such material aid that the experiment may succeed, and perhaps be continued and extended in its working by and by.

Subscriptions (which will be acknowledged in the 'Shetland Times') will be received at any of the local Banks, or by MISS TURNBULL-STEWART, Lerwick.

Lerwick, Sept., 1874 [*ST* 28 September 1874]

Born in 1823, **Grace Margaret Turnbull Stewart** was the only surviving child of the Reverend John Turnbull, of Tingwall. Her mother and youngest sister and brother, aged 8 and 5, had been lost in an accident on Tingwall Loch. Her last sister died on her way to Australia only a couple of years later, her nearest brother, Robert, died at sea between Reawick and Scalloway eight years later, and her oldest brother William again died at sea two years after that. Her remaining brother was dead before 1853, and her father died in 1867. Through her mother, she was a second cousin to Mrs Irvine of the Tingwall Committee. She succeeded (subject to life-rent) to the Stewart estate of Massater, Orkney, through her kinswoman Mrs Mary Stewart Barry in 1853. She was now living at the Old Manse in Lerwick, and taught a girls' class in Sunday School. In 1881, she was listed as a visitor, along with Grace Jane Watson, to the Reverend David Webster and his wife Christian at Fetlar Manse; in 1891 she was living at 7 Commercial Street, apparently tutoring Jean M Campbell, aged 9, the daughter of the Rev Andrew Campbell, Fetlar. From 1896 until her death she's listed in *Manson's Shetland Almanac* as the President of the Church of Scotland Young Women's Guild; she was also on the committee of the Shetland Society of Promoting Reading amongst the Blind. In 1901 she was at 9 Commercial Street, and had both Jean, now a 'student' and her 15 year old sister Lilias Campbell as visitors (their brother James was to marry John and Harriet Leisk's daughter Harriet). Thomas Manson had her living at the Old Manse in Lerwick with Mrs Baynes, widow of the Reverend Alexander Baynes of Tingwall, 'for many years' but this doesn't seem to square with the census returns; they were still in Tingwall in 1901, and Miss Turnbull Stewart died in 1907.

This advertisement was followed on 19 October 1874 by a further letter on female industrial training, enclosing a letter from James Bolt with 5 guineas for Miss Turnbull-Stewart. James Bolt's letter was enclosed in one from Arthur Laurenson, who seems to have taken up this cause with enthusiasm. Born in 1832, he was a merchant in the outfitter and hosiery business and he was one of the early volunteers of the Rev Macfarlane's Lerwick Instruction Society, a joint founder (in the early 1860s) of the Shetland Literary and Scientific Society, and a Trustee of the Anderson Educational Institute. He wanted to give £5 to each school, to be used on sewing materials or to pay for tuition. Letters followed from several School Board Clerks: the Unst and Mid & South Yell Schools could not teach sewing because of the price of the cloth, and Sandsting didn't have a teacher.

The difficulties the School Boards were having were frequently mentioned. On 20 March 1874, there was a letter from George Stewart to Duncan McLaren regarding the impoverishment of education in Shetland, along with McLaren's reply agreeing, and urging Stewart to seek action from his own MP. The Education Act made school mandatory, but parishes could not afford to build schools without considerable costs on the ratepayers, and so School Boards were waiting for the Government to release funds. This was eventually done, and the new Parish schools began to be built in June 1874 – Gulberwick was the first.

Once built, the new schools had a difficult start. Pupils and parents were reluctant, and teacher turn-over high. Miss Gulland, later a member of the 1909 Shetland WSS committee, and a teacher at the Infant School for many years, wrote to the Lerwick and Gulberwick school board asking for an alteration to the rules of admitting children to the infant school, restricting the age from no child over 10 years to no child over 9 years. 'It was decided to allow the matter to lie over in the meantime.' [*ST* 12 April 1884]

She must have taught them well, in spite of the older children, for here are the Inspector's comments just three months later:

'The order is very good. Reading is fair, and a very high pass is made in writing and arithmetic by the first and second standards. The second standard ought to be much smarter in oral answering. As there is no third standard, the grant under Article 19 (C) cannot be paid.' The total grant is £104 15s. The Chairman and the Board had great cause for congratulations with such a report being given now of this school after all the trouble they had had regarding it. It showed that the rules which they had made with the view of improving the school were being carried out by the teacher, and that they were working satisfactorily was evidenced by the fact that the grant for discipline was the highest the school had yet earned.' [*ST* July 12 1884]

Thomas Manson's *Lerwick during the Last Half Century* gives a detailed account of the founding of the new Anderson Educational Institute in 1861. It was opened for boys and girls; 'a mistress qualified for teaching the higher branches of a female education' was specifically mentioned at the Meeting of Parents and Others on 29 February 1862. At that point a potential 59 boys and 21 girls were mentioned. The first head-teacher was the Reverend G W Ellaby, who brought with him 'Mrs Ellaby and a sister, who will undertake the female educational department ... both for imparting useful domestic instruction and accomplishments.' [Letter from Arthur Anderson, 16 April 1862, quoted in *LLHC*, p149]

Academic standards for boys were high. Robert Cowie's younger brother Isaac came second in the First Class at the first Anderson Institute Examination in 1862, after a gruelling public ordeal which included translating a Latin exercise taken at random from a book in the school, being cross-examined on it, an examination on the history of St Paul, an examination in geometry and finally a debate on 'The Influence exercised by the Crusades on European civilisation.' The girls were examined in their own classroom by Mr Ellaby, and Manson does not enlarge on their curriculum, so it's not possible to say whether useful domestic instruction and accomplishments was really all they were taught, or whether that was what was advertised as what parents were thought to want. Sisters Catherine and Elizabeth Linklater came first in their classes. [*LLHC* p 156]

The Edinburgh Orkney and Zetland Association offered school prizes, and these were won by both boys and girls. In 1882, the overall winner was Alexander M Laughton, South Ronaldsay, Orkney, and first prizes went to William Smith of Bressay and Williamina Spence of Nesting. Prizes went to nine others, including four girls: Janet Green, Jemima Williamson, Ellen Sinclair and Grace Matthewson, all of Lerwick (Matthewson later taught Art at the Anderson Institute). [*ST* 14 April 1882]

Secondary age education was more difficult for country pupils, as they incurred the expense of lodgings. Some bursaries were available for this – the County Education Committee had a competitive examination, and in 1893, 72 students entered for this, 39 girls and 33 boys. For a girl, there was the added difficulty of the impropriety of living in Lerwick, away from her family, so that girls without relatives in Lerwick were doubly disadvantaged. The girls from Fetlar staying with Miss Turnbull Stewart were probably attending school here.

For those who could afford to pay for it, private education was also available in Shetland. In the 1870s and 1880s, Mr Walker's school was open to all; later it was run by Miss Sheridan and Miss Ann Sheridan. The *Shetland Times* described the 1890 prize-giving of a school run by Miss Hughson, in Town Hall Buildings. Miss Elizabeth Hughson, born in 1851, gave her profession as teacher of German and French. Other teachers were Miss Mitchell (perhaps the Miss Mitchell who was later involved in the 1909 Shetland WSS) and Miss U K Goudie. Pupils included John Leisk's daughters, their cousin Dottie Sandison and Beata and Daisy Hunter. The curriculum seems to have focused on the arts; prizes were given for English, German, French, Music, Drawing, Singing, Needlework (Plain and Fancy – and no boys in this class), as well as a prize for *Progress in English and Regular Attendance* to Master W S Smith. Bailie Charles Robertson at the close regretted that Miss Hughson did not intend to resume her classes, presumably because of her forthcoming marriage: - 'glad for her sake and wish her every happiness in the new life before her.' [*ST* 1890, from Catherine Irvine's scrapbook.]

Miss Hughson married Robert Bruce Robertson on 14th July 1891, and moved to 3 Burgh Road. They had one son, born in 1892. Her successors in the Town Hall Buildings were Misses Bruce and Goudie – probably the same Ursula Katherine (Kitty) Goudie. There's no obvious Miss Bruce in Bayanne, but the schoolmaster at Urafirth, James Bruce, had two daughters, Elizabeth and Jessie, who married two Robertson brothers in Lerwick in 1895; one of them might have been Miss Bruce.

Another private school, in the Old School Room, continued for the first half of the 1890s. It was run by Mrs Tait and her daughter Alice, along with Fraulein Thumer, German Governess. Mrs Tait was the wife of John Tait, General Merchant of 141 Commercial Street, and Alice was one of the Shetland girls qualified in the St Andrew's University L.L.A scheme. A short-lived school run by Miss Robertson, another L.L.A. graduate, was listed in 1900, the first year that J J Haldane Burgess offered private tuition. [*Manson's Shetland Almanac*]

The *Shetland Times* would have liked to see evening classes to keep young men out of mischief during the long winter nights:

' ... it must be patent to the most cursory observer that most of the spare time of the rising generation is spent at the street corners or in perambulating the town ...' [*ST* 30 November 1874].

The following year it regretted the demise of the Literary and Scientific Society, which had held lectures through the winter. The *Times* appealed to

'our young accomplished and energetic young ladies [to get] a course of lectures on such subjects as amateur lecturers, at their irresistable solicitation, may be constrained to prepare. [*ST* November 1875].

Five years later, there were a number of opportunities on offer:

'Notice: evening classes will be formed in the First Public School - if a sufficient number of pupils offer - for Latin, French, Mathematics, Book-Keeping, Arithmetic, Grammar and Composition, Freehand and Geometrical Drawing. The teacher [Mr Drummond] will meet with intending pupils on the Evening of Monday the 23rd current in the school room. For any one of the above subjects, 2s per month, and 1s additional for every subject after the first.' [*ST* 21 Feb 1880]

Some of Mr Drummond's pupils were perhaps studying for the Aberdeen Local Examinations. These were introduced in 1880, and in that first year, women were 80% of the Preliminary candidates, 72% of the Ordinary / Junior candidates and 100% of the Senior candidates. The Senior certificate was seen as pre-University standard. In all, over the thirty years the examinations were run, over 3,000 women passed the Senior certificate, but only 21 men did. Instead, men sat the University Bursary competition, which was not open to women. Shetland candidates would have travelled to Aberdeen to sit the examinations (a number took both the Preliminary and the Ordinary), and the *Shetland Times* published the lists of successful candidates for that first year.

Ten students entered for Preliminary certificates, four men and six women. The women ranged in age from 19 down to 13. They were:

Wilhelmina Inkster born in 1861, daughter of James Inkster, General Merchant, Brae. She married James Moodie, schoolteacher in Brae in 1898.

Barbara Robertson born in 1862, daughter of Robert Robertson, of R & C Robertson, Grocer, Spirit Merchant in Lerwick, and sister of Robina, below; their uncle, Charles Robertson, became Lerwick's first Provost in 1893. Their father, Robert, and uncles Charles and William had all been involved in the Lerwick Instruction Society.

Robina C Robertson Bina Charlotte Robertson, born in 1864, Lerwick, the sister of Barbara, above.

Anne L Tulloch Anne Logie Tulloch, born in 1864, daughter of William Bruce Tulloch, Shipping Agent, Lerwick, and sister to W A A Tulloch of the Harbour Trust, who was to be the only man at the inaugural meeting of the 1909 Shetland WSS.

Margaret Morrison Margaret Miller Morrison, born in 1866, was a daughter of Hector, and later a member of the 1909 SWSS. A year later a Miss Morrison was assistant to Mr Drummond of the First Public School – it could be this Miss Morrison, as pupil-teachers could be as young as 13, or one of her older sisters.

Margaret A Pole Margaret Ann Pole, born in 1867, oldest daughter of Dr Alexander Pole, Cullivoe, and later a schoolmistress.

Eight of the pupils also achieved an Ordinary Certificate, including five of the women; Robina Robertson was the exception. [*ST* 24 July 1880] There were perhaps students in other years, but this is the only list I've found; I think it's more likely that girls in Shetland moved to the L.L.A. scheme, which could be studied at home.

The L.L.A. examinations:

It wasn't easy for Shetland men to study at University either. Even if their parents were sufficiently in earnest to afford the tuition and book fees, to say nothing of losing the young man's potential income for a further four years, living at home wasn't an option for Shetland students, so lodgings at their University were an extra expense. There were very few Bursaries available each year, for example from the Orkney and Shetland Associations. It's no wonder that only a small number of students went to University from Shetland. Writing for the *Centenary of the A E I, Lerwick*, Andrew T Cluness (at school 1904-9) recalled, 'A very select few went to University.' Among them, though, were scholars like Frank Dalziel and J J Haldane Burgess, who each came top in his year, in all Scotland. The candidate in second place to Haldane Burgess had forty marks less. Each year, student passes were listed in the *Shetland Times*.

'Honours to Shetland students at Edinburgh University ... a number of Shetland students took prizes, with, among them, John Robertson Jun of Lerwick (John Fordyce Robertson, of Viewforth House?) and Francis R Jamieson.' [*ST* 3 May 1884]

Jamieson was elected a member of the University Council. [*ST* 10 May 1884] You wonder how it must have felt to be Francis's equally clever sister, Christina, only two years younger, reading such notices at home in Sandness; she must have felt pride for her talented brother mingled with the knowledge that she'd never go to University. For a girl in Shetland then, the best chance of a University-level education was through the L.L.A scheme.

In May 1881, the *Shetland Times* had a short paragraph giving the numbers of honours and ordinary passes of the L.L.A. (Lady Literate in Arts) Examination in St Andrew's, London, Halifax and Bristol; the wording suggests it was taken from a St Andrews news item.

'In 1877, when it was started, 9 candidates appeared; in the following year, 32 candidates; in 1879, 72 candidates; last year, 92, and this year 179 candidates entered, being nearly double the number that entered last year. The number of centres of examination has been increased this year by the addition of Bristol, and next year Belfast will be added. More women students have come up for examination this year than there were arts students matriculated at the University [of St Andrews] last session. The number of subjects taken up has been greater, and it is stated that some of the honours papers were of exceptional merit. These L.L.A. candidates may be regarded as a virtual addition to the roll of students at the University of St Andrews.' [*ST* 14 May 1881]

The subjects taken were English literature, Latin, French, German, Italian, Comparative philology, History, Education, Logic and Metaphysics, Moral Philosophy, Political Economy, Mathematics, Physiology, Botany and Church history.

The L.L.A. was a home-study course open to candidates across the country. It began in 1876, under the convenership of W A Wright, Professor of Moral Philosophy. He gradually made the course equivalent to the men's M.A., increasing the number of subjects to be taken, and presenting candidates with the same exams on the same day. From 1883, the L.L.A diploma students were given the entitlement to wear academic dress, a sash of the same material and colours as the M.A. hood, and a silver badge. Rural and overseas candidates could also sit the examination; the onus was on the candidate to find a suitable person to supervise the exam, for example a clergyman or headmaster. In 1887, there were 597 candidates. However, although candidates had passed an Honours M.A. paper, the L.L.A was not accepted as qualifying a student for entrance to University classes.

Lerwick was one of the centres of examination for a number of years. Here are these early candidates with Shetland connections. A number of them are primary school teachers. It seems likely that these women taught there to finance their degree; after that, these well-educated women would probably have gone on, as Margaret Craib and Margaret Morrison did, to teach in secondary education.

1883 - 5

Miss Annie Sinclair was the first teacher at Virkie Board School, and taught there from 1880 to 1885. She was the first woman to take the L.L.A. examinations in Shetland. She sat Education, French and History in 1883 in Lerwick, and Honours in Politicial Economy in 1884, achieving her L.L.A. in that year.

Mary Margaret Stephen was born in 1861 at Keig, Aberdeenshire. Her father, John, was a cattle dealer in Inverurie. She taught at Bigton School from 1881 – 1885. She registered for the scheme, but took no examination.

Margaret Simpson Craib was Stephen's sucessor at Bigton School. She was born in 1862, in Aberdeen. Her parents were Charles Craib, mariner and Agnes Bissett. After being a pupil teacher in Aberdeen, Craib taught at Bigton School from 1885-86. She passed Education in 1884 and French in 1885, sitting the latter in Shetland; she also gained her Teacher's Certificate in 1885. She then taught at Stanmore School, Westmorland for two years, and became Headmistress of Wester Hatton Public School,

Belhelvie. There she resumed her studies: Botany and English in 1888, History in 1889, She was awarded her L.L.A. in that year.

Jane Wingate was born in 1864 in Dunrossness. Her father Thomas was the minister in Sandwick, her mother was Elizabeth H Bruce, daughter of John Bruce of Sandlodge. The family moved to Stromness before 1871. Jane went to school in Edinburgh, then took her first papers in English Literature, Honours, and French in Aberdeen in 1884. She went on to take Logic and Metaphysics along with German in 1885, and was awarded her L.L.A. in that year. Her sister, Helen Murray Wingate, went to Girton. Jane died in Orkney aged only 36. Her brother, John Bruce Wingate, seems to have inherited Sandlodge, for he died there in 1939.

'L.L.A. ST ANDREW'S UNIVERSITY - SHETLAND COMPETITORS - At the examination last month, Miss Margaret S Craib, Public School, Bigton, passed in education and Miss Anne Sinclair, Public School, Virkie, passed with honours in political economy, and obtained the L.L.A. degree.' [*ST* 31 May 1884]

1887-8

Jane M Sime, educated at Dundee High School, took French in 1887. A Margaret Sime taught at Sandsound School from 1886-7, and a Miss Sime returned there from 1895-6; the name's unusual enough in Shetland to assume she's the same person.

Margaret Miller Morrison, the daughter of Hector Morrison, had already qualified through the Aberdeen Local Examinations scheme. She took her English and French examinations in Lerwick in 1887, and followed these with History Honours and German, completing her L.L.A. in 1888. By 1892, the date of Manson's first *Shetland Almanac*, she was teaching at the Institute.

Sara Malcolmson of Hillhead, Lerwick, took her English honours in 1890, though not in Lerwick. She was probably Sarah Goudie Malcolmson, born in 1856, teacher, and daughter of William Malcolmson, baker; she was resident in Charlotte Lane in 1861; at 2 Hill Lane, in 1871; at 12 Malborough St, Dawdon, Durham as a governess in 1881; and at 47 Harley St, Marylebone, London in 1891. She emigrated to Canada before 1905, and married there.

1891-3 In 1891 and 1892, again two candidates sat their examinations together:

Mary Charlotte Robertson, of Rocklea House, was born in 1874. She was the daughter of Charles Robertson, first Provost of Lerwick (and so cousin to Barbara and Robina who took the Local Examinations in 1880). She took English in 1891 and French in 1892, both in Lerwick. She was to run a private school in Rocklea House at the turn of the century.

Alice Marjory Tait, of 5 Burgh Rd, Lerwick, was born in 1870. She was the daughter of general merchant John Tait, 141 Commercial Street, and Elizabeth Murray, and one of nine surviving children (three died in infancy). She took English in 1891, and History Honours in 1892. She and her mother were to run a private school in Lerwick from 1892. In 1900 she married Andrew Nicolson of Bressay, and went to live at 7 Inverleith Row, Edinburgh.

Joan Brown, of Burgh Road, Lerwick, was born in 1874. She took her Honours English in 1893. Her father, John Brown, was a merchant in Lerwick, and his mother was Grizel Stout, daughter of Robert who built Stout's Court. She married Thomas Mackenzie Reid, Customs Officer, in 1905.

Margaret Ann Pole had also qualified through the Local Examinations, and now went on to take her Education Honours in 1893, her German Honours and History in 1896 and her French Honours in 1897, the year she was awarded her L.L.A. Her address is given as Craigilea, which belonged to John Harrison and his wife, Andrina Bruce. In 1893, Andrina had just had a fifth son; the others were 18, 17, 15 and 10, and their daughter was 13. It's possible Margaret Pole was governess to the younger children. She went on to become a schoolmistress, and died in Dorset in 1958.

After 1892, women could go to University in Scotland. Shetland women also sat L.L.A. examinations in Lerwick in 1901-2 and 1917, and the L.L.A. diploma continued until the 1930s.

University degree courses:

In 1889, the Universities (Scotland) Act was passed, allowing Scottish universities to admit women to degree courses. This new opportunity was immediately taken up with enthusiasm.

It was women in Edinburgh who were the first in Scotland to graduate. The first female undergraduates at Edinburgh were admitted in 1892, and eight graduated on 13th April, 1893, all having previously studied in Edinburgh Association for the University Education of Women classes. They were: Miss Flora Philip, the first women member of the Edinburgh Mathematical Society, a member of the Greek Club, and one of the first teachers at St George's School for Girls, Edinburgh (an EAUEW enterprise, opened in 1888); Miss Maude Newbigin, author, and member of the Royal Scottish Geographical Society; Miss Amelia Stirling, daughter of the Scottish philosopher James Hutchinson Stirling, and a correspondent of Emerson and Carlyle; Frances Simson, who became Warden of Masson Hall; Lilias Maitland, who co-authored a novel called *Summers and Winters at Balmawhupple* – there is a stained glass window in her memory in All Saints' Church, St Andrews; Mary Buchan Douie, who went on to study medicine at the London School of Medicine for Women, and was very much involved in the rebuilding and extension of the school, and the admission of women to the Fellowship of the Royal Colleges of Physicians and Surgeons; Margaret Nairn, who was involved in a 1908 challenge to Universities of Edinburgh and St Andrews; and Grace Fairley, who was holding a teaching post in Canada, and received her degree in absentia. In 1896, Chrystal Macmillan became the first woman with a Science degree from Edinburgh; by 1914, a thousand women had degrees from Edinburgh University.

Edinburgh does not have the addresses of its early women graduates, so only family tradition could tell us if Shetland women graduated from there before World War I – it would then be possible to look up the names.

In St Andrews, the profits from the L.L.A. scheme began a fund for a women's Hall of Residence, University Hall. It was opened in 1896 with Louisa Innes Lumsden, one of the 'Girton Pioneers', as the first warden. In 1908, she also became president of the Aberdeen WSS, and was to lend Helen Fraser her horse-drawn caravan for a speaking tour of the Borders. After Elizabeth Garrett in 1862, the first woman graduate from St Andrews was Agnes Forbes Blackadder, who began her studies in 1892 and graduated in Arts in March 1895. She went on to study at University College, Dundee, then at the Queen Margaret College for Women, eventually gaining her MD in 1901. As Dr Agnes Savill, she published papers on the forcible feeding of suffrage prisoners, and was a radiographer in the Scottish Women's Hospital in Royaumont, France in WWI. As far as I can find out, there were no Shetland women in residence at St Andrews before World War I.

There had been a dedicated college for women in Glasgow from November 1882. The first head of Queen Margaret's College, Glasgow, was Janet Galloway, who remained in post for 27 years, until 1909; her mother was a friend of the Jamieson family. Their Medical School was established in 1890, and Dr Marion Gilchrist was the first Glasgow University woman graduate, in 1894. She went on to become an expert on diseases of the eye, and an activist in the Glasgow and West of Scotland Suffrage Association. Queen Margaret college became affiliated to Glasgow University in 1892. The University of Glasgow Roll of Honour contains a number of early women doctors and surgeons who subsequently served with the Scottish Women's Hospitals in France, Serbia and Salonika. Like Edinburgh, Queen Margaret's College does not have the addresses of their early graduates.

Dundee had also had a University College for both men and women since 1881. It was founded by a Dundee philanthropist, Mary Ann Baxter, to 'promote the education of both sexes' and was the fore-runner of the present University of Dundee.

In Edinburgh, Dr Elsie Inglis had founded the Scottish Association for the Medical Education for Women in 1889, and in 1898 she opened a Hall of Residence for women medical students. In 1899 she was appointed a lecturer in gynaecology at the Medical College for Women and she also opened a small hospital for women, still continued in the Elsie Inglis Hospital in Edinburgh.

Aberdeen University also opened its courses to women in 1892, and the first 20 women students began their courses in 1894. Four women graduated in arts in 1898, and by 1899 women made up a quarter of the Arts Faculty.

The first woman M.A. to teach at the Anderson EI was Miss Jane G Mackay, in 1906. She was probably from outwith Shetland, and stayed only a year. She was followed, in 1907, by Jennie Campbell, born in 1886, and so just twenty-one when she took her degree. Miss Campbell taught at the Institute until 1925, when she married Arthur Smith. She was probably the first woman from Shetland to graduate, and one of the first women graduates of Aberdeen University; her son Douglas remembers her telling him that when the lecturer called out the register, using only surnames, she refused to answer 'Adsum' to his 'Campbell' and all the male students clapped and stamped their feet until he said 'Miss Campbell.' Although Douglas doesn't remember his mother speaking of the suffrage movement, her younger sister Daisy was to become an active committee member of the Shetland Women's Suffrage Society, and he remembers a number of the committee members meeting at Bridge evenings in their house.

Miss Campbell was joined in 1912 by Miss A Dey, M.A., again probably from outwith Shetland, and another SWSS member. She remained until 1914, when they were joined by Miss Margaret Beatrice Tulloch M.A, born in 1889, who married a fellow-teacher, Edwin Dixon, in 1916. Miss Helen M Chalmers, M.A., taught at the AEI from 1915.

Another early graduate was Winifred Laing, the daughter of Provost Laing, and first cousin to Christina Jamieson. She was born in August 1886, and so probably graduated as a pharmacist around 1907 or 1908.

Shetland's first woman graduate: Jennie Campbell at her graduation.
Photograph courtesy of her son, Douglas Smith.

76

4

The 1880s

Feminist legislation,
continuing pressure,
women serving on parochial boards,
and the municipal vote in Shetland

Lerwick Town Hall at midnight.
Photographed by John Leisk; courtesy of Shetland Museum and Archives [00416K]

Lerwick was changing to the town we know today. Charles Gilbert Duncan had already begun the first of three major public works in the 1860s: the new water and sewer system. In 1876, the second began: building the new Victoria Pier. The initial expense was £715, and the list of Guarantors included a number of familiar names: Wm Duncan, John Leisk, Arthur Sandison, Geo. Reid Tait, John Robertson sen., Alex. Mitchell, Duncan & Galloway, G Harrison and Son, Peter Garriock, James Hunter, Robert Stout, H Morrison, John Robertson jnr, Mr Samuel Laing. A further £10,200 was raised locally, and all these names appeared again, headed by John Robertson, Merchant, £600, Lewis F U Garriock, £400, John Leisk, £400. The pier was finished in 1878, and was immediately an asset to the town, as boats could now unload, and passengers embark, directly to the pier. In 1886, when the herring boom began, Lerwick became Britain's first fishing port, and the harbour dues rose from around £500 to £1178; thereafter, it made a steady profit, which returned to the town coffers.

In 1875, the new County Buildings had been built, and the prisoners were transferred from the Tolbooth to the Fort, leaving the Tolbooth free for the Post Office to return there. In 1878, a Committee convened by John Leisk was set up to produce a revised Feuing Plan of the Trust Property of the town, to make it available for building. The Committe met throughout 1878 – 1881, and a large number of the villas of the Hillhead and on the roads down to King Harald Street were built in the 1880s and 1890s.

The Victoria Pier was followed by the building of the Town Hall. This was first discussed early in 1880, and a Limited Liability Company formed to pay for it. The first chairman was former Chief Magistrate Joseph Leask of Sand, and 2000 shares of £2 were sold. On 13 October 1880 the company accepted the tender of John Aiken to build the new Town Hall for £3240, and appointed a Decoration Committee to organise donations for the interior. Thomas Manson gave a full account of the building, decoration, laying of the foundation stone (by the Duke of Edinburgh) in 24 January 1882, the Grand County Ball which opened it in 1883, and the Jubilee Celebrations in *Lerwick in the Last Half-Century*, chapters 33 and 34.

In 1880, the new telegraph cable had been laid, and the *Shetland Times* was now publishing the latest Telegraphic News.

Nor was the Literary and Scientific Society totally defunct; the *Shetland Times* of 1 May 1880 gave details of a fund-raising concert. The thank you on behalf of the Society was given by Mr Galloway, the Procurator Fiscal; his wife was to be Vice President of the 1909 SWSS.

Women were invading a sacred male preserve:

'THE FEMALE FOOTBALL MATCH IN GLASGOW On Monday night the females who have been peregrinating the country during the last fortnight describing themselves as 'international teams' representing England and Scotland gave one of their football exhibitions in Shawfield park, all the other football clubs in the city having refused the use of their parks...' The women arrived in omnibuses drawn by 4 horses, but a fight broke out among the crowd - 'more interesting than the match ... no club with any regard for their good name would encourage such a humiliating spectacle made of the popular winter game.' [*ST* 28 May 1881]

You wonder how on earth they managed to play football *at all* in long skirts; but then, they managed to bicycle successfully, in fact the bicycle gave women a new freedom.

Women were also considered sufficiently independent to be the target of a scam in February / March 1880, with a large advertisement for the 'Ladies' Co-operative Supply Company'. The Committee was given as a list of ladies' names, but a correspondent, 'Z', from the *Orkney Herald*, was dubious, and a letter from A.P. pointed out that as married women the ladies, 'save as their husbands' agents, are incompetent to hold property or deal in shares ... no possible explanation, in my opinion, can show it to be a sound financial undertaking.' [*ST* 6 March 1880]

On 13 March the advertisement was withdrawn: 'A warrant has been issued to arrest one Mr Stanley, the promoter of the Company.'

Women's suffrage was the butt of a jokey story from America:

'Testing a Woman's Nerve: A tall lady with a saturnine countenance came into the *Chronicle* office today and demanded of one of the reporters if Virginia offered a good field for a series of a dozen lectures on women's suffrage.'

After terrorising the 'small reporter' for calling her a 'female' and insisting she is stronger than he, he routed her by pretending to see a rat, whereupon she emitted a shrill scream and ran. [*ST* 13 March 1880]

The *Shetland News* began in 1885. It was Conservative, rather than Liberal, and similar in shape to the *Shetland Times,* but with double the number of pages. It began with a front page of advertisements, but then two more pages of small ads, followed by two pages of local news, another page of advertisements, including local books and 'for sale', then a page of reviews, a 'wit and Humour' column, a page of political and world news, and finally, a last page of adverts.

By the mid 1880s the original Lerwick Women's Suffrage Committee was diminished to only four members, Mr Walker, John Robertson, Hector Morrison and Miss Spence. Mr Dobson had gone to another parish. Dr Cowie had died, and his wife had gone to Edinburgh. Mr Macfarlane died in 1886, and his wife went to Canada after that. Miss Ogilvie died in 1881, and Mrs Bailie Robertson in 1886. Even given the *Shetland Times'* reluctance to report suffrage activity (it was a great supporter of Gladstone), it seems that there was little or no activity here after the initial enthusiasm of 1873 - 4.

1880 was an election year, and this time the Liberals came in, due to a campaign led by Gladstone, to such an effect that the Party leaders, Lord Hartington and Lord Granville, withdrew in his favour, and he returned as Prime Minister. This was the election of the 'Midlothian Campaign', where Gladstone made a series of fiery speeches (some of them five hours long, good grief!) against continued British economic assistance to the Ottoman Empire, in the light of recent atrocities in Bulgaria.

To everyone's surprise a Tory candidate, Dr G R Badenoch, suddenly appeared in Shetland. He was sponsored by several local citizens, including George Reid Tait and W B M Harrison. He doesn't seem to have been a friend to women's suffrage; after speaking at length on foreign affairs, he focused on the Radicals:

'In the Constitution of our country, there is a large body of truth engrossed, and and it is because of this that we are able to regulate all our beneficial laws, and especially those relating to marriage. There is a class of men who would sweep all this away.'

He seems to have had a rough time, with a number of 'hisses' and cries of 'Laing for ever!' The meeting ended in laughter.

Mr Laing himself came hurriedly up to the isles for a tour. He was warmly received in Walls and given a vote of confidence in Scalloway, but he had a rough ride in Lerwick, including someone blowing a fog horn up in the gallery. He speaks about the County and Burgh Act and redistribution of seats, but not votes for women, nor is it raised in any question. [*ST* 10 April 1880]

The results were published on 1 May 1880; Samuel Laing was again returned for Shetland, standing as a Liberal. The Liberal party had gained 110 seats, giving them an overall majority of 52. The contest seemed to have given local voters a shock, for in May 1880 they formed the Shetland Liberal Association, chaired by Bailie Hay. [*ST* 22 May 1880].

In September 1882, Laing published his end-of Session address to the electorate, as an apology for not being able to come up to the Isles in person. It began: 'GENTLEMEN:' and went on to say how he would like to see the House reformed with less time given to debates now the press reported speeches given at public meetings:

'They are simply the outcome 1st, of deliberate obstruction; 2nd, of vanity and self conceit; 3rd, of want of brain-power to enable to speaker to condense and distinguish between what is worth saying and what is not...'

To avoid this he suggested that the Government should allot closure to bills, and asserts that this would not prevent individual bills being presented:

'I have never known an instance of a man being refused a hearing because his principles or his person were unpopular. Mr Bright was for many years the advocate, and that not always in the mildest tone, of opinions intensely unpopular with the majority of the House.' [*ST* September 1882]

Feminist legislation of the 1880s:

The Municipal Franchise (Scotland) Act(1881) granted women ratepayers in Royal and Parliamentary Burghs in Scotland the right to vote in municipal elections. The Earl of Camperdown, proposing the second reading to the Lords in May 1881, called the Bill another step in the direction of the emancipation of women.

'He knew of no reason why the females of Scotland should be placed in an inferior position to the females of England... there had been no opposition to the measure in the other House of Parliament.' [Hansard, 6 May 1881]

This was extended to Police Burghs, as Lerwick now was, in the spring of 1882.

During 1882, meetings to 'arouse the newly-created electors to a sense of the duties and responsibilities of the municipal vote' were arranged by the Edinburgh society, and speakers included Jessie Craigen, who travelled to Aberdeen, Dundee and other places – not, as far as I can see, Shetland. In November 1882 here, only four candidates came forward for the five seats: Major Cameron, Mr James Hunter, Mr James Tulloch, and Mr Alex Mitchell. Although the election was not contested, the *Shetland Times* still printed a short article taken from the *Free Press*, obviously part of the Edinburgh society's education campaign:

'THE FEMALE FRANCHISE At the ensuing municipal elections women householders in Scotland will for the first time, have the privilege of recording their votes ...' Quoting the Edinburgh NSWS, it reminds householders that as the Town Council controls: '...drainage, water supply, proper paving and lights, it is fairly enough argued that that concern women even more than they do men. Then again, in such matters as the licensing of public-houses ... the interest of women is certainly not less direct than that of men. It is therefore sought to be earnestly impressed upon every woman that she should carefully prepare herself to exercise the right of self-government now conferred upon her intelligently and conscientiously and in the interest of morality and temperance ...' [*ST* 4 November 1882]

The 1882 and 1886 elections were also uncontested; women ratepayers in Lerwick would not get the chance to vote until 1889.

The **Married Women's Property Act** (1882) was one of the nineteenth century's single most important changes in the legal status of women in England. Feminists hoped that it would remove the argument against married women gaining the vote; if her seperate legal existence was recognised, she could no longer be presumed to be represented by her husband. In some ways, *feme sole* status was established, but only to the extent of a wife's 'seperate property'; she was not bound personally. A married woman was now capable of

'entering into and rendering herself liable in respect of and to the extent of her separate property on any separate contract, and of suing and being sued, either in contract or in tort, or otherwise, in all respects as if she were *feme sole*, and her husband need not be joined with her as plaintiff or defendent, or be made a party to any action or proceeding brought by or taken against her; and any damages or costs recovered by her in any such action shall be her separate property; and any damages or costs recovered against her in any such action or proceeding shall be payable out of her separate property and not otherwise.'

Her husband was still responsible for her torts, and she was still not able to make an independent will. She could will away only her personal property; if her husband subsequently pre-deceased her, she had to make a new will as a widow, acting as a *feme sole*. As before, married women were given protection, not independence; their status with regard to voting rights was unchanged.

The provisions of the various English Married Women's Property Acts came to Scotland in stages, but by 1882 Scottish and English wives were roughly equal with regard to property. A wife's right to administer her separate property, and dispose of it without her husband's consent, did not arrive until 1920 in Scotland.

The **Matrimonial Causes Act** (1884) was brought on in part by the case of Captain Weldon. He was willing to provide for his wife, but refused to live with her, and she brought a suit for restoration of conjugal rights. The court granted her plea, but Weldon still refused. Earlier in the century a woman had allegedly gone to prison in Suffolk and died there, rather than return to her husband; the House of Commons had, seemingly, more sympathy when it was a man refusing to live with his wife. The new Act ruled that non-compliance with a successful suit for the restitution of conjugal rights was to be taken as an act of desertion, and the deserted spouse could apply immediately to the divorce court for a separation order, instead of having to wait two years. The court would then order the deserting spouse to pay maintenance, and award custody of children to the plaintiff. The **Married Women (Maintenance in case of Desertion) Act** (1886), gave magistrates the authority to order a husband to pay maintenance directly to the wife he had deserted, instead of the previous cumbersome process of the wife having to apply to the parish, which then sued the husband. Both these Acts applied only in England, but the debates over them were influential in forming public opinion and judicial practice in Scotland.

The **Representation of the People Act** (1884) (the Third Reform Act) enfranchised agricultural workers by eliminating all but the most minimal property qualifications. The Act extended the borough claims into the countryside: all male householders, all men paying £10 in rent or holding land valued at £10. The electorate now totalled 5,500,000, but it was very far from universal suffrage; 40% of adult males were still without the vote, as well as all women. A clause suggesting the extension of the Bill to women was debated on 12 June 1884. Lord John Mannees, proposing the reading of the clause, said:

'To me it is a very simple, a very plain, and almost a humdrum question. It is simply this—Will you grant the Parliamentary franchise to a class of Her Majesty's subjects who, for many years past, have blamelessly, and with great advantage to the State, exercised the franchise with respect to Municipal, with respect to Poor Law, and with respect to School Board elections?'

Comments by Mr Stansfeld and others make it clear how much pressure they were under from Gladstone's government:

'I decline to discuss the subject ... under the conditions created for those in favour of admitting women to the franchise by the action of the Prime Minister the other day. Those of the Liberal Party who take an interest in the subject were told that we may not vote in favour of this proposal, unless we choose to place ourselves under the imputation of risking the passing of the Franchise Bill, or, it may be, of imperilling the existence of the Government itself.'

The vote went against reading the clause, by 271 to 135 (Samuel Laing does not appear to have been present), and women's suffrage was not discussed further. In contrast, there were several divisions taken on the point of whether a felon should continue his disenfranchisement for a year after he had served his sentence.

The **Guardianship of Infants Bill** (1886) also applied to Scotland. A number of cases after 1874 highlighted the anomalies in the previous Act of 1873. One was in Scotland, where a wife was given a separation from her husband on the grounds of cruelty, but was not allowed custody of their four-year old daughter; the judge felt the child would 'introduce a soothing influence to cheer the darkness and mitigate the bitterness of [the father's] lot, and bring out the better part of his nature.' The second decision, widely condemned publicly but perfectly correct in law, was in the case of Mr Agar-Elis. He was a Protestant, his wife a Catholic, and before their marriage he had promised, in front of her family, to raise the children as Catholics. He went back on his word, and their mother had them secretly instructed. When the parents separated in 1878, the father had the children made Wards in Chancery, and they were sent to boarding schools. All their letters to and from their mother were read, and mother and daughters were forbidden to discuss religion. When he refused his seventeen-year old daughter permission to visit her mother, she appealed to Chancery, and her father's rights were upheld: unless the child's safety was threatened, neither mother nor court could interfere with the father's rights.

The Guardianship of Infants Bill was introduced in 1884 by James Bryce, Liberal MP for Aberdeen South, and feminists had prepared for it by giving lectures and publishing articles. By spring 1884, 180 petitions with 19,513 signatures had been sent to Parliament; there was no petition from Lerwick or Tingwall, suggesting again that there was no suffrage activity here. Bryce's bill reflected the desire for parents to have equal custody rights, including joint custody during marriage. Some feminists were arguing that women's natural functions of child-bearing and lactation gave them greater claims to custody; as Jessie Craigen said in one of a series of lectures:

'...The richest woman here tonight that is the mother of children loves them dearly; the poorest no less. And the laws which wrong the mother's love are an outrage on the common womanhood by the bond of which we have all been drawn here.'

The debate on Bryce's Bill showed agreement that the presumption in favour of the father could cause injustice. Joint custody during marriage, however, was going too far for the House of Commons, and that clause was deleted on July 22. In the Lords, the Bill was delayed until the following session; Lord Fitzgerald made one last attempt to restore the joint custody clause in March 1885, without success. The Bill then became focused on a widow's rights to custody; with a few exceptions, members agreed that a widow had the right to custody of her children over her late husband's will or guardian appointees. The mother's appointees, however, would only serve as guardians if the husband could be shown to be 'unfitted to have sole charge'. This measure passed the Lords in 1885, but was blocked in the Commons, and was not passed until after the 1886 election.

Continuing pressure:

Associations and individuals continued to lobby the government over the decade. In 1880, the first Women's Liberal Associations were formed, and it gradually became common to see women on political platforms. The Corrupt Practices Act of 1883 made it illegal to pay canvassers, and so more women became involved in door-to-door politics on behalf of their male relatives. The Women's Liberal Federation was formed in 1887; it did not pass a resolution in favour of women's suffrage until 1890, and was to be split in 1892 over the question of whether married women should be given the franchise.

The Conservative Primrose League created their Ladies' Grand Council in 1884; in December 1886 the Edinburgh Habitation of the Primrose League held a discussion of female franchise, which Edinburgh solicitor James Bruce said 'would add great lustre to the party.' The motion agreeing was carried by a considerable majority. From 1889 the Ladies' Grand Council attempted to forbid discussion of women's suffrage but on 30 October 1891 the Grand Habitation (Scottish Branch) resolved it should petition the Government, calling women's suffrage: 'an act of justice which must come, and great credit would reflect on the Government which carried it into effect.' In 1887, 1890 and 1892 annual conferences of the Conservative Associations of Scotland urged the Government to enfranchise women. Possible Conservative leaders, like Balfour, were also pro-suffrage:

'We have been told that to encourage women to take an active part in politics is degrading to the sex, and that received the assent of an hon. friend of mine below the gangway. It has received the assent of almost every speaker to-day. I should think myself grossly inconsistent and most ungrateful if I supported that argument in this House, for I have myself taken the chair at Primrose League Meetings, and urged to the best of my ability the women of this country to take a share in politics, and to do their best in their various localities to support the principles which I believe to be sound in the interests of the country. After that, to come down to the House, and say I have asked these women to do that which degrades them, appears to me to be most absurd.' (Balfour, 1891)

One possible reason for the Conservative support of women's suffrage, as one letter of 1891 explained, was that it could be a fender against the growing Labour movement. Activists hoped that giving a small number of propertied women the vote would hold back universal suffrage. The next Bill, giving only municipal voters the franchise, was to be introduced by a Conservative MP.

In April 1882, the Convention of Royal and Parliamentary Burghs petitioned Parliament to extend parliamentary franchise to women who had been granted the municipal franchise; the petiton was presented on 5 June by James Barclay, radical Liberal MP for Forfarshire. Twelve town councils followed suit. The Convention was to petition again in spring 1887; this petition was presented by William McEwan, Liberal MP for Edinburgh Central (he founded the brewery). Twenty town councils also sent petitions; Lerwick doesn't seem to have been one of them.

One of the most often used arguments against giving women the vote was that they didn't want it. It was Priscilla Bright McLaren who suggested the idea of a 'Grand Demonstration of Women', to show the government the support for women' suffrage, and she presided over the first, held in Manchester Free Trade Hall in 1880, and organised by Lydia Becker (it didn't make the *Shetland Times*). A large number of working women were present; men were allowed in the gallery, as spectators only, on payment of 2/6 (do I detect revenge for the Anti-Slavery conference, all those years ago?) But look how far the women had travelled. It was only nine years since Jessie Craigen had spoken here in Shetland, introduced and accompanied by clergymen, to emphasise her respectability, in a tour organised by the Temperance League. This was a highly succesful demonstration focused solely on women's issues, organised by women, for women, with a woman chairman and committee, and only women speakers.

There were further demonstrations, including one on 3 November 1882, in Glasgow, and one in Edinburgh on 24 March 1884; in all, nine 'Grand Demonstrations' were held. Jessie Craigen and Lydia Becker both made speeches at eight out of nine of them. Unfortunately, the *Shetland Times* discontinued its Glasgow Correspondent's column during 1882, and gave no mention at all of any of the demonstrations; it was too busy giving the 'Latest Canadian News' and the 'Funeral of the Duke of Albany.'

The efforts of the Manchester society also won women's suffrage for Manxwomen in 1881, when a Bill for Household Suffrage to male persons came up for discussion in the Isle of Man 'House of Keys.' It was extended merely to ' women owners,' but there was much rejoicing at this concession to the principle of Women's Suffrage, and Emmeline Pankhurst (whose mother was a Manxwoman) was later to use it as an example of a region allowing limited women's suffrage without degenerating into the expected chaos.

In 1888 the Central Committee of the National Society for Women's Suffrage was split in two. The Central Committee wished to retain its 'no political affiliation of national political societies' rule, and, for pragmatic reasons, excluded married women from the vote, believing this was one of the stumbling blocks in the House. Lydia Becker and Millicent Fawcett remained with this group; the Central Committee was to lose one of its longest serving members and a tireless worker when Lydia Becker died in 1890. The Central National Society for Woman's Suffrage didn't expressly include married women, and were willing to accept affiliation from organisations who supported women's suffrage (a number of provincial Women's Liberal Associations, for example); the McLaren family were part of this organization.

There was to be a further split in March 1889, when Richard and Emmeline Pankhurst, Josephine Butler, Elizabeth Wolstenholme-Elmy and, later, Jacob and Ursula Bright, broke away from the Central National Society over their support for William Woodall's 'widows and spinsters' Bill. They were to form the Women's Franchise League, which campaigned for universal female suffrage with no property qualification. The WFL was to organise a Women's Disabilities Removal Bill in August 1889, and two conferences: an International Conference on the Position of Women in all Countries in July 1890, and a three-evening conference at the Pankhursts' house in London in December 1891. Their campaigning was important in the 1894 Local Government Act, which created rural and urban district councils; a clause introduced by Walter McLaren and James Stansfeld which allowed qualified married women (those with property of their own) to vote in local elections was an important step in blocking the 'widows and spinsters' Bill.

The 1885 and 1886 Parliamentary Elections:

The Redistribution Act of 1885 introduced the concept of equally populated constituencies. In total, 79 towns lost their MP, and 38 lost one MP; London and large northern towns were given more MPs. 160 seats were altered, the majority of them Liberal, to the gain of the Conservatives through middle-class seats in town. The redistribution is a partial explanation for the end of the Liberals' twenty-seven years in power, and the dominance of Conservatives through the rest of the century.

The first General Election after the Redistribution Act took place in November and December 1885. Rumours of Laing's retirement had been circulating for some time:

The Hon J C Dundas ON HIS POLITICAL OPINIONS declared himself a Liberal, and looked forward to Laing's retirement:

'… it could hardly be matter for surprise if Mr Laing should determine to retire from the strain of public life, though his retirement would be a loss not only to the constituency he has faithfully served, but to the country at large.' [ST July 1884]

Orkney and Shetland's new MP was Leonard Lyell, Liberal; he was to serve as MP for the next 15 years. Although he was to be challenged in the next three elections by a Liberal Unionist candidate, he retained his seat with a sizeable majority each time until 1900, when he lost (by 40 votes) to Liberal Unionist Cathcart Wason. His Liberal Manifesto of 14 March does not mention votes for women. Again the Liberals won the greatest number of seats in the House of Commons – 319, plus 11 Independent Liberals, to the Conservative 247, but the balance of power was held by the 86 MPs of the Irish Parliamentary Party. As the Liberals were divided over the Irish Home Rule question, this led to a split, with Lord Hartington and Joseph Chamberlain leading the Unionist Liberals, and an election in July the following year.

This time the Conservatives, in a pact with the Liberal Unionists, took 393 seats, leaving Gladstone's Liberals with 192, and the Irish Parliamentary Party with 98. The new Prime Minister was Lord Salisbury, and he appointed his nephew, A J Balfour, as President of the Board of Government, then Secretary of State for Scotland, then, in 1887, Chief Secretary for Ireland. In 1891 Balfour became First Lord of the Treasury and Leader of the House of Commons. Like Balfour, Salisbury had spoken in favour of enfranchising women.

Leonard Lyell (Sir Leonard Lyell from 1894) seems to have been primarily a constituency MP. Unlike Samuel Laing, whose voice was heard in debates on a range of domestic and foreign issues, Lyell spoke rarely in the House – six or seven times each year, and on each occasion it was on something directly connected with Orkney or Shetland. He seems to have had a genuine concern for the crofters' welfare, arguing for example, that the right to take seaweed should be part of crofting tenure, and asking about rights as to mussel beds, and the exact provisions as to rent day of the 1886 Act; he visited Ireland to see crofting conditions there for himself. He took a strong interest in education. He asked twice that electoral rolls should be prominently displayed in Post Offices as well as on the door of the Established Church, as many of his constituents were Dissenters. He was also concerned about shipping, speaking on several occasions about lighthouses around Shetland, and he seems to have urged the Vee Skerries light. He spoke several times in favour of the Post Office. He urged travel expenses for County Councillors and asked if the Government was going to reward Betty Mouat's Norwegian rescuers.

The 1886 election was contested here in Shetland, with Mr Henry Hoare standing against Lyell. The *Shetland Times* was very critical of behaviour of young men at Hoare's meeting 'disturbing the proceedings and interrupting the speakers by perpetual stamping and shouting'. They approved of Mr Lyell: 'he has been close in his attendance [in Parliament], and has interested himself in all business that in any way affected his constituency.' [*ST* 10 July 1886] Two weeks later, they gave detailed rebuttal of criticisms of the way he'd voted, and denounced Mr Hoare: 'a candidate brought down by a clique of discontented Whigs who call themselves Unionists because they are in union with the Tories.' [*ST* 24 July 1886]

Women serving on Parochial Boards:

Women were standing as candidates for Parochial Boards almost as early as they stood for School Boards, and in significantly greater numbers. Parochial Boards were constituted by Poor Law legislation of 1845, and their job was to administer relief to deserving cases in their parish. One of the first women to be elected, in Uckfield in 1875, was Marie Corbett, wife of the Liberal MP Charles Corbett. She gradually removed all the children from the local workhouse and boarded them with foster families. Martha Merrington was elected in Kensington, also in 1875. In 1880, there were eight women Guardians in England and Wales (of 28,000 Poor Law Guardians); by 1890, there were eighty. The lifting of the £5 property qualification in 1894 had an instant effect on women standing: the number rose to nearly nine hundred in 1895. Ada Neild, on the Crewe Board of Guardians, was one of the first working-class women to become an elected official, and married woman Emmeline Pankhurst was elected to the Chorley Board. The numbers continued to grow over the next decade, to well over a thousand; by comparison, there were only 200 women serving on School Boards in 1900, and a similar number on Parish Councils.

In Scotland, the work of administering Poor Law Relief was done by an Inspector answerable to the Parochial Board. Margaret Foulton was elected to the Inverkeithing Parochial Board in 1876, but seems to have been a lone example in Scotland; it was not until 1893 that four women were elected to the Edinburgh Parochial Board, supported by the suffrage society.

The Lerwick Parochial Board had been established in December 1845, with the power to levy rates on heritors and occupiers. The *Shetland Times* of 29 March 1884 gave details of the formation of Poor-house board, using the Orkney model. It was to be paid for by all the parishes, who might send paupers at any time, but if the house was full each parish would be allocated a number of beds, according to their valuation. The house was to be for 50 inmates. On 3 May 1884 there was a meeting of delegates from all over Shetland, and a committee was agreed.

The new Poorhouse had its foundation stone laid on the same day as the Grand Hotel and the opening of the Harbour Works, 23 June 1886, and was in operation by June 1887:

'Mr and Mrs Alexander Coutts, the new governor and matron of the Poor-House, arrived here to enter upon their duties, as per ss St Magnus yesterday (Friday).' [*ST* 4 June 1887]

The Parochial Board in Lerwick was exclusively male. In the 1890s, the Chairman was John Robertson Jnr – 'Young John o the Trance', and Hector and Donald Morrison were also members. The only women involved were the nurses: Miss Isabella Petrie was listed as the nurse for the Lerwick Combination Hospital for many years, and there was a Matron and a Nurse for the Combination Poorhouse – the nurse for 1898-9 was Miss Mary Dunn, Donald Morrison's future wife, and a member of the 1909 Shetland WSS. In 1908, the Nurse for the Poorhouse was Miss Hay; the Matron of the Hospital in 1910 was Miss Esplin. Both were to be present at the inaugural meeting of the 1909 Shetland WSS. [*Manson's Shetland Almanac 1892 - 1910*]

1889: Women in Shetland vote at last:

The first news page of the *Shetland News* of 2 November 1889 was devoted to the forthcoming Municipal Elections. These were to be hotly contested between the previous councillors, backed by a long list of familiar names, and the Working Men's Candidates, A J Garriock, J C Grierson, R B Hunter, James Hutchison and Laurence Mouat. **Archibald John Garriock**, Commercial Street, was an accountant, born in Reawick in 1828, and the youngest brother of L F U Garriock. **James Cullen Grierson**, Albert Wharf, was a solicitor, born in 1863. In 1901, he was to be resident at Twagios House, making his family the tenants before the Jamieson family. **Robert Bruce Hunter**, 6 Carlton Place, was a bank agent, born in 1856; his grandfather owned Prospect House, where Grierson was a tenant at the time of the election. **James Hutchison**, above Stout's Court, was possibly the coal merchant's storeman / fisherman, born in 1845; **Laurence Mouat**, Commercial Rd, was a timber merchant, born in 1837. In short, as working men's candidates, they were fairly middle-class, but it was a good gesture. In Shetland, as across the country, the Third Reform Act had enfranchised many more working-class voters, with all male householders entitled to vote in Parliamentary elections, and this gave the working men more confidence in their political power.

The *Shetland News* was firmly behind the 'old guard':

'we think the first consideration should be to get men of experience ... the present members have been managing the town's affairs in the most economical manner possible, having due regard to efficiency. We do not think the four new candidates could effect the slightest improvement in this respect.'

There is no mention of it being the first time women were to vote in a Shetland election, but 'For the guidance of electors we append a form of ballot-paper, which should be marked as follows:' [*SN* 2 November 1889]

The *Shetland Times* was equally unimpressed by the newcomers:

'we think that any diligent ratepayer ... must admit that our present Town Councillors and Comissioners of Police have been, most harmoniously, and at the same time persistently, working [to keep expenditure] within the narrowest possible limits ... It seems to us really quite out of place, considering the whole circumstances of the case, that public money, which is so much required for other purposes, should be spent in a contest. ... we consider that the men who have already served the community, and having thereby gained knowledge and experience, and who are still willing to continue in that service, should have the first place in our regard.'

Clear instructions are given on the next page, along with a picture of the ballot paper:

'Now each voter has five votes, but he cannot give the whole to one man as in School Board voting. He can give *one vote each* (by marking a X or the figure 1) to any five candidates ... [ST 2 November 1889]

Two of the letters in the *Shetland News* show support for the Working Men's Candidates. AN ONLOOKER wrote:

' ... having seen the names of two working men as candidates I thought this was something new in Lerwick, and indeed the more I thought over it, the more it seemed to me worthy of serious attention. It appears that it is the spirit of the age that working men should have more management than they have at present in public affairs. In other parts of the country, working men are bestirring themselves, and successfully, with this view, whereas Lerwick has been far behind, or rather I can say, has done nothing at all in this direction. ... I see from the nomination that two of such men have been secured, eminently fitted for the post, it is to be hoped that success will follow these two candidates... It is the principle I contend for, of allowing the working classes to have more power in the Council, that should animate the election.' [*SN* 2 November 1889]

The second letter was by RATEPAYER, and specifically mentioned women:

' ELECTORS OF LERWICK ... These are hard times ... It is therefore not only your duty but your interest to see that men who have the power to levy and expend the assessments which fall so heavy on you, are not men of party interest but men of the people ... The people now have the power of government, both burghal and national, in their own hands.

The right of women, long fought for, is now in the matter of voting attained, and it is hoped that those of our sisters who have votes will study their own interests, and at the same time aid the right by going to the poll on Tuesday and making their mark for the right man. ...

Ratepayers of Lerwick! Men and women! do not be intimidated by power, nor cajoled by artifice, but show your good sense and independence of judgement by voting for the gentlemen I have named.' [*SN* 2 November 1889]

On the days before the poll,

'the 'Workmen's Party' had been pretty busy ... for the town was placarded everywhere with huge posters... The spelling of these ... showed slight variations from established rule. ... Both parties circulated specimen ballot papers.

The polling took place in the Burgh Court Room, Town Hall Buildings. Mr J K Galloway, solicitor, acted as presiding officer, and Mr Ar Sandison, Town Clerk, as polling clerk. ... There was not a great deal of excitement until in the evening, when the canvassers were beating up every available voter [ie bringing them out to vote], and at eight o clock, when the poll closed, a pretty large crowd had assembled at the Hall. ... about 356 electors had polled, out of an electorate of abut 540. Of this number, however, there are a great many absentees, so that a large proportion of the available voters had come up to the poll. ... shortly before 11 o clock the result was announced...'

Harrison, Halcrow, Hunter, Kay and Leisk were elected with over 200 votes each. 'The support received by the 'workmen's candidates' was extremely meagre...' [Grierson 111, Hutchinson 102, Mouat 92, Garriock 90] [*SN* 9 Nov 1889]

The *Shetland Times* commented: ' ... from our point of view the result has been eminently satisfactory ... ' [*ST* 9 Nov 1889] However, it conceded that the campaigning had been educational and that it was better to have a contest than lack of interest.

The Municipal elections were not contested again until November 1901, when socialist James Robertson stood as a fifth candidate, but was not elected.

5

The 1890s

The new County Councils,
feminist legislation,
the rise of the working class,
women vote in the Commonwealth,
and the 1897 Franchise Bill

The Esplanade, Lerwick, in the 1890s. Photographed by John Leisk; courtesy of Shetland Museum and Archives [R00704]

A schooner at the wharf, late 1900s.
Photographed by John Leisk; courtesy of Shetland Museum and Archives [R00679]

The new County Councils:

The next big upheaval in Shetland administration was the establishing of the new County Council. Lyell spoke several times during the readings of the Local Government (Scotland) Act (Bill nos 187 and 334):

'... I have watched the attitude of the people of Scotland both in the county where I live and in the constituency I represent, and I may say the attitude has been that of perfect indifference and neglect, and a feeling of doubt is conspicuous as to whether it is worth while to alter existing arrangement to adopt a measure which effects so very few reforms. This attitude throughout the country is shared by the majority of Scotch Members. If we thought that the Bills represented the maximum of reform the present Government are willing to allow they would be rejected with scorn, and we would have nothing further to do with them, even if they passed; but the Bills are acceptable to us as a foundation upon which we hope to build up and establish a logical and consistent system of Local Government throughout Scotland.

At the outset there are two great omissions from the Bill, omissions which have been noticed several times already, but are of such importance as to be insisted upon with a view to remedy. I refer to licensing and the necessity for further reform in dealing with the educational machinery of the country. We want in Scotland municipal reforms in counties as in towns. I only refer to education for a moment to say that I regard the great advantages which the larger burghs of Scotland possess in matters of education are due to the School Boards having control of a great number of schools where they are able to grade the scholars and so provide for elementary and higher education. I should like to see a measure of this kind entrusted to County Councils, general supervision in educational matters, and a power to restrict the number of superfluous offices the expense of which now falls on the county with no advantage to education.

The most important duty that under the Bill will devolve upon the new County Council will be the management of roads; in fact the new County Council will, to a great extent, be very little more than a glorified Road Board.'

He is concerned that the new County Council should, unlike the current Commissioners of Supply, represent both owners and occupiers:

'... throughout Scotland the local rates are equally divided between occupiers and owners... Here, in this Bill, with the system of single-member constituencies and a very extended franchise, we shall have County Councils comprised exclusively of members elected by occupiers. ... it is a matter well worthy of consideration, whether on the ground of fairly representing the two interests, it might not be worth while to have two member constituencies sending two members, one elected by the owners and one by the occupiers. I do not think there would be any dislike to that on the part of the people of Scotland; it would be an elective board the people of Scotland are accustomed to see, and they would deal with the matter fairly, the expense falling upon both classes.

The principle of double members has been conceded by the Government, and I cannot for the life of me conceive why, having admitted the principle in connection with the Parochial Board elections, it should not be applied to County Councils where it is more defensible. ... Practical details in connection with this subject can be dealt with in the framing of the Valuation Roll. In that Roll in Scotland we have the name of the tenant and the owner and the amount of the rent paid, and that should be sufficient for all purposes. It ought to be made a thoroughly simple and useful Roll for all elections—Parliamentary, County Council, and School Board. I should like to see the one register for all these purposes. ... It is proposed in the Bill to extend the franchise to all the householders, provided they are willing to pay their share of the county rate.

I note, with great satisfaction, the separation of Orkney and Shetland into two separate district counties for local purposes. I think as the Government have gone so far and have rightly gone so far, in separating two counties which have nine hours of sea voyage between them, and the inhabitants of which are distinct from each other in their habits and views, it would be desirable to create separate counties for the western islands. And, as a matter of detail, I would direct the attention of the Lord Advocate to the date of the election of the first County Councils. December is fixed in the Bill, but that is as very bad date for the islands in the North and West of Scotland. It is about the stormiest month which could have been chosen, and the difficulty of getting proper candidates to come forward, and of getting voters to go to the poll in that month will be very great. I trust, therefore, that the date will be altered.

I would only like to say, in conclusion, that this is no Party matter. On other questions we are divided on both sides of the House, but I trust that all Scotch Members will meet together for the purpose of discussing this question on its merits. We have all a common interest in making the Local Government of Scotland as good as possible, and I think we may all unite in a friendly way, urging our own points, and begging the Government to give a candid consideration to such matters as may come up for discussion. We want to simplify the whole machinery of the Bill, and make it as easy to work as we can, and so as far as possible, perfect the Local Government of Scotland.' (Hansard, 23 May 1889)

In the same debate, Mr Campbell-Bannerman (Prime Minister from December 1905 – April 1908) came out strongly in favour of married women:

'... Even the opponents of giving the Parliamentary franchise to women admit that they may properly have votes in local affairs. They have votes for School Boards, and they also have votes for Town Councils, and they certainly ought to possess the same privilege in regard to county matters. But I wish to pass a little criticism on a phrase used in the clause which confers the female franchise. The clause says:— Every woman who is not married and living in family with her husband, otherwise possessing the qualification for being registered as a Parliamentary elector, but who is disqualified, for being so registered by reason of being a woman, shall, nevertheless, be entitled to be registered as a county elector. I do not know whether these words—'not married and living in family with her husband'—are borrowed from some other Act or Bill, but they do not appear to me to be very happy. Of course, a woman who is not married would not have a husband to live with, but the meaning may be a 'woman who is not married, or who being married is not living with her husband.' But whatever the meaning, I object to it altogether. I object to the exclusion of married women from the exercise of this privilege. Why should a married woman be shut out from enjoying it, while those who have failed to change their condition in life, or, still less, a married woman who is unfortunate enough to be living away from her husband, is to be preferred? I hope that when we come to that part of the Bill in Committee we shall be able to make some improvement in it. [Hansard, 23 May 1889

In the end, however, married women were not entitled to vote for the County Councils in Scotland.

Lyell's impression that his constituents were indifferent to the new County Council was reflected in the *Shetland Times*: '... unfortunately from the larger part of the county there is yet no sign of any public interest.' However, the editor felt there could be benefits from the new arrangements:

' ... if the new order of things has any meaning at all, it is simply that the cultivators of the soil are now given an opportunity of taking a part in Local Government. ... it would only be a reasonable expectation that a large majority of the elected councillors should not be land-owners. ... If sufficient energy and spirit is now shown, much public good will be the result.' [*ST* 21 Jan 1890]

The editor went into detail to prove his contention that certain of the old government namely, the Lord Lieutenant, the Convener of the County, the Chairman of the Board Trust and the Chairman of the County Road Authority could not at the same time offer themselves for popular election. Then to be specific, he suggested that John Bruce of Sumburgh, the Convener of the County, should resign the convenership before his nomination; after the poll, there was another comment about Mr Bruce still standing as Convener to be elected by his tenants (he was returned by a majority of 9 votes).

In the event, thirteen seats of the twenty-seven were to be uncontested, and three more did not put forward a candidate: North and South Walls, and Fetlar. ('Had there been some sort of organisation, such as a Liberal Association, [this] would not have occurred ...' [*ST* 25 Jan 1890]) Further confusion was caused by the candidates of Northern and Southern districts of Sandsting and Aithsting being transposed in the Rolls, meaning they were standing in the opposite districts. Sheriff Thomas refused to transpose the names: 'the Rolls with all their faults must be acted upon by the Presiding Officers as headed.' [*ST* 1 Feb 1890]. The *Shetland Times* of 8 February 1890 printed a number of telegrams between Sheriff

Thomas and the Secretary for Scotland explaining the situation and asking for a delay, which seems not to have been granted. Unst also seemed to have difficulty with north and south voters being transposed into the wrong district: the *Shetland Times* spoke of 'the very incorrect list of voters'. Northmavine (Eastern division) was the most hotly contested, with four candidates standing; there were no contests at all in Lerwick.

Several of the contested districts held meetings, and the suggestion is that these were not attended by women. At Hoswick: 'Mr Clark, on rising, said: - 'Gentlemen ...' In Sandwick, 'Mr Sinclair T Duncan addressed a meeting of ratepayers ... a rather large gathering of men present...' The language for the Dunrossness meeting is neutral: 'Mr Bruce of Sumburgh addressed a meeting of electors ... a small number of electors gathered to hear what that gentleman had to say.' [*ST* 1 Feb 1890]

The numbers eligible to vote were small; the total electorate was 3760 (2879 men, 881 women), or about a tenth of the population, which gives an idea of how really poor many people were. The men/women proportions varied from region to region. The highest number of women, proportionately, was in Quarff, Burra & Havera, where they outnumbered the men (23 men, 27 women). In Lerwick and in Tingwall, a third of the electorate was female; where there were more wealthy families, it's likely that spinster daughters could qualify through inheritance. However, it's a reasonable inference that most of the eligible women in the country districts were widows; unmarried women would stay at home with their parents, and would have no property, older spinsters would only inherit the croft if there were no living brothers. On the west side, women were a quarter of the electorate. In Unst, Northmavine, Delting, Nesting and Bressay, women were less than a fifth of the electorate. In Yell, Cunningsburgh and Sandwick there were fewer, about a seventh; in Dunrossness, Fetlar and Whalsay, the female numbers were tiny.

The turnout varied from region to region. North Unst had a 75% turn-out, and at least one woman must have voted there. Transport seems to have been provided (by the candidates?), as the *Shetland Times* reported, 'Old men and women who perhaps never dreamt of such a day of being 'wheeled in a carriage' were joyous and hearty.' [*ST* 8 February 1890] Tingwall's turnout was around 60%, and again it's likely women voted there. Bressay, Dunrossness S and Whiteness & Weisdale also had a 60% turn-out, but in those places the male/female ratio was lower, and the votes cast well below the male electorate number. In E Northmavine and Sandwick, there was a 55% turn-out; the number of votes cast was again well below the male electorate numbers, and the *Shetland Times* said, 'In Northmavine ... groups of men could be seen all through the forenoon near the pollling booth and along the road leading to it, discussing the merits of the various candidates'. [*ST* 8 February 1890] In S Sandsting & Aithsting, the turn-out was just under 50%, and just over half of the male voters; in N Sandsting & Aithsting, only 25 of a potential 204 people voted, but this could have been because of the confusion over the switched candidates. In N Delting, only 14 people voted, of an electorate of 101. In Whalsay & Skerries and Nesting & Lunnasting the turn-out was also in the teens, but in each case the second candidate withdrew. The Fair Isle inhabitants were disenfranchised by distance: 'as was to be expected, none from the island appeared at the Polling Station at Virkie.' [*ST* 8 February 1890]

In short, there's no evidence that the women who had the chance voted at all, let alone in any numbers. In South Unst, Fetlar, Yell, W Northmavine, S Delting, Walls, and in some areas of Lerwick (that is, outwith the municipal constituency) then women still hadn't had the chance to use their vote.

In April, councillors were co-opted for the vacant seats: 'On Saturday last the Deputy Returning Oficer formally declared the Reverend J A Campbell elected County Councillor for Fetlar and Mr Peter Georgeson for Walls (southern division).' [*ST* 5 April 1890]. North Walls seems to have remained without a councillor.

Alexander Sandison, Gardiesfault, Unst, and his wife Margaret Johnson, from Fetlar. Alexander was voted in as the North Unst member of the first Zetland County Council, in the 1890 election which gave rural Shetland women their first chance at the ballot box. The numbers mean that at least one woman voted in Unst, but women there were less than a fifth of the electorate.

Alexander and Margaret's daughter Isa was to be the second President of the 1909 Shetland WSS. Her husband Tom Mackinnon Wood was Secretary for Scotland at the time. Isa's brother, the Reverend Alexander ('Looie') Sandison, carried the Shetland WSS banner to a meeting in London.

Photograph courtesy of Louis Mackay.

So who were the new Zetland County Councillors? The landed interest was well represented by John Bruce Jnr of Sumburgh, Convener, W A Bruce of Symbister, Thomas Gifford, factor for Busta, Robert Hunter Bell, Lunna, James John Robertson Meiklejohn, Bressay, farm overseer, Zachary Macaulay Hamilton, Symbister, Whalsay, who was the son of the minister of the same name, and factor for the Garths and Annsbrae estates, and Arthur James Hay, Lerwick, Chamberlain for the Lordship of Zetland. There was a solicitor, Bailie John Bannatyne Anderson, Clairmont Place, Lerwick, and eleven merchants: Alexander Sandison, Gairdiesfault, Uyeasound, Unst, Grocer, general merchant; Arthur Laurenson, Leog House, Lerwick, draper and hosier; Alexander Cunningham Hay, Hayfield House, Lerwick (Rev Walker's son-in-law); John Robertson Jnr, Victoria Pier, Lerwick; Thomas Anderson, Hillswick, merchant; Charles Hoseason, Mossbank, Delting, general merchant; Alfred Stove, 19 Hillhead, Lerwick, wood merchant; John Robertson, Strombridge, merchant; Robert Henderson, Scousburgh, general merchant; Peter Georgeson, Walls, merchant; Sinclair Thomson Duncan, Hoswick, merchant. There were four ministers, the Reverend John Love, Mid Yell, the Reverend D Gray, Burra, the Reverend J A Campbell, Fetlar, and the Reverend George Clark, Cunningsburgh. James Anderson, Aithsness, Aithsting, was a stonemason; James McCullie, Schoolhouse, Sand, was a schoolteacher; James Sutherland, Gerraton, Unst, was a mail driver. Archibald Sutherland was the first County Clerk. During this first term of the ZCC, C D G Sandison, Unst, took over from James Sutherland and J M Goudie, ironmonger, replaced Arthur Laurenson for Lerwick S.

The second County Council elections were held in November 1892, and, according to the *Shetland Times,* 'It must be admitted that the interest displayed in the election of the new County Council ... has been of the most languid description.' [*ST* 26 November 1892] Ballots were now secret, removing one of the earlier objections to women voting: ... 'it is scarcely necessary to say that every man and woman can then place their cross where it pleases them, without fear.' [*ST* 3 December 1892]

The lack of interest included the *Shetland Times* itself, as their reporting of the election is decidedly sketchy, and their description of what was happening in which seat unclear. Twenty-one seats seem to have been returned unopposed, and seven of these had new councillors; two had no candidates: Walls S, and Fetlar. The Fetlar councillor, Mr Campbell, was not re-standing due to difficulty in attending meetings; the Walls councillor, Mr P Georgeson, had not come forward again, and no other candidate had presented himself (he was later co-opted, and served for many years). Only four seats were contested: North Unst, Tingwall, Delting N and Dunrossness. There's no table given of the results where there was a contest, but the 'thank-you letters' suggest Charles Sandison (Unst N) and Sinclair T Duncan (Dunrossness) won their seats back.

The new ZCC was even more weighted towards the Lerwick middle-class, with only three men (Bruce, Gifford and A J Hay) representing the landed interest. There were nine merchants, four ministers and three solicitors, including J C Grierson of the Working Men's Candidates from the 1890 Town Council election. Newcomers included R D Ganson, Lerwick, merchant; George Sinclair, Ollaberry, merchant; Mr John Small, solicitor; and the Reverend W Lewis, Nesting & Lunnasting. The Reverend W Glover was co-opted for Fetlar.

From a suffrage point of view, women still had not had the chance to vote in South Unst, Fetlar, Yell, W Northmavine, S Delting, Walls S, in some areas of Lerwick, and, practically speaking, in Fair Isle; Foula is not mentioned, but the inhabitants must have had equal difficulty in voting at their polling station in, presumably, Walls. Women in North Unst, N Delting, Tingwall and Sandwick had had two goes.

The lack of contests was to continue for the next two decades. Women in Northmavine South got their first chance to vote in 1901; with only a 45% turnout, they can't have been hugely enthusiastic. Women in Yell S and Walls had to wait until 1907; Delting South women didn't vote in a County Council election until December 1919, a year after female householders aged over thirty and householders' wives aged over thirty had had the chance to vote in their first General Election. Lerwick Central and North were also contested for the first time in 1919. Unst S and Yell N were at last contested in 1922, and Fetlar women finally got their chance in December 1929, when Sir Arthur Nicolson was contested after an unopposed reign of over twenty years (he won, 37 votes to 23). All women over 21 had been enfranchised a year earlier, and young Fetlar women had already had the chance to vote in a General Election the previous May. Lerwick S was uncontested until 1932, when it joined the rest of the town as Lerwick Landward, a separate five-seat council ward, and not a part of the ZCC. In that year the first woman county councillor was elected unopposed, meaning that there was a woman on the council before some women in Lerwick had had the chance to vote for a councillor.

In November 1888, a Society for Promoting the Return of Women as County Councillors had been established to sponsor Jane Cobden and Lady Sandhurst in the London County Council election in January 1889. Cobden stood for Bow and Brumley, Sandhurst for Brixton. Both were elected, and Sandhurst began to work on the problem of baby farming. However her election was declared void in March, because she was a woman, on the petition of Beresford Hope, the losing Conservative candidate. Cobden retained her seat as her opponent did not take legal action against her, although she was advised not to take part in committee work for the first year. However, as soon as she began to be active, looking at children held in reformatories, a writ was filed, and the case was heard in the Court of Appeal in 1891. Her membership of the council was declared valid, but her participation invalid (huh?) No more women were elected to English and Welsh Town and County Councils until a 1909 Local Government Act declared them eligible. Eleanor Rathbone of Liverpool was the first, in 1909 (as an MP from 1929 to 1945, she was to pioneer Family Allowances). By 1910, 22 women had been elected; in 1914-15 there were 48, and in 1919-20, 320.

The 1894 Act which created elective parish councils and urban and rural district councils took it for granted women should vote and serve as councillors on these; this included women ratepayers and married women, though they could not qualify on the basis of the same property as their husbands. The Home Secretary, Asquith, initially resisted this proposal, but the vote went against the government which then capitulated - an indication of the growing feeling in Liberal circles that enfranchisement should apply to all women. The £5 property requirement for potential councillors was abolished; all that was asked for was qualifying residence. A number of women stood for the new Parish Councils: in 1896, there were 200 women on the 8,000 Parish Councils, and by 1900, there were 150 rural and 10 urban district woman councillors.

The situation was different in Scotland. In 1899 and 1900, the Scottish Women's Liberal Federation focused on trying to get women eligible to sit on town councils, but the Town Councils (Scotland) Act of September 1900 did not admit women as councillors. After it was passed, the SWLF drew up a questionnaire to be given to parliamentary candidates, examining their views on women's suffrage. It was not until November 1907 that women in Scotland were allowed to stand as candidates for their local council. The first was Lavinia Malcolm, in Dollar, Clackmannanshire. She must have been good; in 1913, she was appointed Provost of Dollar Town Council.

Shetland's first woman councillor was to be Elizabeth Tait, who became councillor for Lerwick Landward in 1932, on one of five unopposed seats. Lerwick Landward had just become a separate district council. Elizabeth Davidson, of Gremister, Quarff, was born in 1880, and had been a teacher until her marriage to Thomas Tait, from Sandwick, in 1906. They continued to live at Gremister, and had nine children.

Mrs Charlotte Nicol, the first woman town councillor in Shetland, and a member of the 1909 SWSS, was elected in 1933. Before the election, the *Shetland Times* described her as

'Mrs Nicol, who has considerable experience of public work, though not of municipal office, a lady of independent mind and strong character.' [*ST* 4 November 1933] After the election, the editor wrote, 'We would join in congratulation Mrs Nicol on being the first lady to be elected to the Lerwick Town Council; she has made local history.'

In terms of votes, she came fourth out of eight candidates. Another woman, Rose Sutherland, the English wife of Sheriff Clerk Archibald Sutherland, also stood, but was not elected.

Selina Garriock, the first woman on the Zetland County Council, was elected for Tingwall in 1935; she was re-elected in 1938, but died in September of that year. Selina Darrell was an American, born in New York in 1883; she married Lewis James Garriock, son of L F U Garriock, in 1903, and came to live in Scalloway. After her, there were no more women on the ZCC until 1955, with Grace M T Halcrow for Cunningsburgh, and Amanda T Youngman for Yell North. Even as recently as 1973, there were only two women on the ZCC, Joan Macleod (Cunningsburgh) and Williamina Tait (Walls).

The present council has five women (Laura Baisley, Betty Fullerton, Florence Grains, Iris Hawkins and Caroline Miller) out of twenty-two councillors. Florence Grains was the first female Vice-Convener; we have not yet had a woman Convener of the SIC.

There seem to have been no women serving on Parish Councils in Shetland until after World War I.

However, there were two women serving as Registrars in the first decade of the twentieth century: Miss E G Morrison, Burra and Miss Ann M Mathewson, Mid and South Yell. Miss Morrison was Registrar in Burra from 1908, when she took over from her father William Morrison. Mr Morrison was the Headteacher of Burra School, and the Inspector of Poor for the parish; Eliza Gilbertha was his seventh child, and assisted him in the school. Ann Mathewson was similarly long-serving; her grandfather had been the school-teacher and registrar in East Yell, and she was brought up in the schoolhouse, although her father is listed as a grocer. Manson lists her as the East Yell Postmistress.

There was a large number of other public bodies and committes in Lerwick in the 1890s and 1900s, and very few women seem to have served on them. In the list of organisations in *Manson's Shetland Almanac*, Miss E Spence was Secretary of the Young Women's Christian Association; Miss Turnbull-Stewart was the President of the Church of Scotland Young Women's Guild; Mrs and Miss Cameron were in charge of the Lerwick Sick Aid Society, and Mrs Arthur Hay of Hayfield and, later, Mrs Leisk, were secretaries of the Lerwick Dorcas Society. Mrs Leisk was also listed as the secretary of the Horticultural Society in 1897-8. There were two female librarians in the Lunnasting Parish Library. The office-bearers of the Shetland Society for Promoting Reading amongst the Blind were all male, but in the 1890s a list of female committee members was given, including Mrs Galloway, Mrs Skae, Miss Turnbull-Stewart and Mrs Leisk. All the other clubs and societies, from charitable ones directed at women, like the Shetland Fishermen's Widows' Relief Fund and the RNR Relief Widows Fund, to fun ones like the Lerwick Lawn Tennis Club, the Zetland Burns Club, the Lerwick Amateur Orchestra Society and the Shetland Literary and Scientific Society, had male office bearers and committee members.

The first Ladies' Tent under the Rechabite Order in Shetland was instituted in June, 1894. Officers included Mrs Laing, Mrs Harrison, Miss Harrison and Misses Florence and Jessie Garriock (Sarah Atherton's sisters-in-law). 'The new Tent was named 'St Sunniva' ... and it bids fair to be a success.' [*ST* 16 June 1894]

Feminist legislation of the 1890s:

The question of to what extent a husband 'owned' his wife was widely discussed in the early 1890s because of the sensation caused by the 'Clitheroe' case. In 1891, the Court of Appeal made a decision in *Regina vs Jackson*. Mr and Mrs Jackson of Clitheroe had married in 1887, without the knowledge of Mrs Jackson's family, and had never lived together, as Mr Jackson had gone immediately to New Zealand. In the next two years they had quarrelled (by letter?), and when Mr Jackson returned his wife refused to live with him. He sued her for restitution of conjugal rights, ie that she should return to cohabit with him. At that time, a wife could not sue her husband for 'access to his person and bed' if they were living in the same house, but there was no legal concept of marital rape, so Mr Jackson's demands could include enforcing sexual intercourse, although in this case they did not. In spring 1891, Mr Jackson kidnapped his wife on her way home from church, and took her to his house. There he put her into his sister's charge and had her attended by a nurse and physician. Mrs Jackson's relatives attempted to procure a writ of *habeas corpus*, which would have meant Mr Jackson bringing Mrs Jackson into the presence of the court to declare her own wishes. The Court of Queen's Bench, however, refused to issue the writ, on the grounds that 'a husband had the right to the custody of his wife, unless he uses it for some improper purpose or is guilty of some excess or misconduct'. With regard to his seizing of her, 'he had a right to regain possession of her from those who were endeavouring by force to prevent him from having the custody of her.' [*Justice of the Peace* 55, 28 March 1891, p 199-200]

Mrs Jackson's relatives appealed, and the Court of Appeal issued the writ. Lord Halsbury, the Lord Chancellor, asserted that 'no English subject has ... a right ... to imprison another English subject, whether his wife or anyone else's.' [*Justice of the Peace* 55, 28 March 1891, p 199-201] However a number of legal authorities disagreed, and quoted previous decisions suggesting that a husband had such a right.

Feminists rejoiced at Lord Halsbury's decision. '*Couverture* is dead and buried ... It is the grandest victory the women's cause has ever yet gained, greater even that the passing of the Married Women's Property Acts,' Elizabeth Wolstenholme wrote to a friend on 21 March 1891. She went on during the 1890s to campaign against marital rape, but could not find an MP willing to sponsor so improper a Bill.

The **Custody of Children Act** (1891) was concerned with cases where a parent had given a child to a third party, and then wished to take him or her back. The Act gave the Court discretion to act in what it felt to be the child's best interests.

Not feminist legislation, but ... the 1892 **Burgh Police (Scotland) Act** doubled Shetland's police force to two men.

In 1895, Parliament passed the **Summary Jurisdiction (Married Women) Act**, which was an extension of the Matrimonial Cause Act of 1887; this time a woman could apply for a judicial separation, custody, maintenance and court costs *after* she had left her husband because of his 'persistent cruelty' or 'wilful neglect'. As before, she was not eligible if she was guilty of adultery, but there was a rider: 'provided the husband has not ... by his wilful neglect or misconduct conduced to such act of adultery'. Significant numbers of women apparently took advantage of this; more than 87,000 separation and maintenance orders were granted from 1897 to 1906. Scotland was not affected by this Act, as the principle behind it – that a wife could leave a cruel or neglectful husband, and still be entitled to maintenance – was already recognised here. Of course, as nowadays, many other emotional and economic factors were in play to affect a woman's decision to leave her husband, however appalling his behaviour.

Modern feminist studies suggest that married women in Shetland were more vulnerable to abuse. Unmarried women and widows were more strongly within the 'female network' of support, and, even if they were living in a male-headed household, were more likely to have other women around them to protect them. There were also more of them across the county during this period: the percentages for women over the age of 15 were 50% unmarried, 15% widows and 35% married.

Two Shetland cases show the Sheriff having sympathy for the wife over the husband. In 1886, the Sheriff heard the case of Betsy Nicolson vs Robert Anderson. They had been married in 1870, when Betsy was 19 and Robert 37. By 1885, they had seven children, five girls and two boys. In 1887, after a serious assault on her and her daughter Isa, Betsy brought a precognition against him, but by the time the case came to the Sheriff, Robert had 'found the Lord' and Betsy forgave him. The Sheriff expressed misgivings, but Betsy persisted in dropping the case. Their last child, Harriet Beecher Stowe Anderson, was born in 1890. Betsy eventually left Robert at the persuasion of their grown-up children.

The second case was from 1893: 'Husband and Wife case: Magnus Leask was charged with assaulting his wife Margaret Williamson ... by seizing hold of her by the wrists, pushing her on to a chair and kicking her.' Leask denied kicking her, but even if he was lying, compared to some of the horrors quoted by Frances Cobbe in 1878, it was a comparatively light assault. The Sheriff made him withdraw the words 'in self defence' and then accepted the plea of guilty. He wasn't punished, but given the benefit of the First Offenders' Act. There's no further information about what happened to his wife. [ST 11 November 1893]

However, the sentencing depended very much on the individual Sheriff, so I can't make generalisations; this whole area is a study for another day.

Rollitt's franchise bill:

On 27 April 1892, Sir Alfred Rollitt, Conservative MP for Islington South, moved the second reading of the **Parliamentary Franchise (Extension to Women) Bill** proposing the parliamentary franchise only for spinsters and widows who would be eligible for the municipal vote. His preamble suggests it had been presented in the previous session by Mr Woodall (Liberal MP for Hanley) and passed by the House without division. Like Fowler fifteen years earlier, he emphasised the exclusion of married women as a practicable measure.

He referred to Wyoming, Guernsey and the Isle of Man as current examples, and Australia and New Zealand as coming close to passing such a measure, then pointed out the contradictions of his opponents' reasoning:

'If women press for this extension, then 'they are agitators, and their demand should not be complied with;' if they do not agitate, then 'they are indifferent on the subject.' If many Petitions are presented, then 'they are got up by organisation;' if the Petitions are few, then 'you see women do not want this extension.' If the platform is occupied, then 'there is reason to fear the invasion of Parliament by the advocates of female suffrage;' if the platform is not resorted to, then 'there is no popular feeling in favour of the proposal.' The allegation that it is not wanted has invariably been urged against the extension of the franchise to any class.... May I also point out that the criticisms upon the non-inclusion of married women are generally put in a somewhat illogical way? It is said, first, that the principle of including women in the franchise is objectionable; but, again, it is said, 'If you include married women a great objection to the measure will be removed.' In fact, the argument is, first, that we should not include any women; and, secondly, that we should include more.'

He then stated clearly what his Bill intended:

'Every woman who in Great Britain is registered or entitled to be registered as an elector for a Town Council or County Council or who in Ireland is a ratepayer entitled to vote in the election of Guardians of the Poor, shall be entitled to be registered as a Parliamentary elector, and when registered to vote at any Parliamentary election for the county, borough, or division wherein the qualifying property is situate.'

After the debate, the motion to read the Bill now was defeated by 175 to 152 - only 23 votes. No list of voters is given in Hansard. The Bill does not seem to have been presented again.

After the near-success of Rollitt's Bill, members from all the suffrage societies agreed to organise a petition showing large-scale, united support from women of all classes. Members from across the country were on the Special Appeal Committee, with Priscilla Bright McLaren as President. 140 meetings were held across the country between 1892 and March 1894, with 3,500 members helping to collect 257,796 signatures. The signatures were from women only, 'of All Parties and All Classes', collected in books and pasted onto a long roll of cloth. The Appeal was apparently displayed in Westminster Hall on 19 May 1896, the day before the next Franchise Bill was due to be presented by Faithfull Begg — unfortunately, the Government needed the time for another bill, and Begg's was delayed until 1897. The links created by the Special Appeal Committee were to be an important factor in in the formation of the National Union of Women's Suffrage Societies (NUWSS) in October 1897.

Surprisingly, in view of its size, the researcher in the House of Commons archives can't find any mention of this petition; it seems very strange that it should have been taken to Westminster Hall, yet not apparently presented to the House.

The rise of the working class:

Support for the women's suffrage movement was growing among working class women, particularly through the trade unions. In Lancashire, Sarah Reddish, born in 1850, and a mill worker from the age of eleven, left the mill to become an organiser, first of the co-operative society, then of the trade union. Her speeches inspired two more Lancashire women, Selina Cooper and Helen Silcock, to join her. Silcock was one of the first women to speak in Hyde Park, at a Labour Day demonstration in 1895; she was on the Executive of the Wigan Trades Council, and later became President of the Wigan Weavers' Union. While the middle-class National Societies women were still asking for the vote only for women who would have had it had they been men (a position Chrystal Macmillan was to emphasise here in Shetland as late as 1909), the Lancashire women wanted the vote for all women. Enfranchising propertied, single women was no good to them; they wanted to be able to influence change directly.

There was a lot that needed to be changed. Education in factory areas was minimal, with children of ten passing a simple 'leaving' exam; after that, they could work in the factory in the morning and return, exhausted, to school for the afternoon. Girls were not expected in school on 'washday', or at any other time their help was needed with domestic duties, which were, after all, a far better training for their important future role as wives and mothers. The male trade unions, in the 1880s, had made an attempt to limit women's work to 'suitable' trades, such as needlework, matchbox-making and domestic service. However, as Clementina Black, secretary of the Women's Trade Union League, pointed out at the Trade Unions Congress in 1887,

'Men do not work at these trades, and suffer nothing from the competition of women. The real point to be complained of is the low rate of payment earned by the women ... the only way to prevent the employment of women in any trade they are unfit for is for the men to join in helping them to combine in order that they may receive the same wages for the same work. If employers have to pay women the same rates as men there would be less temptation to employ women to do what they are less fit to do than men.'

She was talking of women chain makers in the Black Country, but the problem was widespread. A man's wage would be at least 17/- a week; an older, more experienced woman could earn as much as 12/-, but some women would take home only 7/-. Those were full time workers; many women working from home were piece-workers, like women who sewed shirts. Their weekly pay could be from 3/- to

20/-, depending on how many daughters could be co-opted to help, but there were also weeks when they earned nothing. Over one and a quarter million women worked as household servants in the 1890s, with long hours, extremely low pay and no trade union to speak out for them. Matchgirls were easily identified by the common 'phossy-jaw', a disfiguring bone disease caused by phosphorus – one of the first successful women's strikes had been that of the match-girls against Bryant and May in 1888. The 'suitable' jobs for women were just as hard as the 'unsuitable'.

The world of work opened up for women through the 1890s with a range of white-collar jobs. The expanding Victorian economy created more paperwork, both in Governmental departments and private firms, and lady clerks were cheaper than men. The new department stores employed lady assistants. The Education Act making schooling compulsory meant more teachers were needed. Figures for Lancashire show a tripling in the number of women commercial and business clerks, a doubling of women employed in local government, and women teachers increasing by a third. In 1891 in Lancashire, there were just under 20,000 women in these jobs; in 1901, 29,000 [*One Hand tied behind Us,* p 102]. Expanded throughout the country, that meant a huge number of young women now able to support themselves without losing their 'respectable' status.

This work was not necessarily an easy option. Since the number of jobs was still limited, and competition for them fierce, employers were able to ask for long hours and give poor working conditions – the Factory and Workshop Acts didn't cover shops or offices. Shop assistants who 'lived in' were poorly paid, because they had their board, and they worked very long hours – 8.30am to 8pm on weekdays, and until 10pm on Saturdays. An woman working in a shipping office normally worked from 8am to 8pm, but found herself staying until after 10pm on 'shipping nights', Tuesdays and Fridays.

'There is no question among women who have to work for themselves about wanting the suffrage. It is the women who are safe and sound in their own drawing rooms who don't see what they want it for,' Dr Elsie Inglis commented in a letter to her father, 1891.

The new secretary of the Manchester WSS (now renamed the North of England Society for Women's Suffrage) was Edith Roper, a young Manchester graduate. Roper set out to incorporate this new, working class voice into the suffrage fight, deliberately taking speakers out of the drawing rooms and into the cotton towns of the north, and enlisting the aid of the local women's working organisations. Working women became a vital part of the fight in the north. By the 1900s, Reddish, Cooper and Silcock were joined by other speakers, among them Ada Nield Chew, who, at the age of eighteen, had taken on her factory employers in a series of letters to the *Crewe Chronicle*. They realised the immense bargaining power of the women's trade guilds – the Cotton Unions of Lancashire, for example, had 96,000 women members to 67,000 men.

The July 1892 election saw power swing again, with Salisbury's Conservatives and the Liberal Unionists gaining only 313 seats between them; Gladstone's Liberals formed a government in alliance with the Irish Parliamentary Party, and Gladstone was returned for his third term as Prime Minister. Keir Hardie gained his first seat, at West Ham South, and founded the Independent Labour Party in the following year. He was to be a staunch supporter of women's suffrage: 'I know of no argument in support of the grant of the franchise to men which does not equally apply to giving the franchise to women.' A number of women's suffrage workers were involved in the ILP, including the Pankhursts and Mr and Mrs Snowden – Mrs Snowden was to visit Shetland in 1912.

In general, Liberal MPs also supported women's suffrage; as Jacob Bright had said two decades earlier, the right to individual liberty and direct representation was a keystone of the Liberal philosophy. In 1892, the Scottish Women's Liberal Federation was formed. Number 4 of the Objects of the Association was 'to secure just and equal legislation and representation for women.' In the summer of

1895, the Scottish Women's Liberal Federation sent resolutions to all the leading members of the Government and to all Scottish MPs, and in 1902, after much discussion, it agreed 'that the official organiser of the Federation be sent to help those candidates only who support Women's Suffrage in the House of Commons.'

The English Women's Co-operative Guild had been founded in 1884. In July 1892, it held a 'festival' in Manchester to celebrate having achieved a hundred branches – the first time that many of the older women had attended anything similar. In November 1892 the Scottish Women's Co-operative Guild was established, and it sent a petition to the government for the extension of parliamentary franchise to women in the following year.

For working class women the Women's Co-operative Guild was what the Literary and Debating societies had been for middle-class women: a place where they could meet and discuss the issues of the day in a supportive environment. A popular magazine with them was the socialist *Clarion*, owned by Robert Blatchford, which published essays for and against women's suffrage along with essays on topics like pay and conditions, and these were read and discussed in the Co-operative Guild groups. 'Clarion cycling clubs' were popular, and as well as letting young women enjoy the freedom of their own transport, they were used by activists as a way of spreading the suffrage message. One keen member was the young Christabel Pankhurst.

In Shetland too, as we saw in the 1889 Municipal Election, working class men were beginning to make their voices heard. Frank Pottinger, who was to be one of Shetland's leading socialists, was converted by his brother James in 1894, and was 'spreading the word' in Lerwick. The *Clarion* was widely read here in the 1990s, along with Blatchford's tracts *Merrie England* and *God and my Neighbour*, Harry Quelch's *Justice*, and pamphlets by Bebel, Marx and Keir Hardie. Unlike Hardie, Quelch was strongly against enfranchising women with a property qualification, considering it a betrayal of the principle of adult suffrage; he was to quarrel with the WSPU for their support of it. There was even to be a Cycling and Rambling branch of the Lerwick Working Men's Association.

The Zetland Cycling Club had been founded in 1897, and the first outing, in late May, to Weisdale, included three lady cyclists, as well as a number of ladies in the accompanying gig. They had a picnic at Sandwater, then went on to Huxter Inn, where they were photographed by R Ramsay [Shetland Museum and Archives Photo Library, Y00073]. They made regular runs thereafter.

Unions had been active in Shetland for many years, and some included women members. The Shetland Branch of the Educational Institute of Scotland had been founded around 1850. The *Shetland Times* of 29 May 1886 gives the account of an Annual General meeting held in the Infant School, Lerwick. Fourteen people were present, including five women: Miss Gulland, Miss Sheridan (St Magnus School), Miss Morren (Clousta), Miss Polson (Sandsound), and Miss Slater (Sandwick). Part of the business of the ordinary meeting seems to have been a discussion on educational matters; 'Mr McCullin, Sand, was appointed to read an essay at the August meeting.' [ST 5 June 1886] *Manson's Shetland Almanac* gives Miss Gulland as the Secretary and Treasurer in 1892.

Other unions are mentioned in the *Shetland Times* and in Peter Jamieson's *Letters on Shetland*. J R Leslie, for example, was the organiser of the Shop Assistants' Union. Propaganda was organised by the members, with a range of educational and social activities. According to Peter Jamieson they were so widespread and finely organised that even the town's message boys went on strike shortly before the outbreak of World War I. Unfortunately, no research seems to have been done in Shetland on the history of the Trade Unions; it would be very interesting to know how much working class women were involved here.

Many Labour voters and organisations were, however, suspicious of the women's suffrage movement. In 1884, the Trade Union Congress had passed the motion that 'this Congress is strongly of the opinon that the franchise ought to be extended to women on the same conditions as men' by a large majority; in 1901, with the Third Reform Act having enfranchised many more working men, delegates were to argue that enfranchising only propertied women would lessen the influence of trade union voters, and the motion to back women's suffrage was defeated in favour of working for full adult suffrage. This debate was to resurface in letters between E S Reid-Tait and Christina Jamieson in the *Shetland Times*, and in the Council debate on whether to support women's suffrage, where Frank Pottinger came out against the women.

The first women vote in the Commonwealth:

On 19th September 1893, the women in New Zealand were granted the right to vote in Parliamentary elections, followed on 21 March 1894 by the women of South Australia. In 1899, the women of Western Australia joined them, and in 1902, the women of New South Wales.

Faithfull Begg's Bill, 1897:

The Parliamentary Franchise (Extension to Women) Bill was to enfranchise women on the same property grounds as men, and was intended to include qualified married women. The Second Reading was introduced by Ferdinand Faithfull Begg, Conservative backbench MP for St Rollox, Glasgow, on 3 February 1897. It was his maiden speech in the House of Commons, and he began by summarising the last thirty years of protest and achievement:

'... by a series of Acts which had been passed in recent years, married women had been given the control of their own earnings—['hear, hear!']—the control of property that accrued to them as next of kin, and the right to hold property which was secured to them by bequest; and in those circumstances he contended that it followed, as a matter of course, that they should be entitled to vote in connection with the management of that property. ... [Women] were regarded as capable of holding property, and, in consequence, paid taxes upon it, and it had been recognised for many years as a principle of the constitution that taxation and representation should go together. ['Hear, hear!']

Further, the right had been extended to them to vote in connection with Parish and District Councils, Poor Law Guardians, County Councils, Town Councils, and School Board Elections, and he ventured to say that they had exercised those functions with credit to themselves and advantage to the country. ['Hear, hear!'] Moreover, women had been recently appointed on Royal Commissions [Margaret Irwin], and had been from time to time called as witnesses in Parliamentary inquiries.

They had also been granted in recent years educational facilities, through which they had distinguished themselves in many walks of life. Nearly 500 women had already taken the B.A. degree at the London University, nearly 400 had passed tripos examinations at Cambridge, and nearly 300 had passed with honours at Oxford. [Cheers.]

... There was, he contended, a large mass of public opinion, both in Scotland and in England, in favour of the principle of this Measure, as shown not only by the petitions sent up to that House by women, but by the resolutions adopted at representative conferences of both the great political parties in the State. He also reminded the House, on this point, of the appeal which was signed last year by no less than 257,000 women from every constituency in the United Kingdom, in favour of the principle of the Bill.

Then they had the experience of their Colonies... A Bill for the enfranchisement of women in connection with Parliamentary Elections was passed in South Australia in 1894, and the working of that Measure had been eminently satisfactory. The first General Election under the Act took place in 1896, and he found that women voted in very large numbers, and that the utmost order and good feeling prevailed. 'The gloomy forebodings,' said his authority, 'of those who had opposed Women's Suffrage have proved entirely groundless.' In New Zealand, too, where such a Bill was passed in 1893, the working of the principle had been satisfactory. Sir John Hall, who was formerly the Premier for New Zealand, stated:— Already the fallacy of the arguments against it have been proved.... Instead of the rough usage and unpleasant associations which they were warned awaited them, never before has an election been conducted with more decorum and order. And Sir John quoted a returning officer, who told him that he would rather poll 200 women than 70 men. ...'

The Motion was seconded by Mr Atherley-Jones, MP for Durham, who tackled the two most common arguments against enfranchising women:

' ...firstly, because women were not likely and could not be called upon to use arms in defence of their country, they ought not to be entrusted with the franchise. ... He should like to ask how many people who were responsible for involving this country in war were ever likely to bear arms in its defence? They, in the House of Commons, and also in the other House, were the persons who in a large measure were responsible for directing that movement of popular opinion which might produce war. And yet, of all the hon. Members in that Assembly, except one or two hon. and gallant Gentlemen, there was hardly a solitary man who would bear arms.... What he claimed for women was, that ... they bore the responsibilities and disadvantages of war. They suffered more acutely in their own persons and the persons of their children from being deprived of their husbands or their sons or brothers by the operations of war. They suffered from the burden of taxes and the general disarrangement of their social condition by war, to as large an extent at least, and probably even to a larger extent, than those who took an active part in carrying on war.'

Secondly, 'that women were indifferent to the franchise, and did not care to exercise it, that there had never been any demonstration on their part of their anxiety for the franchise. ... Women had not control of the Press, women had not control of the platform, it was contrary to the nature of women to take part in those formidable demonstrations which from time to time marked the activity of political enthusiasm among men. But, although they had not these facilities, there were not wanting indications of a strong opinion in favour of this movement among the women of the day. Many women of distinction had given adhesion to the movement, and so far as he could gather the feeling among women was in that direction. So far as vehicles for the expression of opinion offered, petitions and so forth, the evidence was abundant that women did desire the possession of the franchise.'

As for women being degraded by the rough and tumble of politics:

'Not only did Members avail themselves of women's help in political organisations but they dragged their wives through all the dreary, weary election time, from platform to platform, to listen to insipid oratory. [Laughter.] He knew one most charming lady, wife of a Member on that side of the House, who conducted to a successful issue an election campaign during her husband's absence abroad. It was idle to talk about this degradation, all the evidence we had showed that it tended to elevate the tone of elections when women took part in them. If there ever was any force in the argument it had disappeared, and women now took part in District Council, Parish Council, County Council, Boards of Guardians, Municipal and School Board elections, and upon some of these bodies women sat and took part in administration of local affairs.'

Finally, 'The two million women who worked in factories should have the right to bring direct influence to bear through legitimate channels upon Parliament, through Members chosen by themselves to decide this question. Was it not of urgent and vital importance in the interests of sanitation that factory women should be able to bring direct pressure to bear on Parliament to better the conditions of their lives? Was the question of education and employment of children of no moment to women? ... If women possessed the franchise, an honest effort would be made, which, he believed, would be crowned with success, if not to remove, at least to mitigate, the horrible evils which resulted from our unhappy social system. The number of women who would be enfranchised by the Bill was comparatively small. The supporters of the Bill believed that by admitting women to the franchise Parliament would do much to upraise, morally, intellectually, and politically the condition of women, and to make woman what to a large extent she was not at present—a more fitting companion, comrade, and partner to man.' [Cheers.]

Mr Radcliffe Cook's reply first demolished the colonies' pretensions to civilisation:

'Generally speaking, the children followed the example of the parent, not the parents the example of the children ... When other civilised nations began to grant the franchise to women, it might be time for the most civilised nation in the world to see whether it would not be well to follow their example.'

He then focused on the state of the Suffrage societies, particularly on their finances:

'... out of 67 societies who were claimed as affiliated with the Suffrage Society only 11 were Suffrage Societies, and 56 were Liberal Associations of the ordinary stamp. The Parliamentary Committee ... consisted for some time, so he understood, of Miss Cozens, the secretary, and her mother. There was no office, no officials, and no money. ... The Manchester society was the earliest founded of any. ... he found that in a population of 530,000 there were about 160 members all told, both men and women, many of them not residing in Manchester ... the Society was in debt to the extent of £70 at this moment, and yet in Manchester there were plenty of wealthy, intelligent women who were supposed, according to the supporters of this Bill, to be pining for the franchise.'

He finished by calling the travelling speakers 'a stage army':

'The Report of the National Society for Women's Suffrage, 1894, contained a list of meetings which were held—78 in all, of which 25 were drawing-room meetings. There was a drawing-room meeting by invitation of Miss Tickell; a drawing-room meeting by invitation of Mrs. Algernon Joy, with Mr. Joy in the chair; and of these meetings Mrs. Fawcett, the hon. secretary, addressed 34, Miss Blackburn 10, and Miss Mordan 8, and all these women made one attempt after another at different meetings to endeavour to excite enthusiasm among their friends in favour of this movement. In the North, the manifestations were the same. Out of 34 meetings held in the year ending October last, the 'stage army' was again to the front. Mrs. Philip addressed 15 meetings, Miss Hodgson and Miss Edwards each 7... there was no sufficient demand for the Franchise among women.'

Mr Labouchere (Northampton), was also opposed, and showed the kind of ridicule women had to face:

... 'If they did away with the barrier of sex, logically they must give the vote to every woman. [Ministerial cheers.] What would be the consequence? In electioneering the life of a candidate would be absolutely intolerable. [Laughter.] They knew what phase of mind a lady had. She never would understand a plain answer to a question. [Laughter.] He had always observed that ladies, for whom he had the highest respect and admiration, were incapable of argument; when one proved to a woman she was wrong she simply repeated in almost the same words her previous proposition. [Laughter.] A lady, one of the leading members of the Liberal Women's Federation—he believed that was the name of it—[a laugh]—who had been in favour of female suffrage, wrote to him only this morning. She said she was recently founding a Liberal Women's Association when a lady got up and said:— We need a moral vote; no one ought to be allowed to vote whose character does not bear the strictest investigation. [Loud laughter.] He merely mentioned that as an instance of the sort of thing they would be exposed to when women ruled the roast. It must be remembered that women were in the majority. ['Not qualified.'] He was pointing out that if they passed this Bill they would in the end have to give women the vote on the same conditions as they gave it to men. [Ministerial cheers.] His right hon. Friend the Member for the Forest of Dean was perfectly logical in saying that if women were to be electors they ought also to be elected. They themselves would look to that when they got the vote. What would happen? This august assembly would become an epicene club. [Laughter.] They would have men and women sitting here together and discussing matters. Women would claim the right to be on the Executive. They had now a Lord of the Admiralty; they would have a Lady of the Admiralty. [Laughter.] He really believed that the Speaker's seat would not be sacred, and that it was probable they would have a Speakeress. [Laughter.] He took it the Whips would be ladies. If he were allowed to choose the Whips he did not know anything he could not pass through the House. It was a most dangerous and fatal possibility that they would have Whips urging hon. Members, by all the blandishments known to the fair sex, to vote for or against what were their conscientious opinions.'

'...Women had votes at municipal elections. Well, he was sorry they had, but he did not think the few women who had such votes would do themselves much harm by it. But he was perfectly certain that when they obtained those votes they would make the fact an argument for claiming the Parliamentary vote. Nor had he any objection to women sitting on Boards of Guardians and School Boards, because there were matters concerning women and children who were under the control of those bodies, which women were best fitted to deal with but to say that there was no distinction between women having a vote for those local bodies and for the election of Members of Parliament was, in his opinion, to take an exceedingly low view of the Imperial Parliament. ['Hear, hear!'] What hon. Member who was in favour of this Measure would appoint a woman to manage his estate or his business? Not one of them; and to say that, because women were elected to sit on Boards of Guardians and School Boards, therefore they had a right to sit in that House, was in his opinion an utter absurdity.'

'... it should always be borne in mind that the matter was really based on common sense. Nature had made a distinction between men and women, and no Act of Parliament could alter that distinction. [Laughter.] Woman had her province, and he would prefer to leave her to it. For women to exercise the Parliamentary vote, to meddle with Parliamentary elections, or to be in Parliament, was as absurd as for men to engage in the occupations of women. He asserted that women were physically unable to fulfil the full duties of citizenship. ... Intellectually, he said, that women had not these gifts which fitted them for being elected. They had got a certain amount of what he might call instinct rather than reason, but, they were impulsive, emotional, and had got absolutely no sense of proportion. The tendency of women had been to fall under influence. ... He did not want women to take part in the rough wrangles and quarrels that distinguished political life. It had always been the rule, since the world began, that it was most undesirable that women should take that active part in public life that men did. The Greek view of women was that the best woman was the woman who was the least heard of. The Roman view was, 'the woman who lived chaste, made wool, and looked after her own house.' For his part he was of opinion that those views, though old, were sound and solid, and by them he should always stand. He stood there, not only as the advocate of man, but as representing the wishes of the women in protesting against their being given votes.'

The Bill was carried at its second reading by a majority of 71 (Mr Lyell's name does not appear on the list of voters, and there is no mention of it in the *Shetland Times*), but because of the Diamond Jubilee celebrations the movement to Committee stage was adjourned until 7 July. The Scottish Women's Liberal Federation circulated all Women's Liberal Associations asking them to send up petitions from their constituencies; there was none from Lerwick. However, when the Bill came before the House of Commons, it was talked out, and although both Lord Salisbury and Mr. Balfour (then Leader of the House of Commons) had publicly expressed themselves in favour of the principle of the measure in 1891, the Government refused to grant special facilities for discussion of the Bill. There was not to be another Suffrage Bill debated in the House of Commons until 1904.

In Lerwick, celebrations were also planned for the Queen's Diamond Jubilee Day: the handover of the new Gilbertson Park to the town. Among the elaborate planning by the Town Council, the Ladies' Committee was in charge of raising money for refreshments, decoration, sweets for the children and gifts to be given to the poor. They achieved the very substantial sum of £31-9-4 ½ . [*Lerwick*, J W Irvine, p 183] Sending ladies out to collect money would have been unthinkable only thirty years before. The same tactics were to be used in 1912 to collect funds for a concert and dance at the Anderson Educational Institute:

' ... Later two young lady-pupils were instructed to invade the town and cajole funds from the lieges.' [William Sandison in *Centenary of the A E I, Lerwick*]

The revived Lerwick Literary and Scientific Society, according to E S Reid Tait's *Historical Sketch*, took a similar view:

'On 11 October 1893 the Council took, to what many of the members must have seemed a very revolutionary step, that of admitting ladies to membership on the Council. I am afraid the decision to do so was not made so much from the point of recognising the equality of the sexes, but, as was stated openly and shamelessly at the meeting, because they would be very useful as canvassers for new members. The first lady to be elected a week afterwards was Miss M A Cameron, Annsbrae House [Margaret Ann Cameron, younger daughter of Major Cameron of Garths, and niece of the Miss Cameron Mouat who was one of the first women on a Shetland school board. Miss Cameron was to become an Anglican nun in Aberdeen]. Mrs Shennan, wife of Sheriff Shennan, and herself a Shetlander, was also elected, but declined the appointment. In her place it was decided to ask Miss Katherine Irvine, the gifted translator of Jensen's 'Fair Isle' and 'Helga', by Reinhold Fuchs, to fill the vacancy. For some reason Miss Irvine could not see her way to do this, and as Miss Cameron only remained a member for a few months, the Council were deprived or rather deprived themselves of the help and advice of the gentler sex until October 1923, when Miss M A Harrison and the late Miss M M Morrison were elected members [Dolly Harrison and Margaret Morrison were both members of the 1909 SWSS]. Miss Harrison is still carrying on the good work, but the number of ladies on the Council has since them been considerably increased, with obvious benefit to the progress of the society. [*The Shetland Literary and Scientific Society, An Historical Sketch,* E S Reid Tait, President of the Society, Lerwick 1946]

Mr Radcliffe Cook's remarks about the state of the suffrage societies had obviously struck home, for later in 1897 the two Central organisations and the Women's Franchise Leauge reunited under the National Union of Women's Suffrage Societies (NUWSS), led by Millicent Garrett Fawcett, still the organising secretary; she did not become president of the NUWSS until 1907. In the absence of bills to support, the NUWSS focused on building grass roots support through local campaigning.

A herring station in the late 1890s.
Photographed by John Leisk; courtesy of Shetland Museum and Archives [R00620]

6

1900 - 1905

The socialist movement in Lerwick,

Christina Jamieson,

John Cathcart Wason,

working class parliamentary protest

and feminist legislation.

The socialist movement in Lerwick:

Lerwick continued to expand on the money brought in by the great herring boom. By 1901 there were 141 herring stations in Shetland, and the auctions had moved from Garthspool to Freefield. The population had swelled from 4,216 in 1891 to 4,803. The pigsties had been cleared from the Sletts and Burgh Road, and there were pavements around the streets of new houses. There was a hammering of new buildings: the eight-bed Gilbert Bain Hospital (now Goudies Funeral Directors Ltd) and the Central School (now Islesburgh Community Centre) were built in 1902. 1904 added the Volunteer Drill Hall (now the Garrison Theatre). In 1905 the House of David, Victoria Buildings, Islesburgh House and the Harbour Offices were all built, and in 1907, the new Fish Market was built, along with the Post Office and the Old Infant School.

This prosperity was for the merchants and the gentry. Because of the predominance of the herring fishing and the cost of the large boats required, the Shetland fishermen took only a small share of the catch, and emigration rose again. From 1891 to 1901, over 1,500 people left Shetland. Perhaps the bitterness of seeing others take the rewards of their profession accounted in part for the rise of socialism here; perhaps it was a consequence of the working people speaking out for the first time about their life to the Crofters' Commission, and the improved conditions that that achieved.

The Lerwick Literary and Debating Society was founded in 1902 under the auspices of the Reverend James M Crawford and his successor the Reverend A J Campbell. Mr Campbell was minister of the Lerwick Parish Church, or 'Muckle Kirk' from 1902. Thomas Manson said:

'Mr Campbell's personality, as well as his abilities as a preacher ... made a strong appeal to the congregation. He entered with zeal and enthusiasm upon the onerous duties he had undertaken .. and took a prominent and able part in other spheres of activity. In particular he took a keen interest in the Lerwick Literary and Debating Society.' [*LLHC* p 279 – 80]

Manson gave a vivid account of his behaviour at one debate, in the Town Hall, where he listened to the other side, then rose, took off his coat, and launched verbally into his adversaries [*LLHC*, p280]

The Literary and Debating Society met weekly, on Thursdays, in the Rechabite Tent Room, and was immediately infiltrated by local socialists, who came to be nicknamed 'da merry boys o da Debating Society'. In 1903, James Robertson delivered a lecture on 'Socialism: the workers' only hope.' In Edinburgh, the Literary and Debating Society had been very important in the emerging women's suffrage movement, as a place where women like Priscilla Bright McLaren and the Stevenson sisters could practise public debate in a supportive environment. The Lerwick Literary and Debating society was to host Christina Jamieson's opening lecture on women's suffrage in March 1909, and Mr Campbell also chaired the public meeting of Shetland's next Suffrage visitor, Chrystal Macmillan, in October 1909.

Robertson, Frank Pottinger, J J Haldane Burgess and Magnus Manson founded the Lerwick Working Men's Association in 1905. Frank Pottinger was the first chairman, Magnus Manson the secretary. The LWMA invited Tom Kennedy of the Social Democratic Federation (the principal Marxist party of the time) to speak. He gave lectures on the Esplanade, with such effect that the LWMA affiliated to the SDF. Meetings were held first in Monthooly Street, then, as membership was reaching 200, in the Town Hall, and before long the SDF (later the Social Democratic Party and the British Socialist Party) was a power in Lerwick's political, cultural and social life. National speakers like Harry Quelch, Jack Williams and John Maclean came to Shetland, and held meetings on the Esplanade and at the Market Cross. Local members sold pamphlets at these and any other public meetings – Bobbie Jamieson, knowing the minister was interested in ideas, sold the *Clarion* outside the Muckle Kirk on

110

Sundays, and took *Christian Socialist* pamphlets to the young persons' Pleasant Sunday Afternoon club (on one Sunday, he sold 66 of them).

The Socialists had great fun writing 'letters to the editor' under a variety of names; Sammy Anderson's personal best was seven letters under different names in one edition of the *Shetland News*. This shows just how seriously letters to the paper are to be taken; if life was quiet, they would argue against each other, just to keep 'the Cause' in the news. Some of the younger members of the group organised a Cycling and Rambling Club, with expeditions into the country, and a tent at the Sands of Sound with the 'red banner' flying.

Working men's candidates ran for local office on socialist and labour platforms (there was not to be a parliamentary Labour candidate until 1945). In 1905, William Sinclair, baker, and Alex Ratter, librarian, became the first working-class men on the Town Council, with a good share of the votes, although they did not stand again the following year. Their manifesto makes it clear what they wanted:

'a large number of the working-class of Lerwick, as elsewhere, are compelled to live in houses which have long ceased to be habitable, being ill-lighted, badly ventilated, and devoid of necessary sanitation. Not only is this the case, but the houses are let, as a rule, at excessive rents, which these tenants are forced to pay owing to the lack of other ... accommodation.'

The workmen's dwellings they fought for became a reality after World War I.

David Sutherland, watchmaker, was the first working man on the County Council, standing for Sandness in 1907. It was he who proposed the motion pledging the council to nationalise the land:

'in view of the way public improvements and rights of way are so frequently thwarted and blocked by private ownership in land, in this Council's opinion, the time has come when private ownership of land should be abolished, and that state ownership and control of all such land should be established.'

The motion was passed unanimously, and Willie Stewart wrote a column length article on this victory for the *Clarion*. In 1906, Pottinger, Manson and Sinclair all took places on the Lerwick School Board, and in 1911, Pottinger became Chairman. They were successful in securing the first provision of school meals in Shetland, for an average of forty children each school term.

One founding socialist, J J Haldane Burgess (1862 – 1927), was a remarkable man with influence on those around him. Novelist, poet, Norse historian, musician, linguist and scholar, he followed the story of the Russian Revolution with great interest, and had a strong admiration for Lenin and the Bolsheviks.

Christina Jamieson:

It is here, perhaps, that an educated woman with similar literary and historical interests, the moving spirit of the 1909 Shetland WSS, should come into the story: Christina (Tina) Jamieson, who moved to Lerwick in 1899, and who was to deliver the opening salvo of her campaign, a 'Sketch of the Votes for Women Movement', to a packed meeting of the Lerwick Literary and Debating Society ten years later. Although there is no written record of her being linked with these early socialists, there are a number of possible connections. Her family took the tenancy of Twagios House after J C Grierson, a 'Working Men's Candidate' in the 1890 election, and, since 1898, the councillor for Aithsting; socialist David Sutherland was to be councillor for Sandness from 1907. Bobby Jamieson, who'd sold socialist propaganda at church events, was of Papa Stour origins, although not the same Jamiesons as Christina, and his brother Peter went on to found *The Shetlander* and *The New Shetlander* magazines – Tina's nephew Bertie was to write for *The Shetlander*, and there are articles by 'Freya' on fishing that are in Christina's style. From 1911, Jamieson was on the School Board chaired by Pottinger, with E S Reid Tait as a member, and Pottinger and Manson attended women's suffrage meetings.

Christina Jamieson and her family in 1876:
At the back, left to right: William, father of Bertie; Frank, later Chief Inspector of Schools, whose wife was the Shetland WSS representative at Edinburgh meetings; Christina.
Middle row, left to right: Annie, Christina's father Robert, her mother Barbara, and Robert.
Front row: John Kay later Professor of Anatomy at Leeds University, then at Trinity College Dublin, and Edward Bald (the baby) demonstrator in Anatomy at Edinburgh University. The brother Christina eventually joined in New Zealand, James Speid, was not yet born.
Photograph courtesy of John Kay's grandson, Peter Jamieson.

Jamieson and Haldane Burgess were contemporaries, with Jamieson only a year older, and Jamieson too was a writer, having already published articles about life in Shetland in *The People's Journal, the Scotsman* and *The Weekly Scotsman,* as well as short stories under her own name and the pen name John Cranston. Like Haldane Burgess, she took a great interest in Shetland's heritage, and was to be a founder member of the Shetland Folk Society, along with E S Reid Tait and her nephew, Bertie Jamieson, a fervent Communist.

The lovely photo of Tina as a little girl shows her with dark, intelligent eyes and a determined chin. As a teenager, she has a very strong look of her mother; later photos give an air of friendly good humour. She was a west-side lass, born at Cruisdale, Sandness on 30th June 1864, where her father Robert was the teacher. Her mother, Barbara, was also a teacher, and daughter of the teacher Robert Laing. They met when her father, going to an EIS meeting, 'took with him as a walking companion his eldest daughter Barbara.' [*Correspondence from J P S Jamieson*] Her son's description of Barbara was warm:

'She inherited her father's intellect, was as well-read in general literature as her husband; came to have great influence over the people of Sandness by this kind understanding, and remained her husband's right hand for nearly forty years.'

Tina was born in 1864, the second child of a large and distinguished family. Her older brother Francis, born in 1862, became Chief Inspector of Schools in Edinburgh; William, born in 1866, was a Commissions Agent, who emigrated to New Zealand; Robert, born in 1868, was a merchant seaman; John, born in 1873, was Professor of Anatomy at Leeds; Edward, born in 1876, was Professor of Anatomy at Edinburgh; James, born in 1880, became a surgeon, first in South Africa (where he was caught up in a rebellion by the Chinese workers) and then in Nelson, New Zealand. There he became involved in medical politics. Annie, the younger daughter, born in 1871, was an invalid, perhaps with a learning disability; she remained with her mother and sister until her death in 1922.

E B Jamieson, Anatomist and Shetlander, by Jenny and Martin Eastwood, gives a vivid picture of the life led by the young Jamiesons. All studied at their father's school in Sandness, and each boy in turn served four years there as a pupil teacher before going straight to University. Tina taught half a day at the school, and Mrs Jamieson taught sewing and knitting. It was a very literate household; Robert corresponded with friends all over the country, and they sent him books and magazines. Mr Cooper of *The Scotsman* regularly sent boxes of 'review copies' of books, and other friends sent *The Illustrated London News, The Graphic* and *Punch;* the *Times* and the *Scotsman* were taken by the household. All these were

available to pupils as a lending library. A favourite evening pastime of the family was story-telling, and the Norse legends were popular – E B was later to use them in his anatomy lectures, explaining the course of the ulna nerve as the exploits of Olaf the Nervous. As a country girl, Tina would also have done her share of looking after the croft animals, bringing in the harvest and raising the peats.

Barbara (right) and Catherine Laing, 1868. Catherine was apparently the go-between for Barbara and Robert during their courtship. She was still living in Lerwick when Barbara, Christina, Annie and William's son Bertie moved to Twagios House.

Photograph courtesy of Peter Jamieson.

Christina Jamieson, left, with her sister Annie.
Photograph courtesy of Peter Jamieson.

Robert Jamieson died suddenly in 1899. Only Tina, now aged thirty-five, and Annie, now twenty-eight, were still at home to support their mother. The Sandness people installed a nominal certificated teacher in post, and Tina ran the school until the end of the session. Then the three women, along with William's six year old son Bertie, moved to Lerwick; perhaps, since Robert had been an only child, they wanted to be nearer Barbara's family.

Barbara's younger sisters Mary and Catherine were at Seaview Court, Commercial Street; Mary was a dressmaker and had lived with them at Sandness when Christina was a child. Jamieson family tradition has Catherine having acted as a go-between when Robert and Barbara were courting, perhaps with the intention of marrying Robert herself; relations between the sisters were apparently strained in later years. Barbara's youngest brother, Arthur Laurenson Laing (A L Laing, the pharmacist), was also in Lerwick; he had two teenage children, Katherine Winifred (the early woman graduate) and Arthur.

The Jamieson women came first to 1 Seafield Court and then to Twagios House. It became the family gathering place, and the Eastwoods' book gives an account of it: large on the outside, but with only four bedrooms, a sittingroom, dining room and big kitchen, where Alex Johnston and his Papa Stour concert party were later to practise their Sword Dance – a maid there commented on the smell of bleach, from whitening their cross-garters. The house was guarded by a fierce goose, and also boasted a ghost, the 'pin-legged fiddler', who could be heard clumping about the house and occasionally playing a tune or jangling the long-disconnected room bells. In spite of him, the students E B brought home for a country holiday found the house and family welcoming, and enjoyed their time here; in the twenties, Tina must have been glad to have them, for she lost her mother and sister within one year, leaving only Bertie and her at Twagios.

Twagios House, the Lerwick home of Christina Jamieson.
Photographed by J D Rattar, 1948; courtesy of Shetland Museum and Archives [R01085]

Shetland's new MP, John Cathcart Wason:

The September / October 1900 election saw the return of the Conservative / Liberal Unionists to power, with a majority of 402 to 183 Liberals, plus another 84 MPs, mostly Irish Unionists, but including two for the newly-formed Labour Representative Committee (the name was changed to the Labour Party in 1906). They were Keir Hardie (Merthyr Tidfil) and Richard Bell (Derby).

In Shetland, Lyell lost by only 40 votes to Liberal Unionist John Cathcart Wason, who was to

serve as MP for Orkney and Shetland until his death in April 1921. He was born in Perthshire, but after training as a barrister he emigrated to New Zealand, where he was a successful farmer and an MP from 1876. There, apparently, according to a later comment in a meeting in Lerwick, he had been a supporter of women's suffrage. He sold up in 1900 and returned to Scotland. In 1902 he was to resign his seat as a Liberal Unionist and re-stand as an Independent Liberal (as Samuel Laing had been). He was re-elected as a Liberal from 1906. His brother Eugene was also an MP, for Clackmannan and Kinross, and chairman of the Scottish Liberal MPs from 1908 to 1918. Eugene Wason seems to have been in favour of women's suffrage, but Cathcart Wason was adamantly against it, taking any opportunity to fight against women getting the vote, and leading the opposition to Stanger's Bill of 1908.

Most of Wason's speeches in the House were on Orkney or Shetland topics, but he also naturally took a strong interest in Britain's colonies, so that in the Hansard list of speeches for 1903, 'Chinese Labour in the Transvaal' and 'East Africa and Uganda Currency' rub shoulders with 'Inadequate accomodation at Lerwick Post Office' and 'Disposal of Bodies of Whales cast up by the Sea.'

The question of Chinese labour in the Transvaal showed him thinking sympathetically about the situation of women. Various arguments had been advanced for importing Chinese men and women as labour for the mines in South Africa; Wason was strongly against it:

'... an even more serious matter was the proposed introduction of Chinese women into this unfortunate country. Not content with driving 100,000 Chinamen into the country, to the detriment of our own labourers, the right hon. Gentleman was going to introduce 50,000 Chinese women and so many thousand Chinese children. The right hon. Gentleman might salve his conscience with the thought that he had introduced so many thousands of women under the names of Mrs. Ah Sin and so forth, but they would not be the wives of the coolies. No Chinamen, except those of the highest class, ever took their wives with them. What was to be done with the women? Were they to be placed in the compounds, or were they to be let loose on the country to earn their living in any way that seemed good to them? ... He strongly protested against this selling of flesh and blood for the sake of gold, not only to the present but the future ruination of South Africa for generations. The enlightened opinion of the world was against the Government on this question.' [Hansard, 22 February 1904]

He also spoke several times in different years on safe speeds for motor cars, and questioned fatalities:

'I beg to ask Mr. Attorney-General for Ireland if he will inform the House upon what grounds the proceedings against the Marquess of Downshire, for so driving his motor car as to cause the death of a woman, were withdrawn in the Dublin Police Court.' (The Marquess had been cleared of blame.) [Hansard, 15 April 1903]

Working class parliamentary protest:

The new Prime Minister was Conservative Arthur J Balfour, brother-in-law of committed suffrage activist Lady Frances Balfour, and himself in favour of women's suffrage. His election gave suffrage workers new hope that the Government might support a Bill. After the success of the Special Appeal petition, and the interest aroused by it in working women's circles, the Northern suffragists decided to make their own petition, to be signed only by women in the Lancashire cotton mills. It was launched on Labour Day 1900 at an open air meeting in Blackburn, and visiting speakers then travelled by rail to every mill town in the county. Canvassers held meetings and visited the homes of the workers in the evening; some employers allowed canvassers in the mill, and union branches also supported them. In a year the petition gathered 15,000 signatures, and a large number of working women accompanied it to Westminster in spring 1901. A second deputation representing the 66,000 Yorkshire and Cheshire workers was made in February 1902, and this achieved more publicity, with the women carrying their petition right into the House of Commons. Keir Hardie gave them a tour of the House, and in the evening they attended a meeting in Chelsea Town Hall, where Hardie spoke strongly in favour of women's suffrage.

A further boost was given to the women textile workers by the election of a third Labour Representation MP at Clitheroe. David Shackleton, secretary of the Darwen Weavers Union, was chosen as the candidate, and women workers immediately drew public attention to the fact that the Clitheroe women trade unionists each paid 6d into a fund to maintain their MP. A deputation urged Shackleton, if elected, to actively work for the enfranchisment of women, and he agreed. He was elected unopposed in July 1902; he did not, however, introduce a bill until 1910. In 1903 he was followed by two more Labour MPs, Will Crooks (Woolwich) and Arthur Henderson (Barnard's Castle). Will Crooks was to introduce a Women's Suffrage Bill in 1904, but it was not properly debated.

In October 1903, the National Convention for the Civic Rights of Women began a more actively Parliamentary campaign. At it, the NUWSS agreed to ask all Cabinet Ministers and leaders of the Opposition to receive a delegation of women, to write to all MPs, to hold mass meetings in all great towns, to have a committee in every borough/county, to press women's suffrage on the MP / candidate for each borough before the next election, and to press the party associations and selection committees to favour a suffrage candidate. There's no sign, however, of pressure being put on the Liberal association in Shetland – there was no women's suffrage group revived here until 1909, as far as I can find out.

The the working-class suffragists of the north formed their own movement, the Lancashire and Cheshire Women Textile and other Workers' Representation Committee. Its first manifesto was published in July 1904, advertising their determination to send their own candidate to Parliament, voting broadly on Labour principles, but putting the fight for enfranchising women first. They chose to contest Wigan, and began fund-raising immediately, in readiness for the next election. Their initial candidate was Hubert Sweeney from London; he was to withdraw at the last minute, when they were lucky in aquiring a local replacement, Thorley Smith, local councillor, chairman of the Wigan Labour Representation Committee. Smith was backed by his Union, the Stonemasons. Supported by Esther Roper, Mrs Pankhurst and other suffrage workers, he gave his opening speech on 3 January 1906. He was to be beaten at the polls by the Tory candidate, but gained over 2,000 votes.

In 1904 two important working class organisations passed resolutions backing women's suffrage. Although the 1901 attempt to have the TUC endorse women's suffrage had failed, activists continued to work at local level, and by the end of 1903 a number of local unions had voted in favour. These votes were taken to the national Labour Representative Committee Conference of 1904, which passed a motion agreeing the principle that women should be given the vote on the same basis as they had it for parochial elections. Five months later, the question of women's suffrage came on the agenda of the Englishwomen's Co-operative Guild's Annual Congress. After some debate, the Congress backed Will Crooks' suffrage bill, in spite of the fact that their married members would not qualify for a vote, on the grounds that it could lead to fuller enfranchisement.

Feminist legislation, 1900 – 1905:

It was not until the final months of Balfour's government, on 16 March 1904, that Sir Charles McLaren (MP for Bosworth, and son of Duncan and Priscilla; he was later created Baron Aberconway), introduced his Motion to remove women's disabilities. It does not seem to have been an actual Bill, more a statement of intent on behalf of MPs. He pointed out that the subject was a non-party one, and referred to the success of Faithful Begg's bill of 1897 before going through the history of the women's movement in Parliament. Like Begg, he pointed out how far women had come, and gave the example of women voting in New Zeland and Australia.

'On this point he quoted the opinion of Sir Edward Barton, the Premier of the colony, who, speaking to a deputation of ladies in London in 1902, said none of the anticipated evils had resulted from the granting of the suffrage to women in Australia, and that the success of the movement in the United Kingdom would tend to promote the unity of the Empire. The experience of the Colonies was convincing that we might with perfect safety extend the franchise to women.

... He combated the idea that this was a sort of fad on the part of a number of rich and active political women. The question had been taken up very largely by the working women, and especially by those women who were trades unionists. In the borough of Wigan the women trades unionists were supporting a candidate expressly in their own interests. He pointed out that since men had had the franchise there had been a steady growth in the wages of men, from 50 to 100 per cent. There had not been any similar rise in women's wages. They were paid far below the standard of men. The object of trades unions should be to prevent men's wages being dragged down to the level of women's wages, and the best way to do that was to level up the wages of women, which might be expected to follow the granting of political privileges to the sex.'

The Bill was seconded by Colonel Denny (Kilmarnock Burghs), who emphasised the steps backwards for women:

'...Viewed historically, this was one of the solitary cases of reaction to be placed against this House. ...When the great era of local effort and government came, women were recognised as, at any rate, capable of administrative work, of interpreting and carrying into effect laws of great complexity, in the passing of which, however, they had no share. Then came another period of reaction, and judge-made law barred them first of all from sitting directly on county councils, while two years ago they were barred again from sitting on the borough councils which replaced the vestries, on which they could be elected; while in 1902 Parliament again took away from them all powers of sitting on the educational bodies which replaced the School Boards. That was how the matter stood now, and he could not put his case better than in the words of a lady, capable not only of sustained devotion to the interests of her sex, but also of putting her thoughts into eloquent words: 'In these days the trend of modern polities is setting always more and more strongly in the direction of social and domestic legislation, which affects the daily life and interests of women as much, and frequently more even, than those of men. In fact, there is no relation of our lives, whether as members of a family, as private citizens, or as wage-earners, which legislation does not touch, and women equally with men. Large sections of our legal statutes, such for example, as the Factory Acts, affect women and children almost exclusively, and is it not preposterous, then, to say that in respect to laws regulating their own most vital interests, and those of their children, not one woman, and not one mother, is to have any direct voice in the matter. To say that women have no rights or interest in the making of the laws is simply to say they have no rights or interest in the ordinary affairs of the family, or of life itself.

... as this matter had been discussed for sixty years, this evening's debate would only, as it were, form the lens of a great camera focussing the opinion and argument of all these years into a collected and understandable picture. Might he say in conclusion, that he trusted this House would not shrink from doing anything but absolute justice to a claim from a body of would-be electors much more numerous than their own sex, a body, moreover, actuated by the laudable desire to have some share in the formation of laws, which although affecting men, touched women much more, not only in proportion, but in the intensity of results upon their life and happiness.'

The opponent was Mr Labouchere, (Northampton):

'... On every occasion he had come forward as the champion of women against those wild spirits among men and women who wanted to foist a privilege on the vast majority of women who did not desire it. ... What would be the effect of granting the franchise to all women? There were a great many more women than men in the country, and the preponderance was increased at election times owing to the fact that many men were occupied in work abroad. If the Resolution was adopted, therefore, the country would be absolutely in the hands of women. If there was a majority of women Heaven only knew how far they would go when they had the power. Therefore they might take it as a necessary consequence of giving women votes that they would sit in this House. Why was the grille kept in front of the Ladies' Gallery? They were told it was because the sight of so much beauty would so disturb the minds of hon. Members that they would not be able any longer to continue their deliberations quietly. But if ladies were transferred from the gallery to the Treasury Bench and mixed hugger-mugger with hon. Members, it would be difficult to say what might happen. Personally he was an old man, and the transference would not affect him very much. He was speaking more out of sympathy with the young men in the House, and he would not conscientiously submit them to such a temptation. Talk about 'lobbying'! If his hon. friend the Member for West Southwark had a beautiful lady on each side of him urging him to vote in a particular way on a private Bill, he believed that his hon. friend would succumb. So far as he could prevent it there would be no such risk. The hon. Member for Kilmarnock said that women canvassed for him, or, rather, what he said was that he canvassed women.

COLONEL DENNY: No I did not.

MR. LABOUCHERE: Well, there was another danger. Candidates would have to canvass women if they had votes. He saw an account the other day of a case in the North of England where a gentleman was found to be visiting a lady who was not his wife. But what was his reply? His defence was that he visited the lady because he contemplated becoming a town councillor, and that he went to see the lady in order to canvass for her support. Curiously enough that plea was not accepted, and the unfortunate man was condemned to pay damages.

COLONEL DENNY: He was acquitted.

MR. LABOUCHERE said that that was worse. He did not know how domestic bliss was to be continued if a man was perpetually leaving his own wife and visiting another man's wife on the plea that he wanted to be a town councillor. He thought that the hon. and gallant Gentleman would agree with him that that would be a very dangerous state of things. The fact was that though a small number of women wanted the franchise the vast majority of them did not. If women had really wanted it, with all the influence they possessed, they would have got it long before this time. Women were perfectly satisfied with the indirect influence they already exercised. It had been said by a great poet that 'the hand that rocks the cradle rules the world.' That was perfectly true, and the vast majority of women were perfectly happy in their homes, and had no wish to mix in the turmoil and rough work of elections. They preferred to be what they were; and it was as a champion of these women that he now appeared in this House. ... There were many qualities which women had, and which men had not; but these qualities were not precisely those which fitted them to give votes, or to have a voice in this House. The fact was, women were too impulsive, they had too much heart, and were too good for political life. When an intelligent woman had got an idea into her head, it could not be knocked out of it. One might prove to her conclusively that she was all in the wrong, but she would simply repeat what she had said to commence with. It was said that perhaps women would develop if they had the franchise. According to Darwin they had all developed from worms, or monkeys, or other lower animals. How long did the hon. Gentleman opposite suppose that it had taken him to develop from a worm? Millions of years! And were they to give women votes in the hope that in some millions of years they would develop into intelligent voters and proper Members of Parliament? ... His own belief was that, if they gave women votes, and particularly if they allowed them to sit in this House, the domestic peace of many households in the country would be destroyed. The Radical husband and the Conservative wife would be found standing against each other for the same constituency. The hon. Member opposite had said that women canvassed for him at Northampton. That was not true. He would never have a woman canvass for him, for in such work a woman did more harm than good. He thought that one of the worst things ever done for the Conservative Party, to which he did not belong, was the establishment of the Primrose League, and therefore he hoped that that Party would always support it.'

He gave a good example of his tactics in stirring up feeling against suffrage workers:

'Ladies seemed to think that he was their special enemy; they did not believe that he was a friend of women. What happened at Northampton was that a number of women who were members of the Women's Franchise Association came down to that city, took committee rooms, and issued placards inviting his constituents not to vote for him, and they went about canvassing against him. At the meeting of the electors at Northampton he asked the men how they would like their 'missises' to go about like these women, leaving their husbands at home to feed and wash the baby, and the invariable answer was 'No, we won't.' The result was that these women were received everywhere with cries of, 'Go home and look after the baby,' and they soon indignantly retired from the field.'

Then he gave illustrations of how Bills have been deliberately talked out:

' ... those who voted in favour of the Resolution in this House were themselves opposed to it. [Cries of 'No.'] Yes, yes. Everybody knew what happened when this Resolution was to come on. Members were pestered by women in the lobbies, and asked to fulfil their pledge, and vote for the Resolution; but two-thirds of those who would vote in favour of it would infinitely prefer it to be talked out. [An HON. MEMBER: No.] His hon. friend said no, but he was not everybody. What happened in the case of the Plumbers Bill which stood in front of the Women's Franchise Resolution? Everybody at once displayed a deep interest in the Plumbers Bill, and took part in long discussions upon it. Then on another occasion his friend Mr. Hazell, then Member for Leicester, got his Verminous Persons Bill through its First and Second Reading, and through Committee, and it came on for a Third Reading; but it stood in the way of the women's franchise Resolution. Well, hon. Members discussed the Verminous Persons Bill at inordinate length. Someone asked, suppose he had a fox in his pocket, was he to be regarded as a verminous person? Then there were questions asked as to whether the bath was to be warm or cold, or of what temperature. Everybody knew that these discussions on the verminous question were a mere blind to talk out the Bill to prevent the other question of the Women's Franchise coming on. Was it not a positive fact that that sort of thing would not be allowed unless the sense of the House was in favour of putting off the question in that indirect way. There was a Bill down on the Paper that night about Barnet Waterworks. It was a Private Bill. He had studied it, and there were many interesting questions connected with it. He proposed to treat the Bill exhaustively. He was perfectly indifferent as to whether Barnet got that Bill or not, and if it had come on he would probably have taken the side of the minority. ...'

SIR JOHN ROLLESTON (Leicester) had earlier met some of his women constituents, and, like Keir Hardie two years earlier, had tea with them:

'He had the honour to present a petition in favour of this Resolution that afternoon from some thousands of women workers at Leicester and Hinckley, and yesterday deputations attended at the House from Bolton, Wigan, Cradley Heath, Leicester, Hinckley, and other places. Their purpose was to interview the hon. Member who was to introduce this Resolution and other Members interested in their cause; and they clearly and forcibly made out their case. Afterwards the hon. Member for the Loughborough Division and himself had a most interesting and instructive tea-party in the precincts of the House with the members of these deputations. One of their guests, with some reluctance he admitted, told them that she had worked ten hours a day at welding chains and received at the end of the week 5s. for that work. But it was fair to say that she also said that that was not the maximum wage paid to women workers in that trade, as some obtained as much as 10s. a week. Now what these women workers said was that men who had the franchise had a weapon, and could get their wants attended to, and that until they also got this weapon, the women of this country would doubtless have to continue to work under harsh conditions for starvation wages without being able to make their wants felt. That was briefly the effect of what the deputations said, and which he was glad of the opportunity of repeating these at first hand, and of urging upon the House with all the force at his command the acceptance of their plea. He most heartily supported the Resolution.'

He was followed by Labouchere's fellow-member for Northampton, Dr Shipman:

'... his colleague did not fully represent that constituency on this great question. ... The people of Northampton thought very strongly on this question, and they had an association which worked for it. He would strongly support the Resolution. ... There was no doubt that if Northampton was polled on this particular question, it would say, as Northampton's greatest Member, Charles Bradlaugh, said, that they required the intelligence of women to help them to properly govern a country which consisted of women as well as of men.'

In general, the speakers were for enfranchising women, although one dissenter pointed out pertinently that if it were really a burning question, the House would not be 'practically empty' - there were only 250 MPs present. The Motion, 'That the disabilities of Women in respect of the Parliamentary Franchise, ought to be removed by legislation.' was passed by 182 votes to 68; 'Ayes' included William Spencer Churchill, David Lloyd-George and Eugene Wason; opponents included the Rt Hon J A Chamberlain. J Cathcart Wason does not seem to have been present. [Hansard, 16 March 1904] The Motion would be taken further in May 1905, with John Slack's Bill.

The **Education (Scotland) Act** of 1905 put the new Education Authorities in place, with powers to oversee and fund schools and teachers over the whole area. Transport for remote pupils and medical and dental inspections of pupils were also to be organised. The English School Boards had stopped women being elected at this point (although they could be co-opted), but when Eugene Wason asked 'Are ladies eligible for election to the School Board?', A Graham-Murray, Secretary for Scotland, replied, 'Oh, yes.' and the question was not raised again. Captain Ellice (St Andrew's Burgh) pointed out that the Bill did not include the superannuation of lady teachers, and hoped that would be remedied at a later date.

Like Lyell, Wason took a keen interest in education. His comments showed a sympathetic understanding of his Orkney and Shetland constituents:

' ... very glad to understand ... that, under the Bill, it would be possible to do away with some of the disabilities which some teachers in the Highlands and Islands of Scotland suffered through being unable to come under the provisions of the Superannuation Act. ... Another point with which he was delighted was the provision for the conveyance of children to school from remote districts, instead of their having to walk to school on cold, wet days. Many children were blamed for stupidity in school when they were actually suffering from toothache and earache. If more attention were paid to the physical condition of the poor children and if their health were better looked after, there would not be the same outcry as at present for technical education. The Scottish children had plenty of brains if they had only health; and if facilities were provided against their sitting in school with wet feet and wet clothes. He was disappointed at not having heard from the right hon. Gentleman more about cooking lessons—a subject which was almost lost sight of. Girls, as well as boys, went out into the world utterly devoid of knowledge of that science. With reference to the remarks of the right hon. Gentleman the Member for Haddington, he trusted that the right hon. Gentleman would not curtail the powers of the School Boards in regard to holidays in any district they thought fit. All of them were anxious that education should be carried on as far as possible, but there were many circumstances in which it was desirable and absolutely necessary that parents and guardians of the children should have their help in harvest and at other times.'

There was still a marked difference between the education of boys and girls. In 1904 – 9, girls still didn't study science at the AEI, being given needlework instead (as late as 1981, when I began teaching, girls didn't do woodwork). Girls intending to teach did practical teaching at the Central, enrolled as pupil teachers. These pupil-teachers could be as young as 13. There was a number of qualified staff at the Upper School: Mr Kirkton the Headmaster, Mr Allan, Mr Thomson; Miss Morrison and Miss Hunter, for French and German, with Miss Chalmers for assistant French and Latin; Miss Campbell in the English department, which included history, geography and music; Miss Mackay in Maths; Miss Grace Mathewson, for Art [*A E I Centenary booklet*].

John Slack's Bill, 1905:

John Slack (St Albans) introduced a Bill asking for women's franchise on the same property qualifications as men on 12 May 1905. The previous debate had been on whether the vehicle lights regulations in force in various counties should be standardised country-wide. The vehicle lights debate starts with Mr Labouchere illustrating the filibustering tactics he'd described by asking for a count of Members (217 voted, so it must have been hard for him even to pretend that there were fewer than forty). After that, several of the speakers denied, as part of their speeches, that they were thinking of the Women's Enfranchisement Bill to come next. Mr Cathcart Wason was the opening opponent on the vehicle lights, arguing that what would do for Middlesex would not do for Orkney; Mr Labouchere spent so long praising Scotch MPs that the Under-Secretary of State for the Home Department pointed out that very little of what he said was relevent to the measure, and Keir Hardie accused him of being in conspiracy with the government. The vehicle lights debate went to a division.

Mr Slack was then able to introduce his Bill, and his opening speech expressed his regret
'that the measure should have come on at so late an hour in the afternoon, and said that as a comparatively new Member he felt almost appalled at the extraordinary abuse of the forms of the House which that afternoon had been witnessed, manifestly and in some quarters avowedly with a view to preventing discussion of this Bill.'

He was seconded by Sir John Rolleston, and opposed by Mr Labouchere. After the brief debate the remaining time allowed, Slack's attempt to move the question was refused by the Deputy Speaker, and the debate was adjourned 'until Monday' [15th May].

Monday finally came on Friday 2 June 1905. The preceding debates all centred on Ireland, and, as had happened on the previous occasion, a count of Members was asked for (there were 311 there). The Plural Votes Bill was debated at length, three following were withdrawn, and the Women's Enfranchisement Bill was started at last, beginning in mid-speech with anti-suffrage MP Herbert Robertson. He had barely done his first ten minutes when Labouchere asked for a count of Members. Another anti-suffrage MP then spoke, and although Slack and others called once more for a division as time ran out, the Deputy Speaker again refused, and the debate was adjourned. Slack's Bill was finally talked out on 5 December. You can sympathise with Priscilla McLaren's embittered comment: 'They are merely playing with us now.'

A pause, before the new era of protest begins. 112 years since the women of revolutionary France had achieved equal rights with men, and lost them again; 65 years since the Anti-slavery Convention where elected delegates had not been allowed to speak, just because they were women. Women had come so far in the thirty-nine years since that first petition was presented by John Stuart Mill. Now they could vote in municipal, borough and county elections, and a good turnout of women had done so; they could take seats on school and poor house boards. A wife could leave a husband who mistreated her and still be entitled to alimony; she could fight to keep custody of their children. The goods she brought to a marriage, and the earnings she made during it, were hers. Women could now graduate from University; they could study to be doctors and lawyers, although not practise as the latter.

Women could vote for their legislative representatives in Australia, New Zealand, in Wyoming, Guernsey and on the Isle of Man. Women in Britain were now accepted on political platforms; they were seen to organise rallies, speakers and unions.

And yet – and yet - in spite of mass rallies, of petitions with more signatures than Parliament had ever seen, of determined lobbying, the vote seemed no nearer. Supporters in the house had the precedent of municipal voting and the experience of New Zealand and Australia to prove that the sky wouldn't fall on everyone's heads if women were allowed to vote, the anti-suffrage brigade were still bringing out the same arguments that they had used nearly forty years before, and yet bill after bill was talked out or defeated. The Government promised support, but wouldn't give it.

In the 1908 Women's Franchise Bill debate, a summary was given by Philip Snowden, ILP MP for Blackburn, and husband of WSPU activist Ethel Annakin:

'... this was the twenty-third occasion that the question of female enfranchisement had been debated since John Stuart Mill moved his Amendment to the Reform Bill of 1867. On each of those twenty-three occasions the same worm-eaten objections had been brought forward. In the intervening years those objections had been disproved by the hard logic of facts. In Australia, New Zealand, Tasmania, Finland, some of the American States and ... in Norway also, women had the franchise, but in none of those countries had the anticipations and fears which had been so often expressed been realised. The stockings still got darned, the baby was still nursed, women did not spend all their; time discussing politics, and the population continued to increase. ... It had been pointed out that there were more than 400 Members of that House pledged to women's enfranchisement ... Thirty-eight years ago a Women's Franchise Bill passed a Second Reading in that House, and twice subsequently a Bill had been carried through its Second Reading. The Liberal Federation or Council had repeatedly passed resolutions in support of the enfranchisement of women, and quite recently, at its meeting twelve months ago, by seventy-one votes to thirteen, it asked that the Government should at once take steps to press forward this reform into law. Last week, at a meeting of the Federation or Council, the question was again discussed, and in spite of the vehement eloquence of the hon. Member for Loughborough, it was decided by a large majority to continue to press upon the Government the extreme urgency of this question.

... The hon. Member for Plymouth, in trying to minimise the importance of the franchise agitation, had stated that there were not more than 300,000 women associated with suffrage organisations. Might he put it like this? What was the number of men associated officially with Liberal organisations in the country? He ventured to say it was not more than 300,000. They all knew that the membership of an organisation was no criterion at all of the strength of public opinion. ... Every working women's organisation in the country supported the Bill. They were absolutely unanimous in demanding that the vote should be given to women on the same terms as it was, or might be, given to men; and he thought they were wise in confining their demand to that. They concentrated their demand at present upon the simple point of the removal of sex disability. ... His hon. friend had presented a petition from the textile workers in Lancashire, the majority of whom would not be enfranchised by the measure, but all the same they demanded a Bill of this kind, and they were wise, because they recognised that for all practical purposes the granting of the vote to a few women was the enfranchisement of the whole sex. He had only one more thing to say. The Home Secretary had asked for a majority in favour of the Second Reading as an indication of the growing sympathy with the cause in the House of Commons, but he did not think that that would quite satisfy the women outside. He believed a similar appeal was made when a similar Bill was under discussion nearly forty years ago, and they were not satisfied that mere platonic sympathy should be shown with such a measure. However, he hoped that at any rate the vote that afternoon would be of such a character as to indicate that inside that House, which after all was the last place in the country to feel the influence of public opinion outside, there had been since the last division on the question a very considerable advance.'

If the Pankhursts hadn't brought in a new form of protest, would the old tactics really at last have carried the day?

Christabel Pankhurst in 1905, the year she sparked off the militant movement by spitting at a policeman. With her mother, Emmeline, she was the leading organiser of the WSPU.
Photograph from a contemporary magazine, author's collection.

7

1905 - 1909

The Pankhursts,
militancy and imprisonment.

The name that everyone connects with women's suffrage is Pankhurst: Mrs Emmeline Pankhurst and her daughters Christabel, Sylvia and Adela, the heroines of the movement, who handcuffed themselves to railings, suffered persecution, arrest, imprisonment and force feeding for 'Votes for Women'; the myth they wrote themselves in their autobiographies. It's not how their contemporaries saw them, nor do many modern suffrage historians sympathise with them now. Bluntly, Emmeline and Christabel were the despotic heads of a terrorist organisation which planted bombs, vandalised paintings and fired houses, sometimes with risk to those within. Even their 'Votes for Women', as the *Clarion* pointed out, came with the property clause attached. Their suffragist contemporaries were horrified at their behaviour, which they saw as destroying decades of patient demonstration that women were fit to vote, and even those who began by sympathising, like Teresa Billington and Helen Fraser, were to leave the WSPU over their tactics. Other stalwarts, including the Pethick-Lawrences, who had given them financial support over the years, and Sylvia and Adela Pankhurst themselves, were to be dismissed from the WSPU.

Whether the suffragettes did the suffrage cause any good is debatable. Letters in the *Shetland Times* and *Shetland News* show how strongly the general public felt about their actions. They certainly gained publicity, but the government's attitude also hardened against them in the years immediately before the war, and the dilemma of being seen to negotiate with terrorists – as all suffrage workers were now labelled in the public perception – made franchise bills difficult to introduce. Modern writers find it particularly hard to sympathise with Christabel; Emmeline continued to go in and out of prison, at great risk to her health, while Christabel was imprisoned only twice, in 1905 and 1908, each time briefly; she was never force-fed, and when in danger of arrest on the more serious charge of conspiracy, in 1912, she moved to Paris, and directed operations from there.

On the other hand, they, and the many women who followed them, were courageous and determined in their fight for the rights we take for granted. They regularly put themselves in the way of being roughly handled by police and officials. They were given prison sentences just for attempting to enter the House of Commons, or for interrupting political meetings in a way that was commonplace for men. By 1911 there had been a thousand prison sentences, and many suffragettes had suffered the pain and dangers of forcible feeding. The most outstanding is perhaps Annie Kenney, who was not protected by middle-class clothes and accent, but there were many others.

In spite of her husband's links with the suffrage cause, Mrs Pankhurst was not initially interested in 'votes for women' but was a strong member of the Independent Labour Party; in 1894, she was elected as ILP candidate to the Chorley Board of Guardians, and in 1895 she campaigned for her husband when he stood as the ILP candidate for Gorton. Dr Pankhurst died suddenly in 1898, leaving the family in financial difficulties. Mrs Pankhurst opened a small shop and accepted a paid part-time post as registrar of births and deaths. When Hardie was elected to Merthyr Tydfil in 1900, she took a renewed interest in politics, was elected as the ILP candidate to the Manchester School Board, and became an ILP delegate to the Labour Representation Committee. In 1901 she went as delegate to the ILP Congress, and in August 1902 she was a founder-member of a new ILP branch, Manchester Central. Although she spoke at suffrage meetings on a number of occasions it was generally in a Labour context – for example, she backed David Shackleton's campaign in Clitheroe.

Christabel seems to have found the routine work of politics boring; unlike Sylvia, she did not share the drudgery of leaflet distribution and pamphlet-selling. Mrs Pankhurst suggested Christabel take a part-time course at Manchester University, and it was there that she met Esther Roper and her companion Eva Gore-Booth, the leaders of the North of England Society for Women's Suffrage. She joined the society, and spoke on its behalf several times in 1901, before going to University to read law. She proved to be a brilliant student; she was to graduate in 1906 with First-Class Honours, although it would not be possible for her to practise law – the legal profession was to remain closed to women until after World War I. While at University, she continued to meet with the northern suffragists, and became a member of the Women's Trade Union Council – Gore-Booth was its co-secretary. She does not seem to have been an active member, speaking at only one meeting. Her charismatic personality, and particularly her attraction for young women like Annie Kenney, is frequently commented on; the charm can still be felt in the brief film clip of her return from France at the start of the Great War, in 1914. [Pathé News, National Film Archive]

Sylvia Pankhurst was a committed member of the ILP, and, when she moved to London to take up an art scholarship, a close friend of Keir Hardie. She was to be involved in early WSPU militancy, but resigned her position as secretary in spring 1906, although she still lectured on the suffrage cause while also working on her career as an artist; this included a series of paintings of women workers from across the country and a number of designs for suffrage events. Her later suffrage work was predominantly among working-class women in the East End of London. Her memoirs recall that it was Christabel's persuasion that brought Mrs Pankhurst into active suffragism.

Adela was the youngest daughter, and was involved with the WSPU from its earliest days. Like Sylvia, she also kept her association with the ILP. She had been imprisoned twice by 1907, when she came up to Aberdeen to help organise the fight against the Liberals in the by-election there; in autumn 1908 she became WSPU organiser in Yorkshire. She continued to speak with her mother and Christabel until 1912, but a combination of ill-health and dislike of militant tactics made her give up her WSPU work; she was to emigrate to Australia in 1914, and become an ardent pacifist.

At the beginning of 1903, Christabel had become impatient with the lack of progress, and blamed this on the ILP, to the extent of attacking visiting socialists and writing condemnatory letters to generally supportive papers like the *Clarion* and the *Labour Leader:*

'... it will be said, perhaps, that the interests of women will be safe in the hands of the men's Labour Party. Never in the history of the world have the interests of those without power to defend themselves been properly served by others ... I hope the women of England will not have to say that neither Liberal, Conservative, nor Labour parties are their friends.' [*Labour Leader*, 14 March 1903]

She followed this by attacking individual candidates to such an extent that John Hodge, secretary of the Steel Smelter's Union and a member of the Labour executive, put up by the IPL for the Preston by-election of May 1903, complained in a letter to the *Labour Leader* that his candidature had been damaged by her behaviour and poster. Philip Snowden, a family friend and fellow-worker, was vilified for speaking against the property qualification.

In autumn 1903, Mrs Pankhurst formed a small pressure group within the Labour movement, the Women's Social and Political Union. When the WSPU was formed, Christabel immediately transferred her energies from the North of England WSS – somewhat to their relief, one suspects, as her alienating tactics were at odds with their patient building-up of widespread grass-roots support. However, conversely, she now began to be a regular speaker for both the North of England WSS and the ILP. As her attitude hardened she advocated an 'all or nothing' approach to male politicians, and in February 1904 she tried to disrupt the main meeting of the Free Trade League in the Free Trade Hall; the chairman refused to let her speak. In late 1904, a newspaper error led to the Chairman of the Women's Trade Union Council, Amy Bulley, writing to the Manchester Guardian to explain that the WTUC was a non-political body which had no stance on the women's suffrage question. Christabel's rival letter forced the WTUC to make a formal pronouncement: that its subscriptions were levied for the purpose of organizing women's labour, and that women's suffrage, although desirable, was outwith its remit. As a consequence, a large number of suffragists resigned from it, leaving the WTUC with only a hundred members.

Mrs Pankhurst still believed that votes for women could be achieved through the growing Labour movement. In spring 1904, she had been elected onto the ILP Executive. At the 1904 ILP Annual Conference, the Executive instructed its MPs to introduce a private member's bill for women's suffrage. This brought up, once again, the debate of who exactly should be enfranchised. Adult suffragists argued that male suffrage would be easier to achieve, but feminists feared that once all men had the vote they would no longer support votes for women. The North of England suffragists did a survey which showed that a vote on the same property qualifications as for men would enfranchise 80% of working women, but their definition of 'working women' was vague enough for the statistic to be disputed, and the old accusation of a vote only for rich women was brought out. The Women's Co-operative Guild and the North of England women's trades groups came out in support of a limited bill, as the best that could be achieved; the *Clarion* was critical of this. In January 1905, however, at the Labour Representation Committee Conference, a resolution endorsing the Women's Enfranchisement Bill was moved and defeated by 483 to 270 votes in favour of working for full adult suffrage – an about-turn from their support of the limited women's franchise proposed by Wilkinson and seconded by Isabella Ford only the year before. By contrast, the Newcastle and Crewe meetings of the Men's National Liberal Federation both passed resolutions in 1905, on the eve of the General Election, in favour of the removal of sex disabilities 'in the matters of the Parliamentary Suffrage and of election to local bodies.'

Over two hundred women, including Mrs Pankhurst, Christabel Pankhurst and Isabella Ford, had been in the Commons Lobby during the debate on vehicle lights. It was becoming very clear to Christabel Pankhurst that patient lobbying and petitions were achieving nothing, and she resolved to take protest a stage further. In the summer of 1905 local unemployment demonstrations were followed by a relief bill; she looked about for a good opportunity for a suffrage demonstration, and her later comments make it clear her intention was to be arrested, although she denied this at the time.

The venue was the Manchester Free Trade Hall, on 16 October 1905, and the speakers were Winston Churchill and Sir Edward Grey, both likely to achieve a Cabinet post in the next Liberal government. Christabel Pankhurst and Annie Kenney sat through the packed meeting until question time, when Annie Kenney asked, 'Will a Liberal Government give votes to women?' The question was ignored, and Christabel stood up too; together they unfurled a 'Votes for Women' banner. At the request of the Chief Constable of Manchester, they put their question in writing, to be answered at the end of the meeting; when it was not, they renewed their protest, and were marched out of the hall by policemen (granted, they were intending to be provocative, but *Shetland Times* reports have made it very clear how much rowdiness MPs were expected to take from men at meetings). To make sure of arrest, Christabel spat at one policeman.

The arrest and seven-days sentence caused a little comment in the press. Much more publicity was generated by Teresa Billington, who organised a protest meeting and reception crowd of suffrage workers, working women's union members and ILP workers (Billington was the ILP organising secretary). Flowers were presented to the heroines, and letters of support read. However it gradually became clear (partly because Christabel contridicted her own version in speeches) that what had seemed a courageous gesture had actually been a publicity stunt, and over the subsequent months other supporters began to distance themselves. Working women with more experience of real police brutality objected to unladylike behaviour; their dignity under mistreatment was sometimes all they had. Patient grass-roots organisers found their supporters unwilling to be associated with headline-grabbing, and all the other societies seemed unhappy with this new tactic of heckling at public meetings.

Annie Kenney, the Pankhursts' second-in-command, dressed in her working clothes. Originally a mill girl, she was arrested and forcibly-fed many times, but continued to fight for women's suffrage. There were a number of 'mill lasses' strongly involved in the women's suffrage movement, as they saw the vote as their only chance for pay and conditions comparable to those of male workers.
Photograph from a contemporary magazine, author's collection.

Campbell-Bannerman, and the new Liberal government, 1906:

The Conservative government finally resigned in December, 1905, and the election was declared for January 1906. The Liberals were returned with a majority of 124 over the House of Commons; here in Shetland, Cathcart Wason saw off his Conservative challenger, C J Dunlop, by 3,837 votes to 1,021. The suffragists counted 420 supporters across the new House of Commons; the Cabinet was divided, although the new Prime Minister, Sir Henry Campbell-Bannerman, was pro-suffrage:

'... The more I come to close quarters with the social questions which affect the great mass of the people of this country, the more am I driven to the belief that women ought to have the power of expressing their opinions on those subjects and help in their solution.'

The new Government's proposed legislation calendar did not include a women's franchise bill, and this omission provoked a WSPU march to Parliament. It was this march which attracted media attention to the news potential of the WSPU, and after this their coverage increased out of proportion to their membership, which remained small. On the march, their main supporters were working-class women from the East End recruited by Annie Kenney. Forty women from South Ham voted to affiliate to the WSPU – London's first 'suffragette' group.

Scotland became important in the suffrage fight at this point, as a number of key Liberals had their seats here: Campbell-Bannerman himself (Stirling, District of Burghs); the subsequent Prime Minister, Herbert Henry Asquith (East Fife); Richard Haldane, Secretary for Scotland (Haddingtonshire); John Sinclair, 1st Baron Pentland (Forfar); and, from 1908, the President of the Board of Trade, Winston Churchill (Dundee). Of Scotland's 70 MPs, 58 were Liberal. From now there was to be an increasing WSPU presence at by-elections in Scotland.

The second reading of the 1906 Franchise and Removal of Women's Disabilities Bill was introduced by Sir Charles Dilke on 2 March, and again it had been squeezed into the end of the day; Dilke rose to cries of 'There is no time now'. The debate was adjourned, and the Bill does not seem to have been debated again. On 25 April 1906 Keir Hardie presented a Resolution to the House of Commons: 'That, in the opinion of this house, it is desirable that sex should cease to be a bar to the exercise of the Parliamentary Franchise.' During the debate, twelve WSPU members created a disturbance in the Ladies' Gallery, giving anti-suffrage MPs a perfect opportunity to say that women were not yet ready to be trusted with the vote. The Resolution did not make it to a division.

On 19 May 1906, there was a deputation to Campbell-Bannerman. Four hundred women, between them representing 50,000 textile workers, 22,000 Guildswomen, 1,500 graduates and 50,000 women of the British Temperance Association, came to London. Eight women spoke to Campbell-Bannerman, including Emily Davies and Mrs Pankhurst; Annie Kenney was also there, dressed in her mill girl's clogs and shawl. Campbell-Bannerman asked for their patience, and Keir Hardie replied 'Patience can be carried to excess.' The women then held a rally in Trafalgar Square.

Four days later, Campbell-Bannerman refused to give extra time for the Bill allowing women to stand as local and borough councillors, and when the matter was brought up again in July, he simply said that if an opportunity occurred, it would be taken. The Bill reappeared in the Commons in August 1907, having been passed by the Lords; it seems to have been passed in the Commons with regard to single women, but there was to be a further debate in May 1909 on married women and paupers being permitted to stand as councillors in England and Wales.

Annie Kenney was arrested for a second time in June 1906, along with Teresa Billington, for causing a disturbance while attempting to call on Asquith, now Chancellor of the Exchequer (Billington slapped a policeman). They were the first suffrage women to be imprisoned in Holloway. Annie Kenney was now one of the few working women left in the WSPU; under Christabel's leadership it became increasingly middle-class. Ten women, including Kenney, were arrested in October 1906 on a march in protest against the government's legislation programme. This demonstration, where the women resisted arrest by struggling, kicking and lying down, sparked off a good deal of protest among the suffragist societies.

On 3 November 1906, just before she died, Priscilla Bright McLaren dictated a letter – her last - to the WSPU women in prison:

'We send you our heartfelt sympathy in the trying circumstances in which you are placed. We offer you, too, our warm admiration for the noble courage and self-sacrifice which you have manifested in your earnest efforts to improve the conditions of the women of your country. These efforts we feel assured, will bear fruit at a very early date in the passing of real measures of pure justice for which so many of us have now for nearly half a century, by every constitutional mean, strived in vain.'

The break between the WSPU and the National Union of Women's Suffrage Societies came in November 1906, when Christabel Pankhurst and Teresa Billington spoke at a special trade union meeting in London. The meeting was organised by the Lancashire Women Textile Workers' Representation Comittee, and the topic was the reduction of wages at the Royal Army Clothing Factory. Pankhurst and Billington had agreed that they would speak only on that topic, but broke their word and focused on the women in prison. To the great annoyance of the organisers, who wanted to publicise their cause, the papers reported the 'Suffragette meeting on Pimlico Pier'.

Relationships between the WSPU and the Independant Labour Party were also strained. In August 1906, Christabel Pankhurst, Billington and two other WSPU and ILP members had gone up to speak at the by-election in Cockermouth, where Robert Smillie, president of the Scottish Miners, was standing for Labour. They were lodged by socialists, but when they spoke they refused to endorse Smillie, who was an adult suffragist. The Conservatives won the by-election, and the ILP asked for an explanation. Christabel defended herself at length at a meeting in September, but when the same tactics were repeated in Huddersfield a few months later, the topic was raised at the 1907 Easter Conference. A number of women pledged themselves to support the Labour candidate, but Mrs Pankhurst and others resigned from the ILP.

There was to be a further split within the WSPU in September 1907. Mrs Pankhurst and Christabel decided to over-rule Billington's WSPU constitution, which placed power in the hands of branch delegates; they cancelled the next conference and those sections of the constitution. A number of prominent WSPU members, including Billington and Charlotte Despard, broke away; at first they maintained the name WSPU, but the following year formed the Women's Freedom League, a militant society which was willing to accept law-breaking, but did not approve of injury or attack on persons or property. The WFL was to back non-payment of taxes and was to be involved in the Census refusal of 1911.

1907 - increasing action:

In Scotland, the NUWSS and WSPU were still working together; there was a joint meeting in Edinburgh in January 1907. The Glasgow and West of Scotland WSS was also willing to work with the WSPU at this point, and the new WSPU organiser for Scotland, Helen Fraser, toured the west coast with the support of local NUWSS societies.

In January 1907 the WSPU came to Aberdeen for the by-election there. Their tactics were now to oppose any Liberal candidate, even a pro-suffrage one, on the grounds that the Government was refusing to grant women the vote; this was to bring them into conflict with other suffrage organisations. Speakers included Teresa Billington-Greig (she married at this time), Helen Fraser, and, at the beginning of February, Mrs Pankhurst and Adela Pankhurst. The WSPU claimed credit for the Liberal candidate's majority being slashed from 4,000 to under 400, and a WSPU branch was formed in Aberdeen. Mrs Pankhurst returned to Aberdeen in May, then went on to speak in Glasgow, Edinburgh and the west of Scotland.

The first large procession organised by the NUWSS took place in London in very poor weather on 7 February 1907 – it was nicknamed the 'Mud March'. Led by Millicent Fawcett, Lady Frances Balfour and Keir Hardie, over 3,000 women carrying red and white flowers, rosettes, handkerchiefs and banners marched from Hyde Park to Exeter Hall: titled women, graduates, artists and actresses, members of women's clubs, temperance groups and women textile workers. The march showed the strength of the suffrage movement and demonstrated to the many thousands of spectators that suffragists could protest peacefully. Huge processions were to be a feature of the movement from now on; Christina Jamieson was to represent the Shetland WSS at the Coronation Procession in 1911, and the last, in 1913, had forty thousand people in it.

Mrs Pankhurst's 'Women's Parliament' was held in Caxton Hall just six days later. When women's suffrage was not mentioned in the King's Speech, 400 women marched on Parliament. Ordered to turn back by the police, they refused, and police and women clashed. A number of women were injured when mounted police reinforcements arrived, and onlookers protested at the way the police were treating the women. Over fifty women and two men were arrested.

The 1907 Women's Enfranchisement Bill was presented to the House on 12 February by Mr Willoughby Dickinson (St Pancras North), and the debate for the Second Reading was on Friday 8 March. It had a first place on the orders of the day and was given five hours' discussion with no demonstration of any kind in the Gallery, but no division was taken. The reason given in the Lobby and by the Press was that 'the question having got beyond the academic stage and into the region of practical politics, the Speaker felt it to be impossible to allow the closure to be moved on such an important change in the British Constitution.' On 14 March, Campbell-Bannerman was asked if further time would be given to the Bill. He replied that this was unprecedented and impossible under the circumstances.

In late February two Scottish women, both actresses, were arrested in London when they attempted to enter the House of Commons. One was Helen Fraser's sister, Annie; told by the magistrates that she had been obstructing the police, she retorted, 'On the contrary, the police were obstructing me.' The other was Maggie Moffat, from Glasgow; her husband Graham was to found the Glasgow Men's League for Women's Suffrage later that year. Unlike previous suffrage prisoners, both women were put in the second division, that is, they were treated as criminal, not political prisoners, as a later debate in the House of Commons brings out:

Mr Keir Hardie: Is it not a fact that in October, 1906, and from then until January of this year women imprisoned for similar offences were treated as first-class misdemeanants; why has that rule been departed from; and will the Home Secretary [Hubert Gladstone, the Victorian Prime Minister's son] use his influence and authority to have similar cases treated as first-class misdemeanants?

Mr Gladstone: As a matter of fact, the magistrates in their discretion did order first division treatment to the first batches of Suffragists, which were dealt with in 1906 and the beginning of 1907. Then, I think, nearly twelve months elapsed without further disturbances, but in January of this year and subsequently the magistrates, also in the full exercise of their discretion, thought fit to order the second division treatment. As I have repeatedly said, I have no power to interfere with the discretion of the magistrates by giving orders for the removal of prisoners from one division to another.

Mr Dillon (E Mayo): Is it not the fact that in the case of Dr. Jameson and the raiders the Government of that day did overrule the decision not of a magistrate, but of the Judge of the High Court who had sentenced them, and whether, in view of the fact that these ladies have been convicted for what is undoubtedly a political offence he will exercise his power to see that they are treated as first-class misdemeanants?

Mr Gladstone: It is true that in the cases referred to by the hon. Member the prisoners were transferred to what was then the first misdemeanant class, but that was done through the machinery of the prerogative of mercy. The whole situation has been altered by the Act of 1898, by which the discretion as regards the division to which the prisoner is to be sent is specially reserved to the magistrate. [Hansard, 28 October, 1906]

Dr Leander Starr Jameson was a statesman in Africa and a friend of Rhodes. He led a troop in support of a rising against Johannesburg in 1896, and was sentenced to 15 months in Holloway Prison; he served only a year. Suffrage sympathizers regularly referred to this case.

In March, 1907, Lady Steel, widow of a former Provost of Edinburgh, took the first militant action in Scotland when she refused to pay her taxes. A 'roup' (forced auction sale) of some of her goods was held at the Mercat Cross in Edinburgh; local supporters bought the items and returned them. June 1907 saw the launch of a new suffrage journal, *The Women's Franchise*, which included both NUWSS and WSPU news from Scotland and England; the west of Scotland socialist weekly, *Forward,* was already carrying suffrage news, interviews and articles, including some by Keir Hardie under the name 'Lily Bell'.

Scotland's first procession took place in Edinburgh on 5 October 1907. It was organised by the WSPU, but as it was to be a peaceful demonstration the older societies were also involved, and between two and three thousand women took part, including local Women's Liberal Associations, Conservative Primrose League habitations, the British Women's Temperance Association, and Union representatives like the Jute and Flax workers from Dundee. Men from the newly-formed Glasgow Men's League for Women's Suffrage carried a banner saying 'Scots wha hae votes – men'. They were followed by women with a banner 'Scots wha haena votes – women.' Men of the Edinburgh Labour Party acted as stewards for the meeting after the procession.

WSPU members continued to 'heckle' Parliamentary meetings, and one example of the treatment this aroused when it was women doing the heckling was in Aberdeen. Mrs Pankhurst had spoken in Aberdeen on the 16 December, and the rowdy behaviour of some young men in the audience sparked off two letters to the *Aberdeen Free Press*; they were not, however, removed. The following day, Asquith was due to speak, and that morning the *Aberdeen Free Press* carried a letter in support of women's suffrage from the local Liberal Association.

The WSPU agreed that it would give Asquith an uninterrupted hearing if one question on suffrage was put to him, and Mrs Black, president of the women's Aberdeen Liberal Association, rose to make the representation. She was immediately told she was out of order, and had to raise her voice over the audience shouting. When her question was answered brusquely, a minister on the platform attempted to move a women's suffrage amendment to the official resolution. Three stewards tried to eject him until they were ordered to withdraw by MP James Murray. Mrs Pankhurst rose on her seat and attempted to protest; she was removed by stewards. The affair left Aberdeen Liberals feeling that the suffragists had been unfairly treated, and that those in charge had showed themselves as bullies.

On 25 May 1908, Keir Hardie was to raise the issue of this discrimination in the House of Commons, asking the Secretary for Scotland,

'whether his attention has been drawn to the treatment by the police of three women who were distributing literature outside the Montrose Town Hall on the day of the poll in connection with the recent bye-election; and whether he proposes introducing legislation to ensure that women who are denied the franchise shall at least be guaranteed the same facilities as men for propagating their political opinions.

(Answered by Mr. Sinclair.) 'My hon. friend has been good enough to send me the newspaper report of this occurrence. No legislation, however, seems to be necessary, for, so far as the administration of the law is concerned, there is no distinction of sex.' [Hansard, 25 May 1908]

WOMAN – A PERSON OR NOT A PERSON?
Drawn by our special artist S Begg.

A GIRL-GRADUATE AT THE BAR OF THE HOUSE OF LORDS: MISS CRYSTAL
MACMILLAN APPEALING FOR THE RIGHT TO VOTE

Miss Macmillan appeared at the bar of the House of Lords the other day to urge the rights of
women-graduates at the Scottish Universities to vote for the election of University representatives in
Parliament. Much of the argument turned on the meaning of the word "person". Acts passed in
1868 and 1881 gave the franchise to all "persons", other than those subject to legal incapacity, upon
whom one of the four Scottish Universities had conferred a degree. All other franchise law has
referred expressly to "men" or "male persons". Miss Macmillan and the Scottish ladies associated
with her sought to prove that woman is a "person" within the meaning of the Act, and that the
phrase "legal incapacity" could justify no sex-disqualification.

Illustration and caption from the *Illustrated London News*, 21 November, 1908, author's collection.

Crystal Macmillan, Dr Elsie Inglis and others had been involved in a legal challenge to the Universities from July 1906. The nine hundred women graduates of Scottish Universities were, in theory, entitled to vote for the two University MPs; the statute granting this simply said 'persons', and so the women asked for their vote. When it was refused, they took the Universities to court, and when the Lord Ordinary ruled that 'persons' meant 'Male persons' they appealed to the House of Lords. Chrystal Macmillan presented the case in 1907, and although the case was lost there was a good deal of praise for this 'modern Portia'; in the 1920s she was to qualify as a barrister.

The *Shetland Times* didn't cover any of the suffrage events of 1907. It was now a much larger paper: the first and fifth pages were adverts; page two was the serial and 'women's adverts'; pages three and four were local news, now including photos; page six was political news. For the issue after the 'Mud March' it included a speech by Mr Balfour at Hull, and the Derbyshire by-election; the following week, after a number of WSPU members had been arrested, the world news was the discovery of an Egyptian queen's tomb and a miraculous crucifix. The Edinburgh march was also ignored. The *Shetland News* didn't mention the processions either. It's hard to tell whether these events which were so important to suffrage workers were genuinely minor in the context of the time (although other newspapers covered them), if the *Shetland Times* and *Shetland News* generally didn't cover mainland events on the grounds that folk would read about them in London newspapers, or if they were simply refusing to have any truck with this women's suffrage nonsense.

The first mention of the name Pankhurst in the Shetland press comes in the *Shetland News* in late December:

'INTREPID MISS PANKHURST

Miss Pankhurst played the part of a female Daniel in the lions' den at Nottingham on Monday night. A number of mice were let loose on the platform. Miss Pankhurst never quailed. She rose above traditional womanhood, and stooped and caught two or three of them. She held them in one hand and stroked them tenderly with the other, while she gazed reproachfully at her opponents. Then she handed one of the mice down to the reporters for their inspection, and essayed to resume her speech. Her efforts were futile, and at length she was compelled to abandon the platform.' [*SN* 20 December 1907]

The *Shetland News* clearly expected its readers to be familiar with Christabel Pankhurst and the WSPU. I haven't found this incident mentioned anywhere else, and the mice/women joke was a recurring joke.

WOMAN SUFFRAGE SERIES.

FELLOW WOMEN, OUR DAY DAWNS AT LAST.

An early example of a suffrage card, posted in Old Swan, Liverpool on 31 October 1907. The message on the back is to Miss Knowles, Sheriff Hutton Castle, York, and it reads:

'Thought you might be interested in 'Suffragettes' they just abound here! I was very sorry to hear about Eve – I hope she will not find the lying so bad after a while. Gertrude

Postcard, author's collection.

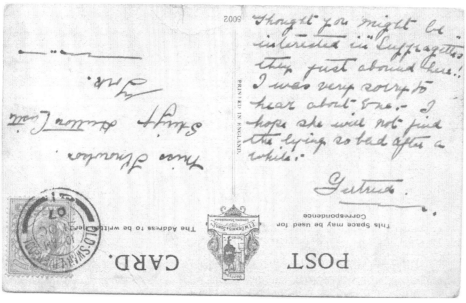

Protests and arrests, 1908:

By the start of 1908, politicians had become so wary of the tactics of the suffragettes that Asquith, in agreeing to meet a deputation of women, had demanded an assurance that no violence would be attempted. The deputation included Emily Davies, now over 80, as well as Mrs Pankhurst, Lady Frances Balfour and two Scottish members of the WFL. From February, women were banned from Liberal meetings, although WSPU members still managed to get in, by hiding beforehand, arriving in disguise or climbing on the roof. Cabinet ministers were given extra police protection, which seems extreme, given that the worst offences the women had actually committed were window breaking; it was the women themselves who had been assaulted by police and anti-suffrage men. Male supporters who spoke up for 'votes for women' at Liberal meetings were also ejected by stewards.

In February, a second men's suffrage association was formed, the Edinburgh Men's League for Women's Suffrage, and Graham Moffat, the founder of the Glasgow Men's League, held a protest meeting against the sentences received by suffrage women. The 'Women's Parliament' was held once more, followed by a deputation to Parliament, where a number of women were arrested. They included Mrs Pankhurst, who was sentenced to six weeks imprisonment in Holloway.

The 1908 Women's Enfranchisement Bill was moved for a second reading on 28 February by Mr Stanger (Kensington N), and seconded by Mr Acland (Richmond, Yorkshire); as Mr Stanger pointed out, it was the same bill as that of 1906 and 1907. The principal opposer was our own Mr Cathcart Wason, treating the question in a humourous spirit, as another MP pointed out during the debate. His speech took advantage of the suffragette tactics:

' ...He asked the House to consider whether this movement was founded on riot or revolution. If it was founded on riot, were they going to yield to clamour? If so, what an example was set before them. Many of them felt very keenly about vaccination, others had strong views about vivisection, and for himself he had specially strong views as regarded the iniquity of trawling and whaling in the Shetlands. Was he to be encouraged to bring his constituents down to break the Secretary for Scotland's windows and tie themselves to his railings? He did not hesitate to say that many of his constituents would gladly put in a certain time in gaol if they could bring any proper and due influence to bear on the Secretary for Scotland. He would not object to a few months hard labour himself if he could bring that pressure on the right hon. Gentleman that his constituents desired. If it was founded on riot, Members would see what a hopeless impasse they were in. If it was founded on revolution, this was one of the most revolutionising measures ever proposed in a great assembly on a Friday afternoon by an absolutely irresponsible person. They were often told what a disaster it would be to the country if they had Home Rule or a great measure of tariff reform. Either Home Rule or tariff reform of the wildest description would be simply a gentle breeze to the tornado that would sweep over the country if they passed this Bill. ... If it were a question of temperance or factory legislation, he would be prepared to say that in such questions women reigned supreme. An hon. Member said to him the other day with regard to the Licensing Bill— I do not know what to do about this question, because I do not know how the women feel about the barmaids. [A Bill was before the House banning women from serving behind a bar; suffrage groups objected to the loss of work for a large number of women] Well, he himself did not know what the women felt about the barmaids, but he knew how he felt about them. If they had their way he believed ninety-nine out of a hundred Members of this House would vote strongly for the suppression of barmaids. [Cries of 'No' and 'Why?'.] He would tell the hon. Member why. Because they refused to allow young, middle-aged, and old men to be tempted by their sexual instinct as well as their natural instinct of strong drink. Strong drink and sexual instinct were the two things most compatible and together made trouble. ... The conclusion at which the hon. Gentleman arrived was that, without votes, women would be treated badly, and driven to the wall. Who had ever treated women badly? They could not bring forward a single grievance from which they suffered, which if they could prove and make it plain hon. Members of this House were not too eager to jostle each other in their anxiety to remedy. ... He thought everybody ought to do all they could to oppose it.

Another point which he appealed to hon. Members specially to consider was this. They had a great and fixed belief in the sanctity of the Holy Scriptures, and there was nothing in the Holy Scriptures to warrant this measure. Indeed, they were against it. Hon. Members who went through St. Paul would find that his whole doctrine and teaching were against it. It was nobody's fault that providence had created a great difference between the sexes.

... Another point was this. If the Bill gave a right to women to vote for a Member of the House of Commons, of course with that went the right to sit in that House and to be elected to an office in that House, even to that held by Mr. Speaker of controlling an assembly which was not always too orderly. Almost every one must shudder at such a possibility as that. ... the one thing which women wanted most was sovereignty, rule, power to put man under their feet and keep him there. Everyone knew that there was never a happy household, no matter what the importance of the household was, unless the woman was the supreme sovereign of the household. No one had a happy home, from the poorest to the highest, unless the woman ruled, absolutely, the household.

The hon. Member who seconded the Motion had talked about women's work. There was no work which women could not perform. They could, and did do everything that man could do. In some parts of Scotland it was the common thing to hear: 'Jean is going to be married. What can she do to keep a man?' There was not a field in which women had not distinguished themselves, but they could not have them in that House. There would not be happiness in the House if they did come in. If women were exceedingly desirous of taking part in the legislation of the country let them be sent to another place. He would give a willing vote to any proposition that would transfer them to another place, and gave them a share in the legislation there. ... he warned the House that they could not have legislative peace unless they kept the sexes as far apart as possible. ... His contention was that the women did not want the vote, and were perfectly satisfied with things as they are. The agitation for the Bill was a bogus one, it would redound to the discredit of the Liberal Party, and it would constitute a grave peril and danger to the country. It was, therefore, with a full sense of responsibility, although accompanied by a feeling of regret that he had to announce that he could not support the Bill and would move that it be read a second time that day six months.'

During the ensuing debate, Mr Pike Pease (the great-nephew of Elizabeth Pease Nichol who had been at that first anti-slavery meeting, and who was a founder member of the Glasgow WSS) retorted,

' ...But an argument which has considerable effect in the country, though perhaps not so much in this House, is that ladies have recently shown that they can act in such, a way as to make it impossible for the men of this country to grant the franchise. That is, that women's behaviour has been so bad in regard to the riots which have taken place lately that we ought not on that account to pass any measure for the extension of the franchise to women. I think that, though we may not agree as to the methods that have been employed, we must all agree that the intensity of their feelings has been shown by the willingness of these women to endure hardship, and also that many of these ladies probably are very well qualified to act as voters in this country. It does not follow that the whole class of women should be prevented from voting simply because a certain number of ladies act in a violent manner. If that were so, then it would be possible to argue that if there were a thousand criminals in the male class in this country all the men should be disfranchised.'

Mr Kettle (East Tyrone) picked up on 'the devil quoting Scripture':

'... The hon. Gentleman had a last argument. He had said the reason he was opposed to it was that there was nothing about woman suffrage in the Scriptures. The Scriptures was a large and extremely interesting book, but it left a great many things untouched. There was nothing, for instance, about the comparative economic value of free trade and protection. There was nothing in it about the Tariff Reform League or about whaling in the Orkney and Shetland Islands. If, however, hon. Members had not texts on these and other questions they had with them in support of the Bill the entire forces of logic, which, after all, ought to have some infinitesimal effect on the minds of hon. Members. ... They had also the up-growing wave of democracy and experience flowing from the improvement of the laws, regarded from the point of view of social reform, that came to them from every country that had had the courage to take this step. ...'

The ensuing debate was a lengthy one, and in the final division, the Bill was put forward to a Committee of the whole house (generally agreed to be a polite way of shelving it) by 271 votes to 92. Mr Cathcart Wason, as one of the opponents, was a teller for the 'Noes'. [Hansard, 28 February 1908]

One Shetlander at least was unimpressed by Cathcart Wason's stand. A lengthy article by P W Hunter of Saltcoats, Ayr, in the *Shetland News* of 14 March 1908 criticised him as being no true Liberal, if he was to ignore basic Liberal tenets such as 'no taxation without representation' and 'force is no remedy'. Peter William Hunter, who was later referred to as an ex-Bailie of Lerwick, and a Councillor in Ayrshire, was a socialist. He was born in 1862 in Billister, Nesting, and a confectionary agent. His wife, Isabella Robertson, was from Aberdeen. He was to be a strong supporter of the 1909 Shetland WSS, coming up to give lectures on suffrage topics, and writing letters to the paper.

As Mr Stanger had pointed out, women in other countries were getting the vote: Finland in 1906, Norway in 1907, Denmark and the last state in Australia, Victoria, in 1908. In Britain, the women's fight for the vote was about to hit a brick wall, in the person of Herbert Henry Asquith, appointed Prime Minister in April 1908 in the place of the dying Campbell-Bannerman. Asquith had opposed women's suffrage since 1892, and in spite of the majority of his new Cabinet being pro-suffrage, he was to continue to oppose it. There were a number of by-elections as the result of Asquith's promotion (an MP appointed to a cabinet post had to re-stand), and all saw the suffrage groups out in force. Four were in Scotland: the Liberal majority was cut by 25% in Kincardinshire, Dundee and Montrose Burghs, and Churchill was booed on polling day in Dundee. Only in Stirling Burghs, the seat of the late Prime Minister, was the Liberal vote increased. While the NUWSS continued their educational work, pressing ministers to support their cause, the WSPU was determined to fight against Liberal MPs regaining their seats until their government would give a firm promise to bring in women's suffrage.

Echoing W E Gladstone, Asquith commented that he saw no great desire from women for the vote. To disprove this, there was an NUWSS procession in London, when 13,000 women marched from the Embankment to the Albert Hall; a week later, on 21 June 1908, seven WSPU processions from different parts of London marched to a demonstration in Hyde Park, where between half and three-quarters of a million people were estimated to be present. These demonstrations had no effect, and on 30 June Christabel Pankhurst announced a policy of greater militancy, inviting men and women to assemble outside the House of Commons that evening in support of the WSPU deputation to Asquith. Thousands came to Parliament Square, and some arrests were made. Two WSPU members, Mary Leigh and Edith New, broke the windows at 10 Downing Street. The Scottish Borders WSPU organiser, Helen Fraser, resigned in protest at these destructive acts - she went to work for the NUWSS instead. Again, neither rally was mentioned in the Shetland press, although the *Shetland Times* later reported a great demonstration in London in support of the Licensing Bill [*ST* 1 August 1908].

The number of middle-class ladies being imprisoned brought a stream of questions about the head of the Secretary of State for the Home Department, Herbert Gladstone:

Mr Lehmann (Market Harborough, Leicestershire]: ... with reference to the case of the women now undergoing imprisonment for having taken part in the recent disturbances in Parliament Square, whether he can now see his way to consult with the magistrate who sentenced them with a view to the mitigation of their punishment.

Mr Gladstone: The answer is in the negative.

Mr Byles (North Salford): ... Do not these punishments go far beyond anything that has the sanction of public opinion?

Mr Gladstone: I hardly think that is a question which should be put to me.

Mr Swift MacNeill: Is the right hon. Gentleman aware that this course of punishment is abhorrent to the feelings of this House, whose servant he is?

Mr Claude Hay (Hoxton, Shoreditch): Why does the right hon. Gentleman refuse in these cases to make a representation to the magistrates when he made such a representation in almost similar cases before?

Mr Gladstone: ... It may be that originally I was rash in making the representation; but I made it under special circumstances, having regard to the fact that it was the first occasion on which the disturbances had arisen... it is no part of my duty to interfere with the discretion of the magistrates. [Hansard, 14 July 1908]

Mr Swift MacNeill: I beg to ask the Secretary of State for the Home Department whether his attention has been directed to the statements of Mr. J. W. Logan [MP] ... that the ladies, of whom his daughter is one, who were sentenced to various terms of imprisonment in connection with the agitation for woman suffrage, are placed in solitary confinement for twenty-three hours out of the twenty-four, have prison dress, have coarse prison food to eat, are not allowed to have letters or books or newspapers, except one book a week from the prison library, which they are not allowed to read until after 5 p.m., and that the one hour out of the twenty-four in which they are not in solitary confinement is spent half in chapel and the remaining half at exercise in a yard where they are not allowed to speak to any person; in what respects, if any, does this punishment differ from the prison discipline enforced on prisoners guilty of heinous crimes; how many ladies are at present subject to this treatment for offences of a political character which has been inflicted on them in the discretion of a magistrate; and whether he will in these cases advise the exercise of the prerogative of the Crown for the removal or reduction of the cruel and humiliating incidents of such an imprisonment.

Mr Gladstone: ... This punishment differs from that of prisoners 'convicted of heinous crimes' in the following particulars: The diet of the latter is not so good, and for the first seven days not so plentiful. They are not allowed letters until they have served two months, and they are not allowed library books until they have served one month, and then only one per week. They are not altogether separated from other criminals. There were twenty-one of the suffragist prisoners yesterday, but as any of them can secure their release at any time by giving security for good behaviour, I cannot say whether the number is the same now. I cannot advise the exercise of the prerogative of mercy.

Mr Swift MacNeill: Are these ladies, whom the right hon. Gentleman has termed criminals, compelled to wear prison clothes formerly worn by ordinary women criminals?

Mr Gladstone: They are under the rules which govern the second division.

Mr Swift MacNeill: Have they not, as a matter of fact, worn the cast-off clothes of other prisoners?

Mr Gladstone: I really cannot quite say. Of course, new clothing cannot be supplied to all the prisoners who come in, but every care is taken that the clothing should be supplied in a state of perfect cleanliness.

Mr William Redmond (East Clare): Are these ladies obliged to take whatever exercise they get practically in association with those who have been convicted of ordinary criminal offences?

Mr Gladstone: That is not the case. They are kept apart from ordinary criminals.

Mr Keir Hardie: Do they have a separate exercise ground or simply march round with the other inmates of the prison?

Mr Gladstone: They are carefully kept from association with the ordinary prisoners.

Mr Leif Jones (Westmoreland, Appleby): What good object is served by limiting the number of books allowed to these ladies?

Mr Gladstone: That is a question that might be asked in regard to the general prison rules, and I am not at all satisfied that the rule is adequate, but I do not think the question necessarily arises now. [Hansard, 15 July 1908]

Mr Brodie (Surrey, Reigate): I beg to ask the Secretary of State for the Home Department whether his attention has been called to the fact that the ladies now in prison for making demonstrations against the Government are, in default of finding sureties, suffering a heavier penalty than could have been inflicted if they had actually been found guilty of sedition, in view of the fact that by the Prisons Act of 1898 a person imprisoned for sedition or seditious libel must be treated as a first-class misdemeanant; and whether, in view of this circumstance, he will recommend the transference from the second division to the first of the ladies now in prison on account of their having made political demonstrations.

Mr Gladstone: Persons found guilty of sedition are liable to imprisonment for two years, and must by Statute be placed in the first division. As regards the prison treatment of these ladies, I must refer my hon. friend to my numerous previous answers upon this subject. [Hansard 23 July 1908]

On 13 October 1908 (the third anniversary of Christabel's first arrest), a further Caxton Hall meeting was held by the WSPU. Handbills were put out beforehand, saying 'Men and Women – Help the Suffragettes to Rush the House of Commons', and Christabel, Mrs Pankhurst and 'General' Flora Drummond were served with a summons to appear on the charge of 'inciting the public to do a wrong and illegal act.' The women marched to the House in small groups, and few arrests were made. After the protest Mrs Pankhurst, Christabel and Flora Drummond sent for the police to have the warrant served on them, and Christabel, who conducted their defence, subpoenaed Lloyd George and Herbert Gladstone. Although both agreed that the scenes outside the House had been orderly – Lloyd George had even taken his six-year old daughter to watch the women - Mrs Pankhurst and Drummond were sentenced to three months in Holloway, and Christabel to ten weeks.

The *Shetland Times* didn't report either meeting or arrests, although it did have an editorial mention of a rally of the unemployed with an 'in-joke' comment that Mr Jack Williams did not ask the crowd to 'rush' the House of Commons. [*ST*, 21 October 1908] The *Shetland News* cracked at last, with a couple of letters to the Editor, one pro-suffrage, from ANTON, and one anti-suffrage, from DIANA, who was to become a regular correspondent on the topic. She urged women to use their influence in its proper sphere. Two weeks later there was a lengthy column headed SUFFRAGETTES IN COURT, a transcript of part of the trial of the two Pankhursts and Drummond. Beneath it was

WOMEN SUFFRAGE - LETTER FROM THE PRIME MINISTER:

'- asked if he will receive a deputation, he replied that as he is fully aware of the facts, he 'does not think that any useful purpose would be served by his receiving a deputation.' [*Shetland News* 31 October 1908]

The following week had two articles, SUFFRAGISTS AT THE ALBERT HALL and SUFFRAGISTS IN PRISON. SUFFRAGETTE replied to the earlier letters; after making disparaging comments about the ability of the sex that wears trousers, she said,

'... The Suffragettes have worked long and patiently along quiet, lawful lines without attaining their object. They have been driven to take the course they are now pursuing - a course which will soon end in their complete victory.' [*SN* 7 November 1908]

The week after that had 'INDIGNANT SUFFRAGISTS

A crowded meeting of indignation was held in the Free Trade Hall, Manchester ... a letter was read from the newly-elected councillor, Miss Ashton, approving the object of the meeting ... condeming the actions of the Gov in refusing women the vote, and expressing its sympathy with the women now in prison ...' [*SN* 14 November 1908]

The last mention of the year:

'WOMEN SUFFRAGE At a meeting held at Westminster ... it was resolved to form a committee to oppose the extension of the suffrage to women...' [*SN* 12 December 1908]

Christabel Pankhurst, Flora Drummond, Mrs Pankhurst. October 1908

(Above) Christabel Pankhurst, Flora Drummond and Emmeline Pankhurst in court, October 1908. They were charged with incitement after distributing handbills inviting women to rush the House of Commons. Christabel conducted the women's defence, and subpoena'd Lloyd George and Winston Churchill.

Photograph courtesy of the Museum of London.

The imprisonment of the Pankhursts again brought a flurry of questions from their supporters in the Commons through October, November and December. Early questions focused on the inconsistency of suffrage women not being treated as political prisoners; later ones gave a vivid picture of the rules of prison life:

... Mr Cooper: I beg to ask the Secretary of State for the Home Department whether Mrs. and Miss Pankhurst, now imprisoned in Holloway Gaol, were deprived of exercise and put on bread and water because they spoke to one another when they met in the exercise yard.

Mr Gladstone: Mrs. and Miss Pankhurst were not put on bread and water. They were both awarded one day's confinement to cell for taking part in a disturbance in the exercise yard. I may add that I have received satisfactory reports of the health of both Mrs. and Miss Pankhurst, and that directions were given on Friday last that they should be allowed to exercise together in the hospital yard without any restrictions as to talking.

Mr Byles: Are these ladies wearing their own garments?

Mr Gladstone: They are now in the second division. [ie No]

Mr Lupton: Would it not be better for exercise if the right hon. Gentleman allowed them to walk outside the prison?

Mr Cooper: Is it not a fact that Mrs. Pankhurst and Miss Pankhurst were put into solitary confinement for one day because the mother and daughter met one morning and spoke, and were reported for doing so by the wardress?

Mr Gladstone: I am informed that there was an offence against the prison rules concerning talking. ... The suffragists now imprisoned at Holloway are in the second division. There are none in the third division. None of them has been required to take exercise with women serving sentences for theft or any other offences, nor have any of them been placed on bread and water, or confined in a punishment cell. The obligation to keep second division prisoners apart from other classes is imposed by the Prison Rules (Rule 232), and does not require any special instructions from the Prison Commissioners. [Hansard 17 November 1908]

[In response to a question from Mr Cooper]

Mr Gladstone: Prisoners of the second division are allowed a library book and books of secular instruction, as well as devotional books, from the beginning of their sentences; those of the third division are allowed books of secular instruction and devotional books from the day of their admission, but are not allowed library books until they enter the second stage, i.e., at the end of twenty-eight days. In the second stage the library book is changed once a week, and in the third and fourth stages twice a week. All prisoners receive slates and slate pencils on admission, but are not allowed other writing materials, except for writing letters to their friends or petitions to the Home Secretary. Female prisoners in the second division have their library books changed at more frequent intervals. Unconvicted prisoners detained in default of finding sureties are, under the Prison Act, 1898, treated in accordance with the rules for the division, whether first or second, in which they are placed under the order of the Court.

Mr Reese: Will the right hon. Gentleman arrange that the third book, in addition to the Bible and the Book of Common Prayer, provided for these ladies in gaol shall be Blackstone's 'Commentaries on the Laws of England. [Hansard 17 November 1908]

Captain Clive: I beg to ask the Secretary of State for the Home Department how many baths with hot and cold water are provided per 100 prisoners at Parkhurst Prison, Isle of Wight.

Mr Gladstone: The Answer is seven. [Hansard, 18 November 1908]

[In response to Sir William Bull (Hammersmith)]

Mr Gladstone: The suffragist prisoners, like other second division female prisoners, wear a distinctive dress. Their diet is that prescribed for the second division by the rules for local prisoners made on the 2nd September, 1901, under the Prisons Act, 1898, the items of which are fully set out in the rules, with such additions or alterations as may be prescribed by the medical officer in individual cases. When the sentence exceeds one month, they may write and receive a letter and a visit once a month, and special letters and visits are allowed to all prisoners in connection with matters of urgent business. They are allowed to exercise for one hour daily, and to work in association for a time daily whenever associated labour can be arranged. In common with all prisoners, they can earn a remission of one-sixth of their sentences by good conduct and industry, if they are sentenced to more than one month's imprisonment. They are subject to the ordinary Prison Rules (number 78, and following of the Rules for local Prisons) as to punishment for misconduct. [Hansard, 30 November 1908]

Mr Swift MacNeill: I beg to ask the Secretary of State for the Home Department what is the number of women enduring imprisonment at the present time owing to circumstances arising out of the Suffragist agitation, and of the imprisoned women how many are suffering imprisonment by a sentence passed by a Judge on conviction after a trial by jury; what is the period of the imprisonment and in what division, how many under sentences inflicted by magistrates, and for what terms and in what divisions have they been placed, and how many for failure to give securities to be of good behaviour although they have been convicted of no offence, and the sentence of imprisonment from which there is no appeal is regarded by law as no punishment; and whether, having regard to the circumstances and the fact that these ladies have not been guilty of any offence savouring of moral degradation, he will consider the desirability of advising the Crown to exercise its prerogative for their release in order to enable them to spend Christmastide in their homes instead of in a prison.

Mr Gladstone: Three ladies are at present imprisoned. They were sentenced by a Metropolitan magistrate, two to three months, and one to ten weeks imprisonment, in default of finding sureties to be of good behaviour. They are being treated under the rules for second division prisoners. As regards the last part of the Question, I must ask my hon. friend to excuse me from making any statement at the present time.

Mr Lonsdale (Armagh, Mid): Are not these ladies treated with far greater severity than the cattle-drivers in Ireland?

[No answer was returned.] [Hansard, HC Deb 14 December 1908]

The WSPU continued to hold rallies in the absence of their leaders. The *Shetland News* published an account of one:

SUFFRAGISTS AT THE ALBERT HALL
WHAT THE CABINET HAS TO EXPECT

The Thursday night's At Home of the Women's Social and Political Union took the form of an Albert Hall meeting. Scarves of purple, white and green were to be seen in all parts of the hall, and in front of the organ was a banner: 'Neither to change, nor falter, nor to repent: Mrs Pankhurst, Christabel Pankhurst, Mrs Drummond, in prison, October 24 1908.' The audience was composed mostly of women, but there was a sprinkling of men. At the call of Mrs Pethick-Lawrence, who presided, the audience stood at the opening of the proceedings, and offered a 'silent salute to those brave women who are in bondage that they may win freedom for their sex, and to those women of another society who so pluckily carried out their demonstration last (Wednesday) night.' Cheers were then given for the three imprisoned suffragist leaders.

Mrs Pethick-Lawrence laid down the following as part of the future programme:

No Cabinet Minister must be allowed to speak in public.

The tin potentates calling themselves the Government must be made the laughing stock of the civilised world.

It must be made impossible for any Liberal candidate to be returned at a by-election.

There must be no false politeness. They must let everyone know what they thought and felt on the matter.

A resolution was passed congratulating Mrs Pankhurst and her daughter, and Mrs Drummond and the other Suffragists, and demanding of the Government their immediate release. Mrs Lawrence referred to Mr Gladstone's declaration that he had no power to have the women treated as first-class misdemeanants, Mr Gladstone's name being received with hisses. Choruses of 'Shame', hisses and groans greeted a reference to the Premier. As to 'rushing' Parliament, they might as well rush the waxworks at Madame Tussaud's, or the Museum mummies.

Mr Pethick-Lawrence also spoke, and it was subsequently announced that £23,000 had been collected towards a £50,000 scheme. [*SN* 7 November 1908]

The article is followed by one giving a brief account of Mr MacNeill's questions in the House of Commons, suggesting that both were sent together, perhaps as a general WSPU news release. The sums of money raised by the WSPU were quite astonishing.

The Pankhursts were released on 19 December. In the meantime, photographs of them in prison uniform, with a white cap, dark blouse and skirt printed with white arrows, and a white apron printed with a dark arrow, were on sale as post-cards. Later, replica arrows would be carried by suffrage prisoners in processions. The Pankhursts were to capitalise on their experience at a fund-raising bazaar at Prince's Skating Rink in April 1909, where attractions included two replica 'Holloway Cells'. One showed a suffragette sewing, scrubbing or knitting, and the other, twice the size, showed a male political prisoner reading. The hall decorations were designed by Sylvia Pankhurst, and decorations and items for sale were all in the WSPU colours.

An indignant kitten in front of the WSPU colours of green, white and purple. Postcard, author's collection.

I want my Vote!

A small triumph: on 9th November, 1908, Elizabeth Garrett Anderson, now aged 72, was elected in Aldeburgh as the UK's first woman mayor.

Otherwise, the suffrage campaigns continued as they had done. In March 1909, Howard's Women's Enfranchisement Bill passed its second reading by a majority of 35, but got no further. A Representation of the People Bill asking for full adult suffrage was introduced by a private member, and supported by Sir Charles McLaren. This Bill had no chance of success – full adult suffrage was not achieved until 1928 - and was not supported by the NUWSS for that reason. The NUWSS continued to focus on education and propaganda, and their magazine *The Common Cause of Humanity,* with reports of suffrage activities from across Britain, was launched in April 1909. In her history *Women's Suffrage,* Fawcett estimated that two or three hundred outdoor meetings were held every week during the summer months. WSPU organisers also worked on 'spreading the message'; Mr Pethick Lawrence estimated that 1,000 meetings were being held across the country every month.

The message was certainly reaching Shetland, as there were Up Helly Aa squads featuring suffragettes and policemen. 'Votes for We-Men' (below) is from 1909.

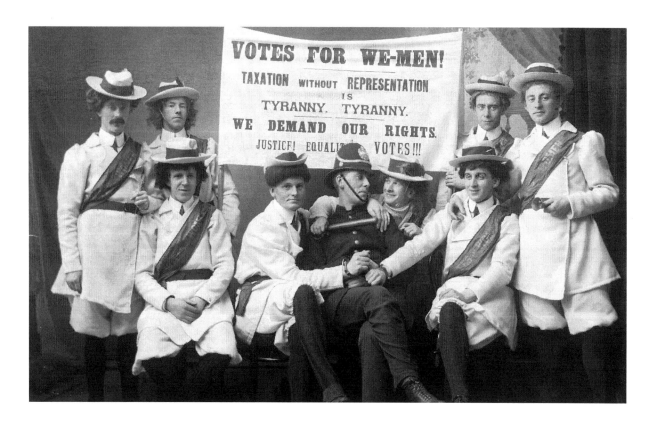

'Suffragette' squad, 1909.
Photographed by R Ramsay, courtesy of Shetland Museum and Archives [UH00060]

146

8

1909

The new campaign in Shetland

Christina Jamieson in the 1920s.
Photograph courtesy of the Shetland Museum and Archives [Z00295, detail]

Christina Jamieson's lecture:

The new Shetland campaign began in March 1909, when Christina Jamieson delivered a closely argued, carefully researched account of women's history at a meeting of the Lerwick Literary and Debating Society, to 'frequent applause'. The *Shetland News* account stressed the size of the audience: 'There was a very large attendance of the members of the Society and the general public, and a great many could not gain admittance. The audience was largely composed of ladies.' The *Shetland News* gave the full text of the lecture, which was also sold later as a pamphlet, price one penny. In it, Jamieson began by contrasting the Eastern world of enclosed women with the western: 'Maritime and warlike peoples often left their women for long periods in charge of affairs. Women therefore had more freedom and scope, and their spheres of action were never defined or limited.' She went on to detail those spheres of action: the warrior queens found by the Romans, the independence of married Saxon women, and the duties of the Norman lady of the manor, whose personal seal was as binding as any man's.

'Women also held public offices in the religious world. The great religious orders gave scope to such women as did not find a satisfying career in domestic life. Abbesses were as powerful as Peeresses. They had great territorial, administrative and educational powers. They could even sit in the House of Lords.'

Jamieson then considered the 'industrial and commercial classes', where the interests of women 'were largely safeguarded by common law. Women free-holders in the counties held parliamentary rights. In towns women with the necessary qualifications were Burgesses or Freewomen with rights of municipal and Parliamentary franchise, which they exercised. ... qualification, not sex was considered.'

She explained that these rights were obtained chiefly through the trade Guilds.

'All Gilds admitted women, who could be apprenticed to and practice, nearly any craft. The widow of a Gildsman could continue his business and exercise his rights in all crafts.'

Jamieson then gave a long list of these crafts, forty-six of them, from aldermen through armourers, barber-surgeons, blacksmiths, butchers, clockmakers, ferryboat keepers, hucksters, jurymen, mariners, masons, tailors, and waulkers to weavers.

However, according to Jamieson, this changed with the Reformation, when the return to the Bible as supreme religious authority brought back Eastern ideas of a woman's place:

'The Man, says St Paul, is the head of the woman, as Christ is the head of the Church. Man promptly assumed the position, without hesitation of his fitness. ... The Religious Orders were broken up, the sisterhoods dispersed, the 'mayde' schools closed, and even the social and religious gilds placed under the ban of the Reformation. From that time to the middle of last century there was no High School, no public Institution of any sort, for girls or for women.

'What shall we do with the women?' asked the reformers, and 'Marry them' said Luther, and set an example.

So women were wholly relegated to private life, taught to practise meekness, patience and silence as their chief virtues; to repress in themselves the desire for knowledge and the ambition that had led the primal woman to eat the forbidden fruit; to regard as their highest privilege the elementary duties of the house... With the women of Elizabethan times who had been reared under the old regime, passed from history the great ladies and self-respecting Free women of British public life. .... The names of women gradually wore off the Gild and Municipal rolls.'

She then went in detail through the protests against the inferior condition to which women were reduced: John Aubrey asking for education for girls in 1670, Mary Astell in 1697, Samuel Heywood's classification of 'women, infants, idiots and lunatics', William Thompson's 'Appeal from one half of the Human Race' of 1825, women's part in the Reform Bill agitation of 1832, Mrs Cobden speaking out for women at a Corn Law meeting and Anne Knight's suffrage pamphlet of 1847.

The next part of her lecture gave a detailed account of the suffrage movement from the 1850s on. She gave a long list of names supporting J S Mill's petition, and detailed its failure, then looked at the reforms achieved by suffrage workers:

'Most of the conditions that now make life more tolerable for toiling women owe their origin to the workers for women's suffrage, and every beneficial national movement owes them impetus. Political effort and ambition instead of making them unwomanly, only helped to strengthen, deepen and broaden all the powers and capacities of their womanhood.'

She explained the 1868 decision against the women householders, and detailed the subsequent suffrage bills, then stressed women's achievements in spite of Parliamentary refusal.

'During the Victorian period women hve emerged from private life and done noble public work in nursing, domestic, hospital, sanitary, social and prison reform; parochial, civic, ecclesiastic, institutional and national development; in commerce, literature, art, drama, journalism, politics, religion, philanthropy, temperance, medicine, science, exploration, research. ... The great women of the nineteenth century, having fought a good fight, are passing away, saddened, and with a lessened faith in men. It is for the younger generation of women, reared in an atmosphere of growing aspirations, to carry on the struggle. And they will carry it on.

They will spare no effort, suffering or sacrifice to establish a principle that is yearly becoming more vital to them – the equal political rights of men and women.

Their claim is an enduring one. It has never abated, and it has grown in insistence. Its basis on right is increasingly recognised. The State must ultimately grant it.

And if in the past our people have looked to their daughters for hope and loyalty and helpfulness; their sisters for purity, rectitude, and comradeship, their lovers for the motives that elevate and ennoble every human impulse, their wives for inspiration, support and comfort in every care, aim and ambition, and their mothers for the supreme lessons of unselfishness and devotion – these qualities will still be forthcoming in the future, when women hold an acknowledged share in the political life of the nation.

Under the domination of man, in the domestic world it was only recently that a woman could call her body her own; in the ecclesiastical world, she dare not speak to say her soul is her own; in the social world her right of moral judgement is not her own; in the work-a-day world the value of her toil is not her own; and in the political world her sense of justice is so thwarted that is is rapidly becoming a sense of mere injustice – she does not belong to the genus homo; she is not a part of mankind; if you call her a person you use unparliamentary language. Can absurdity further go?

Whatever the ultimate relations between men and women, they come together into the world as brothers and sisters – and that first relationship, with its equal footing, should never be forgotten. In happy families the opportunities and advantages of all the children are equal; and the final estimation of their work is based on character and not sex.

The character and capacities of women can never be fully known while it is in the power of men to fix arbitrarily what they must do, or must not do.'

The *Shetland News* account ends:

'The lecture was a very able and instructive one, and Miss Jammieson's remarks were frequently punctuated with applause.

At the close the following ladies and gentlemen took part in the discussion: Miss M Harrison, Mrs Nicol [both to be members of the SWSS], Messrs M L Manson, T Angus, Revs D Houston and A J Campbell, Messrs F H Pottinger, J Allan, R B Hunter, G Emslie, H Brayshaw and H M McLeod.

With the exception of Messrs Allan and Emslie, all the speakers were in favour of the franchise being extended to women, Messrs Manson and Pottinger favouring adult suffrage for both sexes over 21 years of age.' [*SN* 20 March 1909]

It's interesting, given later comments that the ladies of the Shetland WSS did not speak out, that although the audience is said to be mostly ladies, the questions were mostly from men; even in a mostly female audience with a female speaker on a topic particularly concerning them, women were reluctant to ask questions in public.

The text of Jamieson's speech was published in the *Shetland News* on 20 March 1909, and the following week's response, in the *Shetland Times* Current Topics page, was an example of the abuse those advocating votes for women in public had to put up with. The author said that if he had known

'the lecturer on the 'Women's Rights Movement', or whatever it may be called, I would have waited on her some night, borrowed her manuscript and, for her own sake, consigned it to the flames.'

He made it clear he was not at the lecture, but said he had to read the text twice to make sense of it, calling it a 'crude and illogical production ... more of 'special pleading' than sound argument.'

He objected to her using the names of Hannah More and Florence Nightingale (the latter did indeed sign Mill's petition) in connection with women's suffrage: 'Could anythimg be more grotesque ... to [mention these] with Mrs Pankhurst or the other members of the screaming sisterhood?' and refuted her perfectly correct idea that Quaker women were involved. He went on to talk at length about Jamieson's father, who had been a friend of his, and gave a glowing account of his teaching and accomplishments:

'He was widely read and brought a broad, clear philosophic mind to bear on most subjects. His reasonings and deductions were masterpieces. He rarely took anything for granted, but rather weighed the whole phases of a question in the balance, rejecting that which he considered doubtful, and holding fast to that which he conceived to be lasting and true. ... Among the few treasures I possess, are some letters written for me by my late friend. His death made Sandness and the whole Shetland Islands the poorer; and it was that deeper knowledge of the man that made me regret that he could not have seen Miss Jamieson's MS before she ventured before the public with it. Had he done so, I make no doubt it would have shared the fate that accidentally befell Carlyle's first manuscript of 'The French Revolution.'

I hope that underhand blow did not hurt Jamieson too deeply; perhaps the knowledge that she had gained her scholarship from her father helped her to ignore it. The anonymous author's final paragraph sounded a note which was to be heard a number of times on the letters page:

'If women had taken advantage of all the phases of public life open to them, if they could point to a record of work done, as a guarantee of their desire to accomplish more, I would be more assured of their sincerity. ... the County Council, the Town Council, the School Board and the Parish Council. ... it has only been with difficulty that women have been induced to vote in such contests, much less to take part in the work. ... It is the same old story, I suppose, some women are so constituted that if they had all the earth at their disposal, and command of all the universe, they would call public meetings and make indignant protests becasue they could not, over their afternoon tea-cups, appoint a committee of their number to conduct affairs and reorganise the general arrangements of the Kingdom of Heaven.' [*ST* 27 March 1909]

On 30th March, three letters which criticised the 'Current Topics' attitude were published, including one from Ilford:

'We are not many Shetlanders in Ilford, but we are all unanimous in condemning the author of 'Current Notes', for his cowardly and unkind attack on Miss Jamieson.'

and one in Shetland verse, by 'Fiskeske':

'Bit if he tries da lik again,
As sure as death I'll let him ken
He sanna pass withoot correction,
I care no wha may hae objection.
I'll tak mi whittle fae mi pocket,
An' in his gapin' gills I'll sok it,
I'll snee his tail an' rit his muggi,
I'll mak him laek a birsled buggi,
I'll rikkle him, an' whan he's poodered,

I'll rost him, till he's fairly scoodered.
So ye can tell him dis frae me,
An' fu' he taks it, we'll aye see.' [*ST* 3 April 1909]

Jamieson or another supporter must have sent the original article and Current Topics column to the NUWSS, for a further letter appeared on April 24, from Kate Kilburn, NUWSS, which turned the column's purpose neatly on its head:

'One can only suppose that your object in publishing an ebullition so permeated with personal animus ... was to benefit the cause of women's suffrage.'

During the summer, Shetland had two important visitors with New Zealand suffrage connections, Sir Robert and Lady Stout. Sir Robert Stout had been born in Lerwick in 1844. His grandfather James had built Stout's Court, and Robert Stout, Provost of Lerwick from 1913 – 1915, was his first cousin. Sir Robert had qualified as a teacher then as a surveyor before emigrating to New Zealand in 1863. There he studied law and became a successful trial lawyer, then Otago University's first law lecturer before entering politics. He had been Premier of New Zealand twice, and in 1893 had been central to getting the women's suffrage bill passed. At this point he was Lord Chief Justice and Chancellor of the University of New Zealand. Jamieson's brother James was involved in medical politics in New Zealand, and the Jamieson and Leisk families would have been aquainted with Stout family members still in Lerwick.

Lady Anna Paterson Stout, born in 1858, was a foundation member of the New Zealand Women's Christian Temperance Union, the National Council of Women and the Society for the Protection of Women and Children, and a determined campaigner for women's rights, education and welfare. After her visit to Shetland she was to remain in London for three further years, and be active in the suffrage movement nationally. At their official reception, Provost Porteous said of Lady Stout:

'I know that those who have had the pleasure of meeting her here have been impressed by the charm of her manner, with her bright and ready intelligence, and rightly came to the conclusion that Sir Robert indeed is a fortunate man.' [*SN* 21 August 1909]

Sir Robert and Lady Stout arrived in Shetland on 31 July 1909, and a number of functions were held for them. A 'red carpet' Conversatzione and Dance in aid of charity was held in the Town Hall on Wednesday 11 August. The concert part included Misses Campbell and Leisk doing a pianoforte duet, and the dance went on until 2.30am. There was a civic reception held in the Town Hall on Friday 13 August:

'Fully two hundred ladies and gentlemen in Lerwick and throughout the isles [attended]. The reception was timed to begin at 3 o clock ... and was in the main hall, which was laid out in drawing-room fashion, and tastefully decorated for the occasion.' While afternoon tea was served 'the company indulged in animated conversation'.

It is very likely that her contemporaries Mrs Leisk, wife of the previous provost, Mrs Laing, wife of the next year's provost, his sister and niece, Barbara and Christina Jamieson, and Mrs Sandison, wife of the Town Clerk, would have talked to Lady Stout about the suffrage question, asked how women in New Zealand had prospered, and told her of their plans to set up a Shetland Women's Suffrage Society. There were other opportunities for them to meet too; Lady Stout later mentions that Lady (Watson) Cheyne, whom she met in Shetland, gave a dance for her daughter. It's also likely that Lady Stout offered to become President if such a society was started; her social position was such that I think the overture must have come from her.

Sir Robert and Lady Anna Stout. She was
to be the first President of the Shetland
WSS, a choice that was to bring
controversy.
Photographs taken from E S Reid Tait's
scrapbooks, courtesy of the Shetland
Museum and Archives.

An interview with Sir Robert appeared in the *Shetland Times* and *Shetland News* of 7 August 1909. The *Shetland Times* interview does not mention women's suffrage, but the *Shetland News* interview asks

'What is your opinion of Women's Suffrage? I have always been in favour of Women Suffrage, and was one of its first supporters in New Zealand.'

Lady Stout was also interviewed, but only by the *Shetland News*. The interview focused exclusively on women's suffrage, and demonstrated her political awareness. She refuted the idea that women did not bother to vote with actual figures, and stressed the pride women took in their right to vote, and the improvement of life in New Zealand. She also made it clear that women did not neglect their children for the sake of intellectual pursuits, and was critical of the attitude that she found in Britain:

'By giving women the franchise you will make them better wives, better mothers, better sisters, better citizens; you will raise the standard and ideal of citizenship ... In Great Britain you seem to be afraid of giving the vote to women. ... You have more condescending show of politeness to women than we have, but you have none of the real courtesy of comradeship that we have, though you talk about your reverence for women more. Our women attend political meetings in greater numbers than men, and are always treated with consideration and attention. Here it seems that men may ask any stupid question and receive a civil reply, but if a woman asks a simple question she is at once hounded down, ejected from the meeting. From our point of view such treatment is evidence that all your civilisation has only put a superficial veneer on the brute that lies below, that is ever ready when met by intelligence and unanswerable argument to exercise the tyranny of physical force to silence opposition. But you will have to get rid of your prejudices, your sex war, your insular ignorance and aloofness ... the sooner the franchise is granted to women the better it will be for the nation, not only now but for the generations that are to come.' [*SN* 28 August 1909]

The interview is written as one long speech, and shows Lady Stout as a very capable orator. She was later to be asked to speak on behalf of the WSPU, and did indeed speak in Hyde Park on several occasions.

John Cathcart Wason's visit to his constituency took place at this time (there is, alas, no record of a passage of arms between him and Lady Stout) and the transcription of his electoral address shows the socialists standing up for women's suffrage:

Mr W Sinclair asked a question in connection with Women's Suffrage. (Applause) In moving the rejection of the Women's Enfranchisement Bill, did Mr Wason think that women were not capable of exercising the vote? Mr Wason - I did not make any remark of the sort ... Women's suffrage has never been demanded by any great majority of women, and I, in common with the great majority of women, do not think it is at all desirable that women should come down to the same electoral platform as men. They have more than enough to do in their own homes, local councils and local authorities. (Some hissing and applause, and a voice, 'Better go to New Zealand.')

Mr Sinclair - Is it not because of economic circumstances that we have so many unmarried women in our midst? (Loud laughter) And now women are prepared to spend six months in prison in fighting for their rights. Does Mr Wason not think they are entitled to vote, and all men too?

Mr Wason said that women did not go to prison for their political opinions, but because of breaking doors. (Cries of Oh, oh.) Did anyone think that the women who demanded the vote should not be liable to the ordinary laws of the land when they created a disturbance, just exactly in the same way as men? It was an untrue, mendacious statement to say that women suffered because of their political convictions.

Mr Pottinger - Does Mr Wason think women should obey laws when they have no say in the making of them? (Hear, hear)

Mr Wason - My opinion is that the women of this country are perfectly satisfied with the existing state of things. If you think that women should enter the house of Commons and rule the destinies of the country you are entitled to your opinion. I do not think so. (A voice: There are old women there already', and laughter.)

Mr Sinclair - May I ask how it is that women in London, Glasgow and other large centres are imprisoned, and not the women in Lerwick? (Laughter.)

Mr Wason - I should think the answer is very simple. The ladies in Lerwick know how to behave themselves. (Applause)

Mr Manson - Is Mr Wason in favour of men and women having votes at 21 years of age, and if not why not?

Mr Wason - Surely I have already told you that I am not in favour of women's suffrage.

Mr Manson - Are you in favour of adult suffrage for men and women, and if not why not?

Mr Wason - No, I am not.

Mr Manson - Why not?

Mr Wason - I will tell you at the next election. (Laughter) [*SN* 28 August 1909]

On the mainland, women were being ejected from political meetings for asking just these questions. It's hard to imagine that women here would have been treated the same way. Ejecting an anonymous woman in London or Glasgow is one thing, manhandling your provost's wife in Lerwick is quite another. All the same, the ladies of the Shetland WSS took care not to put it to the test, submitting written questions, and taking Mr Wason's 'condescending show of politeness' in silence.

Hunger strikes and forcible feeding:

Militant action continued on the mainland. In June 1909, Scotswoman Marion Wallace-Dunlop was arrested for stencilling the message 'It is the right of the subjct to petition the King, and all commitments and prosecution for such petitions are illegal' on the wall of St Stephen's Hall in the House of Commons. When she was imprisoned, she went on hunger strike, and was released by order of the Home Secretary after 91 hours. Although this was entirely an individual initiative, it was greeted with enthusiasm by the 'War Office' of the WSPU, as a new way to put pressure on the Government; Christabel Pankhurst was learning the truth that outragous conduct becomes commonplace when repeated, and militancy demands escalating action. From now on, hunger striking was a regular tactic, and for the moment prisoners who resorted to it were reasonably quickly released.

Her message was in advance of another WSPU attempt to petition Asquith. When they were arrested, Mrs Pankhurst and the Hon Evelina Haverfield (later to be head of Elsie Inglis' ambulance drivers in Serbia) pleaded that by the Bill of Rights and by the terms of the Tumultuous Petitions Act, they were legally entitled to petition Asquith as a representative of the King. Nearly a hundred women had been arrested with them, and the magistrate adjourned all cases until he could take further advice. The case was heard again on 9 July and sent to a higher court, on the understanding that Mrs Pankhurst would make no further attempt to petition during 1909. The case was finally heard by the Lord Chief Justice in November; he found against Mrs Pankhurst, and she and Mrs Haverfield were each fined £5. The cases of the other women were dismissed.

Fourteen women who had smashed windows in that same raid were tried separately, and each was sentenced to one month in the second division. All went on hunger strike, and were released after a hundred hours of fasting.

In the WSPU's place, the Women's Freedom League picketed the House of Commons from July to 5 October, the end of the session, waiting for the chance to hand a petition to Asquith. A number of women were arrested for attempting to approach him.

The first Scottish arrests took place in Glasgow in August 1909, at a lecture on the Budget by a Cabinet minister. Four women were arrested, including Adela Pankhurst and two American students Alice Paul and Lucy Burns. Paul was a Quaker, and a member of the WSPU. She had already been arrested in June, in London; this is where she met Burns. Both were arrested again in Limehouse in July, at a Lloyd George meeting, and went on hunger-strike. They were released after five and a half days, and came up to campaign in Scotland with Adela Pankhurst. Paul had spent the night on the roof of St

Andrew's Hall, hoping to gain entry to the meeting; she was brought down in the morning, when a number of women attempted to force their way into the meeting. Paul and Burns repeated their tactics in Dundee in September, and when sentenced to ten days imprisonment, they refused either to eat or to work. Press coverage was initially scornful, but when the women were released after three days, visibly weak, public opinion was more sympathetic towards them. Both women were to be arrested again several times. Paul returned to America in 1910, and Burns returned in 1912. There they worked together for women's enfranchisement, using WSPU-style tactics. From 1936, Pauls was to be the USA representative on the Laws Committee of the International Council of Women.

The first forcible or 'assisted' feeding took place in September 1909, in Winston Green Prison, Birmingham. A number of women were arrested for disturbances at an Asquith meeting, and all were forcibly fed. Their accounts, published on their release, caused widespread horror and condemnation. One of them, Mary Leigh, charged the Home Secretary, the prison governor and the prison doctor, with assault. The High Court found against her, on the grounds that their actions were justified to safeguard her life. This ruling gave legality to the forcible feeding of suffrage women.

On 16 October 1909, in Dundee, women had their first taste of what was to become increasing male aggression. Winston Churchill was holding a public meeting, and as he had agreed to meet a WFL deputation the WSPU agreed not to disrupt his meeting, but to hold a separate protest a small distance away. Four women, including Adela Pankhurst, arrived in a car, but as soon as it stopped it was surrounded by men wearing Liberal rosettes. The women were grabbed at, and mud was thrown on them until they succeeded in driving away.

There was a further scene in Dundee three days later, with five women (the sister of an MP and the daughter of the *Scotsman*'s late editor among them) being arrested for disrupting a Churchill meeting in the Kinnaird Hall. All were sentenced to ten days imprisonment, and all went on hunger strike. Force-feeding was considered, for the first time in Scotland, but the prison doctor felt it could damage the health of each woman, and they were released. Flora Drummond compared the 'humanity' of Scots prisons favourably with those of England, where forcible-feeding was now a regular occurence, but the Secretary for Scotland asked for details of 'assisted feeding' with, presumably, the intention of using it.

Chrystal Macmillan's visit to Shetland, September 1909:

In late September 1909, Chrystal Macmillan, the 'modern Portia' who had taken the case of the University graduates to the House of Lords, lectured in Shetland. Her visit was part of a tour which also included Caithness, Sutherland and Orkney. As she mentions Jamieson as the 'secretary of the local society', it seems reasonable to assume that they had corresponded beforehand; perhaps it was through Jamieson's Edinburgh contacts that she was invited to Shetland. 'Several local ladies who support the votes for women movement' helped beforehand to sell brooches and women's suffrage literature, particularly *The Common Cause*, 'a good many copies of which were sold'. She spoke in Scalloway on Wednesday and Lerwick on Thursday, giving a long and closely argued speech.

There is a full account of her lecture in both the *Shetland Times* and *Shetland News* of 25th September 1909. Here's the *Shetland Times*' description of her speaking style:
'... Miss Chrystal McMillan, B Sc, of Edinburgh, is certainly one of the leaders of the movement... The address itself was spoiled by the evident straining after simplicity and clearness ... In a speaker of less experience, it would be put down to nervousness, but in Miss McMillan's case it must be habit. ... mere orderliness cannot hold an audience in the way that the introduction of the speaker's personality and imagination into the words would do.'

Chrystal Macmillan, who spoke in Shetland in September 1909.
Photograph by kind permission of Iain Macmillan and the People's Story Museum, Edinburgh.

The *Shetland News* emphasised how full the Rechabite Hall was:

'every available seat was occupied, and a great many forms and chairs had to be brought into the hall. As it was, many could not gain admission, and had to be turned away.'

The text of Macmillan's speech was similar in both papers. She began with describing women's struggle to win a University education, and the advantages it had gained them, then spoke on the history of men's franchise: 'Even here in Lerwick, men were not born with voting papers in their hands.' Recent bills had been attempted, almost thirty in as many years, but none had been passed.

'Last year, in February, the Bill had come up for a second time, and the House ... had voted by a majority of 167 that Women's Suffrage was just and right, and yet nothing had been done. .. in June last year a procession of 15,000 women of all classes and occupations went through the streets. ... there was another demonstration held in London at which seven processions walked through the streets, and it was said in the 'Times' ... that there were something between half a million and three-quarters of a million of women ... And yet after that, when the Prime Minister was asked to receive a deputation he said he would not do it, and had no done it since.'

She emphasised the illogicality of men's position, and the benefits of women's suffrage to the country, and ended by looking at women's right to work: 'it was becoming a serious question.'

After her speech there were questions. One was on universal suffrage, from Magnus Manson; it was a topic on which he felt strongly, as he had three years ago lost his right to vote. This tension between the adult and the women's suffragists has already been seen in the fledgling Labour party, and was to be re-aired in a series of letters between Jamieson and E S Reid Tait. Macmillan's reply makes the suffragist position clear: 'they were asking for the vote on the same grounds as it was given to men, whatever those might be.' Mr R B Hunter, one of the 'Working Men's Candidates' from the 1889 election, asked her view on lady MPs, and a written question asked her if she supported those who had smashed Mr Asquith's windows. Her reply was that it was very difficult for those outside the constitution to use constitutional methods; 'the House of Commons was imprisoning those people who were asking it to do what it itself said was just and right.'

The vote of thanks was moved by Mr R B Hunter. The Chair of the meeting was the Reverend A J Campbell; this must have been one of the last meetings he chaired, for he and his wife left Lerwick for Glasgow in November 1909: 'His departure was regretted not only by his congregation, but by a large section of the general public.' [*LHCC*, p 280] He later became Moderator of the General Assembly of the Church of Scotland, and his wife continued to support women's suffrage at meetings on the mainland.

Macmillan must have gone straight back to Edinburgh, as she was present at the 'grand procession' of 9th October 1909. The theme of the procession was 'What women have done – can do – and will do.' It was led by 'General' Flora Drummond on her white horse (riding astride, her horse 'under perfect control', according to the *Scotsman*), and included women pipers and groups of trades and professions carrying banners – medical women under a snake and lamp banner, fishwives in their kirtles and graduates in their gowns. There were decorated floats and eighteen 'tableaux' of historical women. The lead piper was a nine-year old girl, Bessie Watson, sitting at the front of the cart which held the tableau of the Countess of Buchan in her wooden cage – her punishment for crowning Robert the Bruce when her menfolk were too afraid to do it. Banner slogans included 'What's good for John's good for Janet', 'A Guid Cause maks a strong Arm' and (aimed at Asquith) 'You manna trample on the Scots thistle, laddie'. An estimated 2,000 took part in the procession, and Press reports spoke of 'tens of thousands' of spectators, with people six-deep on Princes Street. The procession was followed by speeches at Waverley; Mrs Pankhurst was among the speakers.

'Current Topics', on 9th October, was unrepentent. After admiring Macmillan's Scots country lass looks, he said,

'It would be the better for this race, for the country and for the Empire, if such big, healthy, strong lasses had all their attention glued to the nursery, rather than gadding about ... procuring cheap notoriety as 'pioneers' and 'martyrs' in the 'cause'.'

He was joined by W.M. in an equally hostile letter, which sparked off a correspondence with A Andrew. On 23 October, 'Current Topics' returned to the issue:

'A friend of mine ... assured me the other day that the local suffragettes - who he says is is largely composed of old wives of both sexes - have decided to form themselves into an active organisation. ... I often find myself wondering if those ladies who talk so much about the vote are really sincere. But ... the man is not yet born who can say when a lady is sincere.'

At the time he was writing, a number of women were sincere enough to endure 'assisted feeding' in Newcastle for having disturbed a Lloyd George meeting.

The Shetland Women's Suffrage Society:

The inaugural meeting of the Shetland Women's Suffrage Society was held at Twagios House on 23 October, 1909, and the nineteen women and one man present were very clear: their new society

'had no connection with the disturbances which had been caused recently by women suffragists, its object being solely by constitutional means to endeavour to secure to women the Parliamentary Franchise.'

The new group was affiliated to the NUWSS at that first meeting, and it was agreed to put the *The Common Cause* in the local reading room, and to report their proceedings to the local newspaper.

The meeting was convened by Jamieson. Like the members of the first Shetland suffrage societies, the women present were very much 'of the establishment', the wives and daughters of men of standing in Lerwick. Their involvement implies their men's support for women's suffrage – support that was later to be shown in delegations and letters to the Prime Minister from both Town and County councils. A change was the lack of ministers and minister's wives among them; from being a church cause, women's suffrage had become mainstream. Most importantly, with the exception of Mr Tulloch, they were all women.

Here is the full list of names: [Miss Jamieson], Miss Gulland, Nurse Esplin, Mrs Nicol, Nurse Hay, Miss Harrison, Mrs D Morrison, Mrs Morrison, Miss Mitchell, Mrs Sandison, Mrs Leisk, Miss Morrison, Miss J Mitchell, Mrs Harrison, Mrs Laing, Miss Campbell, Miss Leisk, Miss E Allison, Mrs Galloway, Mr Tulloch.

They would all have known each other, given the smaller Lerwick of that time, and the more limited social mix. Mrs Leisk, Mrs Laing and Miss Gulland all sang in the choir at the 1883 opening of the Town Hall; Miss Mitchell was the accompanist. The choir for the 1887 Queen's Golden Jubilee celebrations included Mrs Leisk, Mrs Morrison, Miss Jamieson, Mrs Laing, Miss E Mitchell, Miss Allison, Miss Harrison and Miss Gulland – seven of the nine families involved with the committee. In 1897, the Zetland Quadrille Club held a Masked Ball; Miss Gulland went as a Lady, Louis XIV period, Miss Harrison as a lady of Queen Anne Period, Miss Leisk as Winter; Mrs Harrison and Mrs Leisk were, as chaperones, in Evening Dress (sounds good fun). Their husbands were similarly linked: the list of Brethren of the Lodge Morton for the laying of the Foundation Stone of the Lerwick Harbour Works in 1883 included John Leisk, Alex Sandison, Robert Walker, D Morrison, W A A Tulloch and Brother Laing; subscribers to the new pier included both the men of the old suffrage committee and the husbands and brothers of the new: John Robertson, John Leisk, Wm Duncan, Alex Mitchell, Hector Morrison, J Harrison. The Chief Ruler of the St Sunniva Tent was Mrs A L Laing, the Deputy Ruler, Mrs Harrison, the P.O. Ruler was Miss Harrison; the Secretary was Miss Florence Garriock, Mrs Sandison's sister-in-law; the Guardian was her younger sister, Jessie. [*ST* 16 June 1894]

As with the societies down south, a small number of families formed the core. There were the two Atherton sisters and a daughter; the two Robertson sisters, a daughter and a niece; Miss Morrison and her two sisters-in-law; Mrs Laing and her niece, Miss Jamieson, and two Mitchell sisters. There was a balanced spread of ages, with Mrs Harrison the oldest, at 62. Mrs Leisk, Miss Gulland, Mrs Laing and Miss Mitchell were in their fifties. Miss Jamieson, Miss J Mitchell and Miss Morrison were in their forties, Miss Harrison and Mrs D Morrison were in their thirties, and Miss Leisk, Miss Campbell and Miss Allison represented the young things.

The first President was **Lady Stout**, a choice that was soon to involve the society in controversy. The first Vice-President was **Mrs Galloway.** She was Isobel Ann Robertson, born in 1849 in Chester, and the only daughter of William Robertson, Master Mariner. She married James K. Galloway in Glasgow in 1869, and they moved to Shetland immediately; he was procurator fiscal here for almost 60 years (his mother was Agnes Kirkland, from Ayr; I wondered if he had any connection with Marion Kirkland Reid, author of *A Plea for Women*, or with Janet Galloway, the first head of Queen Margaret's College, Glasgow, from 1882 -1909). They lived in Commercial Street, in the house built by Charles Ogilvy. Mrs Galloway was a member of St Columba's Kirk, and donated a cushion and pulpit Bible in the 1890 renovations. They had three children, now all left home: Andrew, who was a writer and solicitor in Renfrewshire; Isobel, born in 1872, who took advantage of the new educational openings for women to bcome a lecturer for Stafford County Council – she was resident in Stafford by 1901; and Agnes, born in 1875, who went to live with her sister before 1901.

Harriet Leisk, whose Liverpool courtship and early married life we've already followed, was the new Chairman of the SWSS. John Leisk was now a well known figure in the town. He was Provost of Lerwick from 1895 - 1904; he was also chairman of the Harbour Trust and involved in facilitating the building of the new Victoria Pier and Esplanade; Thomas Manson calls him

'one of the initiators of the scheme, as he was one of the promotors and guarantors. He has been its mainspring ... the whole community agrees that as regards an abiding and whole-hearted interest in public affairs as embodied in the Harbour Trust, besides the Town Council and Feuars and Heritors, no one holds a higher record than Mr John Leisk... after nigh on 42 years of strenuous work, he still is at the head of affairs, as Chairman – a position his brother Trustees will not allow him to remit.' [*Lerwick in the Last Half-Century*]

Leisk and Sandison were also shipping agents for the 'Greenland vessels' – the seal and whale fishing boats.

Mrs Leisk was musical; she sang in the choir, and their daughters Hattie and Louisa were involved in the Lerwick Orchestra, along with their cousin Dorothy Sandison. Hattie played the piano, and Louisa and Dottie the violin; Dottie also sang at the opening concert of 1904, with Hattie accompanying. Mrs Leisk was also involved in the Dorcas Society and the Literary and Scientific Society – she was particularly interested in the library.

The first years of the new century must have been filled with wedding preparations in the Leisk household: Bessie married Miles Walker-Pole of Delting in St Magnus Church in June 1903; they emigrated to South Africa, and had one daughter. Hattie married Dr James (Terry) Campbell, the son of the Fetlar E C minister, in St Columba's Church in November 1906; Louisa married W R Durham, Headteacher at the Central School, at St Columba's in July 1908, and had two children, Alice in 1910 and James in 1911. The information I have about the family has come from Louisa's grandchild, John Durham.

The Leisk family in the gardens of 169 Commercial Street in 1912. Harriet Leisk is dandling her newest grandchild, James; on her left are his mother, Louisa, and her daughter Alice. Alice Leisk sits on the ground beside her mother, with her sister Hattie and Dr Terry Campbell behind her. Bessie and Miles Walker-Pole, on a visit from South Africa, are standing with their daughter, and John Leisk is at the right hand side. Photograph courtesy of John Durham.

(Right) Harriet Leisk in 1915.
Photograph courtesy of John Durham.

Christina Jamieson was appointed Secretary and Treasurer. By this time she had been living in Lerwick for nine years, and so would be well aquainted with the townsfolk in her social circle, which included, as we have seen, the Literary and Debating Club. She also had regular visitors from south; her brothers tended to gather at Twageos House each year, and her brother E B brought a group of lively undergraduates up each summer. A letter quoted in *E B Jamieson* shows a strong friendship with one of Jamie's friends, Dr Washbourn; it was written in 1906, when he was studying medicine in Edinburgh, and preparing to return to his native New Zealand:

I have some difficulty in adjusting myself to the altered conditions of our correspondence, and I fancy too that your metaphysical phase of mind will have altered with your environment, and you will no longer be greatly interested in abstract discussions about life and the various philosophies that help or hinder us in our struggle through it. ... I don't [go on battering my poor head against the unyielding walls of the unknowable] as much as I used to. And working in the garden, playing with little children in the fields and shore and reading good novels have done more than any other agencies I know to save me from states of mind bordering on madness or at least hysteria.

[Ostensibly discussing the possibility of marriage being good for EB] But I refuse to endorse what you say about marriage. Granted that given ideal people it is an ideal state, the majority of married people are not ideal, and, that being so, there is no condition more perfectly adapted for the infliction of mutual unhappiness than marriage. Or if there is not unhappiness, what is taken for happiness is often mere comfort. And one can have comfort without marriage. Marriage is really a condition which only the very strongest love can justify, and that too when other conditions are all perfect. Many marriages are absolutely iniquitous. Besides a man's marriage is often a sign of deterioration. A man will start life with very high and pure ideals, and will make a good fight for a time. Then, finding that high standards don't pay, he will slacken down, lower his whole tone, decide that, as he is sure of no life but the present, he will take all the good out of it that he can, marry comfortably and pass on his failures and complexities to the innocent beings who love and confide in him. He says that he is doing no worse than he had been done to. But there is nothing more dastardly than to pass on a wrong, oftener by a marriage than by anything else. They may be scattered all over the world, and their sense of friendship be unimpaired, they will be in touch whenever they meet. But let their wives be uncongenial ...

Moreover love, though it is most exalting and ennobling and gives one a sense of being in touch with omnipotence, is a 'jealous God', and unless all its demands, which are nigh unappeasable, are fulfilled, it is a bondage, obsession, a pain. One longs for freedom, the serenity of the days when one is not in love. Friendship is far better. It is calm and reasonable and sustaining. Even the best love marriages ultimately resolve themselves into friendship.

Mind you, this is not against marriage. It is against marriage on any grounds other than I have pointed out. So, we shall be delighted to see EB married, if the right wife for him can be found ..

Poor Christina! You wonder what on earth she's been seeing to have so low a view of men and marriage, or whether she's trying to convince herself – and him - that since she can't leave her mother and sister to go to New Zealand with him, or since he hasn't asked her, or since she's twelve years older than him, it would never have worked anyway. She ends the letter with a give-away:

so the Lord be with you
Yours ever sincerely
Christina Jamieson
PS I've reread this and I'd never have the courage to send it, if I didn't know I'll never see you again.

In more characteristic mode, the letter to Louisa Leisk on the next page begins with the feminist and modulates to the kindly and practical, and shows her strong sense of humour, which was to come out so strongly in the 'Girzie' letters to the paper:
(Right) Jamieson's letter to Louisa Leisk. Photograph courtesy of John Durham.

Twagios 24 – 02 - 08

My Dear Miss Leisk,

"It fa's afore me" that I have never properly congratulated you on your approaching marriage. I here offer sincere congratulations. You have attained what humanity persists in regarding as the chief end of women. Mr Durham is to be congratulated on the treasure that is his. As I do not know him yet, I can only trust to your judgement that he is worthy.

And I used to think you so safe and sound in your views of matrimony. I have not heard your defence of your new position, but I suspect that what Chesterton would call a rash and elemental influence has been brought to bear upon you, and it is a state of feeling rather than a process of reasoning that has put you where you are.

There are a few points that to my grudging spinster eye are pleasing. A leap year engagement is always suspicious, and in this case the marriage hurried on before the victim can escape south for the holidays gives grievous occasion for the adversary to blaspheme. But these are minor points. I want to direct attention to what I regard as a burning grievance.

Here is an admirable and eligible bachelor under whom numerous women teachers have rendered faithful and doubtless adoring service for many months. They get their salaries. You come in, work a few weeks, lift ten pounds and annex the head master and "all his worldly goods" in perpetuity, for your services. Where is the equity, the fair play, of this? It seems outside the region of equity and fair play altogether.

Now if you have any lingering sense of sympathy with the devoted army of single women whose ranks you are deserting, you will yield up – not the man – the ten pounds, as a thank-offering for the great unearned increment that has fallen to your lot. You might give an entertainment or a treat with it, or bestow it on a charity, or best of all make it the nucleus of a fund for giving consolation presents to women who fail to achieve matrimony, and who so often nobly yield to others the congratulations and gifts that [they] themselves yearn to receive. I fear me this is the voice of one crying in the wilderness – from the lone green solitudes of Twagios I give tongues, but will you, alas, "add ear"?

And now I know full well how the rest of your life will be shadowed by the codes, departments, institutions, boards, councils, conferences, committees, officials, and all the rest of the ponderous organisations that exist for hampering the energies and embittering and harassing the lives of teachers; and brightened by the merits, excellences, perfections, achievements and triumphs of the one man who is worth, or knows, or can do, anything among it all.

For I know married women and I know that you will be blessed, and that life has no better thing to offer you than the happiness that is now yours.

I'm afraid to read this again, written as it is in a mighty hurry before going out.

Yours ever,

Christina Jamieson

Miss Leisk, Assistant Secretary and Treasurer, was John and Harriet's youngest daughter, Alice Lyall Leisk, who was 23 at that first meeting. She was to marry Hugh Macmichael, born in 1886 in Edinburgh, in St Magnus Church in 1915; a wartime romance, perhaps? They had two sons. Hugh died in Methil, Fife, in 1944, and Alice lived on at 94a George Street. John Durham remembered his great-aunt Alice well: 'She was a formidable lady, with very strong ideas. She was the serious one of the sisters, very out-going and out-spoken – I'm not surprised she was the suffragist.' [Photograph, left, courtesy of John Durham]

The Sandison partners of Leisk and Sandison were also involved, through Harold Sandison's fiancee, **Miss Campbell**. Miss Margaret Davidson (Daisy) Campbell of 54 Burgh Road was the younger sister of Jennie Campbell, Shetland's first woman graduate. She was born in 1889, so would have been 22 or 23 when the SWSS was founded. She married Harold Sandison, Alexander's son, in 1916 but they were only married for a short time when he was killed by a sniper in France. She was a non-graduate teacher of modern languages at the Lerwick Central Public School for many years and lived with her spinster sister Flora who was teacher of English and History at the Anderson Educational Institute. Her nephew, Douglas Smith, still has Daisy Campbell's NUWSS badge. Mr Smith recalled her great sense of fun: 'She and Flora were always laughing. I remember once there was a rumour of drug taking at the school, and she said, 'After I left teaching it all went to pot!' [Photograph, above right, courtesy of Douglas Smith]

Mrs Sandison is most likely to be Elizabeth Emily Atherton, the younger sister of Mrs Leisk, who married Arthur Sandison, Town Clerk of Lerwick, in 1883 (he was brother-in-law to Alexander Sandison, John Leisk's partner). They had four children, William born in 1884, who married Marie Becker; Arthur, born in 1884, who married Florence McLaughlin in 1912; Harriet, born in 1885, who married John Crawford and Emily Charlotte, born in 1890. Emily is very likely the Miss E Sandison who was to be put in charge of the Friends of Suffrage committee in 1914. She married William Grant in 1915. Elizabeth was to be a keen member of the Shetland WSS, attending a large number of committee meetings. [Photograph, left, of Elizabeth Atherton as a girl courtesy of John Durham]

Mrs Laing was Helen Robertson, born in 1855, so of a similar age to Mrs Leisk. Her father, Magnus Robertson, was a shipmaster from Whalsay, her mother was Catherine Smith from Bressay. She was the wife of Arthur L. Laing, Druggist and Chemist, and Christina Jamieson's maternal uncle. He was Provost from 1910 – 1913, and an elder of Rev Campbell's church from 1903 - 7. Their daughter Katherine Winifred, born in 1886, took advantage of the new educational opportunities for women to become a pharmacist, and was one of Shetland's first University graduates; their son Arthur, born in 1888, was a doctor. Mrs Laing may well have been active in the SWSS but did not remain a committee member.

Mrs Harrison was most likely Janet (Jessie) Duncan Robertson, born in 1847, and Helen's older sister. She was the widow of William Bailie Mackenzie Harrison, and lived in Prospect House. W B M Harrison, draper, was the son of Gilbert Harrison, Grocer and Spirit Merchant, and one of the members of the first Harbour Trust; he had been in partnership with his father at the north station in the North Ness. After his death in 1880 his older brother John took over the business as Richmond Harrison & Co. In 1885-6, it was taken over by Arthur H Harrison, the youngest brother, who had considerable interests in mining enterprises in Spain; he had also been appointed the United States Consul for Santander in 1881. William and Janet were married in St Giles Cathedral, Edinburgh, 1870, and had seven children in the next eight years; his death left her with six children under ten. The first two, Gilbert and William, seem to have died young; Magnus, the third, married in Spain (presumably he was offered work there through his uncle). Her only daughter Margaret Ann (Dolly) was also present at the meeting. A second Gilbert also went to Spain; her fifth son, Arthur Henry remained in Shetland as a 'draper's assistant', and her last child, John, married Helena Irvine in 1911; his daughter Helen (Nell) became a teacher. Like her sister, Mrs Harrison did not remain an active SWSS committee member.

There were three Morrison women present at that first meeting, two definitely connected to Hector Morrison of the first Shetland Suffrage Committee. The first, **Mrs Morrison**, is a mystery, as Hector's wife Margaret had died in 1892, and Hector himself died in 1903. It's possible she was the wife of his younger son, John Mackay Morrison. She came only to the inaugural meeting.
The other two were his daughter and daughter-in-law. **Mrs D Morrison** was Hector Morrison's daughter-in-law, Mary Stewart Morrison, wife of his son Donald; she was born in 1874, and her father, the Reverend Charles Dunn, was the minister of Lybster. She came to Shetland in 1899 as a nurse in the Combination Poorhouse – Hector Morrison was then the representative for Walls, and Donald was the representative for Yell. They had two children. Mrs D Morrison resigned from the committee in November 1910.

All three of Hector Morrison's daughters became teachers; his oldest daughter Mary Dow Morrison, born in 1860, was registered on the 1881 Census as a lodger on Bressay, perhaps as an assistant teacher; she taught on Foula, 1882-3. She married William D Freeman in 1883; their one daughter died as a baby. Mrs Freeman crops up later in the Suffrage story. Hector's second daughter, Elizabeth Ann, born in 1863, followed Mary as teacher on Foula, 1883-6. She was back in Lerwick for the 1891 census, teaching in the Central School with Miss Gulland (school dates from *A Vehement Thirst after Knowledge*, John J Graham). She married James Thomas Irvine in 1905. **Miss M M Morrison** was Hector Morrison's youngest daughter, Margaret (Maggie) Miller Morrison, b 1866. We've already followed her learning process: Local Education, Ordinary, in 1880, then English, French, History Honours and German through the L.L.A. scheme, qualifying in 1888. She was teaching French and German at the Institute from before 1892. She was to be a committed member of the SWSS committee, attending almost every meeting.

(Right) Margaret Morrison, photographed by J R Irvine, 1910-1912, courtesy of the Shetland Museum and Archives [J00096].

There were three more teachers at that first meeting, all, like Miss Campbell, from the Central Public School: Miss Gulland, Mrs Nicol and Miss Harrison.

Miss Janet Gulland was born in 1853. She taught at the Parochial School (Hunter's School), then was the first teacher of the new Infant Public School, built in 1875. She remained there until 1900, much of that time as headmistress of the Infant Department. A school inspector said of her: 'We can only repeat what we have frequently said before of the admirable manner in which this school is conducted by Miss Gulland, and the painstaking way in which she brings forth the intelligence of such young minds, without having to use a single harsh word.' [ST 2 July 1881] She was an active member of the local branch of the EIS. She attended almost every committee meeting of the SWSS until her death in 1913.

Mrs. Charlotte Nicol was born in 1863, and was also to be an active member of the committee, attending almost every meeting. She was a large lady who lived near the top of Braewick Road, and, Douglas Smith recalled, she had a reputation for being very strict. The Hostel girls had to walk past her house, and they would keep very quiet, otherwise she would come out and tell them off. The were particularly worried at sledging time of year! Mrs Nicol had come from Banffshire, and taught in the north-east of Scotland before marrying A B Nicol, of the herring merchants Smith & Schultz. He died within a few years of the marriage, and Mrs Nicol resumed teaching. At this point she had been on the staff of the Central School for three years. After her retirement, Mrs Nicol was elected onto the Education Committee (from 1928). She became a Fellow of the EIS, and was to become one of Shetland's first women councillors.

Miss Harrison was Miss Margaret (Dolly) Harrison, born in 1874, was a Central School teacher who lived at home, in Prospect House in Law Lane. She's listed as a pupil-teacher at the Infant School in *Manson's Shetland Almanac* for 1892. She was also remembered as being a strict disciplinarian – during the war she gave English lessons to the newly enlisted soldiers, some of whom were barely literate, and I heard a story of the soldiers shivering outside the Hall, scared to go in. Like Mrs Nicol, she attended almost every committee meeting of the SWSS.

(Right): Dolly Harrison. Photograph courtesy of the Shetland Museum and Archive [JS00347, detail].

Miss Mitchell and **Miss J Mitchell** were two of the daughters of Alexander Mitchell, Agent for the Union Bank, and sisters of Alexander Mitchell solicitor, who lived at Southness House, just opposite where Twageos house stood. There were three Miss Mitchells; the oldest, Mary Ross Mitchell, was born in 1859, and was listed in the 1901 Census as a Music Teacher. The next, Jessie Thomson Mitchell, born in 1863, gave her occupation as 'Typewriter'; the third sister, Isabella, born in 1869, married Andrew Leslie of Dunrossness in 1904. A fourth daughter, Jeanie Scott Mitchell, died as a baby. Mary Mitchell attended only the inaugural meeting, but Jessie remained a committee member . Mary and Jessie Mitchell died within six months of each other in 1942.

Miss E. Allison was probably Ethel Allison, born in 1891, and so only 18. She was the youngest of four daughters of Captain George Allison of Dunrossness, Lerwick's first Harbourmaster. Captain Allison was an elder of the 'Muckle Kirk', and gifted a communion chair in the 1890s refurbishment; he died in 1915. His other daughters were Lilly, born in 1878, who married Thomas Stout, chemist, Commercial Street in 1903, and had one son; Annie, born in 1883, who married widower Arthur Murray in 1938; and Jeannie, born in 1885, who married Walter Sloan in August 1914. Ethel also had two brothers, George, born in 1852, died in 1900, and Arthur, born in 1887, who died in Sydney. Ethel was to marry Major John Garriock in August 1917; he died 'of wounds received' in April 1918, in France.

There were two nurses present, **Nurse Hay** and **Nurse Esplin**. Nurse Hay was listed from 1908 to 1912 as the Nurse at the Combination Poorhouse; Nurse Esplin was the Matron of the Lerwick Combination Hospital from 1909 to 1912. Neither of them seems to have been a Shetlander, and neither was on the SWSS committee.

The lone man present, **Mr. Tulloch**, would have been William Arthur Alexander Tulloch of Leog, known as Consul Billy because he was German vice-Consul in Shetland. He was a partner of Laurenson & Co with Mr Peter Laurenson, in a hosiery, drapery, millinery and dressmaking business. His mother was Jane Inches Laurenson, sister of the Arthur Laurenson who was responsible for the Town Hall windows, and aunt of Barbara Laing, Christina Jamieson's mother, making 'Consul Billy' Christina's second cousin. Tulloch's sister Catherine was the last of the family to live at Leog House - she died in 1953, and willed it to the Zetland County Council. As clerk of the Harbour Trust for many years, W A A Tulloch would have worked closely with John Leisk and Captain Allison.

Meetings of the Executive Committee were generally held at 169 Commercial Street; larger meetings were often in the Rechabite Hall. The Minutes are written in a flowing, confident hand, Jamieson's, and countersigned 'Harriet Leisk'.

169/171 Commercial Street, Lerwick, in the 1970s. Leisk and Sandison was the house in the centre of the picture, with the dormer window. The committee meetings of the SWSS were generally held here. Photograph courtesy of Shetland Museum and Archives [SM00688]

The *Shetland News* of 30th November contains a wonderful letter from 'Aald Geordie', railing against the cause as hard as any 'Current Topics' author. Allowing women MPs? That would cause chaos in the House of Commons, for

'..dey canna bear to be kontradiktid, an if ye daur ta spaek against whit dey say, dey're as dorty an tirn as can be. ... Weemin ir no fittid ta tak parit in politics because dey haena brains fir hit ... her wark is at hame attendin ta da hoose wark, da cradle an da typot. Maist o dis suffragists ir weemin id haena muckle wark to du, ir dan he's puirly attendid till.'

Aald Geordie and his wife, Girzie, are clearly a joint production. They pretended to be an old country couple. I'm pretty certain that Jamieson herself was Girzie; the vigorous style, the humour, the one-paragraph statements and sentences beginning 'And' are all repeated in her other writing, and she's the only one in the group who had the country experience. I'd love to think that J J Haldane Burgess was the other, but it could equally well have been E S Reid Tait, or any one of a number of dialect writers. A third writer was to be introduced during Jamieson's illness of 1913-14, when Girzie's place was taken by Baabie Ringinson. Geordie and Girzie reappear in Peter Jamieson's *The Shetlander* in February and March 1923. Their characters had changed, though: Aald Shoordy was arguing with the minister, and Girzie was a very conformable wife, here addressed by her formal name of Mrs Twatt.

Auld Geordie was just repeating the arguments of the time, as used by Cathcart Wason and others, so I'm not sure how immediately obvious it was that he was 'a fun'. Anyone who didn't get the joke would have seen it with Auld Girzie's reply a week later:

' ... An we canna bide contradiction! O whin I tink o da years o contradiction A'm pitten up wi fae dat sinner!' As for women being weaker, 'I nivver fin it said at A'm weaker in mind or boady whin der wark ta du ...'

Lady Stout's letter to *The Times:*

Sir Robert and Lady Stout were in London by October, staying at 64, Lancaster Gate, Hyde Park. As well as launching her daughter into society, Lady Stout made contact with a number of leading suffrage workers. The bundle of letters preserved in the Hocken Collections, Uare Takoa o Hakena, New Zealand [MS0257, Lady Anna Stout papers] all date from November 1909, and concern a letter on the effects of women's suffrage in New Zealand which Lady Stout sent to the London press, and which newspapers initially refused to print:

Sir: Since landing in England last April, I have heard many misleading statements as to the results of the women's franchise in New Zealand. As a native of New Zealand, and one who has been associated with political, social, education and philanthropic societies for thirty years, I think I can claim full knowledge of the subject. With your kind permission I should like to summarize and reply to several of those statements.

1. That women would adopt masculine habits. - No woman, except those of the most abandoned class, is ever seen entering an hotel bar in New Zealand; I have never seen a New Zealand woman smoking; ... Our women play bridge, but usually for prizes, seldom for money. ...

2. That women do not take a broad view of the Empire. - They have been addressing meetings and signing petitions in favour of compulsory military training for men and universal ambulance training for women. ...

3. Women would be treated with discourtesy if they descended from their pedestals as domestic angels and mixed in the rough and tumble of political life. All our experience during fifteen years of of political enfranchisement has proved that women are treated with greater courtesy than in Britain – even in the excitement and strain of election night any woman or girl can mingle with our crowds and be certain of receiving every courtesy and protection. ... Our girl students have equal representation in University, social and athletic unions, and receive the whole-hearted plaudits of their male comrades untinged with jealousy when they achieve any special distinction in scholarship.

Women preside at political meetings, and their ruling is never questioned; they sign nomination papers for candidates and move votes of vonfidence etc. ...

4. That women do not want the vote and do not exercise the privilege. ... In New Zealand the petitions in favour of the franchise never exceeded 30,000 names, but 100,161 women immediately enrolled, and at the first election 73.18 per cent of those enrolled voted. ... The average vote of women to men in 1908 was 79 to 80. ...

5. That women would neglect their homes and children. ... New Zealand women are ... developing a new sense of responsibility of citizenship, which is exemplified by the organization of societies for the promotion of the health of women and children, the objects of which are to "save the babies" and train girls and women in intelligent motherhood. ... We can show the highest marriage rate of any European or English-speaking country except Hungary; a higher birth-rate except Italy, the Netherlands and two Australian states...; and the lowest illegitimacy rate except England, Ireland and the Netherlands; the lowest infant mortality rate in the world.

6. That women would be priest-ridden. – Our education system is free, compulsory and secular, and, in spite of strenuous efforts on the part of certain churches, the women's vote has upheld the system, as they appreciate the benefits their children receive from the absence of sectarian strife.

7. That the vote would cause discord in domestic life. Well, no one has, during 15 years, found a case to prove the statement. ... But in New Zealand we do not profess to be angels, but only intelligent women, who exercise the right to differ from our "lords and masters" occasionally, when it is good for their souls as well as for the benefit of our children and the Dominion.

8. That women's votes would be influenced by their emotions, and that a handsome face and charming manner would tell more than arguments ... I have never heard of a case where a handsome or charming candidate won an election by these qualifications ... women have a keener insight into character than men, and are less influenced by party feelings.

9. That women are not so loyal to their sex as men. – Here women never organized societies to oppose the franchise. Even those who were afraid of the possible results of the franchise were too loyal to their sisters to oppose what was looked forward to with hope by others as a means of advancement in social reform ...

Experience has proved that the women's vote does not cause any revolution, though it steadily improves the conditions of life for the women and children... The comradeship which subsists between the sexes engenders mutual respect, and ensures a strong, industrious and enterprising race, with high ideas of the duties of citizenship and loyalty to the Empire.

I am confident that no one who is conversant with the social and economic conditions of the Dominion, but will bear me out in the assertion that "votes for women" has been an unqualified success in New Zealand.' [Reprinted as from 'a recent issue of the London "Times", *Shetland News* 4 December 1909]

Stout presumably sent a copy of the letter to each of the suffrage societies. One reply was from Millicent Garrett Fawcett, now President of the NUWSS. Fawcett's letter suggested that Lady Stout was already showing sympathy with the militants. It was formal in tone, and gave details of a recent NUWSS quarterly council meeting in which two resolutions were passed, one condemning militant behaviour, and the other condemning the way the Government had reacted. It ended by saying she would keep Lady Stout's interesting letter on the effects of women's suffrage in New Zealand.

The first of WSPU member Lady Constance Lytton's letters was in much friendlier vein, and spoke of Lady Stout having been

'treated shamefully – tho alas! it is only too typical of the press throughout the country. The *Times* has been much better lately. If you will send me your letter I will ask my brother to sent it to *The Times*. I am sure he will gladly do so, for he has been scandalised of late at the press boycott and libels.'

She ends by hoping to meet Lady Stout in London in December. Her next letter, on 7 November, said that her brother was very glad to talk to *The Times*' editor, and

'your letter may possibly have appeared already. Would you kindly send a wire to Lord Lytton saying 'My letter has appeared' or 'My letter has not appeared.'

There was a letter of 9 November from the *Times* editor, G L Buckle, to Lord Lytton, saying that he hoped to find room for the letter.

There was a letter from Mabel Tuke, the Honorary Secretary for the WSPU and a close friend of Emmeline and Christabel Pankhurst, dated 17 November. She mentions Lady Stout visiting on Sunday, and obviously hopes to get her to endorse militant methods:

'The history of the movement is one of blind trust & misplaced faith on the part of women and trickery on that of politicians who hoodwinked and deceived them right through. That is where <u>we</u> score. Our Leaders know the political game and can play it with success –... Dear Lady Stout, do you think you could make a little speech for us, perhaps one Thursday evng will you think it over & let me know.'

Lady Stout's letter appeared in *The Times* on 19 November, and immediately Margery Corbett of 'The Younger Suffragists' wrote asking if their newly-formed group could re-print it as a pamphlet:

'It is such a splendidly conclusive answer to so many common 'anti' allegations that we feel it should have a permanent place in Suffrage literature.'

Corbett was the daughter of the Liberal MP for East Grinstead, and Secretary of the NUWSS from 1907-1909. Her mother Marie was one of the first women poor law Guardians, and the first woman district councillor, for Uckfield. Margery Corbett shared her mother's interest in working class children, and in 1906 and 1907 had helped run vacation classes for Hull dockside children.

A letter dated 24 November from A M Foster of the Leeds Branch of the NUWSS asked for Lady Stout's help in refuting allegations against Women's suffrage in New Zealand. Forster's correspondent was particularly incensed against the temperance work of the women there, and asserted that 'drunkenness has increased 107%... He also stated that the colony was full of hatred, bitterness, underhand dealing etc.'

Lady Constance's next letter, dated 25 November, said 'Your letter was splendid. I have heard so much approval of it.' She had been ill from a neglected cold; she had spent part of October in prison for throwing a stone at a car she believed to contain Lloyd George.

The pamphlet must have been printed quickly, for Lady Constance's next letter, dated 27 November and signed Conny Lytton, began,

'What a supremely good leaflet. I am ordering many copies. And Ld Crewe had the face to tell the Women's Deputation that where women have the vote they don't show an interest in public affairs!' Lytton was still not completely well, but 'Prison itself is not so wearing as the ignorance, indifference & prejudice of people when one comes out.'

Mrs Janet Ashbee, of Woolstaplers' Hall, Clipping Campden, was equally enthusiastic:

'Please accept my thanks for your splendid letter in the *Times* – I have cut it out, and it will be the greatest help to me in convincing provincial opponents – Your arguments seem to me unanswerable.'

On 30th November, a letter from Frederick Pethick-Lawrence, one of the co-editors of the WSPU newspaper *Votes for Women*, asked for permission to reproduce extracts from her letter to make a leaflet.

The Lady Stout controversy:

Fun with Geordie and Girzie had to be set aside when the women of the society read the *Shetland Times* of 4 December. It contained a brief article that threatened to be very damaging to the new Shetland WSS. An indignant Shetlander in New Zealand had sent the Editor a cutting from the *Wellington Evening Post* of 18th October, in which Lady Stout appeared to speak disparagingly of Shetland and Shetlanders:

'In driving down to the quay Sir Robert and Lady Stout passed through the waterside slums, which were awful, and the women there too dreadful to look at. The laziness and shiftlessness of Shetland crofters much impressed Lady Stout, who marvelled that any crops or vegetables could grow under such conditions, for weeds abound, and this disorder is awful. No attempt is made to make the surroundings of the cottages even decently tidy, and no beautifying is ever done. The contrast between the neatness, charm and order of even the smallest cottage in Switzerland contrasted keenly with the dirt, squalor and depression of Shetland farms.

The women too have a hard life. Old women whose life work should have been completed, having only rest and comfort at the fireside, dig peats and carry them home on their backs, and many spend the whole day digging in the field. Women were seen by Lady Stout when in Germany guiding the cow that dragged the plough that the man drove, but she never saw women there doing degrading work, nor acting as beasts of burden, as do the Shetland women. Indeed, there they seem to do all the hard work, all the farming, peat-carrying, and digging, while the men are fishing. New Zealand women have an enviable time in comparison with their sisters in other lands.'

Shetlanders were incensed at such comments from a visitor who had been treated as an honoured guest. Angry letters followed in the *Shetland Times* of the following weeks – the indignation continued until October 1910, with letters still coming in from Shetlanders resident abroad - and there were calls for the new SWSS to remove Lady Stout from her post as their president. Perhaps the new committee felt itself at a loss under this sudden storm, for there was no immediate reply from them in the letters pages. While Girzie said, 'Da Loard iver bliss Lady Stout at's had da courage to spaek da truth' and backed her up in her comment on the unremitting toil of the Shetland countrywoman's life (something Jamieson would certainly have known about), public indignation was focused on Lady Stout's accusation of laziness, and her calling the Lerwick cottages 'slums'. On 25th December, three weeks later, there was a short letter from Jamieson in both the *Times* and the *News*, asking 'why none of Sir Robert and Lady Stout's letters giving favourable and commendable opinions of Shetland have been forwarded to you for local publication?'

Her letter is followed, in both papers, by one from Earl Cromer, President of the newly-formed Men's League for Opposing Women's Suffrage.

The Shetland suffragists rallied their supporters, and tried to focus on what was accurate in the description. On 1st January, 'Justice for all' made the point that 'To Lady Stout, the existing conditions in Shetland and the wretched hovels which do happen to still exist in Lerwick would certainly come as a shocking surprise.'

Angus Park asked the *Times* to publish all Lady Stout's accounts. However a further *Shetland Times* article taken allegedly from an interview with Sir Robert Stout in London had him patronising his wife and ridiculing the suffrage cause: '... all the more disgrace to the English people who give money to such a cause.' Given his record, such a comment seems improbable.

Between 1 and 8 January 1910, Jamieson must have heard from Lady Stout, for on 8 January she wrote to the *Shetland Times* speaking of a 'garbled statement confusing Lerwick and Glasgow'. Lady Stout had a long letter in the *Shetland News,* making it clear that the original article was deliberately tampered with. The comments were from a private letter to her son, and the statement describing the houses as 'slums' was taken from her description of Glasgow, not Lerwick. She enclosed the rest of her description of their stay in Shetland, which was entirely positive. Jamieson followed this with a letter from Lady Stout published in *The Dominion*, also very positive. There were further letters in the *Shetland News* and *Shetland Times* of 2nd April – at least this time the Editor allowed, in a footnote, that the 'slums' were in Glasgow, and in the *Shetland Times* of 16th April, followed by a request for correction from Lady Stout. Unfortunately her letter arrived too late for that week's press, and one suspects the editor was delighted to publish her tart rebuke at it not immediately appearing.

Whether or not the Lady Stout controversy was a deliberate smear by the 'dirty tricks brigade' to damage the women's suffrage cause, as she herself believed, cannot now be determined. Her increasingly public profile as one well qualified to speak on the success of women's franchise in New Zealand certainly could have made her a target. The reported comments must have made life difficult for the new society, which had to share the indignation directed at her.

The parlour of 169 Commercial Street, photographed by John Leisk in 1897. The committee meetings of the 1909 Shetland Women's Suffrage Society took place here.
Photograph courtesy of John Durham.

9

1910 – March 1912

The Conciliation Bills
some scriptural correspondence,
the Women's Coronation Procession,
and the first real destruction by the militants

The first election of 1910:

While all this was going on, there was an election to be fought. Lloyd George's 'People's Budget' had been blocked by Conservative peers in the Lords, and as it was unprecedented for the Lords to interfere with finance bills, this provoked a constitutional crisis which forced a general election. Suffrage workers across the country made it a matter of pride to post 'Votes for Women' across every election poster, WSPU and WFL members gained entrance to halls, and speakers were asked what they intended to do about women's suffrage.

The SWSS's third meeting was a Special General Meeting to discuss their conduct in the General Election. It was held on 16 December 1909 in the Rechabite Hall. There were sixteen women present, including some new supporters: Mrs Ramsay (wife of the photographer, who was also one of Rev Campbell's elders) along with what is probably her sister, Miss [Jemima Catherine] Spence, Miss Donaldson and Miss Manson (perhaps Hilda Manson, daughter of Thomas Manson of the *Shetland News;* she was to marry Miss Campbell's brother in 1923, and knew the Leisk girls well, through school and the orchestra). The SWSS could not send a delegate to the council meeting of the Scottish Federation, but donated £1 to the election fund. The Society decided on what were to become regular tactics: Mr Wason, in London, was to be written to, but Mr Hewsley of the Unionist Party was to be in Lerwick later that month and Mrs Leisk, Mrs Nicol and Miss Jamieson were to interview him on the subject.

The minutes end with a Note whose handwriting suggests that Jamieson was unimpressed: 'The reply of both men being *unfavourable* (crossed out) unsatisfactory, no further action was taken *in the matter* (crossed out) to support either candidate.'

As part of their campaign of persuasion, Jamieson had a two-part article entitled *The Women of Shetland* in both the *Shetland Times* and the *Shetland News* of 22 and 29 January 1910. The first part of the article focused on the importance of their men to Shetland women, and how their lives were focused around them; the second part detailed their keeness to improve their lives, and the importance of the equal moral standard in Shetland. She ended by stressing the support of Shetland men for their women:

'It is quite true that many of the menfolk, in the self-complacency fostered by the uncritical adoration of these same women, take the work of the women for granted, and quite overlook its value. Still, the general feeling of equality is such that Shetland men as a rule 'don't see why women soodna vot'.'

She replied to the criticism that the suffrage movement was led by the middle classes with a comparison between the much-praised brotherhood of man and the emerging sisterhood of women:

'Educated and wealthy women are putting forth more and more efforts on behalf of their toiling sisters, whose bondage to necessity prevents them from striving for their own freedom.'

Norwegian and Finnish women had been granted the vote in 1908; Jamieson finished resoundingly:

'Will not the men of Shetland show themselves worthy of their kinship to those free descendants of the old Norse Vikings whom they yearly unite in commemorating?'

Her words were later echoed by A MAN:

'The apathy of Shetland men on this question has greatly surprised me ... Unquestionably Shetland men owe more to their women than any class of men I know. But for the unwearying toil of Shetland mothers and daughters, two-thirds of the crofts would never be worked ... let the men now exercise that spirit of chivalry which distinguished their Norse ancestors [spirit of chivalry, the Vikings?], and use their influence to enable their women to obtain the freedom to which they are entitled. [*SN* 1 October 1910]

Jamieson's article would have been deliberately timed to come out around Sir Cathcart Wason's address to a well-attended meeting. His patronising comments explain Jamieson's exasperation in the minutes:

'I don't think it would be fair to the women of this country to throw this enormous burden on them ... I have no reason to believe the women of this country desire this extra labour and responsibility ... Let the Government introduce a Bill referring this matter to the women by means of a referendum.'

Mr W Sinclair, the socialist who had asked about women's suffrage in August, was applauded when he asked if Wason had not been an ardent supporter of women's suffrage in New Zealand; Wason's reply was,

'I don't think so ... It was so long ago I can scarcely remember. (Laughter) I have certainly lived to know better.'

Although 'a good many ladies' were mentioned as being present, there's no record of any asking questions, and they certainly didn't make any disturbance; the disruption tactics now in regular use down south weren't being used here in Shetland.

For the first time, women's suffrage is specifically mentioned in a Shetland election manifesto. Wason said:

'Though personally I am opposed to the extension of the Suffrage for women, I an content to rest the case as put by Mr Gladstone: At least it should be ascertained that the womanly mind of the country is, in overwhelming proportions and with deliberate purpose, set on securing it. In view of the division of opinion on the subject, I would vote for referring the question to the women of Great Britain, and be content to abide by the result.' [*ST* 5 February 1910]

The election of January 1910 produced a hung parliament. The Liberals lost 123 seats, but returned to power with just two more MPs than the Conservative and Liberal Unionist Parties. This persuaded Asquith's government to bring in the Conciliation Bill, drawn up by a cross-party group, and offering women's suffrage for an estimated one million unmarried women who passed the property qualification. It was introduced by David Shackleton (Labour MP for Clitheroe), and passed without a division. In response, the WSPU declared a truce on militancy, and arrests ceased for the time being.

By May the Conciliation Bill had still made no progress. The death of the King on 7 May meant that all other Parliamentary business was set aside, and the Conciliation Bill was brought forward again. Asquith had originally said there was no time to discuss it further, but after a ten-thousand strong procession, on 18 June, followed by a deputation from leading suffragists and anti-suffragists on 21 June, he announced that 11 and 12 July would be given as discussion dates. Part of the procession was captured on a still extant Pathé film, which shows suffragettes who had been in prison carrying 'arrows', and graduates in their gowns.

A further procession procession was organized by the WSPU on 23 July, the anniversary of the day in 1867 when men agitating for the Reform Bill pulled down the railings in Hyde Park. This was to have been in conjunction with the NUWSS, but suffragists felt it impossible to work with the militants. Lady Stout was the contact for the WSPU's New Zealand contingent: 'Lady Cockburn and Lady Stout will again receive the names of Australians and New Zealanders...' [*Votes for Women,* 8 July 1910] Subsequent editions gave a map of the 40 platforms, and lists of speakers. Lady Stout was to speak on Platform 35, New Zealand and Australia, chaired by Miss Margaret Hodge, the principal of a large girls' training school in Sydney, and the Vice-Principal of the Women's Political and Educational League in Australia. Lady Stout was the first speaker, followed by Dr Robert Chappell, now MP for Stirlingshire, and a former New Zealand MP. The next speaker was Mrs Mary Gaunt, 'a literary woman who has written much on Australia', and the last was Mr Deacon – no details are given on him. [*Votes for Women* 22 July 1910]

Miss Lamond's visit, July 1910:

Links between the Shetland society and key people in the wider movement continued. The Scottish Federation of Women's Suffrage Societies within the NUWSS had had its first council on 27 November 1909, and the SWSS joined in July 1910. One of its organisers, Miss Lamond, came immediately to hold meetings. Wilhelmina Hay Lamond, born in Scotland in 1883, had attended the University College, London, then trained as a secretary/accountant. She became organizer for the Edinburgh WSS in 1909. In 1911, she was to marry an English war correspondant and travel writer, George Abbott. They had one son.

The *Shetland Times* of 9 July announced forthcoming meetings in Sandwick, Baltasound, Uyeasund, Symbister, Burravoe, Mid Yell, Bressay, Lerwick and Scalloway, and gave an account of her first 'crowded meeting' in the Old Schoolhouse, Fair Isle:

'An interesting discussion followed, but no dissentient voice was raised ... Miss Lamond left the island feeling it was 'fair' in every sense of the word.' [*ST* 9 July 1910]

The following week gave a report of the meeting in Lerwick Town Hall, attended by 150 people, and even the *Shetland Times* allowed that 'The speech was one of the most effective that has been heard in the Town Hall for some time.' The meeting was chaired by Bailie A L Laing, Jamieson's uncle, who said he was 'in entire sympathy with the object of the meeting.', and the resolution of support was to be sent to Mr Asquith and Mr Wason. The *Shetland Times* described Miss Lamond's visit to Whalsay:

'There was a fair turn-out, mostly of ladies, the men being at sea.' [*ST* 23 July 1910]

Miss Lamond stayed at Twagios House while in Lerwick, and the expenses of her visit were paid by Jamieson's brother, John Kay, now Professor of Anatomy at Leeds University.

One of the things Lamond and Jamieson must have discussed was the progress of the Conciliation Bill. In spite of fierce opposition from Asquith, Churchill and Lloyd George, the Bill had been carried by 109 votes. However, given a choice between a standing committee or a committee of the whole house, meaning the Bill would have to wait its turn among other bills, the House voted for the latter by 145 votes. As Miss Lamond said in her Lerwick speech,

'the House of Commons had referred the Conciliation Bill last night to a Committee of the whole House, thereby killing it.'

It was an intense disappointment, when victory must have seemed assured, and suffragists like Lamond and Jamieson must also have been extremely apprehensive as to whether the truce with the WSPU would hold under these circumstances, and what the effect on the suffrage cause would be if there was to be more militant action. For the moment, though, the WSPU waited for the report of the committee, and joint WSPU and NUWSS meetings were held in Hyde Park and on Calton Hill, Edinburgh. Closer to home, the Lerwick Town Council gave a resolution in support of the Bill.

On 8 October 1910 there was a letter from Jamieson, explaining the provisions of the Conciliation Bill, and pointing out Wason's part in its demise:

'It is estimated that it would enfranchise over a thousand women in Shetland, every one of whom is a worker, and responsible for a household.

Mr Wason voted against this Bill, and wholly ignored its existence in his last address to his constituents, many of who had appealed to him to support it.

And the electors tamely accept such contemptuous treatment of a matter in which their women folks, expecially those of Lerwick, are keenly interested, and which has been favourably discussed in many a household.

Is there really, after all, A Man in Lerwick, or even in Shetland ? - Yours, etc, The Secretary, Shetland Women's Suffrage Society.' [*ST, SN* 8 October 1910]

Adult suffrage vs women's suffrage:

A comment at the start of Jamieson's letter, saying that 'adult suffragists would see all men enfranchised before any women' sparked off an indignant retort from E S Reid Tait, pointing out that

'adult suffragists (in contradistinction to woman suffragists, who demand the enfranchisement of a limited number of women only) demand the immediate enfranchisement of all adults, both male and female.' [*ST*, 15 October 1910]

Reid Tait's tone was courteous, and given the Socialists' propensity for writing letters to the paper to keep the pot boiling, and his later association with Jamieson over the Shetland Folklore Society, one does wonder if this correspondence was a collaboration. I don't think so, though; it gets quite heated.

On the same date, a longer letter from ADULT SUFFRAGIST appeared in the *Shetland News*. It criticised Jamieson for

'sins of commission and ommission ... the Secretary misrepresented the the objects of adult suffragists ... the Secretary fails to inform working-class women that the majority of them will be excluded from the franchise under the conciliation Bill ... Removal of sex disability, indeed! ... Why should it be removed for the mistress, and not for the poor, hard-working domestic servant?' The writer ended by regretting that the three Socialist members of the Town Council had supported the motion in favour of the Conciliation Bill 'by voice and vote'. [*SN*, 15 October 1910]

Day by Day, the *Shetland News* equivalent of Current Topics (it also seemed to include letters, although there was a letters page too), was equally critical:

'... the bulk of the suffragists themselves have no real belief in ... the cause. ... [woman] does not gain in influence or power by voting. At best, she votes as her menfolk do. At worst she is victimised into supporting some crank who appeals to her hysteria more than to her judgement. ... Woman's value is so closely associated with the home that away from a home, or without hope of a home, she is a lost unit ... ' [*SN* 15 October 1910]

Jamieson's tart reply to Reid Tait and 'Adult Suffragist' appeared in the next issue of the *Shetland News:*

' ... In view of the fact that adult suffragists admit, when driven to it, that they would accept Manhood Suffrage on the way to Adult Suffrage, I adhere to my statement ... How would Adult Suffragists feel and act about sex disability if existing political advantages were held only by women? ... Let them ... refuse to exercise their right to vote until that right has been conferred on every adult. Then they can come and talk to and about Women Suffragists. – Yours etc' [*SN* 22 October 1910]

E S Reid Tait replied the following week, defending his paraphrase of Jamieson's letter, and answering her last point:

' ... Surely the Secretary of the S.W.S.S. must see, if she carries her statement to its logical conclusion, that in order to be consistent also all women should abstain from using the municipal vote until they have obtained the parliamentary vote?' [*SN* 29 October 1910]

Jamieson's reply chopped logic with him:

' ... Men are very generally enfranchised already. Even if the demand of Adult Suffragists were at once granted, the last man and the first woman would be simultaneously enfranchised. All men would really be enfranchised before any woman. ... Should they not seek to keep women abreast with them all the way?

To be an adult is not to be under a disqualification. An adult, plus a qualification, may vote.

To be a woman is to be under a disability. A woman, plus even a qualification, may not vote.

She is therefore not politically recognised as an adult.

An essential condition preliminary to adult suffrage would be the established political recognition of the fact that women are adults.

This condition can only be secured by the removal of sex disability.

Women Suffragists work for the removal of this disability. Do Adult Suffragists help them?

Are not Adult Suffragists then doubly inconsistent? I am, etc, ' [*SN* 5 November 1910]

C.S. (the new member, Jemima Catherine Spence?) sent a cutting from the *Common Cause* with a more plausible comment from Sir Robert Stout on what he felt the franchise has done for New Zealand women:

' ... its beneficial effect on the women themselves ... their intelligence, their mental horizon and their range of their sympathies have widened, and ... their aspirations, thought and interests have been raised to a higher plane.' [*SN* 5 November 1910]

The Annual Meeting of 5 November 1910 recorded twenty-three members present, although Jamieson's report ended by saying membership had doubled [ie to nearly forty]. None of the members felt confident enough to speak publicly, but Jamieson gave details of their activities: distribution of suffrage literature to the Reading Room and in local booksellers, and personal debate to spread their message. Lady Stout had raised awareness of the issue by letters in the *Shetland Times* (she certainly had!) and 'The Town Council of Lerwick had unanimously passed a resolution in favour of women's suffrage. All honour to the Town Council! (Applause!)'

The AGM was reported at further length in the *Shetland Times* of 12 November. After Jamieson's report of the Society's activities through the year, Miss Leisk read an account of the National Union's work. She explained the three main Suffrage societies, and cited the case of Miss Pankhurst, who qualified as a barrister, yet was not allowed to practise.

'[The Pankhursts'] methods brought into public prominence the movement that had been quietly proceeding for forty years. Unfortunately the notice thus secured was not always favourable, for the public confounded militancy with Suffragism. But, by advertising the movement the militants gave us a great impetus. ... in a few months during last year the thirty-nine Societies of our Union rose to a hundred, and now this year we number two hundred active Societies ... the public man who turns with aversion from the militants, confounding their tactics with their aims, finds himself confronted by a great united body of law-abiding, home-keeping, peaceful, reasonable women, who make the same demand as the militants.'

She suggested the Conciliation Bill might yet be passed through Committee if 'Women Suffragists sufficiently exert themselves' and ended on a positive note by looking forward to the 'great Suffrage Festival to be held in Edinburgh in May.' [*ST* 12 Nov 1910]

November 4th – 11th 1910 was Suffrage Week, marked by a number of meetings. Resumed militancy was announced at the WSPU meeting in the Albert Hall on 10 November, after Asquith had 'vetoed' the Conciliation Bill. An NUWSS meeting was held there two days later, presided over by Mrs Fawcett, and telegrams were received from two newly-elected women mayors, Mrs Lees in Oldham and Miss Morgan in Brecon.

Lady Stout's connections with the WSPU continued. On 17 October 1910 she had spoken at one of their regular Monday afternoon meetings in the Queen's Hall, Langham Place, London, at 3pm, on the success of women's franchise in New Zealand. She referred particularly to the lowering of the infant mortality rate, quoting the statistics which Christina Jamieson was to use in her AGM account of November 1911. [*Votes for Women*, 21 October 1910] Lady Stout spoke again on Monday 5 December 1910, refuting a letter by Lord Glasgow in the *Times*, in which he claimed women's suffrage in New Zealand had been a disaster. Lady Stout pointed out that Lord Glasgow had not been in New Zealand for fourteen years. She was not advertised as a speaker for that meeting, and so may only have commented from the floor. [*Votes for Women*, 9 December 1910]

This was followed by an article in *Votes for Women*. Lady Stout emphasised that New Zealand had the highest marriage rate of the colonies, and an increasing birth rate. She went into detail about working conditions, emphasising that there was no sweated labour in New Zealand, as there was in this country; the miminum women's wage of 5s a week at 16 was increased by 3s yearly to a minimum of £1 at the age of 21. In New Zealand factories, men and women workers were given equal wages for equal work. Women and boys could not do night work, nor a day longer than 8 hours, and they were given a half day holiday per week. Women could not labour longer than 45 hours in a week, and men not longer than 48. [*Votes for Women*, 23 December 1910]

'Black Friday', 18 November 1910:

Difficulties between Asquith's Liberal government and the Conservative-dominated House of Lords had continued through the year, and to get over this Asquith had persuaded the old King to create a number of new Liberal peers after another general election. A further disagreement between the Commons and the Lords persuaded the new King this was necessary. Asquith consulted King George V on 11 November 1910; a dissolution was expected immediately, and suffrage workers feared that if the Conciliation Bill was not named as one of the Bills to be carried forward to the next Parliament, it would be lost. They were right to be concerned; on 17 November, Asquith announced the dissolution of Parliament without any mention of a future Bill for women's enfranchisement. The following day WSPU members marched to the House of Commons in groups of a dozen. The first group included Mrs Pankhurst, Dr Elizabeth Garrett Anderson and her daughter, Louisa. Lady Stout was also present, so Jamieson's account of the demonstration in the Shetland press could well have come from her. Asquith, as always, refused to meet them. The women were manhandled by the police, supported by East End toughs. Later, they spoke of being flung down, of their arms being twisted, and of being pulled aside by men who attempted to assault them. Mounted policemen rode at them. More than 100 were arrested, and those who were deemed to have behaved violently were sentenced to a month in Holloway.

A *Memorandum* forwarded by the Parliamentary Conciliation Committee for Women's Suffrage to the Home Office makes horrifying reading. It gives statements by women of the way they were treated, including being struck on the head, flung to the ground, hurled at a lamp-post, having an arm twisted and being struck on the back. A number of women had a thumb bent backward; one spoke of a policeman forcing a finger up her nostril. The women were also sexually humiliated; several had their breasts fondled while they were being held, and one girl was forced to walk with her skirts held above her head. Several mentioned plain-clothes policemen helping the uniformed police; one spoke of a man who protested against the way she was being treated and was told not to interfere by the plain-clothes men. The women making the statements included a lady of 70 and a disabled lady on a hand-tricycle. It's not surprising that Winston Churchill decided not to take the matter further. [Copy of *Memorandum*, National Library of Scotland, Janie Allen papers] Churchill also announced, in March, that there would be no enquiry into police conduct on 'Black Friday'. The women complaining of injury, he said, should have charged the police at the time. [*Votes for Women*, 3 March 1911]

Press coverage was generally sympathetic to the women, and there was public outrage at published photos of police striking unarmed women. The *Daily Mail*'s front-page photograph of a woman flung on the ground was suppressed as soon as ministers saw it, but by then the general public had also seen it, and read the accompanying interviews. Two women were reputed to have died as a result of police violence. Mrs Pankhurst's sister, Mary Clarke, died of a heart-attack on Christmas day, two days after her release from prison, and her obituary in *Votes for Women* described her as the first suffrage martyr. The second woman, Henria Williams, died of heart failure the following week. Lady Stout could well have known both women, as they were WSPU organizers. Henria Williams' coffin was draped in the WSPU colours.

An extant Pathé newsreel film shows 'Suffragette Riots at Westminster – Scenes in the disturbance in Parliament Square caused by Militant Suffragettes'; a crowd of black-clad men (not all policemen) seem to swamp women carrying banners.

On 10 December, the Shetland papers published a letter from Jamieson which showed a good deal of sympathy with the militants. She detailed what had been done by way of constitutional agitation in support of the Conciliation Bill:

' ... Since the middle of July, no less than 4220 meetings have been held throughout the country. ... No other cause can show such a record of strenuous, widespread and law-abiding agitation. ... On November 18th, Suffragists sent deputation after deputation to Mr Asquith. Many members of Parliament pleaded with him to see them. He refused. He allowed them for many hours to be hustled and bandied back and forth between the police and a mob of jeering, insulting men - a state of things so undesirable that the Home Secretary decided it would not be public policy to proceed against the 117 women who were arrested.

Such, so far as the Government of the last Parliament is concerned, has been the success of a loyally constitutional agitation, embracing the whole kingdom, and unparalled in the history of any cause.

Party men may censure militant methods when they have shown that constitutional agitation succeeds in moving legislation. - Yours etc.' [*SN* 10 December 1910; *ST* 17 December 1910]

'Black Friday', as it came to be known, was a public relations disaster for the Government, and on 22 November 1910 Asquith promised a Suffrage Bill that could be amended to include women if his government was returned to power. A letter to the *Shetland News,* described it as

'entirely unsatisfactory, for he only promised to allow a Bill to be brought forward, which would admit of re-amendment, and therefore, of free killing by wolves in sheep's clothing; and also he completely gave the case away by saying that this Bill should be introduced not next session, nor any fixed session, but 'next Parliament.' The women have learnt from bitter experience that 'next Parliament' ... never comes. .... If ... no sign is given that women's reform is to be brought in during the session, who is there who blames the women for resorting with increased determination to those tactics, which have already brought their question to the forefront of politics? Yours etc W Duncan, Harvey House, Cathcart Hill, Highgate' [*SN* 31 December 1910]

Asquith's non-promise sparked off a second WSPU demonstration with 300 women marching together on Parliament; again, Churchill asked that the 176 prisoners be discharged. The members of the Conciliation Committee deplored the militancy, and stressed that the Bill had not yet been abandoned.

A letter from the *Evening Telegraph and Post* was forwarded to the *Shetland News* by A.B, presumably prompted by the violence reported on 22 November. It gave an account of how Christabel Pankhurst and Annie Kenney came to be arrested in 1905

' ... Liberal stewards hurled themselves upon these two girls, dragged them out with the greatest violence, so that Annie Kenney was seriously hurt, and rushed them out of the building. Outside the two tried to hold a meeting and explain what had occurred. The police refused to allow them to speak and arrested them. ...The women know that they have justice on their side, and a righteous cause, that of human liberty. I am, etc, Emily Wilding Davison (B.A., London)' [*SN* 3 December 1910]

Davison was to be fatally injured while attempting to stop the King's horse at Epsom in 1913.

The second election of 1910 was held from 3 to 19th December, the last in the UK to be held over several days. Since women were still banned from election meetings, members of the Men's Political Union asked about women's suffrage in their place. Lloyd George bore with interruptions, but Churchill gave instructions that any such questioners were to be ejected, and one man was flung out so violently that his leg was broken. Cabinet ministers were given police protection. Suffrage women were particularly outraged by the emphasis on a police escort for baby Diana Churchill, and Wimbledon WSPU sent her a doll as a Christmas present – dressed in green, purple and white, and holding a 'Votes for Women' banner. It's a safe bet that it never reached her.

The Shetland Society had hoped for a visiting speaker in the run up to the General Election, but only constituencies where a Suffrage candidate was standing were being visited. The Society decided, instead, to distribute a pamphlet specially written by Jamieson for the Shetland situation. Leaflets were to be given to shopkeepers, to be enclosed when they were making up parcels.

The women had obviously given up on converting Mr Wason himself, for they delegated three members to approach the Chairman of the Shetland Liberal Association, initially by letter. He didn't reply for some months, provoking a letter from Jamieson asking him 'if she was to have nothing to report to her Society but that she had received no reply'. They also agreed to canvass women entitled to vote in Municipality elections (that is, those who would be eligible to vote under the new Conciliation Bill), and invite them to sign a petition in support. This petition cannot have been very successful, for there is a comment in the ZCC debate on suffrage saying they didn't get signatures from even half of those entitled to vote, nor could the Houses of Parliament archivist find a record of it being handed in.

The election results were again very close. The Conservatives and Liberal Unionists had the larger number of votes, but the Liberal Party had one more MP, and Asquith formed a government with the support of the Irish Nationalists.

In Lerwick, there was a new Town Council, elected on 1 November 1910, and a new Provost, A L Laing, Jamieson's uncle. He was to remain in post until 1913.

The Shetland women were busy fundraising. A Whist Drive, held on 30 December 1910, had raised £4 12s for the Scottish Federation. Organisers for this were Mrs Nicol and Miss Donaldson, along with two more teachers, Miss A Dey, who taught at the Anderson Educational Institute, and Miss Ruby Sandison, who taught at the Central Public School. Sandison was Mrs Sandison's niece by marriage. The intriguingly named 'Conversatzione Dance' had been decided against (the dictionary gives 'conversatzione' as a 'social gathering held by a literary or arts society'). The May Suffrage Festival in Edinburgh was to include sales of craft work to emphasise the femininity of the suffragists, and Shetland goods were to be sent: 'each member is to endeavour to make the parcel a large one!' [Minute Book, November 1910; the next few meetings show Jamieson chasing up hosiery from the members.] In the event, the Festival raised £1,700.

After 'Black Friday' there was an increase in Lady Stout's activities for the WSPU. She gave a solo lecture on Tuesday 2 January 1911 in the Croyden Art Gallery, Park Lane, and spoke again on Thursday 23 February at Horboury Rooms, Notting Hill Gate, along with a regular speaker, the novelist and journalist Evelyn Sharp, at this point organizer for Kensington, and the Reverend WLS Dallas. The meeting was chaired by Georgina Brackenbury, then organizer for Manchester, and the artist who painted the portrait of Mrs Pankhurst which now hangs in the National Portrait Gallery. Lady Constance Lytton made one of her rare appearances in the Queen's Hall on 27 January 1911, and given their friendly correspondence Lady Stout could well have been there; there were also regular rehearsals throughout January and February of the WSPU's official song, Dame Ethel Smyth's 'The March of the Women.'

In February 1911, Norway's first woman MP visited London. She was Melle Roqstav, and *Votes for Women* says she would 'occupy the seat of the president, General Brantlie, during his absence on army organisation.' [*Votes for Women,* 10 February 1911]

There was a jeering letter from HOMO in the *Shetland News* of 18 February 1911:
'What has come over the Women's Suffrage Society? Is it dead? For all it is doing ... it might never have been called into being. ... men at least can and do fight for their principles.' [*SN* 18 February 1911]

Jamieson was swift to reply:

'It will be remembered that Mr Asquith promised facilities for the passing of a Women's Suffrage Bill in the present Parliament.

On Tuesday 7th current, Mr Asquith announced that Government meant to take up the whole time of the House till Easter, and gave a list of days after that date suitable for private members' bills.

Next day, 358 names were given in for ballot. Sir George Kemp proved to be first.

On Thursday he presented a Bill to confer the Parliamentary Franchise on Women.'

Jamieson gave the provisions of the Bill, which was the franchise for women as it was given to men; married women were not excluded, if they had a separate property qualification, but could not vote in the same parliamentary division as their husbands. The Bill was to come up on 5 May 1911, and Jamieson urged every man and woman who thought that women should have a voice in legislation to appeal to members of Parliament and local governing bodies. Her final paragraph pointed out that

'Holding meetings is not very practicable for Shetland women ... The Federation has on hand a plan of literature propaganda, which will be developed later on.' [*SN* 25 February 1911, *ST* 4 March]

Census Day, 1911:

3 April 1911 was Census Day, and in a mass act of civil disobedience across the country WFL and WSPU women boycotted it by spending the night before and until midday on the 3rd, in cafes and houses – having a party, from the sound of the *Scotsman* reports, with Edinburgh suffragists enjoying 'waxworks', skits, songs and music recitals, and a debate: 'Will not giving the vote make woman, man, and man, woman?' Emily Wilding Davison hid in a broom-cupboard in the House of Commons; in London, Mrs Pankhurst spoke at the Aldwych Skating Rink before 'skating and a concert programme.' There was even a census poem in the Bath *Chronicle and Argus*:

> Not till we've got the vote, then I don't mind,
> I'll help the census,
> But while we're trodden down by all mankind
> It discontents us.
> If we but get our votes, our threats we'll cancel,
> If not, no census for Mrs _____. [Mrs Mansel, who hired an empty house in Lansdown Cres for the

night]

> Tis our design obstruction to promote;
> Though our proposal every franchise man cursed,
> I'd not give way – 'No census if no vote.'
> That's quite the final word of Mrs P _____.

> What, fill a census paper? No, not me
> (And I am only one among the many),
> I'll burn the blessed thing; just wait and see,
> I am, dear Sir, yours truly, A ___ K _____.

There doesn't seem to have been any attempt to disrupt the Census here in Shetland; there's no mention of the SWSS in the reports, and the Census seems to have gone normally. The *Shetland Times* specifically mentions the much greater number of females over males. It'd be interesting, though, come 2011, to check the Census returns for Mrs Leisk, Miss Leisk, Mrs Nicol, Miss Jamieson and other stalwarts (Mrs Jamieson was apparently in Leeds, and was noted there). If they're there, then it's certain no attempt was made; civil disobedience would, in any case, have been against their non-militant policy, although many NUWSS members took part in the boycott.

Scriptural correspondence:

In the meantime, Jamieson was busy with theology. On March 18 1911, *Shetland Times* correspondent VERO brought Scriptural authority to condemn the women's movement, accusing ministers of lack of moral courage for not condemning it, and quoting St Paul '... I suffer not a woman to teach or to usurp authority over the man, but be in silence' and John Knox

'To promote a woman to bear rule is repugnant to nature, contumely to God, a thing contrary to His revealed will and approved ordinance: and finally it is the subversion of good order, of all equity and justice.' [*ST* 18 March 1911]

St Paul was certainly a gift for anti-suffragists, and a red rag to suffragettes. An early hunger striker, Gladys Roberts, bolstered her courage before being forcibly fed by reading St Paul on the duties of a wife in her cell Bible.

This time, Jamieson replied under her own initials, rather than as the Secretary; perhaps to take on a religious argument was considered too risky for the society. You get a sense of her delight in the debate - such a pity she was never able to go to University, she would have loved it! Her grasp of Scripture shows adult study:

'...the sole object of women's suffrage is to free them from the arbitary authority of mere men. ... St Paul's epistles were all written in expectation of the immediate return of his Lord. It is necessary to discriminate between his messages which were for temporary and particular occasions, and those which are applicable for all mankind and all time.

The advice to read the Bible is sound. Suffragism will lose nothing by it. Especially should men and women read St Paul. ...

If men make Pauline claims, they must hold them on Pauline grounds.

In every case where Paul enjoins submission on women, he turns round on the men; and reminds them that their behaviour must be Christ-like before they can claim that submission.

And when men can come forward - 'strong sons of God without rebuke' - and truly prove that they hold their bodies 'pure temples of the Divine Spirit' by showing the fruits that are the outcome of wisdom, power, holiness, justice, goodness and truth, they will have no difficulty in winning the homage of all womenkind. - I am, etc C.J.' [*SN* 25 March 1911]

She was supported by P W Hunter:

' ... It is noteworthy of some individuals that when they have a doubtful case to defend they seek refuge in any text in Holy Writ which appears to afford a rallying ground for something which the ethical standards of the 20th century denounces in no uncertain sound. Slavery was upheld in the name of Him 'who came to set the prisoners free' and the liquor traffic has been upheld by a passing remark made ... by St Paul to Timothy. ... ' [*SN* 1 April 1911]

VERO was not convinced. After pretending to recognise C.J. as a woman by her logic (as if the whole of Shetland didn't know who the 'suffrage women' were!), he went on:

' ... Only temporal teaching! Why, never since the first woman brought death into the world was there greater cause for silence on the part of woman, than there is today. ... A proper study of the Bible would be detrimental to Suffragism, although certainly the individual suffragist who read the Bible would gain immensely by it. ... What was Christ's attitude to women? It is evident that Christ did not recognise the equality of the sexes. Otherwise, his twelve disciples would not all have been 'mere men'. In fact, Christ's whole life and teaching emphasised the fact that woman was not man's equal. ...we are neither going to take from the Bible, nor add to the

Bible simply to justify the absurd contentions of certain hare-brained women. ... I question very much whether Paul's letter to Timothy were written in the expectation of the immediate return of our Lord. - I am, etc, ' [*SN* 8 April 1911]

Jamieson's reply again showed her engagement with Scripture, and was a model of logic, taking Vero's letter point by point:

'I know no way of learning other than in silence and subjection. ... The Greeks did not educate their women. Inattentive chatter in the temple and theatre was therefore common ... Paul rightly repressed this in the Christian service and teaching, where men and women were both instructed. Women had to be specially told what men, accustomed to learn, already knew.

... Does Vero have any knowledge at all of the scope and history of the women's movement - of the thousands of good and able men and women engaged in it, of its relation and contributions in human welfare, knowledge, progress ... ? 'A soap box!' Is that really all the man grasps? And he is Biblically endowed with authority over women? ... Did he never read of wisdom crying in the streets?

... [Jesus] chose [His disciples] because he never violently broke with race traditions. He never taught them that men were masters of women. ... Was it a woman who betrayed Jesus? Was it women who forsook him and fled? Was it a woman who denied him? ... Do his remarks, when in the home of Martha and Mary, teach that he considers that women should devote themselves wholly to the duties of house work?

Vero must withdraw his assertion that I deny the truth of certain passages in the Bible. It is an absolutely false assertion.

The closing paragraph of Vero's letter is a rather unnecessary confession of ignorance. The disciples, apostles and early Christians all lived in constant expectation of the return of our Lord. ... ' [*SN 15 April 1911*]

A further correspondent on 22 April picked up on Jamieson's comment that Christianity and Suffrage are essentially reconcileable.

'The women's suffrage movement is rich in assertion, but ... assertion is not argument. ... Christianity has been blamed for a great deal, but I think it is imposing too much on it to charge it with producing what is known as the Women's Suffrage Movement. ... Personally I do not oppose Women Suffrage, but let us be quite honest, and seek to secure equal voting rights for all women, not some women. - I am, etc., S.D.' [*SN* 22 April 1911]

Jamieson began her reply:

'While waiting for Vero's reply, I noticed a letter from S.D. As Vero has not re-appeared, I will, with your permission, deal with S.D's letter now.'

She recommended S.D to read St Paul:

'In Jesus Christ, there is neither Jew nor Gentile, bond nor free, male nor female. ... The distinction between Jew and Gentile is now quite broken down in Christian habits of thought. Christian countries are emerging from the distinction between bond and free. In both cases, political freedom is ultimately involved. Our movement inevitably comes next.'

Again, she showed her symapthy with the suffragettes:

'It is precisely the political ignoring of Christian teaching that has driven the extreme Suffrage party to violence. ... the utmost violence of the Suffragettes are as dust in the balance compared to the coercion, violence and indignities to which they have been subjected by men with the delighted approbation of uncomprehending people [force-feeding was by now common in English prisons]. They have effectively proved that men are not to be trusted with law and justice where women are concerned.'

You can feel her enjoying her final paragraph:

'And, after asserting that Women's Suffrage is anti-Pauline, anti-scriptural, anti-pacific, anti-democratic and anti-Christian, S.D. says he personally does not oppose it. I am, etc.' [*SN* 6 May 1911]

Official support for the Conciliation Bill:

The fight to get the Conciliation Bill through continued, with Sir George Kemp to re-introduce the Bill on 5 May 1911. The Shetland Society wrote to their town, county and parish councils asking them to petition MPs to support bill. The County Council and Dunrossness parish council petitioned; the letter was received too late for the town council's monthly meeting, and Lerwick Parish Council deferred consideration. By the end of April 1911, twenty-four town councils, including Lerwick, had carried resolutions in favour of the Bill. The petitions from the County Council and from Dunrossness were presented by Cathcart Wason on 9 May and 12 May respectively. Each petition only counted as two signatures: the ZCC one was signed by J C Grierson and another, and the Dunrossness one by James Bridge, chairman, and another.

The *Shetland Times* of 6 May 1911 gave an account of the debate on women's suffrage in the ZCC. They had received a letter from the Secretary of the SWSS, requesting them to petition Parliament in favour of the present Bill on women's suffrage. Mr Hoggan (Yell South) moved that they send a petition:

'The trend of opinion was somewhat in favour of this measure. It was only a matter of time, and he did not see why they should lag behind the time and show an unnatural feeling toward women.'

He was supported by Messrs Ganson (Bressay) and Loggie (Nesting and Lunnasting, and the first Secretary of the Shetland Collie Club). Mr Loggie said that

'the women were harder workers, and kept their homes together in a great many places in Shetland, and he did not think it right to debar them from the parliamentary vote when they had the minicipal and parochial vote.'

The vote against was moved, surprisingly, by Frank Pottinger (Cunningsburgh), who showed how much damage the WSPU were doing to the suffrage cause:

'Some of the ladies who were presently conducting the agitation in Britain were in his opinion quite unfit to exercise the vote on account of their hysterical conduct. He was an adult suffrage supporter, but in his opinion this was a most reactionary measure. ... it had not a lodgers' franchise ... the number of women who held the qualifications in the same division as their husbands would decrease very considerably the thousand [women voters] that Mr Loggie mentioned.'

Mr Garriock (Tingwall, son of L F U Garriock, and husband of Selina, who was to be an early woman councillor) seconded him.

Mr Ganson expressed dubiousness about the ZCC taking up a political issue, but was over-ruled by the Convener, who felt that it was their duty to take up a Bill which would benefit the County. Mr J W Robertson (Northmavine South) also supported the motion, although he felt it would have strengthened the SWSS's position if they could have got even a half of the thousand women who would be enfranchised to sign their petition. Mr Fordyce (Gulberwick) and Mr Fotheringham were also in favour, Mr Fordyce saying that 'in social problems the ladies would be more likely to carry out improvements than the men'. The motion was carried by nine votes to seven. [*ST, SN* 6 May 1911]

A letter from Jamieson in the following week's paper thanked the ZCC, the Parish Council of Dunrossness and their male supporters 'who have been helpful to us in our efforts to work as a society without the leadership of men. We must stumble before we can walk, and are conscious of blunders and shortcomings.' [*ST, SN* 13 May 1911]

That last sentence sounds most unlike the militant Jamieson of the Biblical letters; you can imagine the married women of the committee persuading her to put it in.

The Conciliation Bill was passed on 6 May, by a majority of 167; the clause allowing married ratepayers the vote was cut from it. The Government, however, refused to give assurances on its future until immediately before the Coronation, when, perhaps fearing interference with the Coronation ceremonies, Asquith promised full facilities in 1912.

The Women's Coronation Procession, 17 June 1911:

The next big procession was the London march in honour of coronation of George V, to be held on 17 June 1911. The NUWSS offered to pay for a representative of the Shetland society to attend, and Jamieson was unanimously appointed. She herself designed the banner she carried, and Miss J Mitchell painted it.

Lady Stout was the WSPU representative for New Zealand women: 'Lady Stout will welcome heartily all New Zealanders who, as enfranchised women, are determined to help their sisters at home in their struggle for the vote.' [*Votes for Women*, 16 June 1911] The magazine gives a map of the procession, and it lists 25 'sections', only three of which are NUWSS.

There are a number of photographs, posters, leaflets, ribbons and badges relating to this procession still extant in the Women's Library, London, and the Museum of the Ciy of London, as well as a short film clip, which shows parts of the procession: women in white dresses and hats, carrying white pennants, followed by an historical tableau which looks like Queen Elizabeth. The title card reads: *Suffragette Pageant 66,000 women take part in a procession through London. All the famous women in history are represented.*

It must have been an amazing thing to be part of. The women had something to celebrate; given the success of the Conciliation Bill, and Asquith's recent promises, the vote was as near as it had ever been. The procession was led by 'General' Flora Drummond and a 'colour bearer', then, on a white horse, Joan of Arc with a tabard and plumed helmet, carrying a banner. Behind her was the WSPU leadership and the women in white who are seen on the film, the seven hundred women who had been imprisoned, with their banner: 'From Prison to Citizenship.' Behind them were the 'famous women', who included Grace Darling, Jenny Lind, Jane Carlyle, Mrs Somerville and Florence Nightingale.
The four nations of Britain were represented: red roses for England, Welsh women in high hats, frilled caps and shawls; Irish women in their full skirts and tight bodices. The Scottish contingent included women pipers in Highland dress and Scottish women carrying the lion rampant flag. Behind them, a 'Car of Empire' was drawn by white horses, with a draped tent guarded by women representing the King's dominions overseas; suffrage workers from Australia, Africa, Canada, India and New Zealand followed, carrying their banners.

The arts section included the Actresses' Franchise League in their trademark green, white and pink, the Artists' Suffrage League, and the Musicians' section, including Ethel Smythe, who had composed 'March of the Women' (it wasn't popular; the women preferred the 'Suffragette Marseillaise', which was easier to sing. Mind you, they'd learned it under difficult conditions: in Holloway, marching round the exercise yard, with the composer conducting with a toothbrush).

Twenty-nine suffrage societies took part, and the Press talked of 'Five miles of suffragettes'. Here are the instructions for a member of the WFL, written on a green, yellow and white striped postcard, with a map of the route on the reverse:
'WOMEN'S FREEDOM LEAGUE 1, Robert Street, Adelphi. Women's Procession, 17 Jun 1911. Please be at the Victoria Embankment between Temple Station and Blackfriars Bridge at 4.30pm, SATURDAY, JUNE 17TH. We shall be much obliged if you will walk in the ..... Section. Please bring this card with you and ask for Miss..... As we wish our Colours (Green, White and Gold) to predominate, we would suggest that all who can should wear White dresses; if not either Green or Brown, as any other colour would not harmonise with the general scheme. Whenever possible, members are requested to dispense with hats. Please also wear WFL Sash or Badge.'

The 'prisoners' pageant' which headed the Women's Coronation Procession of 17 June 1911. These seven hundred women had all been imprisoned. Their banner was designed by Laurence Housman. The National Union of Women's Suffrage Societies invited the Shetland WSS to send a representative to this procession. Photograph courtesy of the Museum of London.

A decorated balcony in St James Street was fronted by a banner reading 'England's oldest militant suffragist greets her sisters'. It was Mrs Wolstenholme Elmy, now 77. There were various receptions held after the procession; the NUWSS held theirs in the Portman Rooms.

Jamieson could well have been with the Scottish women, photographed opposite, with Lady Stout's Empire suffragists behind her, but the map of the procession in *Votes for Women* also shows two separate blocks of NUWSS women, so if the bulk of the procession was WSPU organized, then she was more likely to have been in one of those sections.

She described the procession at the Shetland AGM in November:

'This year saw in London the greatest procession of women that has ever been known in human history ... this crowning demonstration included 500,000 women. It was over five miles long. It took over two hours to pass a given point. It included women of every nation, race, rank, profession, class, occupation and age, drawn from every corner of the world.'

Shetland members got to see the event for themselves: a Cinematograph film was taken, and Mrs Freeman, Miss Morrison's sister, bought a copy, which the Shetland Society arranged for Mr Calder to show at his next performances. The film cost £1, and Mr Calder would be asked to pay half of this and then keep the film.

A number of people have tried to locate the banner which Jamieson designed and carried, without success. It's not in the Shetland Archives, nor in the collections of banners in the People's Story, Edinburgh, or any other National Museum of Scotland; not in the Women's Library, London, or the People's History Museum, Manchester. It may be in a loft somewhere in Shetland (I hope so!), or it may have been destroyed in New Zealand along with Jamieson's papers. Nor do there seem to be any photographs which might show it. It's not on any of the Museum of London's large collection of Coronation photographs, and there don't seem to be photos of the Glasgow procession of June 1914 in the Mitchell Library. Its last recorded appearance was in Lerwick in January 1915.

There are however a number of surviving banners to help us imagine what it might have been like; the Women's Library has a substantial collection, which can be viewed online. The Edinburgh society later called it 'a particularly beautiful one' – such a pity there is no record of it.

The Scottish section of the Women's Coronation Procession.
Photograph courtesy of the Museum of London.

Women from throughout the Empire joined the Women's Coronation Procession. These Indian suffragists were just behind the Scottish contingent. Lady Stout, the SWSS President, was in charge of the New Zealand suffragists.

Photograph courtesy of the Museum of London.

Asquith's pre-election promise to give time for the Conciliation Bill had not been forgotten. Cathcart Wason held a meeting 'of electors and others' in Lerwick Town Hall in late August, and began by answering written questions. His position was that there should be a referendum on whether women wanted the vote, but he gave a warning which was calculated to alarm islanders:

'.. it was exceedingly probable that the effect of practically universal suffrage would be to wipe many constituencies off the face of the earth. ... he would not like to see Orkney and Shetland obliterated in the wilds of Sutherland or Caithness.

Now Mr Wason said he had another question on the same subject. It was in regard to the Prime Minister's promise to give full facilities for the passing of the Conciliation Bill some time during next year. He rather thought his questioner was wrong there. He thought it was during the course of the next Parliament that the Prime Minister would give these facilities. He might point out the effect of the Prime Minister passing the Suffrage Bill next year. It would mean that Parliament would have to immediately dissolve. The House of Commons could not sit for a day if once a Bill was passed conferring the franchise on a large number of electors. He thought the Prime Minister's statement was that full and ample facilities would be given during the next Parliament for the discussion of the measure, and if the voice of the people and their representatives in Parliament was emphatically in favour of the passage of the Bill then it would be given effect to. His questioner could rest assured that the Prime Minister's pledges would be faithfully, honestly and strictly carried out (Applause.)' [ST 2 September 1911]

Jamieson wrote on behalf of the SWSS on 9 September:

'The Government undertaking for the Conciliation Bill is as follows: 'They will be prepared next session, when the Bill has been again read a second time, either as the result of obtaining a good place in the ballot, or (if that does not happen) by the grant of a Government day for the purpose, to give a week (which they understand to be the time suggested as reasonable by its promoters) for its further stages.

... it was before the Dissolution of the last Parliament that Mr Asquith gave his promise of 'facilities for effectively dealing' with the Conciliation Bill 'in the next Parliament, if returned'. [ST, SN, 9 September 1911]

The AGM of the SWSS was held on 11 November, in the Masonic Hall. After giving a review of the year in Shetland, Jamieson gave her concerns about the Conciliation Bill:

'widening amendments are threatened, ... with the avowed intention of wrecking the bill.'

As in the previous year, she commented on the activities of the anti-suffragists: 'they have given great stimulus to the cause and work of Suffragists'.

Looking at the wider world: 'four more [US] States have been enfranchised, Washington and California being the last.' She quotes falling statistics for infant mortality where women have the vote:

'In 1908, [New Zealand] was down to 67 [from 76 per thousand]. Norway comes second, 86 per thousand. Victoria, in Australia, had in 1909, 70 per thousad. Chile ... 362 per 1000... Russia ... has the highest death rate among children in Europe.'

She then spoke about the National Insurance Bill, currently before Parliament. The scheme was compulsory for all workers between sixteen and sixty; each worker paid 4d. a week, the employer added 3d. and the state 2d. In return for these payments, free medical attention, including medicine, was given. Those workers who contributed were also guaranteed 7s. a week for fifteen weeks in any one year, when they were unemployed. These benefits were paid at Labour Exchanges which provided unemployed workers with information on any vacancies which existed in the area. There seems to have been a separate fund for men and women. Jamieson explained the suffrage objections to the Bill:

' It is iniquitous, to begin with, to include women at all in an insurance scheme on a wage-earning basis. Many employments of women are not insurable. The best and most vital work of women is not done for wages. ... it must be remembered that as a rule women must do three times as much work as a man before she can earn the same amount of money. Then the whole charge of the health of women, apart from the meagre maternity allowance to married mothers from the men's fund, is laid on maidens, old maids, and widows. They must even pay the maternity benefits to unmarried mothers, thus being specially charged with the duty a man has shirked. ... It has been cleverly shown that the whole expenses of the scheme will be eventually borne by the working man. It may be more truly shown that it will fall on working women. For it will not be taken from the workmen's needs or out of his scanty pocket money. It will all be taken out of the household money, which the women must administer, and for any shortage of which they must suffer. But protest from voteless women is useless. The Bill, however modified, remains the same in essence, and will pass. ...'

She moved on to Press coverage in a way which perhaps explains the silence of the *Shetland Times* and *Shetland News* on suffrage events:

'For several years the women's movement was boycotted in the press, except for exaggerated and sensational accounts of the misdeeds of Suffragettes - accounts wilfully calculated to throw discredit on the whole movement. The result has been the establishment of a women's press, and a literature of its own is now growing up round the movement. The general press is now relenting. Favourable notices are now appearing in most of the big papers, and the London 'Standard' devotes a daily page to the discussion of all matters relating to women. *The Common Cause*, the organ of the National Union, is published weekly. *The Englishwoman*, a most able and interesting monthly magazine, is devoted to the cause of women. No one has any real excuse for not knowing what is going on in the world of women. And now for the next few months the energies of suffragists will be concentrated on bringing together all the forces that can be put in action to secure the passing of the Conciliation Bill.'

She ended with a reference to the disenfranchised households of Shetland seamen:

' ... There are four thousand voters in Shetland - how many of them are at here to vote at elections? The enfranchisement of women would enable seamen's wives to qualify for the vote. Shetland women have bitter cause to know how much of the accidents, disease and death among seamen is due to preventable causes. If they realised that the vote would enable seamen's wives to bring pressure on legislation affecting the wages, safety and lives of seamen, surely they would do all they could to show they wished for the political enfranchisement of women. ... ' [*ST* 11 November 1911; *SN,* 18 November 1911]

Jamieson's next letter gave an account of events in London. The Conciliation Bill had run out of time. On 7 November 1911, a deputation of the Parliamentary Council of the People's Suffrage Federation presented a memorial to Asquith, asking for Adult suffrage in its broadest sense, including women. Mr Asquith said that a Reform Bill would be introduced for Manhood suffrage, but, Jamieson quoted, 'speaking for himself and not for the Government, he must part company with them when they said man must include woman.' He then agreed to meet a deputation of representative suffragists, and agreed on the 'strength and intensity that prevails on this subject.' However,

'I am the head of the Government, and I am not going to make myself responsible for a measure that I don't conscientiously believe has been demanded in the interests of the country.'

'He promised however,' Jamieson went on, 'that if the House carried an amendment including women in the Bill, the Government would accept and abide by the amendment as an integral part of the Bill.'

The deputation had taken place on 17 November, when Asquith had met thirty women from various suffrage societies. Asquith's blunt refusal to back women's suffrage had meant the WSPU had resumed militant tactics. Jamieson emphasised that the National Union,

'the oldest and by far the largest body of Suffragists, is, and has always been, peaceful in its tactics. ... The members ... while they keenly feel and resent the injustice against which all Suffragists are striving, deplore and repudiate the violent tactics of the militant suffragists.' [*ST, SN* 2 December 1911]

The Shetland Society discussed the WSPU tactics in their Minutes of 7 December 1911: the NUWSS circular letter condemning the militants was sent to the *Shetland Times.* The same meeting read a letter from Lady Stout, the delegate of the Shetland Society at NUWSS in London. She asked for instructions on how to vote with regard to the proposed Reform Bill, and was told 'this meeting is not anti-Government, but otherwise gives Lady Stout a free hand.'

The Special Council Meeting was held on 11 December, 1911, in the Small Queen's Hall, London. At this meeting, a resolution was proposed condemning the actions of the militant suffragists.

In the press report of the November AGM minutes of the SWSS, Jamieson wrote 'This resolution caused much friction in the Union, among them Lady Stout, who also resigned the Presidency of this Society'. The Minutes of 1 Feb 1912 report a 'communication from NUWSS re Lady Stout' and a 'letter of explanation from Lady Stout', followed by a telegram in which she 'repudiated the tactics of the National Union'. The Committee 'unanimously homolgated the attitude adopted by Lady Stout and deplored the defeat of the Amendment to the Motion of the Special Council Meeting of NUWSS.' In other words, although the Shetland society did not themselves use militant tactics, they did not wish to condemn those who did. Given Lady Stout's involvement with the WSPU and her first-hand experience of official tactics, her strong line on this is not surprising.

The Conciliation Bill was to be re-introduced in March 1912. Lady Stout, Mrs Freeman and Mrs Isbister were appointed delegates to the Annual Meetings on 24 and 26 February, and also delegated to interview Mr Wason. The ladies were unable to make the time he suggested, and Miss Palliser, Parliamentary Secretary, was asked to interview him instead on

'Mr Wason's promise to leave the question to the women of the country and his subsequent voting against the Bill etc' [SWSS Minute Book 1 February 1912]

The Chairman of the Shetland Liberal Association had finally conceded that 'in his opinion, Liberals of Shetland were not opposed to the enfranchisement of women' and wrote this to the Master of Elibank, then the Liberal chief whip. Mr Wason's reply was that he had 'taken note of what he said'; in October 1912 he said that he'd 'received the deputation, but must abide by his electoral address.'

A short article in the *Shetland News* on 2 March 1912 gave the progress of the Bill. It was now sponsored by Mr Agg-Gardener (Cheltenham), a supporter of women's suffrage since he'd entered Parliament in 1874. The second reading was fixed for 22 March, and the Government had promised a week for proceeding with it. Jamieson, presumably, wrote an article for the *Shetland News*:

'... the situation is still sufficiently critical to require the utmost efforts of Suffragists. ... Resolutions are being asked from Liberal Associations, and deputations, armed with memorials, are waiting on MPs, while the constituencies of Anti-Suffrage MPs are sending their resolutions and memorials to the Master of Elibank, the chief Liberal Whip.

The militants, disappointed alike by the King's speech and Mr Lloyd George's deliverance in the Albert Hall, are preparing for the 'greatest militant demonstration ever witnessed in this country.' [*SN* 2 March 1912]

The *Shetland Times* published an account of the Anti-Suffrage demonstration with Lord Loveburn's speech, but not of the suffrage meeting addressed by Lloyd George, as Jamieson pointed out in a letter to the *Shetland Times* editor published the following week. At the Albert Hall, Lloyd George had said that the Conciliation Bill was being 'torpedoed' by the projected Reform Bill, and Jamieson was concerned that the Conciliation Bill would be defeated in favour of a promise:

'The Reform Bill with its chance that a private member's amendment to it may be carried ... is not yet before the House. But the Conciliation Bill, which enfranchises rate-paying women, is. And you, sir, will do yourself infinite honour if you now express yourself in favour of this Bill, which will place the franchise in the hands of a thousand - and if the wives of seamen qualify, of far more than a thousand - of your country women in these islands, than whom there are no worthier women in the Empire.' [*ST* 9 March 1912]

The same issue of the *Shetland Times* carried an account of the threatened 'greatest militant demonstration' under the headline:

WEST-END WINDOW SMASHING
SENTENCE ON MRS PANKHURST

'No less than 124 women appeared at Bow Street Police-court, London, on Saturday, charged with window-breaking in the West End the previous evening. ... damage estimated at £5,000 was done. Mrs Pankhurst and her two fellow prisoners were charged with breaking four panes of glass at 10, Downing Street, and others at the Colonial Office.' [*ST* 9 March 1912]

The three women were sentenced to two months' imprisonment.

After a century, the militant acts of the WSPU have blurred into each other. So far, actually, they hadn't amounted to very much, in modern terms. A number of women had attempted to gain entrance to the House of Commons, and refused to go away when turned back by the police; they'd resisted arrest by struggling, lying down or chaining themselves; they'd pestered politicians in the street; a couple had thrown stones at windows of government offices, and one had grafitti'd a political slogan on the House; they'd heckled at meetings, and smuggled themselves in when banned; they'd unfurled banners in unexpected places; they'd refused to pay taxes or fill in census forms; they'd gone on hunger strike in prison. It was only because they were articulate, middle-class women that anyone took any notice.

This window-smashing was their first concerted attack on non-government property, and opponents of women's suffrage moved from distaste at 'unwomanly' actions to horror at women 'un-sexing themselves'. Suffragists watched in dismay as their years of patient persuasion that women could be intelligent yet still womanly were undone, and their best chance yet of a successful Bill was damaged by the actions of the militants.

Punch published a cartoon embodying their feelings that week. Entitled 'In the House of her Friends': the picture showed a Grecian-dressed Women's Suffrage watching rioting women and saying despairingly, 'To think that, after all these years, I should be the first martyr.'

Clearing up after the WSPU 'window-smashing' raid in the West End, March 1912.
Postcard, author's collection.

On 18 March 1912, Scotland had its first taste of suffragette damage: six windows were smashed in Sauchiehall Street, Glasgow, and Emily Green was arrested. She was not a WSPU member, but a friend of the redoutable Glasgow heiress Janie Allen, who had been arrested in England. In retaliation a mob of 200 men and boys threw iron bolts and weights through the windows of the WSPU Glasgow office, also in Sauchiehall Street, and the WFL office in Edinburgh had its windows smashed.

Mrs Pankhurst and her two fellow-leaders of the WSPU, Frederick and Emmeline Pethick-Lawrence, were served with a warrant for arrest for conspiring to commit damage. Christabel Pankhurst was also on the warrant, but decided to leave the country, saying that she could not lead the campaign from prison. She settled in Paris, where she was to remain until war was declared in August 1914. WSPU members regularly crossed the Channel to meet her, and she continued to contribute articles to *Votes for Women*. A number of WSPU members were to be unhappy with this long-distance control, especially as she commanded increasing terrorist attacks; they felt that she was becoming out of touch with the reality of the suffrage struggle in Britain. As the terrorist campaign intensified, a number of loyal supporters resigned, and others were dismissed. These were to include the Pethick-Lawrences and Sylvia Pankhurst, whose working-class East End Federation had led a number of London demonstrations.

Suffragists were concerned that these terrorist tactics were taking attention away from the reasons why women wanted the vote. 'Notes' on the support for the Conciliation Bill were published by the *Shetland Times* at the request of a 'lady correspondent':

'... If the papers published accounts of the solid work done by suffragists with the same alacrity they publish sensational militant and anti-suffrage news, this would not be the case. Labour, wages, housing, education, drunkness, immorality, and war, are all subjects that concern women as deeply as men. But all the laws affecting them have hitherto been made by men. ...' [*ST, SN* 23 March 1912]

In March, the Scottish Churches League for Women Suffrage was established, with Lady Frances Balfour as President. It included representatives of all the Scottish denominations, and was active until the outbreak of war in 1914.

The defeat of the Conciliation Bill by a majority of 14 (222 against, 208 for) was attributed by the *Shetland News* in part to the defection of the Irish members, who voted against it to give more time for debating Home Rule, and in part to the

'acts of violence recently committed by militant suffragettes. ... Mr Eugene Wason voted and spoke against the Bill; Mr Cathcart Wason apparently did not vote, or was not present in the House.' [*SN* 6 April 1912]

The same issue carried a protest from R.T. against what the writer considered the betrayal of the suffragettes:

' .. To desert them now, as some societies talk of doing, seems to me to paralled the base desertion of Joan of Arc [regularly invoked as a suffrage heroine] by those whom she had helped and blessed. I am, etc, R.T.' [*SN* 6 April 1912]

The Bill's defeat also weakened the NUWSS traditional links with the Liberal party, and by April 1912 they were involved in formal negotiations with the Labour Party, who had passed a resolution in January committing the Party to supporting women's suffrage. The NUWSS planned to raise an Election Fighting Fund to support Labour at by-elections. This caused some re-shuffling of personnel; Emily Davies, the founder of Girton and a Conservative, resigned from the NUWSS, and a number of women, Dr Elsie Inglis among them, resigned from their local Liberal Associations. It was however agreed that Liberal party candidates who had been firm in their support for women's suffrage would not be opposed – an inducement to the government to put up pro-suffrage candidates (it didn't work in Shetland). By July 1912 EFF committees were established within each federation, and as by-elections like Holmfirth, Crewe and Midlothian showed the policy was working, links with the Labour Party became closer. The

WFL also backed Labour in by-elections, and there were joint demonstrations by the NUWSS, WFL and ILP in Edinburgh and Dundee in July 1912.

The reminder of one suffrage /Labour link is still prominent today: the red rose icon. This came from a poem 'Bread and Roses', by James Oppenheim, which was published in *The American Magazine* in December 1911, and used as a slogan in the textile strike in Lawrence, Massachusetts, January to March 1912. Modern sung versions include one by Judy Collins, which was used as the soundtrack for photographs of the 2009 Centenary Guid Cause march in Edinburgh,

```
http://picasaweb.google.co.uk/hayakawaheren/Videos02#5391110970471377682
```

Suffrage cat in the WSPU colours.
Postcard, author's collection.

10

April – December, 1912

The effects of increasing militancy

This is "THE HOUSE" that man built,
And these are the Members who've been sitting late
Coming out arm in arm, from a lengthy debate,
Women and men 'neath the shade of Big Ben
In the Year — well we cannot exactly say when;
But the brave Suffragette very shortly must get,
Into "THE HOUSE" that man built.

A pro-suffrage example of the 'This is the House that man built' series.
Postcard, author's collection.

198

By now, women's suffrage had become mainstream. Postcards abounded; a quick scan of 'suffragette postcards' in e-bay shows the variety. Most gave the stereotyped view of suffrage workers as ugly women with glasses and deranged expressions rather enjoying being carried off by policemen. Several showed harrassed fathers dealing with small children, while Mama addressed a meeting in a corner, or, more plaintively, a distressed baby above the phrase 'Mama's a suffragette'. The 'This is the House that Man built' series showed both sides – for example, one 'anti' showed a picture of a steretypical large, be-spectacled woman struggling with a policeman in front of Holloway gaol, with the verse below:

> This is the House that Man Built
> And this is the House of the poor Suffragette
> And there's room for a great many more in it yet;
> When they racket and riot,
> And will not keep quiet,
> We place them on plank beds and very low diet;
> To stop all their din,
> We just run them in,
> Into this House that man built.

However, this series also had more positive pictures, like the one of a committee sitting around a table. Both sexes are there, and the standing Judge at the table-end is a woman.

> This is the House that man built,
> But oh what a wonderful change inside
> The women as well as the men preside
> They both hold the reins & no one complains
> For the men now admit that the ladies have brains
> And are every bit quite as fitted to sit
> As themselves in this House that man built.

There had been a number of plays on the subject written and produced, generally with the suffragette as the heroine, and novelists writing on suffrage themes included Arnold Bennett, Ford Maddox Ford, John Masefield, H G Wells and, later, Rebecca West and Virginia Woolf. There was even a race game, with picture cards and a board. It was called 'Pank-A-Squith'. A card game, Panko, or Votes for Women, had Trumpeters, Suffragettes, Trials and Commons as the Suffragist suits, and Police, Politicians, Magistrates and Prisons as the anti-suffragist suits. The Pankhursts, Lloyd George and Churchill were among the figures on the pictorial cards, which were drawn by Punch cartoonist Tennyson Reed.

The WSPU now had a number of shops around the country, featuring items in their 'trademark' colours of green, purple and white (hope, dignity, purity): postcards and cards, posters, motoring scarves, china, jewellery, badges. Much of it was designed by Sylvia Pankhurst. The colours had now become high fashion, and so were seen in shop windows everywhere – an early example of a marketing brand.

Dr Inglis' visit, April 1912:

In mid-April 1912, Shetland had a visit from Dr Elsie Inglis, now Honorary Secretary of the Edinburgh WSS and Secretary of the Scottish Federation. Her name has already cropped up a number of times in this history: she was an early doctor in Edinburgh from 1894, treating working-class women, and was involved with Chrystal Macmillan in the graduates' challenge to the Universities. There are a number of biographies of her. Accounts by those who knew her portray an inspiring personality who did not admit defeat; if Dr Inglis said something should be done, then those charged with the task found, somehow, that it could, whether it was speaking from a platform, transporting an entire hospital to India or breaking a strike in revolutionary Russia. She had been born and brought up in India, then went to school in Paris. She trained as a doctor in Edinburgh, Glasgow and London, where she became involved in suffrage work. She set up in practice in Edinburgh in 1894, and in 1898 she opened a hall of residence for women medical students. From 1900 she travelled around Scotland as a suffrage speaker. She and her fellow-doctor Elizabeth Garrett Anderson were to sign the letter of protest against the militants' actions which was published in *Votes for Women* in July 1912.

'Dr Inglis spent her Easter holidays in visiting the Northern societies and giving public addresses. The date of her visit here made it impossible for her to address a meeting unless it could have been held on the afternoon of Monday April 15, when a meeting was impracticable. Dr Inglis was, however, so pleased with the state of the Society, the work of which in getting public resolutions passed in favour of Suffrage, had been carried out without any of the hostility and bitterness that had been realised in many other places, that she promised that Mrs Snowden should include Shetland in her autumn tour. Immediately on her return south she sent notice that Mrs Snowden would speak here in August, the date being fixed for the 29th.' [*ST* SWSS AGM report, 2 November 1912]

Dr Elsie Inglis, founder of the Scottish Women's Hospital. She visited Shetland in April 1912, and the Shetland WSS raised money for the Serbian and French hospitals during the war.
Image courtesy of Lothian Health Services Archive, Edinburgh University Library
LHSA/EUL/LHB8A/9/1

More correspondence:

The previous month's window smashing in London and Glasgow provoked another scriptural correspondence, which was begun by OBSERVER on 20 April:

'... we have it on record of some women who took authority over men with very bad results. There was Eve ... Jezebel ... Athaliah ... Herodias ...' He invoked St Paul again before concluding: '... woman was disqualfied by God himself, and they must get His act repealed before Mr Asquith can do anything. I cannot see that women in authority would be any better than in days gone by; for, as I read of them in the streets of London every now and again, fighting the powers that be like a lot of wild cats, I think that they are far enough just now.' [*ST* 20 April 1912]

This time Jamieson answered as the Secretary, SWSS. She repeated her argument that learning requires silence: "Let the women learn', by all means.'

Her conclusion shows her growing frustration at the arguments brought up against women's enfranchisement:

'History shows that insubordination and rebellion in those ruled are the result of incapacity in the rulers. Are men equal to their eagerly accepted tasks when under their political methods good women are maddened into lawlessness? Are men like 'Observer', to be entrusted with the destinies of womanhood when their outlook is so shallow that they believe, because politicians have driven some 200 women desparate, none of the millions of law-abiding women, who build up the homes of which the nation is an aggregate, are fit to have a vote?' [*ST* 27 April 1912]

ANOTHER OBSERVER also waded in:

'Observer's jibe at ... 'women in London fighting the powers that be like a lot of wild cats' shows that, even if it were a sensible jibe, he is claiming very little for such powers that be in the 20th century of the Christian era, in its disgusting treatment by means of forcible feeding, etc, of those who are at least willing to suffer for their principles.' [*ST* 4 May 1912]

Magnus William Colvin ('P.S. - 'Observe' my name stands below my words') of Vancouver Island also wrote in support:

'In Canada, our cities and municipalities have votes for all property owners, whether men or women, and are happier for it. Many of the states of the Unites States of America have votes for women, and are now discovering that it is beneficial ... Women will get the vote in Great Britain if it takes them hundreds of years. They must get it. ... And it will be the best thing that ever happens. It is my hope they get it soon. I cheer to their success.' [*ST* 2 June 1912; Colvin's mother was Jermina Robertson from Sandsound, his father Robert was from Sandwick]

OBSERVER's reply contrasted Biblical descriptions of the 'virtuous woman' and the 'strange woman', and noted that neither Hannah nor Mary, in their hymns of praise, mentioned voting.

'In contrast to this, the Suffragists will exclaim: My soul doth rejoice in the little hammer, and my sprit in smashing windows. Thus we see that Suffragists do not belong to the righteous class, as it is well known that they do not stay inside, but are found at street corners.' [Honestly, I'm not making this up: *SN* 6 July, 1912]

At this point, the previously warm-side-of-neutral *Shetland News* became critical. Perhaps the editor, Thomas Manson, organist and choirmaster at St Columba's Church, was offended by Jamieson presuming to argue her feminist interpretation of the Scriptures (could 'Observer' have been a minister?); perhaps he'd been annoyed by the suggestion that the newspapers boycotted suffrage news, as the *Shetland News* did publish some. Whatever the cause, the Day by Day column in the *Shetland News* on 25 May showed unexpected animosity towards the Shetland WSS:

' ... Are they making any effort to further their cause? If so, no one hears of it but themselves. ... Did Joan of Arc ... go forth to fight her country's enemy with gloves on? Did Grace Darling pause to see whether the humblebaand were of the exact length before she launched her frail boat into the boiling surf?'

He expressed his admiration for the suffragettes, who were at least willing to act in expression of their beliefs.

'...they have compelled public attention to the question. ... when a Women's Suffrage Bill is passed, the Suffragists will have to thank the militants for achieving a large part of the victory.'

He then suggested the SWSS needed to persuade more people of the rightness of their cause through lectures at the Town or any other Hall to make the whole question 'thrashed out like any other question of interest and importance.' [*SN* 25 May 1912]

Day by Day's comments must have been particularly annoying, given that the chance of getting Dr Inglis to hold a public meeting had just been missed. For her reply, Jamieson brought Girzie back to life; perhaps the women of the SWSS were concerned that they were seen as lecturing the men, perhaps Jamieson felt his praise of the suffragettes' behaviour was so absurd that she could not resist the impulse to ridicule it (this is of course assuming that Jamieson was Girzie). While amusing though, Girzie's forthrightness turns to contempt in places.

'... An me tinkin you a proper, daecent, sensible body. Da Loard gie you wit ... Here dir been nothing but peace an' reason, women shawin wi der guid warks an' proper behaviour at dey wir fit ta be trusted wi da vote. But na. Du'll no be persuaded unless dey lift an' tak a fore dem. Did ye du dat fir votes?

Oh! dat dey wid tak you at your wird! An dey wid joost rise and go an brak every window belanging you. I sood gaff. ... Dan dey sood go trow Commercial Street an' lay in every window dere. Dat wid be da day!

Everybody wid see at once dan at dey hed a perfect right ta vote. ...

An dis is da coonsel of a man 'of full age and competent understanding.' Hoo can dat hae da wit da cast a vote?

An as fir meetings. Da weemon'll need ta get mair time an money ta demsels afore dey can hadd meetings. ... Bit dey wid only speak reason and sense. Wha wid come to hear dem? An dan dey wid be a soond dat dey wir a lavin der rightful place an der rightful wark ta tell folk what dey kent afore. A'm seen da laek.

So gude help da thing at tries ta please da men. ...' [*SN* 1 June 1912]

The letter was a mistake. Day by Day's reply poured scorn on Girzie's reasoning and the Shetland suffragists convictions:

'Women cannot reason, and Girzie's arguments are typical of the sex... For years we men have been waiting to see the women coming out in the open in support of the cause they espouse, and to show the public that by the manner they conducted meetings, by their speeches, and by their business capacity, they were fit to be entrusted with the guidance of public affairs.

We have been waiting in vain, however. The Suffragists do not even have the courage of the women of the Salvation Army ... who do not hesitate at the Market Cross and other public places to proclaim to the world their spiritual convictions. [Shetland suffragists are merely] ... sitting still and saying 'Behold how good we are! Our patience and long-suffering should appeal to your sense of chivalry!' Little wonder the cause makes slow progress.'

He then looked at Wason's majority at the last election:

'... had their own convicions been strong, had their feelings been deep, had they considered the advancement of their cause to be of paramount importance, they would have moved heaven and earth to get their men folks to vote against Mr Wason. ... they could in a variety of ways have prevented their men folk who were Wasonites from at least going to the poll.'

[Is he suggesting food poisoning here, a multitude of urgent domestic tasks, or just Mata Hari methods? Quite apart from the moral dishonour of suggesting that women fighting for their own vote would stop their menfolk voting as they chose.]

He agreed that Shetland women are in need of the vote, if any were, because of their living and working conditions - 'as Lady Stout pointed out'. He ended by commending Mrs Philip Snowden's

202

projected visit: 'the Suffragists have made one move' (he was not to know, of course, that she had been booked back in April) and suggested that she and Mr Wason be put 'head to head' to debate the issue. [*SN* 8 June 1912]

Jamieson's reply to Day by Day, as the Secretary of SWSS, was polite and positive; you can feel her and Mrs Leisk doing several drafts to get their points across without offending further. She stressed the importance of literature as a means of education, and the way that newspapers could help with this:

'The work of the County Education Committee ... is never reported in the Shetland papers. The facilities offered to young women and girls by Agricultural and Domestic Colleges have never been insisted on. The desirability of the establishment of model crofts and homesteads, where young people could be trained, and the best possibilities of crofting life opened up to them, has never been touched on. You could help women greatly there.

You could also at least have an occasional column, as the Weekly Scotsman has adopted, keeping your readers in touch with what women are doing all over the world. ...

The vote does not mean the guidance of affairs. It selects those who are to hold such guidance.'

With regard to voting against Cathcart Wason, she pointed out that

' .. the last Unionist candidate .... would vote for a Reform Bill that did not include women. ... The Shetland Society, though it does not cater for the sensation-loving, has done much good work, and hopes that the growing strength of the Scottish Federation ... will enable it to bring north good speakers from time to time.' [*SN* 22 June 1912; this letter was held over from the previous week.]

A new correspondent, ARGUS, focused on Girzie: 'Poor Girzie! I must confess to feeling a little sorry for her. ... I cannot but feel a twinge of pity as I behold her repeatedly put her head into the noose.' He recalculated the numbers of women who could vote in Shetland, looking at the Municipal vote: ' ... the total number of voters in Shetland is 5298, not 4078, and of this number 1211 are women ...' and compared it to the number who do: 'I doubt if five per cent of the female electors ever take the trouble to go to the poll in elections where they already have the franchise'. He suggested that they should serve as members of the various public bodies: 'Having failed in this, how can they hope to prove their case for the granting of the Parliamentary vote?' [*SN* 22 June 1912]

A MALE SUPPORTER replied on behalf of the SWSS:

' ... It is in my personal knowledge that the local suffragists have been doing a lot of quiet, but very effective work. They have distributed literature; they have in many unobtrusive ways brought their views before others and have succeeded in securing many supporters. They have held public meetings, and are arranging to hold another soon.' [*SN* 29 June 1912]

Argus turned his attention to Jamieson in the following week.:

'The letter from the Secretary ... is simply an admission that the criticisms ... were fully justified. I accept the apology, for such it is, and hasten to express the hope that seeing the suffragists have done so little, comparatively, in the past, they will make an effort to do better in the future. ... Let me see what they will do during the next twelve months, say.'

His suggestion was that they might 'Prepare the way to get one of ther own number put on the School Boards in Shetland ... a matter the women should and can tackle.' [*SN* 29 June 1912]

Given that Jamieson was listed in *Manson's Shetland* Almanac as serving on the Lerwick School Board from 1911 on (i.e. she began serving in 1910), this was surprising, as was Girzie's answer:

' ... a woman might serve on a Board or Cooncil till she was deaf an' blind an' bald, an she coodna alter a Ack or change da Parliamenters da lent o' one vote. She wid be a mere tool i' der haands. Na, na. Commend me til da women 'at keeps oot o' it till dey get da Parliament vote.'

She sympathised with the busy widows and spinsters he'd like to see on the Boards, and, with regard to council votes, pointed out how few men there were willing to sit. She then refuted his suggestion that fewer than 5% of women voted.

'When onything is on 'at maiters, [women]'re joost as keen as da men. Look at Lerook! Shaw me a poll whaur da women didna vote.'

203

She pointed out that he began by talking about the Parliamentary vote, before trying to side-track and suggest her figures were wrong: 'An 4087 men in Shetland hev it, and not one woman. Noo, I'll awa tae hoe da taaties, - Yours etc GIRZIE' [*SN* 6 July 1912]

ARGUS took this as a climb-down, and repeated his point about the school boards: 'They have failed to show the public that they are really in earnest over the matter, because they have not used the votes they already have.' [*SN* 13 July 1912]

Aald Geordie was also still alive and kicking, with a long letter giving his 'noshons - dis siffragitts agen' He thoroughly agreed with Argus, who he called 'Maister Eeditor':

'hits maistly ooseliss ta try an' raison wi weemin at ony time, bit ken ye, I tink id dis siffrage dirt whin dey tak hit afore dem, maks dem mair ill-natird and kampshius, an' dey canna bide ta hear ony opeenyun ava oonless hit agrees wi dirs.'

He offers his sympathy: 'Puir sheeld! I doot id du tu maybe is joined till ane o' dis siffrage baand; an if sae du'll no have dee sorros ta seek. An dat's da kaise, dan I'll grip dee haand in simpaty. Gude held dee an' me, we ken what we ken!' [*SN* 29 June 1912]

An old adversary, DIANA, now joined in the correspondence:

'Personally I do not think the Suffrage movement will ever succeed in this country, and I sincerely hope it will not. ... It seeks to make women independent of man, to go out on her own, to fight for herself, to live for herself, to measure swords with men in the battle of life, instead of collaborating with him to make the perfest unit that Nature decrees. ... Rightly understood, and rightly used, woman possesses vast influence over men, and through them over human affairs. She should take care that in seeking to obtain the tangible, she loses that which is subtler but in reality more powerful.' [*SN* 20 July 1912]

Girzie, on 3 August, was still answering Argus:

' ... Public bodies canna [mak Acks o Parliament]. So if da public bodies was a' women, hit wid be da sam'. They could at best only pass resolutions an' send petitions. Last year, hundreds o dem did it. Da Toon Council an' da Coonty Council here baith did it. ... Tink you did Asquith or Wason care one hair?'

As for Diana, two could patronise: ' ... dear ting, gude gie her a breadwinner an' a nursery. The best Suffragist we ha'e, Mrs Fawcett, nursed and helpit a blind husband mony a lang year, an' hed a doughter, 'at wan abune a' da men wi her laer. Der baith doin gude wark fir humanity still, thouugh da bread-winner an da nursery ir baith awa.' [*SN* 3 August 1912]

ARGUS and DIANA joined forces in the 'Day to Day' of 10 August. Argus focused on the Hunter meeting, Diana on the way women were neglecting their households in their quest for 'Votes for Women':

' ....The habits and conduct of many of the children, most of whom are running about outside when they should be at home, conclusively prove that the duties and responsibilities of wifehood and motherhood do not press very heavily on a very considerable number of women. There is too much laxity, too little restraint, a lack of discipline amounting to licence among the rising generation to build up strong character.' [*SN* 10 August 1912; she's speaking about the young men who were to endure the trenches of the Great War.]

P W Hunter's lectures, August and November 1912:

Two lectures were given in Lerwick in early August by P W Hunter, of Saltcoats, Ayr, who'd previously written to the *Shetland News* condemning Cathcart Wason's stance on women's suffrage. The first was entitled 'Some objections to Female Suffrage examined and Dealt with', and there was a 'fairly large audience ... of whom a good many were well known members of the Shetland Women's Suffrage Society.' The meeting was chaired by Mr Loggie. There is a brief account of his speech, in which he made it clear he was an adult suffragist; questions were asked by Messrs M Manson and F Pottinger.

The second lecture was under the auspices of the Lerwick Branch, BSP, on 'The Housing Question and State Aid for Fishermen', in which Hunter spoke on the need for council housing; at the end of his speech, the chairman, Mr Manson, asked for a collection for the wives and children of the transport workers then on strike in London. Hunter then spoke of the importance of state subsidies for fishermen, and the need for Shetland men to unite with those of the east coast.

A letter by FRANCHISE backed up Argus. Its author had been to Mr Hunter's meeting that Monday, with Councillor P W Hunter of Saltcoats as the speaker, and was disappointed that the chair was not taken by one of the local suffragists:

'A mere man should not have presided over that meeting. ... If they lack ability to fight their cause, or if they are deterred from doing so by mistaken feelings of respectability, they are incapable of making a good use of the vote, and so it should be kept from them. ... I noticed that one of the local Socialists readily took the chair ... other Socialists also spoke, took up collections, and distributed literature. ... The Suffragists should be inspired by the action of the Socialists. As things are, the meeting on Monday evening only helped to demonstrate the utter collapse of the Suffrage movement in Lerwick.' [*SN* 13 July 1912]

ARGUS was equally triumphant:

' ... It was really a men's meeting. A man [Argus himself] first suggested that it should be held - a man addressed it; and a man proposed the vote of thanks to the speaker, That is to say, that among all the able women present, not one could be found to speak on the subject for which the meeting was held; neither was there one with sufficient courage to propose even a vote of thanks. Had some of the women present possessed the training which even a term in one of the public bodies could give, such a fiasco, such a humiliation from the point of view of women, could never have occurred.' [*SN* 10 August 1912]

These comments totally ignored the facts that both men must have known: Mr Hunter was clearly invited by the Socialist party in Lerwick, and, respectability or not, it was proper that he should be introduced by men known to him, who had had a hand in inviting him, than by the women who were there as part of his audience.

A further meeting on women's suffrage was held by P W Hunter in the Rechabite Tent Room, and reported in the *Shetland Times* of 23 November 1912. After Argus's comments, the SWSS women were careful to be prominent; the meeting was chaired by Mrs Galloway, Miss Harrison made a short criticism, and the vote of thanks was moved by Jamieson.

Forcible feeding in English gaols:

While Girzie, Argus and Diana were arguing, the suffragettes were enduring. Forcible or 'assisted' feeding had become common in English gaols, and details of the process were explained in lectures by women who had endured it. Early in 1910 Lady Constance Lytton had been imprisoned as 'Jane Warton', an assumed identity to test the different treatment given to 'ladies' and to 'working women'. Lady Constance had a weak heart, and had been handled with care; Jane Warton had neither heart examined nor pulse felt before the doctor and wardresses, after a struggle, managed to insert a steel gag which fastened her jaws wider apart than they could naturally go. This caused her intense pain. Then a four-foot long tube which felt too wide was pushed down her throat. The food was poured down it, so quickly that she felt sick immediately, which made her body and legs double up. The wardresses instantly pressed her head back, and the doctor leant on her knees. She was sick over them, and it seemed a long time before they took the tube out. As the doctor left, he slapped her on the cheek, in contemptuous disapproval.

Alice Pauls, the American student who had been arrested in Glasgow and Dundee, told an American audience about her experiences in English prisons:

'They tied us down with bonds around our legs, chests and necks. Then the doctors and warders held us down and forced a tube five or six feet long, about the size of a finger, through the nostrils to the stomach. ... It always caused my nose to bleed and brought out a perspiration all over me. I had fits of trembling, and I never went through the experience without weeping and sometimes crying aloud.' [*The New York Times,* 18 February 1910]

Her fellow American, Zelie Emerson, had had the bones in her nose broken by this treatment.

Another account was given by the daughter of Gyrithe Lemche, a leading Danish suffragist:

'One day when I was about seventeen my parents had a guest for dinner at Lyngbyhus, an English lady, beautiful, cultured and possibly in her twenties. One eyetooth was missing! She was Sylvia Pankhurst. Was it strange that a seventeen-year-old girl was inflamed when hearing Sylvia Pankhurst tell about England's brutal treatment of the suffragettes? We are speaking about the atrocities of the concentration camps. In England suffragettes were arrested and when they then went on hunger strikes, the English doctors ripped the teeth out of the women's mouths to get a rubber hose with liquid food pushed into the women's mouths. I remember Sylvia Pankhurst's words: 'The corridors in the prisons echo with the women's screams! English doctors behave as the prison's executioners!' [Family newscutting; she was a distant connection by marriage]

Although the word 'rape' was not used, the accounts of force-fed victims stressed similar feelings: the overwhelming physical force used (up to nine wardresses held the victim down), the invasion of throat or rectum by tubes which would have been used on others, the pain, the sense of degradation. Many women who were force-fed were seriously ill for many months afterwards – illnesses included pneumonia, from food getting into the lungs. One eminent surgeon, Sir Victor Horsley, campaigned against forcible feeding, pointing out that the Government was using prison doctors as torturers, but he was backed by only a few others in the medical profession.

Mrs Pankhurst and Frederick and Emmeline Pethick-Lawrence had been sentenced on 22 May 1912 to nine months in the Second Division. They proclaimed their intention of hunger striking unless they were transferred to the First Division, along with the other seventy-five WSPU members then in gaol. Janie Allan barricaded herself in her cell; it took three men with crowbars half an hour to get the door open. Later she said it took her five months to get her normal strength back after being forcibly fed for a week. Emily Wilding Davison also barricaded herself in her cell, using the beds to wedge the door; the authorities turned a hose on her through the window.

By 6 July, all prisoners had been released, and it was the last attempt the prison authorities were to make to force-feed Emmeline Pankhurst, although she was to be arrested several times more.

Militancy continued over the Irish Home Rule Bill, which did not include women as voters. A hatchet was thrown into Asquith's carriage – the first example I can find of a suffragette doing something which might result in serious injury to someone else - and suffragettes attempted to fire the Theatre Royal, where he was speaking. One of them was Mary Leigh, who had taken the Home Secretary to court over force-feeding her. She and her fellow arsonist were both sentenced to five years penal servitude, but were released within nine weeks after hunger-striking.

The question of forcible feeding was brought before the House of Commons in the first week of August, with members debating the difficult choice between forcible feeding and letting offenders go free. Cathcart Wason emphasised his feeling that the House of Commons could not be a court of Appeal against the Home Secretary. This inspired a gleeful letter from ARGUS, wondering what the local Suffragists were going to do when he came to Shetland in August to give his electoral address.

' ... He has done as much against their cause as anyone can do ... the whole force of their organisation should be at work against him.'

To help them out he offers some questions: why Wason supported suffrage in New Zealand, yet is now opposed to it, on what ground of morality or justice he refuses the vote to women, if he considers women intellectually inferior to men, and what he means to do with the million women in Britain who have no hope of getting a husband, and so a home.

' ... I would put [him] on a girdle so hot, I would so roast him that he would writhe and twist and wriggle, and would soon be yelling for mercy. ... Will the local Suffragists do this? We will see.' [*SN* 27 July 1912]

Mr Wason's address to the electorate was reported in the *Shetland News* of 17 August 1912. Again, the women gave a written question, asking whether Mr Wason abided by his last election address, in which he advocated reform on the question of female suffrage in Britain. Mr Wason repeated that he felt there should be a referendum, and turned to the ladies present.

'We have set you up on a pinnacle far above ourselves. (Laughter). We bow down to you and worship at your shrine (Laughter).' He said that they did not need the vote: ' ...what measure [have they] asked from Parliament that they have not got, except the question of the vote?'

He pointed out that there would be a huge increase in the electorate if women were enfranchised; men's mercantile and other hazardous occupations were the reasons why there are so many more women: 'Surely that is a consideration that will weigh with women.' He repeated his offer of a referendum, and was challenged by J W Robertson, who pointed out that when it had been suggested in the House that Mr Wason had opposed it on the reason of cost.

It must have taken a lot of self-restraint to sit quietly under such patronising dismissal, especially after Argus's taunts. It's obvious though that Cathcart Wason would not have answered questions from a woman seriously; the women would simply have been setting themselves up for ridicule from him, disapproval from the floor, and perhaps physical ejection from the building, none of which would have done the reputation of the Shetland society any good.

DIANA crowed.

'As I expected the local suffragists practically left Mr Wason alone. ... I rather admired Mr Wason's reply. Much of it was silly, but a good deal of it embodied the sentiments I hold and have frequently expressed regarding the position of women.' [*SN* 24 August 1912.]

A long letter from P W Hunter called Mr Wason's comments 'an insult to the women of Shetland' and he went on to make a number of points against Mr Wason's care for the isles, as their MP. [*ST*, 31 August 1912]

Jamieson's letter of the same date pointed out that Mr Wason's reply ignored the many demonstrations and pressure from the Women's Liberal Federation. She then gave a list of wants that Parliament had not given:

'The Parliamentary restrictions on the work of women florists, the decision of the Edinburgh printers (enforced by the men on the masters) that women should no longer be apprenticed to the trade, the proposed reduction of pit-brow girls, the minimum wage for men but not for women, the fact that girls of sixteen can be held responsible for immoral acts of grown men, the unspeakable horrors of the White Slave Traffic, all show the need of women's viewpoint in legislation. As things stand, the 'shrine' of womanhood is as open to desecration as to worship.

In regard to 'Argus's' criticisms of local suffragists, I may point out that in Norway, it is since women were enfranchised that they have become active in local government. The same holds true of Australia and New Zealand. ... [he] also makes the mistake of assuming the suffragists are a political party.' [*SN* 24 August 1912]

She ended with the announcement of Mrs Snowden's public meeting, on Thursday 29 August, in the Town Hall, at 8.15pm.

Mrs Snowden's visit, August 1912:

In Scotland, the summer campaigning had been from June to August, with both the NUWSS and the WFL touring. The NUWSS came up to Sutherland, to Dornoch and Bonar Bridge, then took advantage of the Banff Agricultural Show to hold more open-air meetings. Shetland must have been one of Mrs Snowden's last visits. It had been announced in a report in the *Shetland Times* of 1 June 1912, which also gave the SWSS membership as 44.

Ethel Annakin was born in 1881. She was the daughter of a well-to-do Harrogate builder, and became a pupil-teacher, then attended the Pupil-Teacher centre in Leeds, along with Mary Gawthorpe, later to be one of Yorkshire's most inspiring WSPU activists. She went to teacher-training college in Liverpool, then, in 1903, got a post in Leeds, where she became a member of the Independent Labour Party. There she met Philip Snowden, and they were married in 1905. In 1906, he became the Labour MP for Blackburn. Mrs Snowden was at this point a member of the WSPU, and published a *Manifesto for the Women's Social and Political Union* in the New Year *Labour Leader* of 1907:

'We, the undersigned women of the Independent Labour Party, desire to place on record our warm appreciation and high admiration of the work done for woman suffrage by the women of the social and political union. In particular do we admire and congratulate the brave women who have had the courage to suffer in prison for their convictions, and we assert, with them, our profound belief that no real and lasting progress will ever be made apart from the complete enfranchisement of women.'

The Manifesto was signed by over 500 women. When the WSPU split away from the ILP later that year, Snowden remained a member of both, and she and Keir Hardie carried the ILP banner, 'The World for Workers', in the WSPU procession of June 1908. In the summer of 1909, she toured America as a speaker. However as militancy increased she moved to the NUWSS.

Snowden was also an author. She wrote several pamphlets on women, advocating co-operative housekeeping and child-minding, and arguing that the state should give salaries to mothers. She wanted easier divorce for women, and also advocated state control of marriage to ensure the healthiest possible children – she believed the mentally ill and those aged under twenty-six should not marry. She had published her first political book, *The Woman Socialist*, in 1907, and was currently working on a second, *The Feminist Movment*, which was to be published in 1913.

Like Dr Inglis, Ethel Snowden was one of the members of the recently-formed NUWSS Election Fighting Fund committee, and like her, she had just signed a public letter of protest against WSPU militancy, one of the rare instances of one group openly criticising another.

Mrs Snowden's address was reported in the *Shetland News* of 31 August:

' ... Despite a very wet and stormy night, there was a large audience, but it was unfortunate that more people did not take this opportunity of hearing Mrs Snowdon, who is an exceptionally fine speaker. It is no exaggeration to say that no more eloquent, graceful or convincing speaker has ever before addressed a meeting in the Town Hall. Her command of language is extensive, and in clear, virile words she clothes strong and irrefutable arguments in favour of women's enfranchisement. The sentiments behind her remarks were often beautiful; and combining commonsense with hard facts and logical reasoning, interspersed with graceful touches of humour, she held her audience almost spellbound.'

A brief account of her speech was given. The meeting was chaired by Provost Laing.

(Right) Ethel Snowden at a formal dinner with her husband Philip in 1929-30. He was then Chancellor of the Exchequer for Ramsay Macdonald's Labour government.

ARGUS's next Day by Day called for a public thanks, as he was responsible for Mrs Snowdon's visit. It must have taken a fair bit of teeth-gritting to ignore him:

'To all appearances [the Shetland WSS] were dead. ...The movement has received a filip through my intervention, and the 'dressing up' I have given them, which has put some life into it ... can [they] deny this?' [*SN* 7 September 1912]

CONTINENTAL, meanwhile, enclosed a cutting from the London *Daily Express* quoting a letter in the *Times* in which a G M Godden held up hands in horror at suffrage literature:

'no paper other than the medical or scientific journals could publish full quotations from these pamphlets, which are 'sold, with no injury, to young girls'.

OBSERVER began a rather pointless correspondence on why a woman in a print gown has to be treated differently from the same woman in a ball dress. [*ST* 24 August 1912]; INDIGNANT and OBSERVED replied to him the following week. [*ST* 31 August 1912]

The WFL based their west-coast campaign at Rothesay, and over a hundred meetings were held. One organiser commented that women in crowds were taking a more active interest; a new branch was formed in Rothesay, and 140 dozen copies of the WFL magazine *The Vote* were sold; however the comment was also made that the WSPU tactics were damaging their constutional work, with the public not distinguishing between suffragists and suffragettes – a distinction Jamieson had been careful to explain in letters to the *Shetland Times* and *Shetland News*. In late September, the secretary of the Men's League for Women's Suffrage also held a series of open-air meetings, centring on Inverness, to large crowds of working men, and a new Highland branch of the Men's League was formed.

On 7 Sept 1912 there was a second act of damage in Scotland: the glass case containing the Wallace Sword at Wallace Monument, Stirling, was broken. 'Edith Johnston' was arrested, the first Scottish conviction of Ethel Moorhead. At this point she was in her mid forties; she was the daughter of an army surgeon, and was herself a painter who'd studied art in Paris. Her protests so far included throwing an egg at Churchill and being Dundee's first tax resister.

Ethel Moorhead.
Photograph courtesy of Martin Emmison.

Moorhead was to be one of the most destructive Scottish suffragettes, involved in a large number of terrorist attacks, and she did her best to be as obstructive as possible while in prison; the Perth governor described her as insolent and defiant. Her fellow glass-smasher on this occasion was Fanny Parker, the WSPU organiser for the Dundee area, and Lord Kitchener's niece (his comment apparently was, '... she might have some consideration for her family.') Parker, certainly, and Moorhead probably, went on to smash windows in Dundee on 30 October 1912.

Two WSPU members also avoided the police guards at Balmoral Castle (while the Royal family was in residence, too!) to replace the marker flags on the golf course with messages about forcible feeding attached to purple, white and green flags; Asquith and the Home Secretary, McKenna, were harangued by the same WSPU members while playing golf at Dornoch. Asquith was staying at Oversteps, Dornoch, the house belonging to Mrs Hacon – she'll come into the Shetland story later.

On 12 October, a Pilgrimage March from Edinburgh to London began with a rally in Charlotte Square. The march was organised by the WFL and supported by the WSPU and NUWSS. Only six women walked the whole way, but many others walked part of the route with them. Meetings were held during the walk, and a petition was signed. The women arrived in London on 16 November.

In late October, a Liberal meeting was held in Edinburgh, and the WSPU organised a series of interruptions. The nine women who rose to speak were all roughly ejected, along with a man who protested that the treatment they were meeting 'was not like Scotland'. Letters about the way they had been handled continued in the Edinburgh papers for some days, with some correspondents feeling they had 'only themselves to blame' while others felt they had been making legitimate points, and been roughly used in a way that men would not have been. One of the protesters was Ethel Moorhead; she had been hit in the ribs by the teacher sitting next to her. Twenty days later she marched into his classroom, carrying a horse-whip; when he led her to the headteacher's office, she punched him, then, in custody, fought against being searched, and broke a window in her cell.

The SWSS obviously felt the escalation of events on the mainland, for it was agreed at this point to hold a general meeting quarterly.

The SWSS AGM was held on 24 October 1912. Lady Stout's resignation as President, was 'received with regret.' She returned to New Zealand around this time. Two women were proposed: Mrs Mackinnon Wood, wife of the Secretary for Scotland, and Mrs Saxby, from Unst, who was present at the meeting. This Mrs Saxby is more likely to be Mrs Jessie Saxby, the author, although her daughters-in-law Helen, Stephen's wife, or Julia, Thomas's wife, could also have been in Shetland at this time. Mrs MackinnonWood was the first choice, and she accepted the post.

Mrs Mackinnon Wood was a Shetland lass, born Isabella Mill Sandison, and known as Isa in her family. She was the daughter of Alexander Sandison of Gardiesfauld, Unst, who was one of the merchants on the first ZCC. Two of her brothers, Alexander and Robert, were ministers, and her sister

Caroline married a minister, the Reverend Bird. Isabella was a first cousin to John Leisk. A family biography compiled by her nephew described her as 'graceful in form and movement, quick-witted, at times sharp-tongued; a dignified and charming hostess; an invalid in her later years.'

Letters from her brother Alexander, (known as Looie) who was later to carry the Shetland banner at a Men's Deputation in the Albert Hall, gave a vivid impression of the young Isa:

'[In 1874, when Isa was aged 13] Isa changes fast, childhood is already past ... a quiet face with thought in her grey eyes, yet no lack of laughter or fun. Indeed, she possesses a dislike to sobriety in general, and any manifestation of it in me in particular! Thinks brothers are very troublesome and it is unfortunate that sisters can't help loving them. ... My Isa is very dear to me.'

In 1877, when Isa was 16, and his mother was ill, Looie said that

'Isa looks anxious, and he wishes she had less to do; she refuses to read 'Aurora Leigh' or poetry of any kind. Her governess had told her that Ladies must read the poets and be ignorant of what is found in the newspapers. Looie commented, 'Nothing wearies me so much of anyone as to find they are behaving, not living.'

A year later Looie sympathised with Isa who taking on more and more of the household management and was having difficulty with the servants.

'The servants take very much their own way and liberties which your Mamma would not think of allowing. ... I often hear Isa come in from the kitchen in consternation – all of the three girls have gone out to visit some of their neighbours without even mentioning their intentions. When they come in they have, of course, some excuse or other. I rather take the servants' side I think. You know I always was a Radical and they must often feel lonely and out of temper. Isa then, as in later life, was calm and matter of fact. She laughingly demanded that Looie should teach her to be sentimental; all young ladies, she found, were expected to be that, but she couldn't quite manage it. Isa already shewed the beauty of face and form that were always hers.' [from the biography of Rev Looie, by his son Alexander Sandison (1885-1972) - 22 copies published privately, 1967]

Isa's husband, Thomas Mackinnon Wood, was the Liberal MP for Glasgow St Rollox. His father was an Orcadian, and Tom was a member of Looie's church at King's Weigh House. Looie took Tom to Gardiesfauld, where he met Isa; they were married in 1883. Mackinnon Wood stood unsuccessfully for Orkney and Shetland in 1902, his third attempt to get into Parliament.

Tom and Isa's household was described by their nephew, Alex, who stayed with them in the summer of 1904:

'Living with my aunt's family was both an aid and an incentive to these aims (his wish to achieve a London BSc and the scholarship at Cambridge which he needed to be able to fulfil his ambition of going there). My uncle, Tom Wood, was a London graduate in honours and his mind was as attached to scholarship as it was keen in business and politics. My elder cousins were at Highgate School, Hugh already marked out for the Balliol scholarship he won in 1902 and Louis, two years younger, a good runner-up. In the evenings we worked together; I deep in biology, chemistry and physics, they in the classics, and the relative values of Science and the Humanities were in constant debate. My uncle was interested in all our work and widened our knowledge of English literature by talk and reading aloud, giving us also an insight into the pros and cons of national and municipal politics and the administration of the LCC, then in the hey-day of its early ambitions and controlled by the Progressives of whom my uncle was the Leader. It was an intimate, self-sufficient family life: my aunt Isa as charming and understanding with me as with her own children. We rarely sought entertainment outside the home; there were hard and grass tennis courts in the garden and room to drive a golf ball; we had dancing classes from a charming teacher in the large drawing room and there were often dinner parties for political and other friends. Music and drama were rather in the background, for neither appealed much to Tom or Isa and though Tom liked buying expensive pictures, there was little practice of or discussion on art.' [from the biography of Rev Looie, by Alexander Sandison]

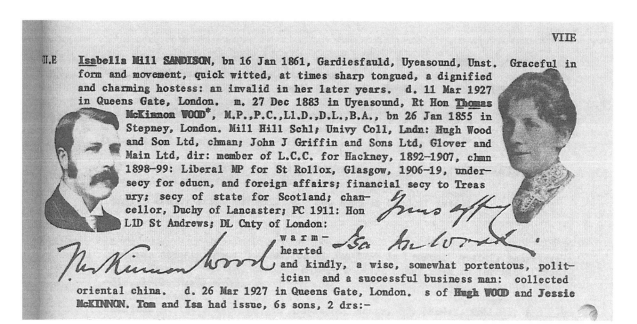

II.E Isabella Mill SANDISON, bn 16 Jan 1861, Gardiesfauld, Uyeasound, Unst. Graceful in form and movement, quick witted, at times sharp tongued, a dignified and charming hostess: an invalid in her later years. d. 11 Mar 1927 in Queens Gate, London. m. 27 Dec 1883 in Uyeasound, Rt Hon Thomas McKinnon WOOD*, M.P.,P.C.,Ll.D.,D.L.,B.A., bn 26 Jan 1855 in Stepney, London. Mill Hill Schl; Univy Coll, Lndn: Hugh Wood and Son Ltd, chman; John J Griffin and Sons Ltd, Glover and Main Ltd, dir: member of L.C.C. for Hackney, 1892-1907, chmn 1898-99: Liberal MP for St Rollox, Glasgow, 1906-19, under-secy for educn, and foreign affairs; financial secy to Treasury; secy of state for Scotland; chancellor, Duchy of Lancaster; PC 1911: Hon LlD St Andrews; DL Cnty of London: warm-hearted and kindly, a wise, somewhat portentous, politician and a successful business man: collected oriental china. d. 26 Mar 1927 in Queens Gate, London. s of Hugh WOOD and Jessie McKINNON. Tom and Isa had issue, 6s sons, 2 drs:-

Isa and Tom Mackinnon Wood, from the family tree compiled by their nephew, with thanks to Alec Sandison and Louis Mackay.

(Left) A photograph taken by Alexander Sandison, thought to be of his sister Isa. Photographs courtesy of Louis Mackay.

Mackinnon Wood was finally elected to Parliament in 1906, and went on to hold a number of offices: Parliamentary Secretary to the Board of Education, Under-Secretary for Foreign Affairs, and Financial Secretary to the Treasury. He had been appointed Secretary for Scotland only eight months earlier, in February 1912.

The AGM was reported in full in both *Shetland News* and *Shetland Times* of 2 November. Lady Stout's resignation was announced, and an account given of the visit to Wason. Dr Inglis' visit in April was also described, and her influence in bringing Mrs Snowden up pointedly explained. The Society's educational work was stressed:
'the Society had sent literature to every parish in Shetland ... the need for funds for literature is great, as it is our best means of propaganda in the Islands.'
The article then looked at the National Union (membership 350,000) and the Scottish Federation (now nearly 60 societies), and explained the decision to support Labour candidates at by-elections: 'the Labour party is the only one that includes Women's Suffrage in its programme.'
The AGM had ended with
'a very interesting discussion ... on the feasibility of women entering public bodies at the present stage of the women's movement. ... while it was a good idea, the restrictions of the Municipal Register and the very large amount of social, philanthropic and temperance work already resting on women, and made more difficult by present political interference, made it impossible for women to undertake any more work than they were already doing. [*SN, ST,* 2 November 1912]

The latest militant activity was attacks on pillar boxes in both England and Scotland. On 18 November a bottle of brown fluid was poured into an Edinburgh postbox; on 28 November, corrosive fluid in an Aberdeen post box; 2 December saw a co-ordinated attack with inflammable fluid on Edinburgh, Leith and Kirkaldy post boxes, followed by another on 6 December on two Glasgow pillar boxes. Jessie Stephen, a domestic servant and Trade Union member, was later to describe the organisation of this: the acid was supplied by a woman chemist, and they met at a specified time to receive it and be told when and where to attack. It's likely such organisation was the work of a local group, rather than under specific orders from London. This tactic was a mistake; it didn't harm the Government, and annoyed the people whose letters had been destroyed.
In Aberdeen, five women were arrested: three, including Fanny Parker, for being in a hall where Lloyd George, now Chancellor of the Exchequer, was due to speak, Emily Wilding Davison for horse-whipping a minister she mistook for Lloyd George, and Ethel Moorhead for throwing a stone at the window of a car she took to be his. One of the women, May Grant, later spoke publicly in Dundee of her reasons for militancy, and from now Scotswomen were behind many of the militant attacks in Scotland. The backlash against such tactics was intensifying; when suffragettes interrupted a University meeting, a group of students wrecked the Glasgow WSPU office. On 11 November, George Lansbury, Labour MP for Bow and Brumley, stood down from the House of Commons for re-election as a Women's Suffrage candidate, but in spite of strong support from the WSPU, he was defeated by 751 votes on 26 November 1912.
An Anti-Suffrage meeting was held in St Andrew's Hall, Glasgow, in late November; speakers included Lord Curzon and the Marchioness of Tullibardine (later the Duchess of Atholl, and, ironically, one of Britain's first women MPs).
The same venue was used by the Scottish Federation for their Meeting on 9 December. Shetland delegates were Mrs Francis Jamieson, Edinburgh (Jamieson's sister-in-law), and Mrs A J Campbell, Glasgow, the wife of the Reverend A J Campbell who had chaired Chrystal Macmillan's Lerwick meeting in 1909. The meeting was presided over by Lady Frances Balfour, and the Earl of Lytton (Lady

Constance's brother, who had persuaded *The Times* to publish Lady Stout's letter) was the principal speaker. The SWSS promised a 5 guinea donation, stipulating that it 'be earmarked for Federation work in Shetland'. Later, Jamieson wrote to ask if part of it could be in knitted goods for sale.

The socialist / suffrage links were still strong; J J Haldane Burgess published his poem *Suffrage* in his collection *Rasmie's Buddy*, published by T & J Manson, 1913.

Suffrage

Ay, it's time wir parlamenters
Got it eence inta dir skults,
'At da only kind of suffrage
Is da suffrage for adults.

When ye spaek o votes for women,
Some MPs can only girn;
Idders tells you 'at it's nonsense;
Idders still gets fairly tirn.
Nane need lippen siccan bodies
Ta hae sense ta jee a jot;
Bit why sood da men o raeson
Still keep women frae dir vot?

Votes for women – it's bit justice;
So, god luck attend dir caase.
If da women mann obey dem,
Lat dem help ta mak da laas.

If da women mann pay taxes
Lat dem help ta lay dem on:
Wi da bulk o social matters
Dey know weel what sood be done.

Some folk, god aald-fashioned bodies,
Bids da women bide at haem,
Mak da maet, an rock da cradle,
Wash da claes and clean da laem;
Bit da same folk backs a system,
An dey never tink it wheer,
By which haems is gettin fewer,
An mair sordid every year:
An dat's for da mass o wirkers,
Aa da wy 'at it can be,
Till dey hae da sense and courage
Ta mak Labour raelly free.

Some says it unsexes women
Ta do certain kinds o wark –
What dey ca men's occupations,
Even wirkin as a clerk.
Let us see noo what it comes till,
For da sake o argumint,
When dey say dey want da women
Ta be just as dey wer wint.

I da days when men wis hunters,
Feghters i da east and west
Dey made only dir ain weapons,
An da women did da rest.
Women cleaned da skins an dressed dem,
Shaped, shooed dem inta claes –
Wis da curriers, and tailors,
An shomakkers dan-a-days.

Women wi dir whorls and spinnies
Startet every textile trade;
Women planted coarn, and grund it,
Made it inta bursten bread –
So 'at dey wer da first fermers,
Millers, bakers, so ta spaek:
An dey wer da first clay-potters,
Made da hoose-loms, an da laek.
Some says women haes nae trainin
For affairs; yea, weel I wat:
Bit supposin 'at it wis sae,
Tell me wha's ta blame for dat.
Men is made da laas for ages,
An some men is siccan swabs,
'At dey're always makkin women
Drudges, stucca-dolls, or drabs.
True men wants dem for companions,
Ta walk wi dem, side by side,
Takkin coonsel sweet tagedder,
Till aa life be glorified.

Some says women, if enfranchised,
Wid da pooer dey got abuse;
Folk o sese kens 'at da great mass
Wid dir votes for progess use.
Even dir one bit o waekness
Wid help up da social heichts –
For dey can't staand ean anidder,
So dey're strong for equal rights;
An da man 'at grudges women
Equal pay for equal wark,
Is no better dan da sweaters
In Hood's sang aboot da sark.
Men gets votes even tho da lowest,
O society da dregs,
Whin dir only claim ta manhood
Is da breeks upo dir legs.
Aboot what da women aims at,
We're nae langer i da dark;
Peace an plenty for da nation,
Happy haems, an joyous wark.

Votes for women – it's bit justice;
So, god luck attend dir caase,
If da women mann obey dem,
Lat dem help ta mak da laas.

If da women mann pay taxes
Lat dem help ta lay dem on:
Wi da bulk o social matters
Dey know weel what sood be done.

Ay, it's time wir parlamenters
Got it eence inta dir sults,
'At da only kind of suffrage
Is da suffrage for adults.

A teachers' outing on Mousa, 1908. Only Miss Harrison can be identified with certainty (on the right, behind the front seated lady), but other suffragists of the Shetland WSS are certainly among this holiday group. Early teacher members were Mrs Nicol, Miss Morrison, Miss Campbell, Miss Gulland and Miss Harrison. They were joined in 1912 and 1913 by Miss Dey, Miss Ruby Sandison and Miss Christie.

Photographed by R Ramsay; courtesy of the Shetland Museum and Archives [JS00347]

11

January 1913 – August 1914

The Reform Bill,
bombs and burning,
forcible feeding in Scotland
and the declaration of war.

The failure of the Reform Bill:

In November, 1911, Asquith had promised a Manhood Suffrage Bill with the potential for including women. Jamieson had explained its provisions at the AGM in November:

'[It is] so drafted that it can be amended to include Women's Suffrage. This really means that there must be two amendments ... [Firstly] to delete the word male from 'every male person' ... There is little doubt this first trench will be carried.'

The second amendment would decide what form Women's Suffrage would take:

'The Labour party will move and vote for Adult suffrage. This Amendment will be carried only if the Opposition vote for it with the intention of wrecking the whole Bill. In the present state of public opinion, the passing of this amendment probably involves the downfall of Government.

This failing, the Dickenson amendment will be moved. This would enfranchise women ratepayers and the wives of men ratepayers – Household Suffrage.

The last amendment, failing the two others ... would enfranchise women on Municipal Register.'

Jamieson urged electors to send deputations to their MP, particularly anti-suffrage MPs, so 'they shall not have it in their power to say that they have not heard from their constituents on the question.' [*SN, ST* 2 November 1912]

Now, in January 1913, the Reform Bill was coming before the House of Commons. A letter from Jamieson, as the Secretary, SWSS, appeared in both *Shetland News* and *Shetland Times,* explaining the need for an amendment to the bill, and urging Shetland electors to write to Mr Wason:

'The sacredness of motherhood, the value and dignity of human labour, the universal interests of men and women are all involved. Law-makers are yearly interfering more and more with the lives, the occupations, and the homes of women. All this applies especially to Shetland women and their self-reliant labours. And on their behalf the Suffrage Society appeals to every Shetland elector to write and ask Mr Wason to vote for the Women's Suffrage amendment to the Reform Bill, or to refrain for voting against them. – Yours etc' [*SN, ST* 11 January 1913]

This is followed by a reminder, different in each paper:

'The cause, if delayed, cannot be effectively brought forward again for years. ... Unionist men and women ... will [you] accept without any protest Mr Wason's hostile attitude to a just claim? Yours etc' [*SN*, 18 January 1913]

' ... Liberal men and women should both write. Liberal women if they had all along concentrated on this Reform, could now have been helping their Party with their vote. ....' [*ST*, 18 January 1913]

On January 23, the Speaker of the House of Commons caused an uproar by announcing, in answer to a question from Asquith, that the Reform Bill could not continue with its suffrage amendment – it altered the Bill too much. A new statute would have to be drawn up for a 'future session'.

The *Shetland Times* editorial of 1 February 1913 was predictably sympathetic to Asquith in its account of the happenings in the House:

'There has nothing come as a greater surprise to Liberal and Tory alike, than the extraordinary development in connection with the Franchise Bill. When the Bill was first introduced it was for the abolition of plural voting, and also to simplify the means of registration for Parliamentary voters. But the Bill got burdened with amendments. ... [including] the opening up of the Parliamentary Franchise for women, and in answer to a question put by the Prime Minister on Thursday of last week, the Speaker of the House of Commons indicated that, if some of these amendments were carried they would so change the character of the Bill that it would become a new Bill and would therefore have to be withdrawn. This announcement produced a profound sensation in the House. The matter was adjourned till Monday evening, when it again came up. The House was crowded on Monday afternoon in every part, not merely the benches, but the galleries, when the Prime Minister rose to give an account of how the Government intended extricating itself from the polition in which it found itself, owing to the Speaker's ruling ... Mr Asquith's reply was a closely-reasoned, cogent exposition of the position of the Government in face of the new conditions which had arisen, and showed that they were desirous of standing by all the pledges given by membersof the Government on the question of Women's Suffrage. It was quite clear, according to the Speaker, that no suggestion of Women's Suffrage could be made in a measure to dealing with votes for men, and the Government had no intention of introducing a measure to give votes to women. However, an opportunity would be given in the coming session for any private member to bring in a Bill dealing with that important matter. It was agreed to form a non-Party committee, drawn from both sides of the House.'

The *Shetland Times* thoroughly approved:

'The wisdom of withdrawing the Bill is quite obvious, the judgement shown in appointing such a Committee is equally clear ... The decision of the Cabinet to give facilities in the next session, which commences in March, for the introduction by a private member of a Women's Franchise Bill is one that can be commended in all quarters. It will give the House an opportunity of a free expression of opinion by all phases of thought and opinion in the House.' [*ST* 1 February 1913]

ARGUS sympathised with the women:

'I really feel sorry for the Suffragists. Again, the Liberals have 'diddled' them. .. Votes for Women will not be heard of in Parliament for goodness knows the time.' He didn't believe it was unforseen: 'Now – only now – is it found that by tacking on Women's Suffrage to the 'Manhood Suffrage Bill' the whole character of the latter is so greatly altered that it cannot be 'proceeded with in its present form' and that a new Bill will have to be introduced ... Now, will anyone seriously say that the Prime Minister and the other 'antis' in the Cabinet did not foresee this long ago? Does not the whole thing have the appearance of being carefully planned – of a trap having been set for the Suffragists, and when they had innocently walked into it, the spring which cut them through the neck was released. ... Mr Asquith is an old Parliamentary hand. No man knows better the tricks of the trade, or how, behind a smiling face and a smooth and unctuous manner, to lead the unsuspecting to their doom. ... The Manhood Suffrage Bill ...was meant for window-dressing purposes only ... they did not wish it to become law.

It was unutterably mean, however, to use the question of Women's Suffrage as a pawn in the game of trickery by which the Franchise Billl was to be withdrawn. The women have fought hard, courageously and persistently, for the Parliamentary vote. They were led to believe that some measure of enfranchisement would be passed. At the last minute, just as they were lifting the cup to their lips, it has been dashed to the ground. The very men who told them the Promised Land was certainly in sight were those who took steps to prevent them entering it. Little wonder the Suffragists have no faith in Liberal promises. No wonder they are driven to desperation.' [*SN* 1 February 1913]

Suffrage workers accused the government of betrayal. Christabel and Mrs Pankhurst promptly proclaimed a new WSPU policy of guerilla attacks and secret arson; in response, a kiosk in Regent's Park was burnt down, and a bomb damaged Lloyd George's newly-built house. The National Union tried to keep the solidarity of the non-militant movement, and asked for messages of support for their president, Millicent Garratt Fawcett, and small contributions towards cost of a presentation badge. The SWSS sent a message of support and 2/-. In all, forty-nine societies sent notes of appreciation, including one in Gaelic from Inverness.

Immediately after the failure of the Reform Bill, Asquith was in Scotland. In Leven, 'Margaret Morrison' (Ethel Moorhead) attempted to rush the hall where he was speaking, and threw cayenne pepper in the face of the policeman who arrested her. At Methil Police Station, she smashed a window and poured water over the officers. She was sent to Dundee, where she went on hunger strike, then transferred to Perth for forcible feeding. The governor was reluctant to force feed, and she was released on 4 February 1913, but the possibility caused a number of letters in Scottish newspapers. Asquith moved on to be given the Freedom of the City in Dundee, and again there were protests, with several arrests.

The same *Shetland Times* editorial had made the Bill's failure sound like the women's fault:

'Meanwhile what is the attitude of these unsexed hooligans, the militant suffragists? Surely, the spirit they have displayed since the ruling of the Speaker of the House of Conmmons became known, has been sufficient to convince the most casual thinker that they are unworthy of any concessions whatever ... It is a pity that the Authorities could not seize such vixens as Mrs Pankhurst and Mrs Despard and send them off to, say, Foula, and allow them to develop their physical abilities by climbing the hills there, or attempting to pull to Walls in an open boat in the face of a stiff south-wester. Europe had an easier mind when Napoleon was safely housed in St Helena; the suffrage movement would have better chance of recognition if the fire-eaters of the party were removed, and it was left to some womanly women to strive for the rights they claim on fair and rational lines.' [*ST* 1 February 1913; what does the editor think the suffragists had been doing for fifty years?]

Jamieson's reply to the *Shetland Times* reflected her sense of betrayal and frustration:

'Dear Sir, I read your last week's leader with some interest, as I believe this is the first time you have editorially taken notice of Women's Suffrage, and I naturally look for some worthy pronouncement on the subject. Your first paragraph sets forth the action of a Government who during the last fifteen months have deliberately and carefully, step by step, approached a situation they themselves created, of absolute imbroglio, which, arrived at, they are not statesmen enough to deal with or to abandon. Then, a private member's bill, which they propose you say 'will give the House an opportunity of a free expression of opinion by all phases of thought and opinion in the House.' And this, when it was instantly pointed out that the 'free' vote would be at once crossed by party considerations relating to the Parliament Act. This, in the face of our repeated experiences of private members bills, with or without facilities. This, in the face of Cabinet ministers' repeated assurances that our only chance lay in inclusion in a Government bill. Is your paragraph a vindication or a condemnation of your position?

As to your second paragraph [on the militants]: Raw hobble-de-hoys (not self-respecting youth) and people whose minds have not got beyond the hobble-de-hoy stage regarding the women's movement, concentrate appreciatively on the militants and their methods, because they understand them and feel able to cope with them. They are wise in keeping to matters within their capacity. But, may I ask, is it because you think hooliganism right and natural in members of your own sex that you have no word of blame for their savage treatment of these frenzied women?

And why would you thrust these women, the result of political blundering and trickery, on the Foula folk, who are equal to any of our isles folk in kindliness and fairplay? Would it increase their good opinion of statesmen, or of you?

Europe produced but one Napoleon, and he did not seek redress for grievances. But a continuance of Parliamentary injustice and impotence will produce a steady crop of these unhappy women, and counter-hooligans have not, so far, shown themselves effective in repressing them.

The press has its share of responsibility for their existence – the press, which publishes full and flaring accounts of their misdeeds, and seems to regard them as the only advocates of Women's Suffrage – the press, which persistently ignores the enormous amount of work done for suffrage on peaceful and law-abiding lines by every other organised body of women, in their hundreds and thousands.

True politicians, like true physicians, deal with the causes, not the symptoms only, of disease. And those who fail in this merely prove their own incompetence – Yours, etc, THE SECRETARY, Shetland WSS. [*ST* 15 February 1913]

DIANA's criticism of the militants in the next Day by Day gave a sense of the chaos they were causing:

'To read accounts of the disgraceful scenes that have taken place in London and elsewhere within the last few weeks, causes me to blush for my sex. To think that Ministers of the Crown have to be protected by the police from the savage attacks – often brutal and cowardly – of women, many of them educated, and accustomed to all the refinement of the best society; to think that these same women have been going about deliberately and maliciously destroying the contents of pillar post boxes, smashing windows, setting fire to buildings, acting more like hooligans and untutored savages than civilised beings, is to bring the blush of shame to the cheek of every woman worthy of the name.' [*SN* 22 February 1913]

This sparked off a new skirmish between DIANA and ARGUS. ARGUS's reply to DIANA descended to name-calling:

'... In all probability she is once of those very estimable 'young' women whom men leave very severely to themselves – they are too 'touch-me-not', too cold, too dignified for ordinary mortals. I'll lay ten to one she has never been in love, except perhaps, in her school days, and that only for a fortnight; that she is not married, and has little prospect of ever entering into that state ...'

His final paragraph returned to his old argument:

'Let the women show more activity, more ability, more energy and earnestness in looking after affairs needing attention at their own doors; then and only then, will their claim for the Parliamentary vote be ripe for consideration and settlement.' [*SN* 1 March 1913]

DIANA's reply showed the goose could hiss as loud as the gander:

'I imagine that 'Argus' is young, that he is a person who reads a good deal, and thinks he knows a lot about about everything ... he will find that all he really does know about anything, and especially about women, is extremely little.' She will not deign to reply to his comments on her personally, except to say that he 'is wrong in every particular. Further, that I am married ...' [*SN* 8 March 1913]

Another correspondence between HAMLET and an ALARMED PARENT in these same weeks discussed whether women teachers should get equal pay with men. HAMLET feared that equal wages would mean 'giving of the prizes of life to women who were willing to shirk the primary duties of life' [*SN* 1 March 1913]. ALARMED PARENT felt 'There are far too many women teachers already, and the only way to keep them down is to pay them a good deal less than men.' [*SN* 8 March 1913]

The first of the SWSS quarterly meetings was held on 24 Feb 1913 with sixteen members present. The Suffrage pamphlets had been distributed through Shetland in the first fortnight of January, and Mrs Fawcett's appeal for letters to MPs was sent to representative people in every parish. Mr Wason was written to again, and he 'replied courteously saying that the matter was receiving his earliest consideration.' Mrs Mackinnon Wood and Mrs Freeman were to act as delegates at the NUWSS Council meeting in London on 27 and 28 February.

A fall-out, perhaps, from the Lady Stout affair: 'the Committee resolved that minutes of the meetings of the Executive Committee of the National Union be no longer sent to this Society.'

However the SWSS was determined to be present at events on the mainland from now on: 'it was decided that if there was to be a procession organised in Edinburgh in Assembly week, this Society would attempt to send representatives and their banner.' This meeting also gave the first mention of 'Friends of Women's Suffrage' who were non-member supporters. A letter from the NUWSS Secretary was read; it concerned the Government's offer to give space for a private member's bill. [SWSS Minute Book, 24 February 1913]

On 14 March, the annual Council Meeting of the Scottish Women's Liberal Federation was almost entirely taken up with the discussion of women's suffrage.

The March SWSS committee meeting discussed the offer of a speaker from the Scottish Federation, Mrs Stetson Gilman. Mrs Galloway offered to host her, but the SWSS couldn't defray her travelling expenses, so asked that the Federation use the 5 guineas donated. Miss Campbell gave in her resignation, which was 'received with regret' [SWSS Minute Book, 25 March 1913].

It's a pity Mrs Stetson Gilman didn't make it to Shetland, for she'd have been an interesting visitor. She was Charlotte Anna Perkins, feminist novelist and poet, and the great-niece of Harriet Beecher Stowe. Her younger brother was christened Thomas Adie, so I wonder if there was a distant Shetland connection.

Terrorist tactics and Emily Davison's death, June 1913:

On the mainland, the militant attacks had escalated. Through February and March a number of pillar-boxes and telegraph wires were interfered with. On 13 March 1913 Mrs Pankhurst spoke in Glasgow, supported by a number of clergymen and their wives. There had been rumours of students creating trouble, so Jessie Stephen used her Trade Union connections to enlist fifty dockers and twenty carters as stewards. The disturbance lasted less than ten minutes; one particularly strong docker picked up a student in each hand and lifted them out. Mrs Pankhurst spoke in Edinburgh the next day. She had at this point been on bail, on condition of refraining from 'incitement to violence'; since this public speaking broke those conditions, she was re-arrested.

Mrs Pankhurst was sentenced to three years in prison on 3 April, and immediately there were increased attacks on property. For example, on the day of her sentence, four houses were fired in Hampstead, the glass of pictures damaged in Manchester, and an empty railway carriage bombed; the next day a mansion near Chorley Wood was destoryed by fire, and a bomb exploded at Oxted station; the following day, Ayr and Kelso racecourses were attacked, the first of a number of attacks on sporting facilities; the next day, two houses were destroyed, at Potters Bar and Norwich; the next, an attempt was made to fire Cardiff racecourse, a house was burned in Hampstead, and a cannon was fired from Dudley Castle; on the sixth day, 'Release Mrs Pankhurst' was cut in large letters in the grass of Duthie Park, Aberdeen.

Extant newsreel film of 13 April 1913 shows the burning of the house of Mr Arthur Du Cros, MP for Hastings. It is a substantial Tudor-style building, gutted by the fire; the roof is badly damaged, and the windows burnt out. A workman brings a ladder over and pries damaged stonework from the eaves. This is followed by an interior shot of the burnt-out building, with smoke still rising from the floor. Other footage from 1913 show the remains of Yarmouth Pier and Pavilion (there was a bomb in dressing room; the comment of the owner was, 'I never thought my show was as bad as all that ...') and St Catherine's Church, London, completely destroyed by fire – the roof and windows are gone, and the interior gutted. [Pathé News, National Film Archives]

Open-air suffrage meetings were prohibited on 15 April 1913; two weeks later the staff of the WSPU magazine *The Suffragette* were arrested, and all copy confiscated. Demonstrations on the freedom of the Press followed, but all those arrested were sentenced to terms of imprisonment ranging from six to twenty-one months. Two months later a notorious 'White Slave' procuress whose victims included young girls was sentenced to only three months, and *The Suffragette* began a campaign against prostitution.

The first Scottish bomb was on 2 May, in a Dundee billiard room, followed by another in the Duke of Buccleugh's private chapel; both of these were discovered before they went off, but in May one exploded in the Royal Observatory, Edinburgh. A school in Aberdeen was set on fire in early May, and Farringdon Hall, Dundee, was burnt down.

On 17 May 1913, ARGUS detailed some of their activities: 'The destruction of pillar boxes, the ruination of golf greens, the interruption of public meetings and all the other nefarious tactics which the militants have recently employed ...' He also mentions an attempt to bomb St Paul's Cathedral, and ends by repeating his remedy: for women to use their places in municipal affairs. In the same edition Aald Geordie was back, putting off casting his peats, for

'da very tocht o' tacklin' hit maks me faerd; yeis, as faerd is a policeman ill be whin he haes ta tackle a siffragit! Mercy faadir: Maister Edeetir, what is gaain tae be done wi' dis suffragits? Hit wis toght ill enyoch whin dey tried ta burn doon Loyid George's hoose; bit noo id dey're geen an' brunt doon da hoose o da Loard, hit passes a' boonds. ... Dat ill be laek a' da rest o' hit; jiust fir spite id dey canna git der will oot. ... Bit I tink dir nae faer o dis

Lerook siffragits duin' onyting desperate, fir dey're muckle laek what's said ida Testamaint aboot da kirk o Ladiegea; dir nidder cauld nor haet.' [*SN* 17 May 1913]

There was a more serious correspondence in the *Shetland News* in early April, following on a letter from Cathcart Wason (to the *Times,* perhaps?) which is quoted along with the reply from Mrs Flora Annie Steel, the writer of a number of books on life in India, but now living in Scotland. Wason pointed out that men's chivalry towards women was exemplified by a woman not now being flogged, not being legally bound to support her parents, not being liable to imprisonment for refusing to pay her debts, that she can sue her husband for desertion, and that if she drinks or breaks up his house, he cannot desert her. Steel pointed out tartly that 'no woman worthy of the name' would desire:

'1. To batten, scatheless, on the ruin of her sisters.
2. To leave her parents to starve without fear of punishment.
3. To defraud her fellows and laugh in her sleeve.
4. To be able, unscathed, to neglect her paramount duties.' [*SN*, 5 April 1912]

A SUPPORTER OF WOMEN'S SUFFRAGE pointed out, more pertinently, the financial reasons that underpinned men's 'chivalry' to women:

'The law does not wish the parents or the deserted wife and family to come on the rates, therefore it sues the person most likely to be able to support them.'

The author then pleaded for women's rights:

'At present a woman who has her living to make is handicapped in almost every walk of life by the obstacles that men put in her way ...' [*SN*, 19 April 1912]

At this point the Health of Prisoners (Temporary Discharge for Ill Health) Act, or 'Cat and Mouse' Act, was travelling through Parliament; it was to receive Royal Assent on 25 April 1913. It gave prison governors authority to release hunger striking prisoners for a short time to regain their strength, avoiding the need for forcible feeding; they would then be re-arrested, to continue their sentence. For the present, suffragettes who did not re-offend would not be particularly looked for. From now until the outbreak of war, Mrs Pankhurst, Sylvia Pankhurst and Annie Kenney were regularly arrested and released; they continued to speak publicly, being smuggled into halls for meetings. On occasion, each had to speak from a wheelchair or a stretcher, the effect of repeated hunger and thirst strikes.

A number of 'safe houses' were established throughout the country for prisoners on the run to use as a refuge. One Scottish refuge was Hoprig Mains Farm, East Lothian, belonging to Catherine Blair. She was a staunch member of the WSPU, but not able to go to prison herself because she had children. She wrote letters to the paper in defence of the militants, and her husband resigned as vice-president of the local Liberal party because of the government's treatment of suffragettes. Blair was later to be the founder of the first SWRI branch in Scotland, in Longniddry in 1917. (Right) Catherine Blair. Photograph courtesy of the SWRI.

The promised private member's bill was brought forward; on 6 May, Sir Willoughby Dickinson's Women's Suffrage Bill was defeated at its second reading, by 267 votes to 221. The Scottish Home Rule Bill was also going through Parliament. In its first draft, women were included as electors, but this clause was taken out before it was presented to Parliament; the Scottish Women's Liberal Federation, the Scottish Federation of the NUWSS, and the Scottish Council of the WFL all protested at this. The second reading was to take place on 15 May 1914, and again the debate centred on women's suffrage. The anti-suffrage league saw a federal system as a solution to the 'woman problem'.

Mr Mackinnon Wood made a strong statement in favour of the inclusion of women. In the end the Bill was talked out.

The destruction of Farringdon Hall was followed, in June and July, by attacks on Stair Park House, Tranent, a wing of a laboratory at St Andrews University, Leuchars railway station and Ballikinrain Castle, Killearn. In most cases suffrage literature was left at the scene, and the WSPU was happy to claim credit. As with the pillar box attacks, the fires and bombs did not harm the Government, but caused considerable public animosity against all suffrage workers. Speakers regularly reported being shouted down or pelted with mud, vegetables or rotten eggs; male students seem to have been particularly hostile, perhaps in resentment at the still-recent invasion of 'their' Universities. In Edinburgh in June, a group of Church Guild women out walking were surrounded by a hostile mob when some children called out that they were suffragettes (the Lanark children were more robust, asking speakers to 'burn our school doon and gie us a holiday!'). The hostility seemed to be an urban phenomenon: when the summer touring began, speakers in the country commented on their warm reception and courteous hearing.

On 4 June 1913, at Epsom, Emily Wilding Davison was fatally injured when she stepped out in front of the King's horse during a race. The jury is still out on whether she meant to commit suicide; the verdict at the time was 'Death by misadventure', and on balance it seems likely that she meant to divert the King's horse in some way, by catching at its reins – perhaps to pin the suffragette rosette she carried on it. She died on 9 June. There was a huge funeral in London, and a memorial service in Albert Square, Dundee. There is a series of short newsreel clips showing Emily Davison's death and funeral (14 June 1913). The race had been filmed as part of the news, so it begins with a cheery clip of policemen drinking beer and the runners coming to the stands. There is a caption: *Tattenham Corner* and the horses coming around the corner and passing the camera. Then, *Suffragette killed in Attempt to Pull Down the King's Horse* We see the horses coming round, a dark figure run out, and shockingly quickly the horses are past, and the figure on the grass; the jockey too is lying still, twenty yards further on. The crowd surges on to the course. The final race clip shows the runners arriving, and the crowd coming around them at the finish.

Emily Davison's Funeral shows a horse-drawn hearse, mounded in flowers, with women in white dresses and coloured sashes, walking on each side of it. Behind them, two motors, also heaped with flowers, then a guard of women in white with black sashes and armbands, each carrying a lily. *The Scene at St George's, Bloomsbury* has a chain of policemen holding the crowd back, with some difficulty; the 'guard' salute as the coffin is carried down railed steps. *The Journey to the Churchyard at Morpeth* has another clip of the funeral cortege; now the banner behind the flowers is clear: 'I have fought the good fight.' [Pathé News, Nation Film Archives]

The SWSS must have discussed Davison's gesture at their next meeting on 7 June, only three days later (she was not yet dead), but it's not mentioned in the minutes. Jamieson was unwell, and the minutes continued in two different hands until March 1914, which suggests a long illness. There are no letters from her, or from Girzie, in the papers; the next AGM report is very brief, and the first longer report is on 11 April 1914. She is known to have suffered from asthma, but that should not have put her out of action for so long. Miss Mitchell resigned at this meeting, but Miss J Mitchell, who had painted the banner, continued as a committee member. [SWSS Minute Book, 7 June 1913]

Emily Wilding Davison, who was fatally injured at Epsom, June 1913.
Photograph courtesy of the Museum of London.

More religious correspondence, summer 1913:

There was another religious correspondence across the *Shetland Times* and *Shetland News* through May, June, July and August. John Robertson, F.R.G.S, and schoolmaster at Sullom, had spoken up for women in a letter on 31 May, citing notable modern women –

'Madame Curie holds a professorship of note in the Sorbonne; Fanny Workman, on the other hand, has climbed to the summit of the Nun Kun Himalaya group to the highest elevation ever penetrated by mankind' - as well as Queen Victoria, Boudicea, Janne d'Arc, Charlotte Corday and Florence Nightingale. [*ST* 31 May 1913]

Matthew S Smith of Lerwick, in the *Shetland News,* denounced the suffragettes as anti-Christian:

' ... the claims of these vote-crazed creatures are not only out of harmony with the Christian religion, but are actually a flagrant setting-aside of its fundamental principles, ie, the basic truths of humanity's fall through a woman's fault, and humanity's salvation through a man's suffering.'

However, he was at one with the *Shetland Times* editor on the treatment of suffragettes:

' ... have these skirted hooligans incarcerated in asylums or removed to places where they can no longer constiute a menace to society.' [*SN* 7 June 1913]

Robertson's reply through the *Shetland Times* went through a list of Old Testament women who were not to be taken as an example, and continued with his own experience:

'Girls are openly sold by their parents at an annual fair in the state of Patiala at so many rupees, according to their charms of beauty ... a Britisher's money is as acceptable as a native's, as I can testify by having had the personal offer of some choice lots. It is really dreadful to think that women can be purchased like pieces of furniture at this era of the world's age. ...'

He pointed out how in previous times

'... young ladies were sent to school to learn sampler sewing, angular writing, deportment and demure manners. Now, they take to typwriting, shorthand, commerce, language, medicine, teaching and architecture ... The tennis court and the golf links have turned out women with figure far more handsome and with bodies more robust than the sickly, insipid misses of the last two centuries. The 'turkey trot' and the 'buck ragtime' have taken the place of the minuet, as the sewing machine has displaced the distaff and the needle. ... The Lord Chancellor has been forced the other day to elect the chairwoman of the West Ham Board of Guardians as a J.P., the first woman so honoured.' [*ST* 14 July 1913]

The 'official' first women JP was Ada Summers, the Mayor of Stalybridge, in 1919; the chairman of the West Ham Guardians from 17 April 1913 to April 1914 (the normal term of one year) was Miss Emily Cecilia Duncan, who represented the High Street and Broadway ward of Stratford. It was usual for the Chairman of the Board of Guardians to be appointed as a magistrate for the purpose of certifying lunatics, and in Miss Duncan's case the Board applied for this appointment. The Lord Chancellor sent an Order agreeing this, so Miss Duncan was, in effect, a certifying magistrate for the time she was Chairman.

'This is the first time a lady has been allowed to officiate in this capacity in England. When a lady was appointed Chairman of Bethnal Green Board of Guardians some years ago the ex-Chairman was appointed to adjudicate in lunacy cases.' [*Stratford Express* 31 May 1913]

Robertson finished,

'... [Woman] was surely meant to be more than the pet and plaything of man, so by and by, as sure as the earth revolves on its axis, will the woman have her round in the cycle of state management as well as that of the domestic hearth.' [*ST* 14 June 1913]

He got a good number of replies: OBSERVED noted that Robertson is 'clearly rejecting the word of God'; PORTIA pointed out that he had 'evidently forgotten to state that it was with the modern instruction in the higher branches of education that 'hooliganism' had to be added to the many qualifications of the latter day Suffragette.' [*ST* 21 June 1913]

In the *Shetland News*, P W Hunter asked if Matthew S Smith honestly believed 'that in the light of the condition of thousands of women in our industrial centres, Christ would have condemned the Suffragists? ... Let us have the manliness to say that we are opposed to it, and do not let us show lack of backbone by sheltering behind the fathers of the Church.'

A new character, Baabie Ringinson, appeared in Girzie's place. Aald Geordie's next letter makes it clear she was in on the fun. Her Biblical criticism and the general style of the first letter recalled Jamieson's, as if 'Baabie' had consulted her before writing. I'd guess at one of the other committee members, perhaps the outspoken Miss Leisk.

Baabie Ringinson sorted Smith out in a way that recalled Jamieson's scholarship:

' ... he wishes people to study and obey the Mosaic Law. This shows he is a Jew ... the Bible states that by Adam all fell. ... He attacks Mr Hunter [... as] an unbeliever. ... I can inform Mr Smith that Mr Hunter is of the highest type of Christian, namely an elder, and that of the Established Church as well.

Mr Smith quotes ancient saints, such as St Basil, as persons whom Christians should follow, which shews that he is not a Jew and the last Christian, but a Roman Catholic too; in fact, of that mixed up kind of class which is neither fish, nor flesh, nor good red herring. I am, etc' [*SN* 21 June 1913]

The *Shetland Times* of the following week had two more letters against Mr Robertson, and another from him. LOVER OF TRUTH cited some more acceptable Old Testament women, like Queen Esther, Ruth, Hannah and Deborah, and picked Robertson up on saying Noah's daughters, instead of Lot's; PATRIARCH explained that women do better for being whipped:

'The Egyptian taskmaster with his whip over the woman is not a nice picture. But you never know. At least, if women are loading coal they are not breaking windows or destroying property.' [*ST* 28 June 1913]

Robertson's letter was a reply to Observer and Portia of the previous week, and mentioned the death of Emily Wilding Davison:

'...There are more cowards than Belshazzar; the woman who faced the King's jockey at Epsom a few days ago was certainly not lacking in courage but in prudence.' [*ST 28* June 1913]

The *Shetland News* of 5 July had Aald Geordie back, blaming Girzie for Baabie Ringinson's letter: ' .. da bodie is haaf doitin, and yit Girzie is no ashemed to geng an mak a skipgoat o her ...' Geordie's letter was followed by a very long letter from Matthew S Smith, taking Baabie entirely seriously and refuting (to his own satisfaction, at least) both her and Hunter's points. It ends by urging them to write again:

' ... Their second attempt may prove better than their first, since it cannot, by any process of natural, or acquired stupidity, prove worse.' [*SN* 5 July 1913]

The correspondence continued in the *Shetland Times* of 12 July. DAPHNE A.D.O.S felt that to bring Biblical criticism into a discussion of female suffrage showed 'a lack of good taste, and is extremely bad form. ... I am heartily ashamed of members of my sex, who madly clamour for 'Female Suffrage', and also of the man who could advocate, or tolerate, the same.' P W Hunter picked 'Patriarch' up on his approval of Solomon's polygamy: '...immorality – yes, immorality which strikes at the very basis of family life ...' [*ST* 12 July 1913]

Robertson pointed out that 'This discussion is now entirely 'offside' and has become an ink-splashing of Biblical criticism.' After picking up several of Patriarch's points, he got back to the point:

'Women have been voters at municipal and school board elections, and why they should exercise such privilege and be debarred from parliamentary elections is a paradox. Just as in medicine there are occasions when women should, if only for decency's sake, perform such duties for which they are naturally suited, so also are there matters of a public nature which are pre-eminently their own and not those of men. ... Give the women a chance. They have not been proved incapable of judicious manipulation of public affairs. What do the Edinburgh people think of the late Flora Stevenson as School Board Chairman, and she is only one of many such women. I am, etc'

He added a PS: 'Please convey my sympathy to Patriarch's wife in her thraldom and servitude.' [*ST* 12 July 1913]

Baabie Ringinson was back, at length, in the *Shetland News* of the same week, smartly and rather bluntly cutting Smith down to size. After two paragraphs of retort, she went into Genesis, and the effects on Eve, followed by an anecdote:

'... the male dude, saying at a meeting – 'Now, Miss Pankhurst, wouldn't you just like to be a man?' 'No,' replied Miss Pankhurst, 'but wouldn't you?'.

As for women's untruthfulness, did he never hear ... the sailors' boast that they left a sweetheart in every port, and the soldiers' boast that they left a sweetheart in every town?'

She finished by complimenting Smith on noticing that Baabie is a woman's name. The letter was in English throughout, and the overall effect was rather leaden, totally out of style with the previous letter, and lacking Girzie's lightness of touch, as if Jamieson had been unable to be involved this time. [*SN* 12 July 1913]

Smith's reply was equally blunt, and equally rude, without adding anything to the debate. He ended,

'Votes for women! Yes, but not till woman has evolved into an intelligent animal ... not till Baabie Ringinson has brushed the ashes of Troy off her hobble [skirt] ...' [*SN* 26 July 1913]

DIANA was also back; during the last few months, she had been so

'disgusted, shocked and ashamed' at the actions of the suffragettes that she had been 'incapable of putting pen to paper ... The setting fire to mansions, the destroying of pillar-boxes, the horse-whipping of innocent men, the destruction of golf-links, in short the whole reign of terror ... is intolerable in a civilised community.' She pointed out the damage they were doing to their cause: 'it will be years before [it] regains the position it held a year or two ago' and ended by reminding women of their womenly influence 'if they like to exercise it.' [*SN* 26 July 1913]

OBSERVER returned on 26 July, with a letter packed with Biblical references. He reminded Robertson of Cain, also a religious man, King Manasseh, and the false prophets of King Ahab, and pointed out that by denying Genesis was written by Moses, he branded himself an atheist. Hunter, another false prophet, was affected with wind, and compared to Goliath of Gath. PATRIARCH also returned to defend himself against the charge of approving polygamy, but said Mr Hunter '... seems to lack the saving grace of humour.' With regard to Robertson, his wife, 'had a hearty laugh over his sympathy' [Poor woman, she probably had little choice but to take it as a great joke]. He still insisted, however, that '...we are not going to see our women going full speed to the devil if a word or a gentle fatherly touch will put things right.' [*ST* 12 July 1913]

P W Hunter was back with another long letter to Mr Smith in the same week's *Shetland News*, and this time his tone was entirely serious, contrasting sharply with the previous points-scoring exercise. He began with concern over the idea that socialism and Christianity are seen as opposed, and quoted the disciples running to tell the Lord that others were casting out devils in His name; should they stop them? Christ said, 'He that is not against us is for our part.'

'Nineteen hundred years later history repeats itself. In the county town of the Shetland Islands we find that the Socialist party and the Suffragist party both have a large following. Why have they such a following? ... There are causes, and very alarming causes, why these movements are in existence.

I only need to refer to low wages, bad housing conditions, and the nefarious white slave traffic. Surely the stamping out of these evils should appeal to every man and woman with a spark of patriotism in their bosom, not to speak of those like Mr Smith and myself who are professed followers of Him who went round doing good.'

He regretted that, in the case of socialism, the churches did not speak out against social evils, and pointed out that many men had moved away from the church. He was concerned that suffragists also would feel they had to choose between their suffragist principles and the church:

'... A very large majority of those who take an active part in Church work are women. Many of these women are convinced that under our present franchise they are being unfairly treated. They demand that the inequality shall be redressed. The suffragists urge them to insist on their demand being made when Mr Matthew S Smith appears on the scene and warns them that if they persist they can have no part or lot in the work of

Christianity. ... Their conscience will tell them that the demand for the vote is a righteous one. If so, Mr Smith must be representing an unrighteous cause. The danger is that some people may mistake the voice of Mr Smith for the voice of Christianity.'

After a tribute to Smith's wide reading and intelligence, he wrote,

' ... the Almighty will hold each of us accountable for the talents which he has given us. Now, permit me to ask, without the slightest impertinence. What is Mr Smith doing to further the cause of his fellow men? Is he working for the cause of temperance, the cause of better housing, or for the Christianising of the Socialist movement? ...'

He ended with a courteously-worded challenge to a public debate on whether a Socialist can be a Christian, with Mr Smith or, if he has not 'been much in the habit of public speaking', any representative that he cared to name, when he was next in Lerwick in October or November. [*SN* 26 July 1913] The challenge didn't seem to have been taken up.

The first letter of August was mercifully short:

'Sir: - I saw Mr Matthew S Smith's exhibition in your last week's 'News'.

If women's intellect is beneath that, it must be very low. I am, etc LYDIA' [*SN* 3 August 1913]

There was a further letter from P W Hunter replying to Observer and Patriarch, Argus took a last snipe at Diana, and the correspondence ceased for the moment.

June – December, 1913:

The Shetland WSS had noted at its June meeting that it could take no action with regard to proposed Summer Schools in Oxford and St Andrews, or the Suffrage Pilgrimage to London nor appeal for funds. The Secretary was to procure 100 Friends of Women's Suffrage cards for distribution among members, and to notify the papers of Mrs Mackinnon Wood's acceptance of the presidency. Regret was noted at Miss Jamieson's illness. [SWSS Minute Book, 12 June 1913; I presume the handwriting is Miss Leisk's, as she was Assistant Secretary]

The Pilgrimage was held during June / July 1913, and a film survives of the meeting in London. Captioned: *Law Abiding Suffragists journeyed from all over the country to hold a gigantic demonstration in Hyde Park.* it begins with two women on horseback coming through the crowd; one is on a white horse, and riding astride. The camera then moves on to the crowd, who are predominantly men; they wave their boaters at the camera. Ethel Snowden isn't on the clip, but she was one of the speakers.

The Scottish Men's Deputation was timed to coincide with the Hyde Park rally. Over thirty councillors, bailies, JPs, ministers and teachers went to Downing Street on the morning of Friday 11 July 1913. Asquith refused to see them, but they met the Scottish Government Whip and the Prime Minister's Secretary, and spoke to a crowd in Downing Street. In the afternoon they met Scottish MPs in the House of Commons, but walked out when the MPs began joking about the Cat and Mouse Act. On Saturday, some of them spoke in Hyde Park; Councillor Crawford, from Edinburgh, spoke of the 'Westminster Gas Works' and called Asquith pig-headed, a humbug, a flea, and an ass. On Monday, the men made another attempt to see Asquith or Churchill, and in the evening they had an interview with Mackinnon Wood. The Prime Minister's refusal to meet them, and the attitude of the MPs, strengthened their feeling for their cause, and the Northern Men's Federation for Women's Suffrage was founded. It was to hold a number of meetings through the autumn, including a mass meeting in Edinburgh in November 1913.

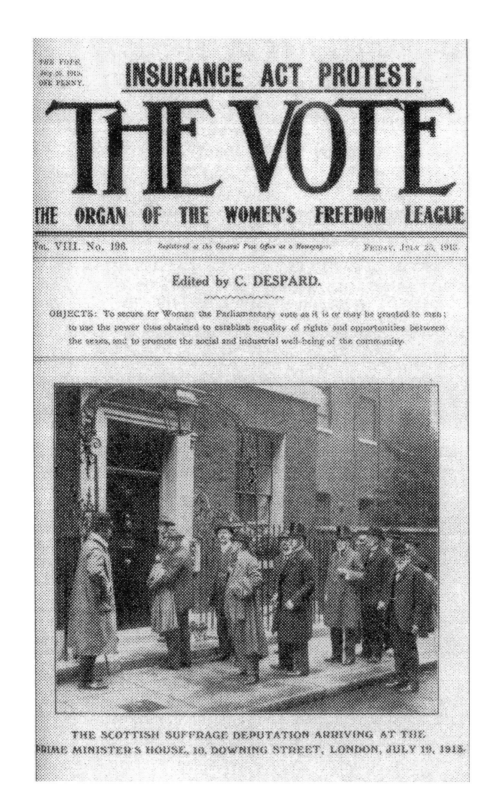

The front page of *The Vote*, 23 July 1913, showing the Scottish Men's Deputation to Asquith. Photograph courtesy of the People's Story Museum, Edinburgh.

The Suffrage summer schools at Oxford and St Andrews were organised by the NUWSS. The Oxford one was 11-25 August; the St Andrews one was run by the Scottish Federation, and speakers included Mrs Fawcett and Louisa Lumsden. It was so successful that it was repeated in 1914 and 1915. A smaller summer school training women in public speaking was held in Conwy Valley in 1913, and in July 1914 a suffrage camp near Weymouth deliberately mixed working class and middle-class suffragist; this, too, seemed to have been successful. The socialist / suffragist links were revived at the South Lanark by-election in the autumn of 1913, with Ada Nield Chew of Lancashire coming up to speak among the mining and farming communities there.

During the summer of 1913, many churches and public buildings had been closed to the public for fear of attacks by suffragettes. The WSPU attacks continued in August and September with fires at Moreland House and Fettes College, Edinburgh, and damage at a Bridge of Allan bowling green and Kilspindie golf links. On 15 October 'Margaret Morrison' (Ethel Moorhead) and Dr Dorothea Chalmers Smith were put on trial in Glasgow for intended fire-raising in a house in Park Lane. They were sentenced to eight months imprisonment, and went immediately on hunger strike. This sparked off the first of a number of church prayer protests, in St Giles, Edinburgh, on 19 October 1913. After the intercessionary prayers, a group of women stood up and chanted: 'God save Annie Kenney, Margaret Morrison and Dorothea Smith. Their enemies torture them, for they know their cause is righteous.'

Sylvia Pankhurst also spent much of 1913 in and out of prison after demonstrations with her East London Federation of Suffragettes, and a film clip from 10 August 1913 shows one of these arrests. It's captioned: *Trafalgar Square Riot Some ugly rushes to secure the rescue of Sylvia Pankhurst* and begins with a procession. A crowd of men come purposefully forward; a boy in a Norfolk suit is being led away by his father, rubbing one eye as if crying. Two women are being marched by a policeman on each side; the first one, Pankhurst, is either arguing or singing. An aerial shot shows the open-topped buses backed up, and a huge crowd beyond. [Pathé News, National Film Archives]

In late August, Sylvia, Mrs Pankhurst and Annie Kenney went abroad, and on October 11, Mrs Pankhurst left for her third tour of the United States. The others returned in November, and spent the last of the year in and out of prison; it was at this point that each had to be brought to meetings on a stretcher.

In Shetland, the SWSS expressed their 'profound regret' at the death of a founder member, Miss Gulland, 'whose ready services and generous subscriptions would be greatly missed by the Committee.' A tribute paid to her by Frank Pottinger, as Chairman of the School Board, is referred to in one of P W Hunter's letters: '... in a few well-chosen and appropriate remarks in referring to the late Miss Gulland [he] urged on the children to be kind and truthful and lead noble and brave lives.' [*ST* 12 July 1913]

The minutes of 1 October also show a strong disagreement with the Scottish Federation. After the Federation promising a speaker, the Secretary had twice written, but had no reply, and now the last issue of *Common Cause* contained an account of Miss Bury's tour in which Kirkwall had been included - but not Shetland.

Anyone who's ever been on a committee knows exactly what the ominous words 'after much discussion' mean. The committee

'agreed that some explanation was certainly due from the Federation Office and the Secretary is to write making certain proposals, and stating that if the Federation did not deal with these proposals the Society would be recommending at its annual meeting to reconsider its adherence to the Federation'.

A letter from the delegate, who wrote under the assumption that a speaker had been in Shetland, was then considered, and it was agreed that she be asked to represent the Society at the half-yearly council meeting, and to put their case strongly before the council. [SWSS Minute Book, 1 October 1913, a different hand from the June minutes]

Presumably the Scottish Federation was suitably influenced, for the AGM of 20 October 1913 reports that Miss Bury, who was to have visited in October, had to postpone her visit to November on account of the election in Northern Burghs. A programme was drawn up for her visit, which seems to have been delayed again, for the January meeting was to discuss 'an exhibition of Women's Industries she wished to bring north' and in February there was mention of her bringing 'lantern slides.' Lantern slides were a popular way of showing regional societies events and people they would not otherwise see. Surviving NUWSS photographs include the April 1909 Pageant of Trades and Professions, the 1911 Coronation procession and the 1913 Pilgrimage. There were more WSPU photographs, as they deliberately courted publicity.

The Secretary reported that there were several new members, but three had been lost by death, and several had left the the islands. After that, the meeting focused on national business. Their new representative on the Scottish Federation Executive Committee was Miss Florence Hilliard, the NUWSS organiser who had formed the Perth society, now living in Edinburgh. The Agenda paper of half-yearly NU meeting was read, and the decision taken on which motions their delegate was to support, and on which to abstain. There was to be a week of prayer in favour of women's suffrage - 'no further action.' A circular from the *New Statesman* was read, and six specimen copies of this publication ordered.

After that, the office bearers were appointed: all were re-appointed, including Jamieson as Secretary, so although the minutes were also in Miss Leisk's hand, she must have hoped to be back in harness soon. [SWSS Minute Book, 20 October 1913]

At this point the New Zealand women were trying to get a Bill for women MPs through Parliament – Lady Stout would certainly have been involved in this. [*Common Cause* 24 October 1913]

Support from the men:

On 11 Sept 1913, the inaugural meeting of the Northern Men's Federation had taken place in Glasgow. The men planned to travel from Scotland to London in February 1914, to make a deputation to Asquith, urging women be enfranchised under the Scottish Home Rule bill. A letter from the Scottish Federation asked the Shetland Society to approach public organisations of men with a view to them sending representatives to this public deputation; no immediate action was taken. [SWSS Minute Book, 1 October 1913] The matter was raised again in January 1914, and it was agreed to ask Town and County Councils, and to 'consult certain menbers of the Lerwick Presbytery to see whether it would be advisable to bring the matter before them at their next meeting.' [SWSS Minute Book, January 1914]

In mid-January 1914, the ZCC discussed sending a representative to the London march: VOTES FOR WOMEN!

The Vice Convener [J W Robertson] said that he had been requested to ask the Council if they would appoint a delegate to attend a demonstration in the Albert Hall, London, on behalf of the women's suffrage movement. He did not suppose any of the members would go for that purpose, but they could appoint a proxy. In the event of none of the members being in London at the time of the demonstration, he moved that they appoint Rev Mr Sandison, who, he understood, was in favour of the movement, and who was brother of Mrs Mackinnon-Wood, President to the Association.

Mr D Sutherland seconded, and this was agreed to.' [ST 24 January 1914]

Alec Sandison, the Reverend Alexander Sandison's great-grandson, recently found a box of family papers which included Alexander Sandison's copy of 'The Non-Conformist Minister's Ordinal', containing suggested forms of services and identifying the bits that are essential and, by default, those that are not. The book suggests that the Minister should say at one point 'Wives, be in subjection unto your husbands, as unto the Lord. For the husband is the head of the wife, as Christ also is the head of the Church.' Mr Sandison had scored through the whole paragraph. His great-grandson commented,

'I was terribly impressed that a Minister should have done this in the late 19th century and suddenly wished I knew more about his parents, who had created a climate in which this sort of belief (and the willingness to demonstrate it) was at least accepted. That he was Isa's sibling makes it clear that he was not alone.'

On 14 Feb 1914 the male suffragists travelled from Scotland to London, and, as agreed, the Reverend Alexander Sandison represented Shetland. The Northern Men's Federation held an afternoon meeting in the Memorial Hall, Farringdon St and the NUWSS held one in the evening in the Albert Hall, which was the one Mr Sandison attended, displaying the society's banner. Later, Jamieson wrote a letter of thanks [SWSS Minute Book, 14 March 1914]

The Presbytery also considered the cause of women's suffrage, with a bit more acrimony:

'A letter was read from the Northern Men's Federation of Women's Suffrage, asking the Presbytery to send an overture in favour of women's suffrage to the General Assembly of the Church of Scotland.

Mr Milne [the Reverend D G Milne, Whiteness] moved that the letter lie on the table, which was seconded by Mr Crawford [the Reverend David Crawford, Bressay], who said he did not think this was a matter which came within the purview of the Church. It was a political matter, and whatever views they might have on it individually they should not deal with it as a Presbytery. Mr Love [the Reverend John Love, Yell] said Mr Crawford expressed his sentiments also.'

The Clerk [the Reverend Archibald Mackintyre, Tingwall] moved as an amendment that

'while the Presbytery were unable to overture the General Assembly they desired to express themselves favourable to the principles of women's suffrage as laid down in the letter just read. ... The Presbytery could surely make up their minds on what was right and what was wrong, whether it was a political question or not. If any political action was wrong, outrageous and disgraceful, the ministers as the leaders of the people, which they pretended to be, should voice their opinions very strongly. ... The housing of the poor was a political and economic question ...; he was competent to judge the morality or immorality of it, and he was prepared to say that the housing of the poor was a shame and a disgrace. The Presbytery were quite entitled to say that to tax women when they did not have the vote was unconstitutional and unjust, and that they were, individually, in favour of women getting the vote, and being placed on the same status as men.'

The motion was amended to 'The Presbytery could not see their way to overture the General Assembly on women's suffrage, and that they expressed sympathy with the aims of the Federation.'

A lengthy and somewhat animated discussion followed, the principal speakers being the Clerk and Mr Crawford. Eventually, the Clerk in criticising Mr Crawford, used the words 'mighty seconder', which Mr Crawford took exception to. ... [and left] the room.

...The motion was carried by three votes to none.' [SN 31 January 1914]

Other Scottish presbyteries had also been debating whether to support women's suffrage. Glasgow and Irvine were strongly supportive; the rest debated the issue, but voted against support. The Town Councils of Scotland also debated support; Glasgow and Inverness sent representatives, but not Edinburgh. Dundee and Aberdeen expressed moral support, and St Andrews decided to take no action. Dollar Town Council would certainly have been sympathetic; it had just appointed Scotland's first Lady Provost, Mrs Lavinia Malcolm.

January – March 1914:

On the mainland, the militants were still at work. 1914 opened with a bang: a bomb in the glass Kibble Palace, Glasgow. On 5 February, there werre three house fires, all in the Strathearn area; in one of them, there were servants in the house, who narrowly escaped. In February and March 1914 new WSPU tactics were tried, with women speaking during the interval at theatre performances and in restaurants.

On 17 February, Ethel Moorhead was re-arrested under the Cat and Mouse Act; she was in the grounds of Traquair House. She was sent to Calton Jail, and forcible feeding – the first in Scotland – commenced on 21 February. When Janie Allen protested at the risk to Moorhead's health, the prison doctor, Dr Devon, replied that if her health could only be preserved by allowing her to set fire to other people's houses, then her health would have to be risked. The doctor responsible for the 'artifical feeding' was Dr Ferguson Watson, who had had experience of forcibly-feeding asylum inmates. Moorhead was released on 25 February with double pneumonia, due to food getting into her lungs, and her account of her ordeal caused such horror that a question was tabled for Mr Mackinnon Wood in Parliament, and queries were sent to the prison governor by the commissioners. Moorhead was due back in prison on 9 March, but walked through the police guard round the house where she was staying.

On 27 February 1914, only a few hours after Moorhead's release, the ancient Whitekirk near Edinburgh was destroyed, a medieval building targeted in retaliation for medieval torture. The destruction of this ancient church caused widespread outrage, and further public alienation from the suffrage cause, even though a number of suffragist organisations wrote to the papers repudiating the act. It is very likely that the arsonist was Fanny Parker.

Whitekirk, Haddington, burnt down by suffragettes on 27 February 1914, in retaliation for the first Scottish forcible feeding in Calton Gaol, Edinburgh.
Postcard, author's collection.

234

On 9 March 1914, officialdom gave some of the sympathy back by police heavy-handedness. Mrs Pankhurst, at liberty under the Cat and Mouse Act, was due to speak at St Andrew's Hall, Glasgow. There had been warning that she would be arrested, and the platform was ringed with barbed wire, covered by flowers. She was smuggled into the hall earlier in the day, in a laundry basket. The hall was filled, and Mrs Pankhurst was just beginning to speak when the main doors opened, and a squad of police officers with truncheons marched in. Accounts varied as to who began what; within seconds there was a riot, with the police laying about with truncheons, women on the platform throwing flowerpots and hitting back with Indian canes, and Janie Allen firing blanks from a revolver into the melee. Letters to the papers urged a public enquiry; a deputation of men complained to Scottish MPs, who sent them back to the Glasgow Town Council. The Council had no jurisdiction over the police, and an internal police enquiry found (surprise!) that the police had acted properly. The WSPU in Glasgow gained 203 new members in the following month. Janie Allen took witness statements with a view to making a private prosecution; these are among her papers in the National Library of Scotland, and in spite of her loaded questions it's clear that the police were unnecessarily rough with spectators, and had no real need to intervene so publicly. Witness comments included:

'[The police were] all round the platform and on the stairs at the sides. ... They acted as if they had come to seize an armed criminal who was being protected by a bunch of dangerous men. ... They marched into the hall with drawn batons – I saw them on the stair when they were held back by pistol shots.' [Statement by Elizabeth Duncan, Janie Allen Papers, National Library of Scotland]

A supporter slashed the Rokeby Venus in the National Gallery in protest, and seven women were charged with breach of the peace on 30 March when they interrupted prayers in St Giles to add a prayer for Mrs Pankhurst.

The SWSS were also thinking about Mrs Pankhurst on their meeting of 14 March 1914:

'Miss Hilliard was asked to act re interview between Mrs Pankhurst and the Scottish Federation.' The banner was to be sent to the Women's Exhibition, as requested. [SWSS Minute Book, 14 March 1914]

A letter from CIVES in the *Shetland Times* encouraged female voters to register:

'Dear Sir, - It is not generally known that young women, as well as young men, can claim to be enrolled as Municipal as well as Parish Council voters under the Lodger Franchise. ... Young women who are earning their own livelihood and living in lodgings should experience no difficulty in securing the vote as lodgers, and young women who are of age and following some employment, but residing with their parents, are also entitled to apply for the vote. ...

This privilege is well worth securing. Everyone interested in temperance work, for example, should be anxious to have a share in carrying out temperance legislation. This they can do by becoming municipal voters. Those, too, who have this qualification may use it for controlling Sunday trading.

The lodger vote must be claimed every year. Forms for this purpose can be had from the Assessor of the District ... the person applying must be 21 years of age, and have occupied the premises in respect of which the vote is claimed for the twelve months preceding the 31st of July of the year in which the claim is made.' [*ST* 2 February 1914; *SN* 21 February 1914]

Aald Geordie was back in the *Shetland News* of 7 March 1914, with a chatty letter to 'Mansie', welcoming him back and congratulating Tammie and Sibbie on their marriage. He lamented Girzie's being taken up 'wi dis suffrage dirt' and hoped 'dy Girzie' hasn't been infected like Baabie Ringinson:

'Faider o paece! fir whit a spaekalation hit made, and nae winder. ... But boy, Sibbie is maybe a suffrigat (Loard forbid!), an I'll maybe be gein me my kail troo da reek... ' [*SN* 7 March 1914]

I can't see any way these personal details could be relevant to Thomas Manson; there were no marriages in his family about that time, and none of the names fit the family. Perhaps it's just Aald Geordie giving local colour.

Miss Bury's visit, April 1914:

In Shetland, the SWSS was still preparing for Miss Bury's visit. She had sent a letter with enquiries to be made before coming to definite arrangements regarding an exhibition of Women's Industries she wished to bring north. [SWSS minute book, January 1914, same hand as 1 October 1913]

The SWSS's next quarterly meeting was held on 4 February 1914. Business included the Edinburgh society's request for a loan of their banner for their summer school, 'as they consider it one of the most beautiful of the Scottish banners, besides being that of the most northerly society.' Two or three members also hoped to attend. There was a letter from Miss Bury - 'decided she be asked to bring lantern slides as suggested. Letter from Miss Hilliard - no action – Miss Hilliard left to own discretion.' [SWSS Minute Book, 4 February 1914, Miss Leisk's hand]

The secretary notes that the SWSS was strongly of the opinion that politics should not enter municipal affairs - 'one reason being it lessens the possibility of women being elected to local bodies, as politically they have no value.'

A letter from the Lerwick British Socialist Society asked members to participate in a meeting of protest against the action of the South African government in deporting Labour leaders; the SWSS decided not to take part, but the request shows the sense of common cause between the the socialists and the suffragists. [SWSS Minute Book, 4 February 1914, Miss Leisk's hand]

For Miss Bury's visit: 'The Secretary is to procure a supply of literature, Friends of Women's Suffrage cards and samples of badges and ribbons.' [SWSS Minute book, 14 March 1914, Miss Leisk's hand] She was well-advertised beforehand:

'Miss Bury, the distinguished Women Suffrage organiser for the northern districts of Scotland will be in Shetland from 25th March to 8th April. She will address public meetings in Lerwick, Scalloway, Walls, Whalsay and Baltasound. Miss Bury is bringing with her a series of magic lantern exhibits of women's sweated industries and will hold exhibitions of which further particulars will be given later. Miss Bury is a peaceful propagandist, and is sent from the Union, which strongly condemns the exasperating and sacriligious methods of militancy.' [ST 14 March 1914]

The Scalloway advertisement also stressed the NUWSS's non-violent stance:

'SCALLOWAY NOTES: WOMEN'S SUFFRAGE ORGANISER: Some considerable stir is being caused in the village this week by the visit of Miss Bury, one of the N.U.W.S.S. organisers. The association is strictly non-party, and non-militant, and in these latter days when the militants are doing much to sicken the country and bring what should be a perfectly legitimate claim into disrepute, the visit from the representative of a union which is trying its hardest to rescue the suffrage question from the unworthy hands of the militants, should be appreciated by all.' [ST 4 April 1914]

DIANA was not convinced:

' ... Although the Association this organiser represents vehemently repudiates the militants and all their actions, she ... will find that in the mind of the general public they are classed as one – they are all Suffragists ...

The outrageous, almost fiendish conduct of the militants ... fully justifies all that I have ever said about women and the suffrage in this column. I said, and I repeat, that once women enter into the rough and tumble of politics ... [they] invariably unsex themselves...' [SN 4 April 1914]

Jamieson picked her up on that assertion in the following week, under the initials C.J. She cited the examples of orderly government in Wyoming, Colorado and other states, emphasised the peaceful work done by the NUWSS., and pointed out that nobody can escape politics.

'Politics operates daily on the lives of even Shetland women, in their homes and at their work. The report in one of your columns on the conditions under which fishworkers live is an outcome of the Insurance Act.... [SN 11 April 1914]

A WOMAN retorted:

'I can inform 'Diana' and all who think as she does, that such views of women as she expresses will not hold water for a moment in these days. Women are only gradually and slowly coming to their own. Centuries of bondage and oppression have not crushed their spirit, although it might well have done so. They have the brains, the ability and the energy to take their part, along with men in most of the walks of life, and in many of these walks they can do, and have proved themselves to be able to do, better work than men. In art, literature, music, in business, in the professions, in industries of all kinds, women have shown conclusively that they can hold their own. That being so, what right have men to deprive them of the power of legislating and making and shaping laws as well as men? Why should not women have the Parliamentary vote as well as men? What defence can 'Diana' bring forward to justify such a piece of injustice? All that women ask for is to have a voice in the making of the laws by which they are governed. This measure of justice cannot be much longer delayed. Women want no more, and they will be satisfied with nothing less.' [*SN* 11 April 1914]

The fishworkers Jamieson referred to was a current case. Mrs Margaret Ogilvy Gordon of Aberdeen had led a deputation to the House of Commons to complain about the working conditions of the herring girls, who generally worked outdoors on the pier, without any shelter against the weather, and with wet conditions underfoot. 'Current Topics', in the *Shetland Times*, had little sympathy, speaking of Mrs Gordon's

'self-appointed task (and I rather think she has a keen desire to appear in the lime-light)' and saying that when 'girls are engaged to be at their posts to commence work on a certain date, it would seem that an even stronger advocate than Mrs Ogilvy Gordon would be required to appear on the scene to regulate the weather.' As to their living conditions: '... it seems there were reasons for complaint as the the reception these girls get when they arrived at Lerwick. ... what might seem a hovel to Mrs Ogilvy Gordon, would be a comfortable abode for less favoured people. This I do know ... that these fishcurers carrying business in Shetland are ever anxious to do their utmost to safeguard the creature comforts of the girls they smploy. And those who see and hear those same girls during the fishing season ... are invariably struck with the idea that they have not a care in the world, for their song and laughter fill the air, and make glad the heart of the listener.' [*ST* 11 April 1914]

The same week's *Shetland Times* reported Cathcart Wason asking the Home Secretary about the conditions under which the herring girls worked, and the accomodation of the steamers which brought them to Shetland. He also made the point that mortality among the fisher girls had been very largely increased on their return from the fishing, and asked whether Mr Burns, President of the Board of Trade, would enquire further into this. Burns said he would. [*ST* 11 April 1914.] The following week has Mr Mackinnon Wood detailing the steps being taken. A related court case was reported in the *Shetland Times* of 14 July 1914. Miss Isobel Meiklejohn, the Inspector under the Factory Acts, led the prosecution of behalf of a number of herring girls. The defendants, James Flett, Sons & Co, of Holmside, Lerwick, and D A Wares of Wick, working from Scalloway, were charged with having breached the hours laid down in the Factory and Workshops Act, 1901; the girls in Lerwick had been asked to start work at 4am, instead of 6am, and the girls in Scalloway had been kept working until 7pm, instead of stopping at 6pm (ie, they'd been asked to work longer than their normal 12-hour day).

The Sheriff agreed that working hours had been breached, but the evidence made it clear that it was an individual act by the foreman against the orders of the firm's owners. He did not feel it was a serious breach of the Act, and admonished the firm, but did not award costs to Miss Meiklejohn.

One woman who was also concerned about the fisher girls was Edith Catherine Hacon. Mrs Hacon is an intriguing figure, and I'm indebted to Mike and Pat Loynd for sharing their extensive research work on her with me. She was probably born Edith Catherine Broadbent or Bradshaw to a middle-class provincial family around 1874. Her parents died when she was an adolescent, and her relatives threw her out when she became pregnant. She worked in a laundry for a time then, after the child died, she was set up in a flat, and became an habitué of the music halls. She became the mistress of poet and critic Arthur Symons (she is the 'Muriel' of his poem *To Muriel: at the Opera)* and of his friend Herbert Horne, a poet and architect. Symons and Horne introduced her to artists Charles Shannon and Charles Ricketts, and she became their hostess at the Vale, Chelsea. There, she met the avant-garde set of the day: Toulouse-Lautrec, Beardsley, Whistler, the younger Pissarro, George Bernard Shaw, Oscar Wilde, John Gray. The painter William Rothenstein later described her 'rich auburn hair and a heart of gold' and called her a 'gracious and radiant mistress'. W B Yeats met her at Horne's studio, and recalled her in his elegiac *The Municipal Gallery Revisited:*

> Before a woman's portrait suddenly I stand,
> Beautiful and gentle in her Venetian way.
> I met her all but fifty years ago
> For twenty minutes in some studio.

The portrait was Charles Shannon's *Lady with a Green Fan*, now in Dublin City Art Gallery. Other portraits call her Amaryllis, or Ryllis.

It was through Rothenstein that she met William Llewellyn Hacon, a rich, widowed barrister. He had been a cavalryman in Austria and was an excellent swordsman and horseman; he was also a keen sailor. Romantically, he saw a pastel drawing of Amaryllis by Rothenstein, and told friends he was going to buy the drawing and marry the woman. Rothenstein arranged for Amaryllis to spend the day with Hacon on his yacht on the Solent, and they were married soon afterwards. The marriage was registered at Westminster, and Edith gave her age as 21. Hacon took over 2, the Vale, went into partnership with Ricketts to found the Vale Bookshop and continued the tradition of open house. In 1896 he built a house at Dornoch, Sutherland, called Oversteps, near to the fashionable golf course, and handy for deer-stalking. His first visits to Shetland were perhaps by yacht. The Aberdeen Art Gallery has paintings by Charles Condor of Mrs Hacon on the beach in Caithness, along with the decorative sign for the Vale Bookshop.

Llewellyn Hacon had a stroke around 1900, and was an invalid thereafter. He died in the summer of 1910, and Edith inherited his entire estate. Her letters from this period speak about 'doing work for seasonal herring workers in Shetland' and 'doing charity work in Shetland.'

Llewellyn Hacon was a committed Catholic, and Edith converted on their marriage. 1910-11 saw the building of Shetland's first Catholic church since the Reformation, for the Irish fisher girls (there were no Catholics in Shetland outwith the gutting season), and Mrs Hacon seems to have been one of the key figures in this. The altar tabernacle is inscribed 'In memory of Ll. Hacon by his wife', and she provided flowers for the opening ceremony. She was also involved in parish administration – when a local doctor, Dr Robertson, wanted to rent the parish house over the winter, his solicitor wrote to her, and she in turn wrote to Bishop Chisolm in Aberdeen about rent and changes of use.

Mrs Hacon stayed at the Grand Hotel with her companion and secretary during 1912 and 1913, while she was working on a project for a rest house for Catholic fishergirls at Gremista. The building was designed by Mrs Hacon's architect, and was built in sections. It included a reading room, a clinic and a room for prayer meetings, and was known as 'The White Rest.' It was staffed by nurses from the Aberdeen branch of the Catholic Women's League. It stood where the Power Station is now, on land lent by Sir Arthur Nicolson of Brough Lodge, until the early 1950s, when it was sold for materials for £200. The building is clearly visible in Rattar's 1930s photos of Gremista.

Mrs Hacon was to be in France with the NUWSS-sponsored Scottish Women's Hospital during World War I. There she met and married a Canadian, William Robichaud. They adopted two boys, but the marriage was not happy, and Mrs Hacon returned to Dornoch, where she lived quietly in the cottage attached to Oversteps. She died in 1952, and was buried in the East Kirk, Dornoch, beside Llewellyn, under the name 'Amaryllis Hacon'.

The minutes of the SWSS General Meeting of 26 March 1914 were once again in Jamieson's decisive handwriting. This meeting was particularly to allow everyone to meet Miss Bury, who had arrived the previous day. Jamieson's letter asking the Town and Council delegates to arrange a meeting of protest against the treatment of the Scottish representation to Asquith had arrived too late for those bodies' meetings but Jamieson had interviewed the Provost, Robert Stout, (husband of the Shetland WSS Vice-President) and she read a letter from the Vice Convener of the Council, saying that if a meeting was decided, it was probable a Shetland delegate would be sent. The final Agenda of the Scottish Federation AGM was considered, and Miss Hilliard appointed as their delegate. Mr P W Hunter sent a letter saying that he was not able to address a meeting. The Shetland WSS accepted the NUWSS's offer to send samples of literature as published on payment of 3/6 annually, and Mrs Mackinnon Wood was to be their delegate to the Annual Council meeting. Stewards were appointed for Miss Bury's meetings.

Miss Bury's Lerwick lecture sounded like a modern-day Fair Trade presentation:

'In the Rechabite Hall on Tuesday evening, Miss Bury, organiser N.U.W.S.S. delivered a lecture on sweated industries, especially in relation to women. Mrs John Leisk presided, and there was a large audience, the Hall being quite filled.

After being introduced by Mrs Leisk, Miss Bury delivered a most interesting and instructive address on the sweated industries which were carried on in the Black Country – her remarks being almost entirely confined to conditions prevailing in England. She showed the conditions under which work was carried on, the rates of pay, and also displayed specimens of the handicraft in which women and young persons were engaged. The lecture was illustrated by a series of fine lantern views, which gave an excellent idea to the audience of the conditions under which these women were compelled to work. In the course of her lecture, Miss Bury made it clear that the Association of which she was a representative, had nothing whatever to do with the militant section, whose methods they greatly deprecated, but were confident of success by means of constitutional methods.

At the close of the address, Mr F H Pottinger and Mr M L Manson put several questions to Miss Bury, which were answered in a satisfactory manner.

Mr J A Loggie then proposed a vote of thanks to Miss Bury, which was seconded by Mr Pottinger, and heartily accorded. A similar compliment to Mrs Leisk, on the call of the lecturer, terminated the proceedings.' [*ST* 14 April 1914]

The *Shetland News* reported Miss Bury's speech in full.

THE NEED FOR FEMALE SUFFRAGE

Striking lecture by N.U.W.S.S Organiser.

Miss Bury, an organiser of the National Union of Women's Suffrage Societies, who arrived at Lerwick a fortnight ago, and has conducted meetings at Walls, Scalloway and Bressay, spoke at an open-air meeting at the Market Cross last Saturday evening, when she dealt with the suffrage movement in relation to wages, and said great help could be given by men, because by competing with men women kept wages down all round. There was a good attendance, and the lecture was much appreciated.

LECTURE ON SWEATED INDUSTRIES

In the Rechabite Hall on Tuesday evening, Miss Bury delivered a lecture on 'Sweated Industries' illustrated by lantern slides. There was a very large and representative attendance, and Mrs Leisk, President of the Shetland Women's Suffrage Society, occupied the chair. Prior to the commencement of the meeting, badges and suffrage literature of various kinds were sold to members of the audience.

The Chairman, in introducing the lecturer, alluded to the general apathy of the public in regard to sweated industries and expressed the hope that Miss Bury would arouse the interest and sympathy of everyone with those thousands of poor sweated workers in our great industrial centres.

Miss Bury said that before showing the slides of sweated industries in which women worked in this country, she would like to say a few words about the Society which she represented. The National Union of Women's Friendly [sic] Societies was established in 1867 through the agency of John Stuart Mill and Mrs Henry Fawcett. Mrs Fawcett was still President of the Societies, which, she might add, always worked on constitutional and law-abiding lines. (Applause) In answer to the oft-repeated query, 'What is your programme?' Miss Bury said women wanted the vote for a definite purpose, and not as a plaything. At election time they supported their friends and opposed their foes. In a three-cornered contest, they supported the Socialist or Labour candidate, because that party was unanimously in favour of women's suffrage. They sometimes opposed the Conservative and sometimes the Liberal, according to the attitude of either candidate on this question. She did not know how Liberals could call themselves by that name when they were opposed to one of the greatest of all Liberal principles, viz., no taxation without representation. (Applause) The motto of the N.U.W.S.S. was 'Freedom', freedom for the women workers of the country, the workers who had to go out into the world to earn their living, although she did not for a moment mean to say that those who worked at home were not 'workers' also. There was the large body of women workers who toiled in their homes in producing articles of various kinds, and the lantern slides to be shown tonight would illustrate the conditions under which these women worked. For various reasons, these women could not actually go out into the labour market. They had their families and their house work to attend to, but in order to live they were obliged to take work to their homes.

A SERIES OF REVELATIONS

The pictures which were then thrown on to the screen and described and annotated by Miss Bury came as a series of striking revelations to the audience, and all around expressions of extreme surprise, pity and indignation could be heard. These pictures threw an impression on the mind which cannot possibly fail to have a powerful effect, and if they did not immediately result in largely increasing the membership of the Lerwick society (though many women and men did join at the close of the meeting) they at least succeeded in showing and proving to a large number of Lerwick people the sordid slavery in which thousands of British women are engaged today.

The pictures showed women chain-makers, a hard, arduous occupation, formly paid for at the appalling rate of 1d per hour, but now, thanks to the Trades Board Act, increased to 2 ½ d and 3d per hour. This Act, Miss Bury said, had resulted in increasing the payment of women to some extent, in a number of sweated industries, though certainly not in all as yet. Other heavy sweated work depicted was fire-brick making, paid for at the rate of 3s and 3s 4d per 1000 bricks, and the lecturer stated that a gang of six 'carriers' had to remove 10,000 bricks per day, while each woman lifed and handled 28 tons per day; hollow-ware trade, showing the dangers of galvanising tin goods; box-making, one of the most exacting and worst paid of the sweated industries; flower and glove making; fur-pulling; brush-making; beading work; regimental badge making (for soldiers' uniforms, ordered from manufacturers by the Government, but made by women outside the factories where the 'fair wage clause' did not apply); button and hook and eye carding; the clothing trade, boot trade, etc., etc. In all these industries the payment of the women workers ranged from 1 ¾ d to 3d per hour, and rarely exceeded 10s per week, even after prolonged strikes and recommendations of the Trades Board Act. Women, girls and chiildren worked 10, 12, 14 and 16 hours per day for a mere pittance at 1s 6d or 2s, and then had considerable outlay for materials, paste, string etc., required. From beginning to end, it was a harrowing story that Miss Bury told, not the least tragic aspect of it all being the baneful effect on the health of the workers: partial blindness, heart trouble, undermined constitutions, tuberculosis etc.

THE CAUSE OF SWEATED INDUSTRIES

Proceeding, Miss Bury said the cause of this state of affairs was that the laws of the country were in the hands of a class and not in the hands of the community. Women were striving to get what men fought and struggled for in the 30s and 60s. They must break down class legislation now just as men did it many years ago. Women were the only unrepresented class in the community, and despite all that had been done on their behalf their conditions and wages still showed a tendency to become worse. She maintained quite confidently that all these evils would be remedied if women were enfranchised. If women had equal rights with men they would not be driven into these low-paid occupations, and they would not compete with men. When they did the same work as men they should be paid the same as men. Such crying evils as the housing question would be largely mitigated if women had the vote, but how could they bring pressure to bear on M.P.s when they could not vote at elections? At the close of an eloquent, clear and impressive speech, Miss Bury said that the woman who did not support the demand for a vote was a far greater disgrace to her sex than the most ardent of the militant suffragists or their opponents. (Applause). She appealed to everyone present not yet members of the Lerwick Society to come forward and join tonight.

A number of questions were asked by Messrs M L Manson and F H Pottinger, chiefly as to whether the Conciliation Bill intended to enfranchise only women with the property qualification and not all adult women.

Miss Bury said that Bill did not contain the limit of her hopes, but it would place women on an equal footing with men. 90 per cent of the women who would be enfranchised by that Bill would be working women, and though all the wommen in the sweated industries would not get the vote those who did get it would help then.

Both Messrs Manson and Pottinger said they favoured universal adult suffrage.

Mr Loggie proposed a vote of thanks to Miss Bury for her admirable lecture, which was seconded by Mr Pottinger in a vigorous speech, in which he said he would never rest until this country had universal adult suffrage, although he was equally desirous of putting an end to a system which compelled women and little children to toil as the pictures had shown tonight.

The motion was unanimously and heartily agreed to, and Miss Bury, in reply, said that women were much needed in the councils of Lerwick.

The proceedings terminated with a hearty vote of thanks to Mrs Leisk for presiding.

A large number of articles of various kinds, made by women in the sweated industries, were exhibited on the stage, and the audience had an opportunity of inspecting the excellent workmanship of them, and of comparing their prices with the mere pittance paid to the women for their work.

A considerable number of women and men thereafter joined the Shetland Society.

The lantern was efficiently manipulated by Mr D Sutherland, and the pictures shown were excellent. [*SN* 14 April 1914]

Close on a hundred people gathered to hear Miss Bury in the Scalloway Public Hall; her visit to Walls also went down very well, although 'she did not convert us, for much water has passed under the bridge since we realised the injustice done to women by the unconstitutional policy of the British Government.' [*SN* 11 April 1914]

Miss Bury's visit was an unqualified success. Forty-five new members (taking the membership up to around eighty-five) and 17 'Friends' were enrolled. Owing to the larger membership, it was decided that meetings would be called by advertisement in the *Shetland Times*. The SWSS gave a donation of £3 to the Scottish Federation in recognition of Miss Bury's services. The cost of her visit had been £3 16/1, and they had taken in £2 13/10. They asked that she come again in July-August, and a 'Hearty vote of thanks was given to Mrs Galloway for her kindness to Miss Bury during her stay there.' [SWSS Minute book, 15 May 1914] The minutes were countersigned by M M Morrison, who was Vice Chairman from now - perhaps, as the Provost's wife, Mrs Stout felt she could not continue in so prominent a post.

M M Morrison
Vice Chairman

(Above) An open-air meeting at the Market Cross in the 1890s, taken here by a preacher. Miss Bury held a similar meeting during her visit in April 1914.
Photograph by John Leisk, courtesy of Shetland Museum and Archives [R02616]

April – June, 1914:

There was a brief meeting on 11 April 1914 to discuss the Final Agenda for the half-yearly council meeting of the NUWSS. Mrs Mackinnon Wood was instructed to vote against Miss Rathbone's policy: 'the most important question on the agenda.'

In 1913, Eleanor Rathbone, secretary of the Liverpool SWS, had been strongly opposed to the establishment of the Election Fighting Fund whereby support was given to Labour or Socialist candidates. Once the fund was established, in 1913, she did donate towards it, but became opposed once more in early 1914. Her policy was defeated, and she resigned from the Executive Committee in protest. She was to become an MP in 1929, and campaigned for family allowances.

Miss Hilliard had resigned as the Shetland WSS's Scottish Federation delegate, and Miss Caw was appointed. [SWSS Minute Book, 11 April 1914] Miss Caw was unable to act, so Mrs Stout of St Andrews was asked instead [SWSS Minute Book, 15 May 1914] - perhaps Mary Stout, the wife of Robert Stout's brother John Alexander.

The SWSS banner was to be 'sent to the Women's Exhibition as requested'. In the May minutes, referring to a demonstration in Glasgow, the SWSS agreed to 'send the banner to be carried in procession and to ask 'Friends' resident in Glasgow to join procession to carry it. Ask that members of Orkney and Shetland Association do same.'

The *Shetland News* carried more details:

'SUFFRAGE NOTES

A conference in Glasgow, following on the refusal of the Prime Minister to see the men's deputation in favour of women's suffrage, resolved on holding a public demonstration in support of the movement. This announcement met with such encouraging response that it was decided to make it an all-Scottish National Demonstration, and all organisations of men and women are being invited to send representatives. Individual friends of women's suffrage are asked to help in making the demonstration as effective as possible.

All the Scottish W.S. Societies are sending representatives and banners for the procession, which will march to Glasgow Green, where a resolution demanding a Government measure enfranchising women will be put from numerous platforms by leading speakers.

It is to be hoped that all Shetlanders in Glasgow who are interested in the welfare of their countrywomen will come forward in support of the banner of the Shetland W.S.S.

Anyone wishing to help should communicate with Miss K Lindsay, Glasgow.

The enormous amount of work done by the Scottish W. S. Federation escapes public notice becasue it is not sensational, but its extent will be shown when its forces are mustered on an occasion like this.

The struggle for the vote is proving very educative to women, and the constitutional party never allow themselves to lose sight of the questions that specially concern women – housing; wholesome conditions for child-life and for women workers; and temperance.

The provisions of the new Temperance Act should be specially studied by women, against whom the charge is often brought that they do not fully use the powers they already have, and they are prone to neglect informing themselves what these powers are. Young women should specially notice that if they are supporting themselves they are entitled to the parish and Municipal vote, whether they are living with the ir parents or in lodgings. This vote must be claimed every year, and the claim, duly signed and witnessed, sent to the Assessor before September 21, each year. [*SN* 30 May 1914]

In late May women of the WSPU, led by Emmeline Pankhurst, attempted to present a petition to the King. There were brutal attacks on the women by plain-clothes policemen, and over sixty arrests.

Mrs Pankhurst being arrested outside the gates of Buckingham Palace, 21 May 1914.
Press photograph, author's collection.

Forcible feeding in Scotland, summer 1914:

June 1914 saw the longest attempt at force-feeding in Scotland. In early May a Scottish WSPU member, Arabella Scott, one of the women arrested the previous year for attempting to set fire to Kelso race-course stands, had been arrested in a WSPU demonstration. She was sent to Calton Gaol, Edinburgh, where she went on hunger and thirst strike. She was released again on 8 May, and went straight back to London, to campaign during the Ipswich by-election as a 'Mouse'. On 18 June she was re-arrested in London and sent, fighting all the way, to Perth Prison. On her previous arrest she had promised her school board (she was a teacher in the Borders) that she would not again take part in further militancy, and nor had she; she was arrested as a WSPU organiser. The English police were now actively seeking suffragettes released under the 'Cat and Mouse Act', partly because of the defiant behaviour of women like Scott.

On 22 June Scott was joined by Frances Gordon, arrested for 'housebreaking with intent to set fire'. Both women went on hunger strike, and when they were not released immediately the WSPU organised protests. These included a visit to the gaol by Arabella's sister Muriel, picketing and vigils around the prison, singing hymns and suffrage anthems, and megaphoning messages of support. The prison governor complained that his staff could not sleep for the noise. Local support was also strong; crowds of sympathizers joined the picketers, and a special meeting of the Perth Trades Council petitioned MPs on the subject of forcible feeding.

The prison doctor in Perth was Dr Ferguson Watson, who had forcibly-fed Ethel Moorhead in February. Frances Gordon's nose was too narrow to insert tubes easily, and she vomited so much that she was fed rectally for some days before being released on 3 July, in a 'pitiful state'. On 4 July, Maude Edwards joined Arabella Scott; she had a heart condition, which should have meant she would not be force-fed, but Dr Watson ignored her certificate, because it was issued by a lady doctor. She was released a week later after promising not to take part in further militant activity.

There was a Royal visit to Scotland during July; the King and Queen arrived in Edinburgh on 6 July for a week-long tour of the Lowlands. During the visit there were a number of incidents referring to the forcible feeding taking place in Perth. Rubber balls labelled 'To remind HM King George V that women are being tortured in prison' were thrown at and into the royal carriage in several cities, banners were unfurled as they passed, petitions were thrown, and at the Clyde a woman with a megaphone implored him to stop forcible feeding. Prayers for the prisoners in Perth interrupted church services and cinema performances; in London Mr Mackinnon Wood was attacked by two women with a dog whip.

On 9 July, Fanny Parker was arrested during an attempt to bomb Burns' Cottage, and sent to Perth; she was forcibly fed for three days, until 16 July, then released because of the persuasion of her brother, Captain James Parker, not a suffragette sympathizer, and taken to a nursing home. Like Gordon, she had been rectally fed, and the examination by a second doctor, which her brother insisted on, showed swelling and rawness in the genital region, which the doctor attributed to rough and faulty introduction of instruments. Parker's account suggested there had also been attempts to feed her vaginally. On 28 July, the nursing home doctor informed the police that Parker had walked out of the home the previous evening.

Arabella Scott remained in prison until 26 July; she had been forcibly fed for over a month. She had been kept in solitary confinement, generally under observation, she was not allowed letters or books, and was kept lying down so that she would not vomit. When she was released, she insisted in a letter to the *Glasgow Herald* that the only effect of the forcible feeding had been 'to strengthen her principles'. [*Glasgow Herald* 28 July 1914]

On the day that Scott's letter was published, Archduke Franz Ferdinand was assassinated in Sarajevo. For many, this was not immediately seen as affecting Britain; there was more concern about possible civil war in Ireland. However, when Belgium was threatened, Britain sent an ultimatum to Germany, and when that was ignored, war was declared on 4 August 1914.

Life in Shetland had already changed. On 2 August, all Shetland Royal Naval Reservemen were called to report to HQ in Lerwick; on 3 August, a number of men of the Shetland Companies the Gordon Highlanders (TF) were called out for special duty in Lerwick, and the A Company was called to HQ for 3pm the next day. They were ordered to take their kit and equipment. On 5 August, the B Company was also called out. Manson wrote in his Roll of Honour,

'During these three eventful days, the town resembled a small armed camp. RNR men arrived in hundreds, and the unwonted and significant sight of so many navy blue and khaki uniforms brought vividly home to the people the first impressions of war.'

Miss Bury had returned to Shetland in late July. A committee meeting was held on 4 August 1914, and the minutes began with her own account of her visit: 'Miss Bury attended and gave report of work done by her during visit. Meetings in Fetlar and Yell, propaganda work undertaken in Unst - new members enrolled in each place.' Miss Bury also gave suggestions for running the Society: 'increase committee, separate Secretary and Treasurer, and create a Literary Society (Mrs Macmaster) and a 'Friends of Suffrage' Society.' These were formally taken up at the AGM in January 1915, with Jamieson remaining as Secretary, Miss Leisk becoming Treasurer, Mrs Macmaster heading the Literary Society and Miss E Sandison taking on 'Friends of Suffrage'.

However there were more important things to think about.

'In view of the present critical condition of international affairs, it was decided that no further suffrage work be undertaken meantime, and that the energies of members of the Society be directed instead to making preparations for the suitable accomodation of wounded men, should a naval engagement take place in the vicinity. It was hoped that it might be possible to form a Red Cross detachment. Miss Bury undertook to find out what steps it would be necessary to take and those present agreed to meet again the following evening to further discuss the subject, and to make the project known to their friends.' [SWSS Minute Book, 4 August 1914]

The announcement of war was made in London that day. The North Road police station officer, Gifford Gray, received the telegram at 4pm on Wednesday 5 August 1914.

12

August 1914 – June 1919

Women during the war

Lerwick during World War I: Victoria Pier and Bressay Sound.
Photographer E Forster, courtesy of Shetland Museum and Archives [V00062]

Signing up

Recruitment for men started immediately. By 6 August 1914, Lieutenant Colonel H C Evans RMLI had arrived to take charge in Lerwick, and the troops trained there as the Shetland Section Royal Naval Reserve. The first to go were the original RNR, who left for Portsmouth on 26 October 1914. There were over 1,000 Shetland men enlisted by February 1915; the next ones to go went to Chatham. The 240 Territorials who left Shetland in June were in the trenches by Christmas of 1915. More left in July. In all, there were 1560 RNR volunteers from Shetland, mostly men from the country, and a large number from Lerwick joined the Gordon Highlanders, as well as 3,000 men in the Merchant Service, which suffered huge casualties during the war.

Throughout the country women were also mobilizing themselves. The suffrage groups had become friendship groups too, and many of them converted themselves to volunteer organisations. They had become used to doing things without the help of men or against their active hindrance, and this experience was to stand them in good stead: where they couldn't get official sanction, they went ahead without it.

Many of the Suffrage societies offered their services to their local council. The Dundee WSS offered its entire organisation to aid in municipal schemes for the relief of distress caused by the war; the Edinburgh WSS undertook the visiting and care of wives and dependents of fighting men of the city. A large number of women suddenly found themselves out of work: milliners, laundresses, dress-makers, seamstresses and workers from the cotton and lace industries. The Edinburgh and Glasgow branches of the Women's Freedom League turned their shops in to workrooms for these girls to make garments for Belgian refugees. The Glasgow and West of Scotland Association opened an exchange for voluntary workers; Scotland's two most prominent militants, Fanny Parker and Ethel Moorhead, worked with the WFL National Services Organisation, 'to bring women workers in touch with employers and find the right work for the right women'.

The Shetland WSS 1915 AGM meeting gave a long list of work done by the London society: 'Bureau for Voluntary Workers, Municipal work among the Belgians, Queens' Work for Women Fund, Help for the Wounded etc,

'as instancing the valuable work done by Suffrage Societies, and receiving recognition as such by Government Officials. The progress of the women's movement throughout the world, and the fact that opposition to women's suffrage was becoming more and more confined to those interested in liquor traffic, gambling, and white slave traffic was pointed out.' [SWSS Minute Book, 30 January 1915]

Throughout the war, *The Common Cause* published a column entitled 'What some of our societies are doing'. It stated, 'In Shetland, the Suffrage Society has initiated (under Miss Bury's lead) the organisation of medical relief work.' [*The Common Cause*, 14 August 1914] and on 16 October 1914 there is '**Shetland:** The Lerwick WSS is practically controlling all the work there.' If this is true – and as *The Common Cause* was widely available in Lerwick, it would have caused great offence if it was untrue – it suggests that the main movers in the various societies formed for war work were SWSS members, which in turn suggests that the society was much larger than the names we know.

The Shetland women formed the Emergency Helpers, with Harriet Leisk as Convener, and Jessie Mitchell as the first Secretary/Treasurer; she served until 27 April 1916, when Mrs A J P Menzies took over until 16 October 1917. The last Secretary / Treasurer was Mrs J W Laurenson, a niece of 'Young John o the Trance', who remained in post until the group was disbanded on 25 May 1919. *Manson's Shetland Almanac* 1917 lists them as:

Emergency Helpers, Lerwick (Approved by the War Office and registered under the War Office Charities Act). President: Colonel Phillips; Convener: Mrs Leisk; Secretary and Treasurer: Mrs Menzies. Meets on Saturdays from 4 to 8 in the Tent Room of the Rechabite Hall.

The group had a committee of seventeen, and fifty other women were registered as helpers, all from Lerwick. In her speech winding up the Emergency Helpers, Mrs Leisk gives details of their work. They had been given the old Post Office to work in, and had begun by collecting old linen, cotton and underclothes. A house-to-house visitation was made to ask what each household would do in case of necessity. Some promised beds and beddings, others undertook to take convalescents, and a few placed their houses at the disposal of the Authorities if required. Screens, hot water bottles and all things necessary for the comfort of the sick were freely offered. They had daily (later, weekly) meetings to prepare surgical dressings and knit comforts: 'It was truly a busy scene, day after day, some rolling bandages, others mending clothes or knitting.'

At the start of the war they held nursing and first aid classes:

'Drs Graham and McVittie kindly undertook to give first-aid and ambulance lectures, which were well attended. Mrs Duncan and Mrs Morrison kindly lectured and gave practical lessons upon nursing.' An article in the *Shetland News* of 29 May 1915 recounts the 'very interesting ceremony ... in Mrs Galloway's house ... when a number of St Andrews' Ambulance Certificates and armlets were presented to members of the Lerwick Emergency Helpers who had passed the recent examination'.

The armlets were made by Jessie Mitchell, who'd painted the banner, and reference is also made to Mrs Hacon

'who was now in France [at the Scottish Women's Hospital at Royaumont], and whose work there had been eulogistically referred to in 'The Common Cause'.

There is a description of how the Emergency Helpers had been put on alert by the recent explosion, and had made five beds ready in case of an overspill from the Gilbert Bain.

'Our next ambition,' [Mrs Leisk said,] 'was to provide a Lerwick bed in France. You may remember the Scottish Women's Suffrage Society offering to provide and staff a Hospital in France. The War Office declined the offer, as they did also the help offered by the V.A.D. The Government were perfectly able to provide for all wounded men likely to require treatment. Naturally the offer was made to France, and was accepted with open arms, and, every assistance given, 'Royaumont' became one of the best equipped and most up-to-date hospitals in France, the whole staff being women. We raised £204 12/- and paid for a Lerwick bed there for four years, ending in December 1919. (Applause).'

Mrs Leisk then detailed the clothing knitted and donated. By the end of the war they had supplied over 2,400 articles to servicemen, the Gilbert Bain Hospital, the Fever Hospital, the Church Army Hut and Dr Walker's Hospital, as well as making 2,427 bandages. They collected used clothing, which was given to men and women from ships torpedoed in Shetland waters, and from April 1917 they took up duty at the Church Army Hut in Lerwick (on the Alexandra Wharf), giving first aid, food and clothing to rescued men and women. They carried on there until the hut was closed on 10 April 1919.

'I have no record of what clothing was given to the crews of torpedoed ships who were landed here. ...We worked on shifts of about three hours, two ladies to each shift, from 10am to 9pm, and later when necessary. We were several times called out at night or early morning to prepare food and clothing for crews of torpedoed ships, and truly it was a pitiful sight to see men landed, often in the thinnest clothing, the water pouring from them, and blue with cold, having more often than not been in open boats for hours in a bitter east wind and rain. We all felt thankful to be able to do all we could for the men who, just as surely as the men in France, saved our nation from ruin. (Applause).

Emergency Helper members also tended the graves of naval men buried in Lerwick:

'The graves of the men who were killed in the raid upon the Norwegian convoy were in a disgraceful state, the sods just heaped upon them. Mrs Menzies and Misses Mitchell and Jamieson undertook to attend to them. The initial work was too heavy for women, and they asked for one or two R.N.R. men to do the heaviest work. The answer they met was that no man could be spared to do it. Misses Mitchell and Jamieson worked away rather than see them left a standing disgrace to the town. After they had got all the heavy work done and the graves in order, they received word that the authorities would take charge of them. Truly a case of putting the cart before the horse.' [*SN* 24 April 1919].

In London, the WSPU immediately declared a truce. Christabel returned from Paris (there's film footage of her arrival) and she and Mrs Pankhurst began a recruiting drive for soldiers. Their magazine *The Suffragette* was re-named *Britannia*, and white feathers (meaning cowardice) were handed out to men who weren't in uniform.

Sylvia Pankhurst was a committed pacifist, and was shocked by their extreme pro-war attitude. She was to focus on social welfare work in the East End during the war, and after it joined Chrystal Macmillan as a member of her pacifist organisation, the International Committee of Women for Permanent Peace. Based in Amsterdam, the ICWPP (later the Women's International League for Peace and Freedom) endeavored to persuade neutral countries to work for a peace settlement. Philip and Ethel Snowden were also pacifists, joining the Union of Democratic Control. The NUWSS as a whole was pro-war, and in May 1915 was to pass a resolution not to send delegates to their International Congress of Women at the Hague. Eight members of the National Union resigned over this decision, but the Shetland WSS agreed with it: '... this meeting of the Executive Committee of Shetland WSS endorses the decision of the Executive Committee of the NUWSS in declining to send delegates to the International Congress of Women at the Hague, and considers that the wishes of the Council have been correctly interpreted.' [SWSS Minute Book 22 May 1915] Millicent Garrett Fawcett focused instead on what women could do for their country, and the few speakers who continued to tour took this as their theme.

As the men went, the women had to take over. In rural Shetland, women had always run the croft while their men were at sea, but now all over Britain, wives, mothers and sisters took over family businesses; women became postmen, bus drivers and conductors, railway porters, window cleaners, painters, journalists, taxi-drivers (under stiff opposition); refuse collectors, road-menders, blacksmiths, millers. All of this work had previously been considered too tiring, too physically demanding, too difficult for women; the women got on and did it, to the surprised admiration of the Press. Dr Elsie Inglis found it ironic that it had taken a war to make men notice women's work: 'Where do they think the world would have been without women's work all these ages?'

DIANA was outraged:

'...women have shown – and why should they not? – that they consider they have as great a stake in the nation as men. I may here say that I consider a mass of drivel has been written and spoken about the 'noble' conduct of the women of Britain in this war of barbarism against civilisation. I for one protest against it. The inference underlying the fulsome praise which has been bestowed upon we women is that in a great crisis women might fail; that they could not be depended upon to do their duty. What a supreme insult! I indignantly call upon any man or any woman to prove from history, either ancient or modern, an instance where when their nation was at war women failed to perform their part, aye, even going to the fighting line, or very near it, to assist the men. ...' [*SN* 26 April 1917]

Having said that though, the only change in the long list of male names as officials in *Manson's Shetland Almanac* of the war years is in the Parish Council Registrars of 1917 and 1918: Mrs E Drummond, Papa Stour, Miss Joann Charleson, Sandsting and Aithsting and Miss H Nicolson, Whalsay were added to Miss Mathewson in Yell and Miss Morrison, Burra. Miss Charleson could have been one of the sisters who taught in Clousta School. Mrs Drummond was Elizabeth Sharp Archer, born in Polmont in 1887, and the teacher on Papa Stour; her husband, David Drummond, gave his occupation as 'gamekeeper.' Miss Harriet Nicolson was the daughter of John Scott Nicolson, of Symbister, who was the manager for Hay and Co, and Sub-Postmaster.

Jamieson remained on the Lerwick School Board; she was joined in 1915 by Mrs J Brown Jnr - perhaps Jeromina Brown, nee Stout, whose mother-in-law came from Sandness; her husband, Daniel Brown Jnr, died at sea in 1915. From 1915, Jamieson also served on the County Committee on Secondary Education. The *Shetland News* of 1919 spoke of her as having acted as Chairman of the Lerwick School Board in the absence of Mr M L Manson. On returning the Chairmanship, she gave a lively speech:

MISS JAMIESON'S SPEECH

Miss Jamieson:- Gentlemen, I have not been heard in this Board for my much or other speaking [sic], but I feel that now is the time to put in my little oar, and I shall plunge it into a sea of metaphors. I feel that the vessel of the School Board has just been steered through the perilous passage between Scylla and Charybdis; and in that passage we have lost three oarsmen [three members had just tendered their resignations]. We are still not clear of rocks, and I lost these three oarsmen with infinite regret. I had hoped that we would be able to bring our barque into safe waters, or founder, all together. I regret exceedingly the loss of these oarsmen, and am now glad that the helm has been taken from me by the competent hands of the Chairman [M L Manson]. As I am not speaking to a motion I suppose I can speak fairly at large. We have had before us the trememdous question of finance in a very concentrated form, with such small results that I am reminded of a proverb about a mountain and a ridiculous mouse. (Laughter)'

She went on to speak about the new Craik settlement for teachers. 'I have every respect and sympathy for the profession. I have an hereditary interest in it.' However she is aware that ratepayers may grudge the expense of better pay for teachers.

'[Parents] should shoulder the consequence of being parents, and in paying the school rate they get enormous value for money. The ratepayers I sympathise with are small householders of meagre means, usually elderly women with no future before them and a past of devoted toil behind them ... these conditions would not have existed if the work of women had been properly valued and paid for in the past. The progress of civilisation is greatly impeded by the poverty of women, and I am exceedingly glad that women's work is to be more valued in the future. (Hear, hear.) ... I am come of a race that always strove how much and how long and how far they could do without money, and I think it is chiefly when money is not a consideration that the greatest work of the world is done. I hope the education of the future will tend to make us first of all serviceable to our fellow creatures, and then, as far as in us lies, active in productive and creative work, without concentrating on money as an end. (Applause) [SN 13 March 1919]

Another woman was listed on a School Board, for Dunrossness, Sandwick, Cunningsburgh and Fair Isle: Mrs Leslie, of Quendale. Mrs Nicol became the Vice-President of the Lerwick Literary and Debating Society; from 1915, Miss Harrison was its Treasurer. 1917 is also the first year of the North Star Cinema Co Ltd, with Miss Mann as the General Manager. Otherwise, there is no sign that women stepped into official positions in Shetland while the men were away; it seems more likely that the clubs simply remained suspended for the duration of the war.

Nursing volunteers

The first volunteer to offer nursing services at the Front was Mabel Stobart, who formed a 'Foreign Service' with women doctors, nurses, cooks, interpreters and all the workers needed for running a hospital in war. She'd already formed the Women's Sick and Wounded Convoy Corps, which had served with the Bulgarian army in the Balkan war of 1912. She began recruiting the day after war was declared, with astonishing success. Sir Frederick Treves (of *Elephant Man* fame) was then chairman of the British Red Cross, and when she went to offer her unit's services he responded that there was not work fitted for women in the sphere of war. She immediately left for Brussels and set up a hospital with the Belgian Red

Cross. Her organisation was followed by the First Aid Nursing Yeomanry, thirty-five aristocratic, fur-coated ambulance drivers who enlisted with the French and Belgian armies. They'd been founded in 1909, and training included first aid, home nursing, veterinary work, signalling and camp cookery; their motto was: 'I cope.' They soon grew from thirty-five to four hundred strong, and gained a reputation for keeping going under fire. The FANY women gained, between them, ninety-five decorations and fifteen Mentions in Despatches.

Mabel Stobart was followed by Millicent, Duchess of Sutherland, who established a Red Cross hospital at the front line - initially on the wrong side of it, where she treated wounded French and Belgian soldiers, then evacuated them all to Britain under the bemused eyes of the Germans. Her hospital was at Calais; the Duchess of Westminster ran one at Le Touquet. The latter patrolled the wards with her wolfhound at her side, and she and her lady helpers would greet the wounded in full evening dress, including tiaras (one hopes they had more humble helpers so the wounded didn't die while they were changing back). It was at her hospital that psychiatrist Charles Myers studied victims of the trenches, and defined the syndrome known as 'shell shock'.

Dr Louisa Garrett Anderson, Elizabeth's daughter, went to Paris as the chief surgeon of a trained team, the Women's Hospital Corps. Her mother said that had she been twenty years younger, she'd have led them herself. Elsie Knocker and Mairi Chisholm, who starred in Radio 4's recent 'book of the week', *Elsie and Mairi go to War,* were involved as ambulance drivers before they set up their Advanced Field Station at Pervyse; while there, they met Marie Curie and her daughter, who set up X-ray posts in 'mobile radiological cars.'

Dr Elsie Inglis, who'd visited Shetland in 1913, offered the War Office a field hospital unit, staffed by women. The reply was 'My good lady, go home and be still.' Naturally, she took no notice. Instead, she wrote to Millicent Garrett Fawcett, asking if the NUWSS would sponsor her field hospital. There was some discussion over what it was to be called; Inglis felt that mentioning women's suffrage would deter potential donors, and so it was named the Scottish Women's Hospital for Foreign Service. By October 1914 enough money had been raised to form the first unit. Her first hospital was at the Abbaye de Royaumont in France. The second unit went to Serbia. In all, a thousand volunteers worked behind in France, Russia, Roumania, Serbia, Macedonia and Corsica. Miss Bury, Shetland's last suffrage visitor, was the Organising Secretary, Personnel Committee and Edinburgh, in charge of passports and travelling arrangements, etc, for members of hospital units going overseas; there are files of her correspondence from 1915 in the Women's Library. Miss Lamond, now Mrs Abbott, who spoke in Fair Isle in 1910, gave fund-raising lectures in India, Australia and New Zealand, and raised over £60,000.

These women were not officially part of the Army, but even as volunteers they wore uniform; the work they were doing didn't fit with sweeping Edwardian skirts and ostrich plumed hats, and their own safety required they be recognisably respectable. Nurses wore white veils and red crosses. The FANY women supplied their own fur coats and gauze motoring scarves; the Scottish Women's Hospital nurses were dressed in 'hodden grey' with tartan facings. The many women drivers, who had to push their Ford ambulances out of shell-holes on non-existent roads, began by wearing breeches and gaiters under their long skirts, but it didn't take long for the skirts to be exchanged for greatcoats; the small start of a women-in-trousers revolution. Motorcycle drivers too wore breeches; the land workers settled for corduroy breeches and smocks.

The Common Cause ran a regular column on the work of the Scottish Women's Hospital, and the Shetland women would have followed the details each week. The newly-aquired Abbaye de Royaumont was described as 'some nine miles from Chantilly, a fine house, with ample accomodation, good drainage and water supply, and electric lighting.' [*The Common Cause,* 11 December 1914] It had previously been a convent, and had been empty for ten years.

Scenes from the Scottish Women's Hospital at Royaumont, where the Shetland WSS sponsored a bed throughout the war. (Above) An orderly, Mrs Harley, chats to recovering patients. (Below) An alfresco lunch for the fitter patients of the Marguérite d'Ecosse and Jeanne d'Arc wards. Photographs from *The Common Cause,* 12 November 1915.

The Transport Column of the Scottish Women's Hospital aboard HMS *Huntspill*, on their way to Roumania. Photograph: Ysabel Birkbeck.

The Transport Camp of the Scottish Women's Hospital in Medegea, with (centre) Mrs Evelina Haverfield. She was arrested with Mrs Pankhurst on 29 June 1909, and was a committed WSPU member. Haverfield was head of the Transport Corps; Ysabel Birkbeck was chief mechanic with the unit. The breeches and short hair of the transport unit caused a good deal of comment.
Photograph: Ysabel Birkbeck.

A page from Ysabel Birkbeck's Serbian diary. The top watercolour shows 'the road to the front, shells ahead.'

The first Scottish Women's Hospitals workers arrived in France a week later, led by Dr Alice Hutchinson and organised by Miss Cicely Hamilton, who was an actress, playwright, novelist and founder member of the Women Writers' Suffrage League. Here's Hamilton's first report back:

'In surroundings of medieval grandeur – amid vaulted corridors, Gothic refectories and cloisters – we proceeded to camp out with what we carried. The Abbey in all its magnificence was ours; but during these first few days it did not offer us very much beyond magnificence and shelter ... Its water supply had been practically cut off when the nuns left it for Belgium. Hence we carried water in buckets up imposing stairways ... our only available stove ... was naturally short-tempered at first ... our equipment ... was in no hurry to arrive; until it arrived we did without sheets and blankets, wrapped ourselves round in rugs and overcoats at night, and did not do much undressing. We borrowed tea-cups from the village ironmonger and passed the one knife round at meals for everyone to take a chop with it. ... we wandered about our majestic pile with candle-ends stuck in bottles. ...

One thing I should like to impress on those who have contributed ... is the pleasure of the folk round here when they learn that our hospital is intended primarily for the service of their own people ... 'nos petits soldats' ...' Cecily Hamilton, Abbaye de Royaumont, 17 December, 1914. [*The Common Cause,* 20 December 1914]

The new hospital had four wards: Blanche of Castile and Millicent Fawcett, with 25 beds each, and St Margaret of Scotland and Jeanne d'Arc, with 18 beds each. It had three motor-ambulances and a touring car. *The Common Cause* published photographs of each team as it went out, and on 29 January 1915 there were photographs of the Abbaye. It had now been approved by the French authorities, had acquired an X-ray machine and was ready for patients. The authorities were sufficiently impressed by the standards of care to ask the women to set up a typhus fever hospital as well – typhus was rife at this point, and *The Common Cause* of 16 April 1915 announced the death of a third woman worker in the Serbian unit. A fifth ward was opened in April, the Queen Mary ward. Extant Pathé film footage shows women stretcher-bearers working in the snow, the X-ray unit and the operating theatre.

Mrs Hacon, who had built The White Rest for fisher-girls in Shetland, was praised in an article by Miss Vera Collum, clerk of the 'vêtements' department at Royaumont. Soldiers could not get new uniforms, so when the wounded were brought in, all their possessions were carefully stored, and their clothes washed and repaired. Collum describes how they were separated, labelled and hoisted up to the roof using a pulley rigged up by one of their drivers. After laundering, the linen items were mended by Madame Fox.

'We ourselves tackle the uniforms with the noble assistance of Mrs Hacon, an NU worker well known in the Shetlands, through whose ingenuity I have seen the 'veste' of an artilleryman, minus half a sleeve, made into a wondrous garment with warm woollen cuffs – all because there was nothing in the world to mend it with but a pair of navy-blue bed-socks - and an old scarlet sock repair a breach made by shrapnel in a pair of infantryman's trousers!

Indeed, we are earning a good name for this Women's Hospital for turning out our men not only mended in body but repaired in equipment ... It sounds prosaic, but if only people at home knew the moral and physical importance of a clean set of underlinen and cleansed uniform to these poor fellows, who have to go back, most of them, to face the mud and misery, the monotony, and the filth of trench life again ... ' [*The Common Cause* 21 May 1915]

It must have been a far cry from the life of Edith Hacon, wealthy widow and philanthropist, and further still from Amaryllis, the artists' model and muse of London's avant-garde.

The Shetland WSS continued as a separate society, and all its fund-raising efforts were directed towards the Scottish Women's Hospital. The first meeting after war was declared was held in the Emergency Helpers' Rooms, with 19 members present. They discussed a Whist Drive which raised £7.12/- for the SWHFS. The delegate to the Scottish Annual Council was Mrs Freeman [SWSS Minute Book 22 December 1914]. Here's the *Shetland News* advertisement for the Whist Drive:

Suffragists and the War The Shetland Women's Suffrage Society are having a whist drive in the Masonic Hall on Wednesday January 6. The proceeds are to be given to the funds of the Scottish Women's Hospital for Foreign Service. The Union to which this society belongs offered its entire organisation and staff for national service when war was declared, and has ever since been engaged in every kind of emergency and relief work throughout the country. Besides being thus engaged, Scottish suffragists have organised a hospital for Foreign Service, of which two units have been already sent to the front. These are at work, one in France and one in Serbia, equipped, staffed and supported by Suffragists, and a third is about to follow. Each unit costs about £1000 a month and it takes £10 to equip a bed. Help is therefore urgently needed. [*SN* 2 Jan 1915]

The Whist Drive was reported the following week as having been 'highly successful and enjoyable'. It was

'attended by a large company, numbering about 60 couples. The beautiful banner of the S.W.S.S., emblematic of their movement, adorned the south wall of the room. ... A short dance followed the whist, and was entered into with the utmost enthusiasm. Mrs Nicol made a capital M.C., but refused to allow more than three 'last dances.' From start to finish this function [was] organised and carried out by Lerwick suffragists.' [*SN* 9 January 1915]

The AGM was held at the end of January, along with a cake and candy sale. Mrs Leisk was not present, but the Secretary thanked the men for their support in connection with Miss Bury's visit. She gave details of the founding of the Emergency Helpers. £1 was to be sent to the Scottish Federation in payment of arrears, and the Secretary gave a general report from the National Union since the outbreak of war. [SWSS Minute Book, 30 January 1915] A Serbian Flag Day was held on 5 June 1915, and another on April 1916:

'During the afternoon practically every house in the town was visited by Girl Guides selling flags, and in the evening brisk business was conducted in Commercial Street, where a large crowd assembled to listen to the Brass Band.'

A long list of thank-yous followed, including the *Shetland News* and bill-poster for reducing their charges, shops who placed collecting boxes in their premises for the day, and the staff of the bank who received the boxes and counted the proceeds – an impressive £29.16s. [*SN* 7 June 1915].

In June 1916, the committee voted to 'pay to [the Treasurer] £3 1/2d being the balance required to complete £25 collected to name a Lerwick bed at Abbaye de Royaumont, France for six months.'

A number of Shetland women also nursed in France. Two sisters, **Martha** and **Jessie Aitken** of Burgh Road, were Red Cross nurses:

Lerwick Nurses on Active Service Two daughters of Mr Chas. W Aitken, Lerwick, Misses Martha and Jessie Ann, are at present engaged in their professional duties as nurses with the Red Cross. The former is stationed at Boulogne and the latter at Aberdeen. A picture in a recent issue of the 'Daily Mail' showed Miss Martha tending to a wounded British soldier, treating him, as the paper says, to the 'smile that won't come off'. The work of the nurse is equally as important as that of the soldier fighting in the trenches, and each of them is rendering a service to her country the value of which cannot be estimated.' [*SN* 2 January 1915]

Martha Aitken was born at Aitkens House, Burgh Road, Lerwick, in 1881, making her thirty-three when war broke out. She was awarded the 1914 Star, or 'Mons Star' for her work early in the war. This medal consisted of a 6cm high bronze star with the hilts and points of crossed swords making four of the star points. An oak-leaf wreath circled the words Aug 1914, and there was GV at the bottom, and a crown at the top. The ribbon was red, white and blue. To have been eligible for this, she must have enlisted before midnight of 22/23 November 1914.

A number of Shetlanders wrote letters from the front which were published in the *Shetland News* and *Shetland Times*, and Martha Aitken's are among them, giving a vivid picture of her work:

HELL COULD NOT BE WORSE

Nurse Martha Aitken, writing to her parents in Lerwick, says, 'Just a short note to say I am perfectly well and safe. All the fighting is in this direction at present, and I am sure Hell could not be worse. We are very, very busy. The men tell some ghastly tales of the cruelties of the Germans to our poor wounded and helpless men. Every man who can fight should be here to avenge the fallen. I will write when I can, don't expect a letter as long as this lasts.' [*SN* 29 May 1915; this was the end of the second battle of Ypres, and a month after the first use of poison gas.]

Her second letter is much longer, and is headlined:

Lerwick Nurse in France.

An Interesting letter.

Pathetic and Humorous Incidents.

A Dream of the Slate's Pier.

'Many a time I thank goodness I am a trained woman and able to do my little bit for my country. These men (the soldiers) are expected to do their best, and they do it, and why not the women too? Often I wish I were a man and then I would be of more use. It makes my blood boil to read of these slackers at home, who don't believe, even yet, that there is a war out here or anywhere else. It is no picnic for the men in the fighting-line, and no one who has been there can want to face an attack again, but still they are too manly to shirk their duty.

When I used to watch the firing-line on a dark night, many thoughts passed through my mind. It was an awful picture, even in one's imagination, what destruction one bomb could do, and what a caravan of agony would come, like greyhounds, to this clearing station in a few hours' time.

Here, it is the fever-stricken ones who come under my care [she has charge of a ward of 22 beds]. They are splendid fellows, and never utter a single word of complaint. One poor fellow has enteric fever and face wounds as well. One eye was blown out, and the sight of the other very much injured. Yet he never utters one word of complaint. It almost makes me weep to look at him. But he is a fine fellow and we like him so much.

...One Scotch boy, she proceeds, was quite delirious, and talked and rambled away all day and night. One time he was at home and another moment in a charge. Poor thing, he was distressed about his pals, and in his delirium kept on beseeching me to 'pull me out of this awful mud. I'm sticking – choking.' He had such a look of entreaty and struggled to get out of bed. Then he would see a bomb coming and would call out to someone to save his pals. Again, he would fancy someone had been killed, and he must avenge his death. Then anyone who was with him came in for a severe mauling. I got several. It was so sad to see him, and yet occasionally he would say something so comical that it was beyond everyone of us to keep from laughing.

The Captain, our medical officer, was examining him one day, and sounding him all over, and as he went on the boy got more impatient and disgusted. At last, he took hold of the Captain's hand and threw it from him, and hauled up the bed clothes. 'Ach, go awa' wi' ye and ga a fella some peace. D'ye hear, ga on.' The Captain said to me, 'That's done it, Sister,' and so left him. He could not help laughing all the same.

... Well, to change the subject, we are in a very nice place and there are some lovely walks through the woods and sand dunes. ... One afternoon I began to scour the woods for leaves, etc, and was busy hauling at some lovely scarlet leaves and berries when from the depths a French officer appeared. He said I was on his property and was trespassing. 'Where do you come from?' he asked. It flashed through my mind that I would get landed before the Colonel for it, so said ... 'No comprez'. He wanted to take my leaves from me, but the expression above saved them. He could not speak one word of English, but I understood every word he was saying to me, but nevertheless stuck to the 'no comprez' and departed, almost double with laughter, and the officer none the wiser.

We are all under canvas here, and it is frightfully cold at times. On a windy night when in bed I often picture my house blowing away and my belongings being scattered to the four winds of heaven. The canvas shakes and flaps, the tent pole rocks and sways, and every minute is making a bigger hole for itself. Then the canvas gets on top of my head and bed. That finishes me, out of bed I hop, and hunt for an unoccupied bed in the compound. Usually one of the night Sisters comes in handy. The Sergeant on duty is then hunted for, and he pegs up my house again and life is resumed till the next gale arrives.

It is the limit to try and find one's way on a dark night. Many a nasty bruise I have got by tripping over tent pegs and ropes. One moment on one's feet and the next wallowing, like a pig, in the thick mud.

... One night I was lying asleep and dreaming I was standing on the Slate's Pier, and that the rain was beating on my face. I awoke and discovered that the rain was coming through the canvas in fine style and pattering on my face. My bed could not be moved, as there was no room, so up I got and put my mackintosh on in bed, my souwester on my head, and held up my umbrella. I could not get the latter fixed, so had to hold it in position and sleep at the same time. I did both, and was none the worse. What life, and yet I love it!' [*SN* 2 December 1915]

However, the huge scale of the casulties meant that hospitals at the front were only for the severely wounded, or for those who would soon be able to go back to the front. Troopships were bringing large numbers of wounded men home within weeks of the war beginning, and hospitals here could not cope either. A number of new ones had to be opened, and halls and schools also had to be used. All over the country, women's volunteer groups were nursing, catering, and cleaning.

Several women from Shetland enlisted in the nursing units attached to the army, which had field posts overseas and hospitals at home. Queen Alexandra's Imperial Nursing Service was founded in 1902, to replace the Army Nursing Service. Members were over 25, single or widowed, and had undergone three years training. Before 1914, there were just under 300 QAIMS nurses serving across the world; during the war, 11,000 more Reserve nurses were recruited. One of these was **Margaret Louisa Robertson**, from Scalloway, who was a Staff Nurse; her father was the head-teacher of Scalloway School, and she was only 22 when war broke out, so she must have already trained as a nurse, to hold so senior a post. A Shetland woman was also in the smaller Queen Alexandra's Royal Naval Nursing Service, again as a reserve: **Margaret Sandison**, Chromate Lane, was a Nursing Sister at the Haslar Royal Naval Hospital, Gosport, an existing pre-war military hospital. She was a niece by marriage of Harriet's sister Emily, and in her late twenties at the start of the war. A *Shetland News* announcement gave more details:

'**Service Appointment for Lerwick Nurse** Miss Margaret Sandison, Lerwick, has just been appointed to the Haslan Naval Hospital at Gosport. Miss Sandison received her training at the London Hospital, and holds the full certificate of training. After almost five years service, she qualified for and attained in October last the certificate of C.M.B. since when she has been on the private nursing staff of the 'London'. Miss Sandison, who is the elder daughter of Mr Andrew Sandison, Chromate Lane, is to be congratulated on receiving this appointment.' [*SN* 6 Feb 1915]

The Territorial Force Nursing Service was formed in 1908, and expanded to over 8,000 women during the war; over 2,000 of them served overseas. **Nellie Gilbertson** was a Sister in the Territorial Force Nursing Service, stationed in 1915 at the 5th Northern General hospital, Leicester; this was a Territorial Force hospital, with beds for 111 officers and 2,847 other ranks. Gilbertson was to receive the Royal Red Cross in 1917. This was awarded only to a fully trained nurse who had shown exceptional bravery and devotion at her post of duty during an incident. The medal was a golden cross, enamelled red; it can be seen in the Shetland Museum, pinned to her scarlet and grey uniform.

Helen Andrina Gilbertson was born in Lerwick in June 1889, and so was just twenty-six when war was declared. She married Lollie Sinclair, one of the owners of Malcolmson's bakery, in 1926, and they had one daughter, Olive. They lived in a bungalow at the foot of Harbour Street, and her niece Margaret Kemp remembered visiting her there: 'She was a very decided person, a real Matron, very particular, very houseproud, and spoke her mind. She had a great sense of humour.'

Mrs Kemp thought that her aunt had nursed in France, and it was there that she had been awarded the medal.

Staff Nurse Nellie Gilbertson, of the Territorial Forces Nursing, who was awarded the Royal Red Cross in 1917.
Photograph courtesy of the Shetland Museum and Archives [NE03257]

The Royal Army Medical Corps was the oldest of the army medical services, founded as medical attendants to accompany the Duke of Marlborough's troops in the early eighteenth century. At the start of the war it had 9,000 'other ranks'; by the end of the war it had 13,000 RAMC officers and 154,000 'other ranks.' One of these was **Jean Yule**, from Scalloway, daughter of Dr Robert Yule, the examiner for the Emergency Helpers' certificates. Jean was a Medical Orderly attached to the RAMC Military Hospital at Colchester. Like Haslar, this was an existing pre-war military hospital at Aldershot. When war broke out, she was in her early thirties; after the war she qualified as a doctor.

In October 1915 an English nurse, Edith Cavell, was shot by the Germans for organising an underground escape route for British and Allied soldiers from her Red Cross hospital in Brussels. Her funeral cortege included a Guard of Honour from the FANY unit. Her death was a public relations disaster for Germany, expecially in America. Suffrage workers must have been wryly amused – or just plain annoyed – when Asquith declared, 'She has taught the bravest man among us a supreme lesson of courage; yes, and in this United Kingdom and throughout the Dominions there are thousands of such women, but a year ago we did not know it.'

'Wilfully blind,' was Millicent Garrett Fawcett's comment.

At the time of Cavell's death, Dr Inglis' unit was behind enemy lines. Inglis risked imprisonment for refusing to sign a German 'blank document' saying that she and her nurses had not been ill-treated; it was only after she learned of Cavell's death that she understood the reason for the German commander's insistance.

Canteen work

The huge numbers of men recruited into the army also needed to be fed: the Red Cross-trained Voluntary Aid Detachments, the Women's Volunteer Reserve, the Women's Legion and the Women's Auxiliary Force were all involved in this, as were many volunteer groups. Canteens were established at training camps and transit points, like King's Cross station. There were also canteens set up overseas; **Mrs Ellen Hepworth**, Parkfield Rd, Lerwick, was an Adjutant, Salvation Army Hut; she worked in France for three and a half years. The Salvation Army established a number of front-line posts to offer comforts to the troops, not the officers, and their website gives several accounts of what her life would have been like. One description of an SA Officer's work at war ranges from frying sausages and making endless cups of tea to the harder tasks of writing letters for wounded soldiers, laying flowers on graves for relatives at home, visiting military hospitals and conducting services. Another account describes an American band of volunteers from 1917, the 'Doughnut Girls'. They made doughnuts because that was what they had the ingredients for, and because they could be made in frying pans over an open fire. Their experiences included being involved in attacks and attending the funerals of soldiers after a battle. They would then cross 'No-man's Land' to say prayers for the buried German soldiers.

The SWSS minutes make regular references to members being away, and they could well have been involved in war work elsewhere, as the war history of one Shetland family illustrates: the **Stout** family of Medical Hall in Lerwick. Margaret Stuart, from Walls, gave me an account of what the women of her family did in the war.

'The girls were all educated at the Anderson Institute and all went on to college or university in Edinburgh or Glasgow, and pursued careers at a time when careers for women were in their infancy. They travelled widely with a self assurance that stems from supportive parents and a secure family home.

Their eldest daughter Anne set the educational pattern for all six girls, she went to the Anderson Educational Institute, then to college in Edinburgh. Although there's no sign that the second daughter, Elizabeth, was involved in the Shetland WSS, she would clearly have approved the principle of women's suffrage. From a young age she wrote articles, poems and accounts of concerts and plays for the *Shetland News*, and won a number of literary competitions. She was a leader of the literary and dramatic life in town and she was one of the first to write plays in Shetland dialect for public performance, often by members of the Pickwick Club. Elizabeth spoke fluent French, and the sisters talked in French at mealtimes. There's a story that she was the first woman to enter the male-dominated reading room in Lerwick [on the sea side of the Tolbooth]. 'Women can read too,' she announced, and she and her sister Margaret marched in, to much rustling of papers, but after that women began to use the reading room regularly.

In 1913, after college in Edinburgh, Elizabeth was appointed headteacher of Hamnavoe School, with Anne as her assistant. They were creative and innovative teachers, the first in Shetland to hold after-school clubs and socials for their pupils. When new regulations came in requiring all skippers to hold a certificate of seamanship, Elizabeth and Anne attended classes in Lerwick during their holidays and at their own expense to gain the qualifications to teach navigation and seamanship. They were very successful, and all their skippers passed the examinations and were awarded the all important certificates.

She was also a keen archeologist. In 1911, she was awarded the Chalmers Jervise Essay Prize for 'Some Shetland Brochs and Standing Stones', illustrated with her own drawings and watercolours, and was made one of only six corresponding members of the all-male Society of Antiquarians of Scotland. Her recognition of the gold Viking Armlet found on Oxna led to its aquisition by the National Museums of Scotland.

(Right): Elizabeth Brown Stout, who left her job as headteacher of Hamnavoe School to spend the last two years of the war in France. Her first job was helping in a canteen in Dormans, then she worked as as an assistant in a hospital under the auspices of the Croix Rouge Francaise. In this photograph she is wearing her C.R.F. uniform.
Photograph courtesy of her niece, Margaret Stuart.

263

In 1917 Elizabeth resigned her teaching post and became a voluntary worker under the Oxford Women Students' Society for Women's Suffrage. This group was affiliated to the Croix Rouge Francaise. It was started by a French tutor at Oxford, who had been horrified by the lack of provision for the French troops at war. She raised money for canteens to be established for French soldiers at the front. Elizabeth Stout arrived in Paris and was assigned to Dormans behind the Rheims front. At first it was relatively quiet but they could hear constant gunfire in the distance, and by 1918, the stream of refugees warned the canteen workers that the Germans were advancing, and they had to evacuate. In a letter to her sister Margaret, Elizabeth said,

'... the enemy are only two kilometres from our place and everyone hurriedly quitting. Our leader fleeing with a wagon, no trains. Some nurses have lost everything. Isn't it rotten when I'd troddled the bike and tin kettles safely through!'

Their canteen was completely destroyed, but the kettles came into use again in Paris, where the C.R.F. was desperate for workers. Elizabeth worked as an assistant nurse in the Hotel Astoria, on the Champs Elysées, which had been turned into a hospital for French soldiers. Air raids on Paris were constant. Each night Paris was bombarded by 'Big Bertha', one of the massive German guns. Plans were made for their evacuation if the Germans took Paris.

Elizabeth was there until the end of the war. On her days off, she took 'Tommies' on historical tours of Paris and Versailles. An American officer, Nathan Levy, joined one Versailles group, and was captivated by this intelligent, vivacious young woman. After a whirlwind romance they were married in Paris on 22 May 1919. Elizabeth wore her C.R.F. uniform, and Miss Myvanwy Rhys of Jesus College, Oxford, was her Maid of Honour. After the armistice Elizabeth Stout and Myvanwy Rhysthe were seconded to the Italian army in Belgium to organise a canteen for General Garibaldi's Brigata Alpi. They scheduled their work so that each had free time to visit the battlefields and see for themselves the terrible destruction of war.

In the Second World War Elizabeth was living in America, but six families enjoyed her amazing food parcels from America, which got past Customs and Excise by persuasive notes about her starving relatives in Shetland.

In 1918 Elizabeth's sister Anne resigned from her teaching post at the Central School, Lerwick, for voluntary work with the Scottish Churches Canteens in Cologne for the British Army of Occupation. The third sister, Francisca, also a teacher, had died in 1913, aged only twenty-three, in a bicycle accident outside Lerwick. Margaret, my mother, taught in the East End of London after graduating from Atholl Crescent, Edinburgh, and keen to 'do her bit' ran a canteen in King's Cross Station for troops in transit. She rose at five to do the early morning shift, taught all day and then did another shift after school closed. She had wanted to join the WRNS, and had been offered a commission, but she thought she was too small to wear uniform! She was awarded the Red Triangle for her war-work. Harriet had qualified as a Princess Louise Nurse in Edinburgh, and served as a theatre nurse in the Gilbert Bain Hospital during the war. The youngest sister Alexandra took a degree in Pharmacy and practised in the family business.'

Only Elizabeth Stout is in Manson's *Roll of Honour*, for her nursing work, but all these young women, and hundreds of thousands of others, went straight from a comfortable existence to the dangers and distress of a world at war.

Three of the Stout girls, (left to right) Harriet, Annie and Margaret, dressed for the Buckingham Palace Garden Party held in honour of those who had done war work. Their tussore suits were bought in London.
Photograph courtesy of Margaret Stuart.

Other war work:

Shetland women in both town and country turned their hands to knitting and sewing for the troops. The Shetland branch of Queen Mary's Needlework Guild was formed on the 3rd September 1914; the presidents were Mrs. Bruce of Sumburgh and Lady Nicolson of Brough Lodge Fetlar. Whereas the Emergency Helpers were predominantly Lerwick, the QMNG also involved country women; there was an organiser for each district, and local committees.

The headquarters of the Lerwick branch was in the County Hall, and members gathered there to knit. Margaret Stout, mother of the girls, was a prominent member of the guild, and told her daughters that they made many strange and poignant garments for wounded men including one-legged trousers and one-armed shirts. In the course of the war over 15,000 garments were made: pairs of socks, scarves, helmets, jerseys, wristlets, mittens, gloves, operation stockings and sleeping socks. Money was also raised, £406 12s 1d, and when the war ended, the balance of £60 19s 3d was put towards the War Memorial.

At the end of the war the Shetland Branch of the Guild received an invitation from Queen Mary to attend a Garden Party at Buckingham Palace in recognition of their war work. No one was available to go at such short notice, so Mrs Stout suggested that her three daughters, who were in London, and had all participated in war work, could represent Shetland. The committee agreed, and so Harriet, Margaret and Anne went. They said one of the best moments of the day was when they climbed into a taxi and said the magic words 'Buckingham Palace please.' The event was reported at length in the *Shetland News* of 31 July 1919.

Other ways in which country people could help were 'National Egg Collection' and 'Moss Days' The National Egg Collection for the Wounded gave eggs to soldiers in hospital; people gathered up their eggs and sent them to Lerwick, then Aberdeen. During the war, 3,000,636 eggs were collected, and £216 19s 7d was raised. There were two 'Moss Days', on 9 August 1917 and in August 1918. Spagnum moss was in demand for anti-septic dressings, and the Shetland moss was said to be the very finest and purest quality. On the first 'Moss Day', men, women and children went out into the hill and gathered, between them, 2,500 large sackfuls. The following year they managed 3,000 sacks.

The *Shetland Times Cigarette Fund* sent 1,589,500 cigarettes to the Front; the *Shetland News* Christmas Pudding Fund of October 1916 raised £281 11s 6d. Putting all these funds together, the amount that was raised here in Shetland, from a population that was on average less well-off than people south, is truly awe-inspiring.

Nor was Shetland generosity confined to its own men; at the end of the war, in January and February 1919, the 'Save the Children' fund for the destitute and starving children in Germany and other defeated countries received 1518 garments and £122.

Shetland Branch, Queen Mary's Needlework Guild, outside their headquarters, the County Buildings. The branch was formed on 3 Sep. 1914. They knitted garments to send to sailors and soldiers. Photographed by R Ramsay, courtesy of the Shetlamd Museum and Archives [SM00072]

The National Egg Collection: Cunningsburgh school pupils collecting eggs for soldiers in hospital. Photographer G Robertson, courtesy of Shetland Museum and Archives [NG00724]

Other specialist groups on the mainland included the Lady Instructors' Signals Company, at Aldershot, the Women's Forage Corps, which had eight thousand women baling hay, chaffing, making sacks, guarding forage stores ('If you have a dog, you may bring it with you') and driving horsed transport. The Women's National Land Service Corps and the Women's Defence Relief Corps did all the work the vanished men had done: ploughing, planting, weeding and harvesting, as well as the daily round of milking, animal care and forestry work. These women insisted on men's wages - £1 a week – so as not to lower the wages for men when they returned.

In June 1915, after a Cabinet split and the disastrous defeat at Gallipoli, Asquith formed a coalition government. A J Balfour replaced Churchill at the Admiralty; Bonar Law became Secretary of the Colonies. Lloyd George became Minister of Munitions and conduct of the war was given to Generals Haig and Robertson. Shortage of munitions was then becoming a serious problem, and Lloyd George realised that women would have to be recruited to make shells and fill them with explosives, and to produce cartridges and hand grenades. The work was heavy – shells weighed 35lb empty – and dangerous. There was a large rally in London in July 1915, led by Mrs Pankhurst and financed by Lloyd George, to show 'Women's willingness to work.' This rally was captured on a Pathé film. The women also learned precision engineering: how to set and grind tools, mill the breech mechanism of the howlitzers, make all the different gun parts, and use logarithms and slide rules for calculations. There's film footage of this too, including women leaving their children at the 'Munitions Day Nursery', filling shells, factory engineering and heavy work. The life wasn't as positive as the film suggests. The munitions workers soon earned the nickname 'canaries' from the yellow shade of their faces and hair, caused by toxic jaundice. Fainting was common, and the chemicals also ruined the women's teeth.

In the last eighteen months of the war, women became involved in the most staunchly male industries. About five hundred women were involved in the ship-building industry, mostly in unskilled jobs, though a number managed to be trained as painters, welders and riveters. The last industry to succumb was coal-mining; it was not until 1917 that the pit-lasses with their shawls and clogs were permitted to come back to the mines, after a government appeal: Men and women of Britain, your country needs you.

The appeal was echoed in the Day by Day column of the *Shetland News*:
'NATIONAL SERVICE
The nation is making an urgent appeal to all, men and women alike, who being unable to undertake military duties, can in other ways assist in bringing this cruel and devastating war to an end. The appeal has not been made in vain, for already a large number of volunteers of both sexes have come forward: but more is needed in order to take the place of men engaged in the various industries of the country, and release them for active service. The problem is a complex and intricate one, because skilled workers cannot be replaced by those who have no knowledge of the work, however willing they may be to learn. Time must elapse before they can be of any real use; but from this very fact it is self-evident that the earlier volunteers come forward to undergo training the better. So many men are of course already on service at the front or otherwise engaged on work connected with the war, that the appeal is more directly made to the women of the nation. Probably no county in the United Kingdom could show a greater proprtion of its women folk doing active work of national importance than Shetland. The women of Shetland are no strangers to hard toil on the land; in fact, but for them many of the crofts could not and would not have been worked at all. In other branches, such as knitting underclothing of all kinds, fishcuring, peat-cutting and peat-carrying, and in many other ways, Shetland women certainly 'do not eat the bread of idleness', and the call to National Service in the present crisis can hardly be said to apply to them, for the bulk of them are doing all they can already. Nevertheless, there must be some men and women in the islands not engaged in work of importance, who could render valuable service to the nation – not so much here as in the south, where their abilities can be utilized to the best advantage. By such the appeal of the nation will not, I hope and believe, remain unanswered.' [*Shetland News*, 19 April 1917]

The Women's Services:

It was in 1917 that the Government created the first women's Services: the Women's Royal Naval Service and the Women's Army Auxiliary Corps (Fanny Parker went on to become deputy controller of the WAAC at Boulogne). Over a hundred thousand women joined up, ready for a life of adventure, and a wage. The Government was more worried about the morality of mixing women and men soldiers, and the adventure was limited. The WAACs were kept busy catering and cleaning; the Admiralty wouldn't allow WRNS anywhere near ships, although they were given some training in, for example, wireless telegraphy. They were not allowed to go to sea until 1990.

Lerwick was a Naval Base from 1914, and typists and telephone operators were needed. **Lena Mouat**, of 75 Commercial Street, was the first, in March 1915, followed by **Mary Inkster** in September 1916, and **Maggie Clarke** and **E A E Smith** in March 1917. By the end of the war, sixteen women worked under the charge of Lena Mouat, now the Assistant-Principal, WRNS, and her fellow AP, **Muriel McKenzie-Grieve**. Apparently the Navy would have liked more women operators, but there were not enough Shetland girls with the training. Nine of them were telephone operators, and most of these were in their mid- to late twenties when war broke out; only two were under twenty, and all were single. The enrolment dates for almost all of them are between May and August 1918. The clerk, **Margaret Agnes A Sinclair**, enrolled on 30 September 1918. There were three typists and two shorthand typists; three of these enrolled on 31 May 1918, one on 8 August 1918, and the last, **Elizabeth Shearer**, who was only born in June 1901, enrolled in January 1919 – although hostilities ceased on 11 November 1918, the final peace plan was not signed until June 1919.

The Shetland Museum and Archives have a number of photos of the WRNs, by an anonymous photographer, and they're a very cheery looking bunch. The 'official' photograph, by R Ramsay, gives more details of where each worked. **Margaret (Peggy) F J Aitken** of King Harald St, **Kate** and **Ruby Anderson**, of 16 St Magnus St, **G Dorothy Anderson** of 'Laarsund', Hillswick, **Mary A Garriock**,

Mounthooly St, **Maggie Irvine**, Albany St, **Christina Janet Williamson Kerr**, Moors, Sandwick, **Britta Astrid Laurenson**, King Harald St, and **Nellie J Tulloch**, King Harald St, were telephone operators, in the Telephone Office. **Pauline Moorcroft**, who's not in the Roll of Honour, was in the Store Office; Maggie Clark, also not in the Roll of Honour, was in the Captain's Office. **Florence Ogilvy Inkster**, Charlotte St, was a typist in the Sailing Office; **Elizabeth M Shearer**, Hillhead and **Annie E Smith**, North Ness were listed as typists in the Roll of Honour, but are not in the photograph; Mary L Inkster and Edith A E Smith were shorthand typists – Edith was in the Admiral's Office. The two officers, Lena Mouat and Muriel McKenzie-Grieve, are wearing rather dashing tricornes, and have gold-braided sleeves. Mouat received the MBE for her work. She went on to become a Business Studies teacher. Some of these WRNs marched in the Victory Parade in London, on 19 July 1919.

(Left) Edith Smith at work in the Admiral's Secretary's Office at Brentham House. Photograph courtesy of Shetland Museum and Archives [NE05251]

The Women's Royal Naval Service, Naval Base, Harbour St.
Back: Nellie Tulloch, Mary Garriock, Chrissie Kerr, Dorothy Anderson, Britta Laurenson, Edith Smith, Pauline Moorcroft, Ruby Anderson.
Middle: Katie Anderson, Maggie Clark, Maggie Irvine.
Front: Lena Mouat, Florence Inkster, Peggy Aitken, Muriel McKenzie-Grieve.
Photographer R Ramsay; courtesy of the Shetland Museum and Archives [SM00063]

Joann B Hawick, MA, PO, of 10 Derby St, Leith, and **Mary Laurenson**, Gorie, Bressay, were also in the WRNS but seem to have served elsewhere.

Women from Shetland also served in the WAAC. **Alexina Nicolson**, of Sellafirth, Yell, was in the Queen Mary's Auxiliary Corps, (re-named from the Women' Army Auxiliary Corps in April 1918) and served in France. Many men suffered from shell-shock, and Nicolson was perhaps affected with something like that too, for, as her great-nephew, Willie Halcrow, told me, after sending a beautiful tinted photograph of herself from France, and saying she'd write once she'd moved to her new address, she didn't communicate with her family again. They thought she had lost her life until 1955, when the local minister received a letter from her asking for a record of her birth, as she was coming up to pension age. The minister told her niece, who got in touch with Alexina. She'd married late on in life, but was now widowed, and living in Bedfordshire. She and her elder sister, Jessie, met up in Aberdeen in 1963, 'but,' Willie said, 'my grandmother never asked her where she'd been, or what had happened.'

Alexina Nicolson in France and (below), in 1963, reunited with her sister Jessie (left) shortly before Jessie's death.
Photographs courtesy of Alexina's great-nephew, Willie Halcrow.

The RAF and WRAF were created simultanously in 1918, and it seemed more acceptable that women should want to learn to fly, as well as doing secretarial and storekeeping tasks. Four Shetland women were in the Women's Royal Air Force. **Charlotte (Lottie) W Robertson**, born in 1897 at Voehead, Weisdale, began as a clerkess with the WAAC, on 29 October 1917, then, when it was formed in April 1918, she transferred to the WRAF at no 1, Fighting School, RAF Turnberry, Ayrshire; her service no. was 6851. After the war she married John Gilbert Williamson, of Bixter.

Her son, Brian, said that his mother rarely spoke about her wartime experiences, but did mention that a plane coming in to land had crashed into the hut where they were stationed. They could look up into the rafters and see the crashed plane! She had also spoken about knowing a Jimmy McCudden who was killed in a plane crash – Major James McCudden was the most decorated pilot in the RAF at the age of only 22: VC, DSO and Bar, MC and Bar and MM. He began flight training in 1916, and was swiftly promoted to Flight Sergeant in 20 Squadron, then to 29 Squadron, Instructor, then, in August 1917, to Flight Commander in 56 Squadron. One of his best known exploits was a dog-fight which downed the German air ace Werner Voss. His final total was 57 'kills'. He died in July 1918 when his plane crashed during take-off.

Lottie Robertson in her WRAF uniform and (below) her certificate of discharge on demobilisation. Photographs courtesy of her son, Brian Williamson.

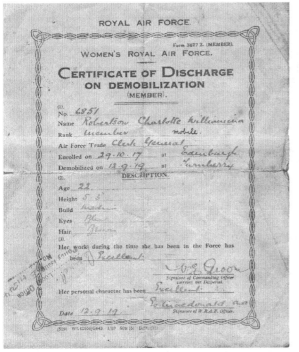

Georgina Josephine Scott [service no 3532], born in Agnesville, Sandness, 1896, then living at 99a Commercial St, signed up to the WRAF on 1 October 1917, and became a Sergeant. She later married Thomas C Spence, Telegraphist. There's a link here with the earliest women on a School Board in Shetland; her great-aunt was Clementina Webster.

Barbara Catherine Henry of Hillhead, Gutcher, North Yell, was a Section Leader in the WRAF. Her father was Davie Henry, the shopkeeper at Gutcher; one of her brothers died in 1916, at the Somme, and another died in 1918, at Cambrai.

Agnes G Tait of Nesthouse, Aith, was also a Section Leader – her discharge certificate adds 'Mobile' She enrolled in August 1918, in Edinburgh, when she was 22, and was demobilized on 15 October 1919 – at that point she was at the RAF Depot, Uxbridge. Her Air Force Trade is given as 'Cook'. There is however a family tradition that before she joined the WRAF she was a nurse in France. She went into service with a Mrs Silver when the war was over, then met and married Harold 'Tiny' Gibbs. They moved to Kenya in the 1920s, where Aggie had an adventurous life, culminating in the MauMau insurgencies, where she slept with a gun under her pillow, in case of night attcks on their cattle. She returned to Aith around 1970, and lived there with her brother and sister until her death in 1981. Her great-niece, Betty Ferrie, remembers a leopard skin draped over the back of her settee: 'She had shot it herself. She was a real character, very adventurous – she'd have been game for anything.'

Aggie Tait in her WRAF uniform, 1918-1919.
Photograph courtesy of her great-grand nephew, John Smith, of Burra.

By the end of the Great War, over a hundred thousand women had enrolled in the official services, and a much greater number had been involved as volunteers. As well as that, huge numbers had kept keeping Britain going while their men were fighting and dying overseas. In the suffrage debate of 19 June 1917, Sir John Simon, MP for Walthamstow, paid them this tribute:

'Nobody to-day can say that the fact of sex has resulted in the women not being able to make a contribution as great, involving as much sacrifice, and producing as much support to the State even as the sacrifices made by men—

HON. MEMBERS No, no!

Sir J. SIMON Even as the sacrifice made by the men! Yes, and for this reason: why is it that everybody's calculation as to the extent to which one of the communities engaged in the War could hold out has been falsified? Those who made these calculations never allowed enough for the extent to which women were able to maintain and support the State in order that the War might go on. I say nothing about the obvious and practical contribution made by mothers and wives—that is a matter which is better left to be thought of than spoken. But the contribution which women have made to support and maintain the working of the State during all these years is a contribution as necessary to the carrying on of the War as the actual contribution of the men at the front. ... You have got now tens of thousands, hundreds of thousands, and even millions, of women who are working in industry who were not so doing before the War began. You have 1,000,000 of them, I think, according to the estimates of the Board of Trade, actually taking the places of men while the men are away. You have another 2,000,000 of them who, although they are not actually taking the places of men, are none the less contributing immensely to some industrial or military effort. ... That is the real reason why the argument from the experience of the War is so strongly reinforcing the whole case for women's suffrage.'

When the Bill reached the Lords, on 10 January 1918, the Archbishop of Canterbury expressed similar admiration:

'I deprecate in the strongest possible way the allegation that those who are in favour of passing these subsections want to do so as a reward to the women for having behaved well in the war; as something that is to be given as a reward to them for being good. It is nothing of the kind. ... It is given to women as a recognition of the part which they are now taking in our national life from top to bottom; not for the part that they have taken in doing women's work—nursing, and the rest—but for the part which in our whole social system, fabric, operations, administration, they are taking to-day, permeated through and through as these things are by the agency and the activity and the effective, daily work of women. I am not speaking of the fact that the women have nursed our wounded men, or that they have done the things which we all knew from the beginning they would do. ... Nobody is surprised at their self-sacrifice, at the outpouring of everything that is highest and best in what the women have done. I venture to think that many are surprised, however, at the way in which women have conducted themselves in entering into the Civil Service work, the industrial work, the educational work, the commercial work, the agricultural work, and so on, all through the kingdom, and are carrying their responsibilities alongside the responsibilities of men, exercising for the public welfare the trust that has been given to them, and, therefore, showing their fitness for and, as I think, showing their claim as a right to have, the further responsibility and trust of exercising the vote.'

Peace celebrations in Lerwick, 30th June 1919.
Photographed by C Coutts, courtesy of Shetland Museum and Archives [SM00218]

13

The vote at last.

War-time campaigning for the vote:

The NUWSS continued to campaign for women's suffrage, holding smaller 'at home' and open-air meetings, which were advertised in *The Common Cause*. The Women's Freedom League still sent speakers round the country, and held rallies in London and Edinburgh in January 1915, after discriminatory measures had been passed - soldiers' and sailors' wives were to be placed under police surveillance, to prevent them from passing on confidential information when drunk. The Northern Men's Federation held an open-air meeting in Edinburgh in May, led by J Wilson McLaren, and another, larger rally there on 18 July, the second anniversary of the men's deputation to Asquith.

Sometimes it felt like women's rights were going backwards. One issue of *The Common Cause* gave an account of the suggestion by the Plymouth Watch Committee of reviving the Contagious Diseases Acts, and recalled Josephine Butler's campaign to have them repealed in the 1870s. [*The Common Cause* 16 October 1914]

The NUWSS still held committee meetings, and the Shetland WSS continued to take an interest in these. A Special Council Meeting was held in Birmingham from 17 to 19 June 1915, and Miss Mitchell offered to ask a friend to attend it as the Shetland delegate. They received a letter from the Brighton & Hove WSS asking this society to support the candidature of their nominees, and decided their delegate would be asked to do this 'provided their views were in agreement with the NU Executive decision of 18 March.' Mrs Lockwood was unable to act for them, but Miss Bury had offered to obtain a proxy. [SWSS Minute Book March 1915] The quarterly meeting of June 1915 went through the preliminary agenda for the NUWSS Council meeting. The Shetland WSS generally supported suggested changes to rules, but went into detail for their delegate of what to support, to vote against and where to abstain. A list of people to vote for on the Executive Committee was also given. [SWSS Minute Book, 3 June 1915]

Numbers attending meetings were falling; nineteen in March, ten in June, and only seven at the next, held nine months later, in March 1916. The Treasurer, Miss Leisk, resigned due to her frequent absences from Lerwick, but was persuaded to retain her office meantime. She had married Hugh MacMichael in November 1915; other wartime marriages were Daisy Campbell and Ethel Allison. Jamieson was away, and Miss J Mitchell was asked to act as Secretary. The funds were very low, because many subs had not been paid in the previous year, and none had been collected this year; it was decided to defer the Federation donation until they had been collected. [SWSS Minute Book, 6 March 1916] At the following meeting, in June, only five members attended. Jamieson was still absent. [SWSS Minute Book, 1 June 1916]

The annual electoral register review had been suspended in 1914, and now few men would be found at their addresses for a full year, meaning the men away fighting for their country would not qualify for a vote. To get over this, and to meet the increasing demand for manhood suffrage, Asquith was considering widening the franchise. In spring 1916, Millicent Garrett Fawcett wrote to him, urging women's claims to the vote, in view of their important role in the war effort. Asquith replied that no legislation was contemplated, but that he appreciated the magnificent contribution by women. However, in August 1916 Asquith gave up his opposition to the vote for women, and an all-party conference of Members of both Houses, presided over by the Speaker of the House of Commons, was appointed to draft proposals on franchise and registration of voters. The death of Kitchener, the battle of the Somme and the 1916 Easter Rising in Ireland all contributed to Asquith's resignation; Lloyd George took over as Prime Minister on 7 December 1916.

A demonstration in Glasgow on 25 June 1915 had called for full adult suffrage for everyone over 21, but MPs were still nervous of how women would vote. They had outnumbered men even before the war, and the continuing casulties increased that imbalance. The proposal when the cross-party conference reported back at the end of January 1917 was to restrict the vote to female householders and the wives of householders over a certain age – 30 or 35. Under pressure from the NUWSS and the WFL, 30 was agreed.

Nine members of the Shetland WSS met at 169 Commercial Street to discuss the new Electoral Bill. Jamieson was still absent. It was agreed that the Society would communicate with Mr Wason, and that the Town and County Councils be asked to repeat their resolutions in favour of Women's Suffrage and forward copies to Mr Wason. [SWSS Minute Book, 1 May 1917] The LTC and ZCC don't seem to have done this – there were very few petitions in 1917. The NUWSS, WFL, Scottish Churches League and Conservative and Unionist Women's Franchise Association got together for a mass meeting on the Mound, in Edinburgh.

DIANA still wasn't in favour:

'...although the women of this country have done their duty, are doing their duty, and will always do their duty, as no one but an entire ignoramus would ever dream they would not, and have taken up work hitherto performed by men, and done it well and in some cases better – still all this does not convert me to the cause of Women's Suffrage. Indeed, it has convinced me more firmly than ever that men's work and women's work are different, and should as far as possible be kept separate. I for one do not wish to see women masculined, if I may use the word, nor men feminised. Each has her and his own sphere, duties and functions to perform to the body politic; to ignore this fact is to go direct in the face of Nature, who, take my word for it, will exact her revenge, remorsely and surely.

When normal times come again, I hope and pray to see fewer and fewer women in the workshop and the factory, and more in the home. As for politics, the less women have to do with them, the better for themselves and the human race.' [SN 26 April 1917]

HAMLET replied two weeks later, speaking more bluntly than the MPs in the House of Commons:

'I would like to ask [Diana] who, especially after this war, is to make the home, and keep the home? The surplus of women over men before the war was something like 2,000,000. After the war this number will be enormously increased; and, alas! besides those who have been killed – the young, strong and brave, the flower of the land – how many will come 'home' mutilated, blind, helpless, a burden to themselves and, sad to say, to those belonging to them. Who is to provide for them, earn money to keep them alive, and get them the comforts and delicacies their condition demands? Who but the women? And how can women do this unless they work, and work at trades and industries hitherto carried on practically exclusively by men. Are the women who have come forward so willingly, eagerly, and in such vast numbers, and aquired skill in many branches of trade and industry to be cast adrift when the war is over? A thousand times No. And if women do not have the vote to enable them to look after themselves, to secure fair treatment, proper conditions, and equitable pay, what will their lot become? Have not men through the franchise, and by means of trade Unions, ameliorated the conditions of labour, and secured for themselves fair renumeration for their work? Without the franchise, they were practically powerless; with it, their voice has been heard. The same thing will happen with women.' [SN 10 May 1917]

The Representation of the People Bill: Clause 4 (Franchises (Women)) was the subject of a seven-hour debate on 19 June 1917, beginning at 4pm and ending close to 11pm. Its main clauses were:

(1) A woman shall be entitled to be registered as a Parliamentary elector for a constituency (other than a university constituency) if she has attained the age of thirty years, and is entitled to be registered as a local government elector in respect of land or premises in that constituency, or is the wife of a husband entitled to be so registered.

(2) A woman shall be entitled to be registered as a Parliamentary elector for a university constituency if she has attained the age of thirty years and would be entitled to be so registered if she were a man.

279

(3) A woman shall be entitled to be registered as a local government elector for any local government electoral area where she would be entitled to be so registered if she were a man: Provided that a husband and wife shall not both be qualified as local government electors in respect of the same property.

Immediately there were several amendments suggested, and the Speaker gave the order in which they would be discussed. The first, which the Speaker did not permit, citing an 1893 ruling, was that it should go to a referendum, and there was some discussion of this. After that, F Banbury suggested omitting 1 and 2, that is, allowing only women of separate property to vote in local, but not Parliamentary, elections. His speech introduced the arguments which were developed during the debate:

'... it must be remembered that in 1912 and 1913 the House decided that it was not advisable to admit women to the franchise. ... We had been recently returned ... and we were in full possession of all the powers that the electorate had given us. In that position, and after two Debates in two consecutive years, we came to the conclusion that it was not advisable to give the vote to women. ... how much more am I entitled, with regard to a House which ought to have died eighteen months ago, and which has prolonged its life upon its own intitiative with the sole object of carrying on the War, to say that it has neither any mandate nor any fitness for introducing a revolution of this character?

The next question we ought to consider is whether women are fit for the vote. ...While it is indisputable that women have rendered valuable service during the War, there is no ground for assuming that women who want the vote and the women who have done the work are the same. The women who want the vote wanted it before the War, and they want it on grounds apart from the War ... they are exploiting women's service during the War as a means to attain the object which they desired to attain before the War. There has been no Referendum taken and it has been impossible to ascertain how many women are in favour of the vote and how many are against it, but I do not think there can be any doubt that there are a large number of women engaged on war work who do not want the vote, and I would like to ask whether the anti-suffragists are to find, as a penalty for their patriotism, that it is made the very ground on which the revolutionary change which they do not want is to be thrust upon them?

This, to my mind, is the most inappropriate time that could have been chosen for bringing forward this particular matter. It has been stated that women require the vote in order to prepare for the change of circumstances which will take place after the War, and that without the vote they will not be able to exercise that influence which they are entitled to exercise on their own behalf. The vote, in my humble opinion and in the opinion of a much greater than myself, is not a reward to be given because somebody has done something which is meritorious. It should be given because the people to whom it is given have shown that they are fit and capable to exercise the duty which is thrust upon them— that is to say, that they are fit and capable of using the-vote, not in their own personal interests, but in the interests of the country as a whole.

... the right hon. and learned Gentleman the present Attorney-General... has told us that so far from women having suffered from the fact that they did not have the vote, or have not been able to pass laws for themselves, they are in a far better position through that very fact than they would have been if they had held the franchise and had been able to pass laws for themselves. ... women do not suffer from the fact that they have not got the vote, and that, as a matter of experience, it is clear that they gain every advantage by the position in which they now are. No one can deny that women exercise a very great influence over their relations, and it is not at all certain that, if they had the vote, there might not be difficulties between them which do not occur at the present moment.

It is perfectly certain that, if my Amendment is defeated, we are not going to stop here. The mere giving of the vote to women carries with it a great deal more than the right to go to the poll or the election booth and place a cross against the name of a certain person. [Mr Gladstone] said: The woman's vote carries with it, whether by the same Bill, or by a consequential Bill, the woman's seat in Parliament. That is a question which has always been raised, so far as I remember, in the Debates we have had on this subject ... It is a matter that has to be faced, and it will be extremely difficult for this House to carry on its work if we have in your place, Mr. Whitley, a lady instead of yourself. It is quite clear that once you have women Members of the House, they are not going to stop as Members of the House. They are fit and will be fit to take the place of Mr. Speaker, of the Chairman of Committees, or to take a part in the government of the country. Mr. Gladstone said: A capacity to sit in the House of Commons, logically and practically, draws in its train capacity to fill every office in the State.

...There is another aspect of the matter which deserves serious consideration, especially at the present time. I do not know whether a few years ago hon. Members opposite would have paid much attention to it, but now, when everybody in this House and in the country is a supporter of the Empire, what I am going to say deserves consideration. We have an Empire containing 450,000,000 people, of whom 300,000,000 are Orientals, distrusting government by women. Yet this is a time when the Oriental part of our Empire is behaving as well as any woman in the War—no one has done better—when we choose, to do something which undoubtedly is likely to destroy our influence over our great Empire.

Colonel GREIG That Empire was ruled by Queen Victoria.

Sir F. BANBURY: That is a very different thing from allowing a large number of women to come in and control the whole of the affairs and business of the State. We had one of the greatest Queens in modern history, and perhaps the hon. and gallant Gentleman will allow me to point out that she was not an absolute monarch. She carried on the Government acting on the advice of her Ministers, who were men. It might be, if this Bill were passed, that not only should we have a Queen, but a Queen who would carry on the Government of the country not on the advice of her Ministers who were men, but on the advice of her Ministers, who were women. ... [Quoting Asquith] 'I oppose this on the broad and simple grounds that, in my opinion, as a student of history and of our own public life, experience shows that the natural distinction of sex which admittedly differentiates the functions of men and women in many departments of human activity ought to be recognised, as it always has been recognised, in the sphere of Parliamentary representation.' That was the late Prime Minister in 1912. What on earth has arisen to change the opinions of the right hon. Gentleman? I must admit I had hopes that he would have been here and would have been able to show some grounds why, having given such a considered opinion as that, he has thought it right to change it.

I should like to draw the attention of the Committee to what has happened in America, where there are something like twelve or fourteen States which have women suffrage. Those States returned President Wilson at the last election on the ground that they were against war. The only woman—Miss Rankin, I think her name was—who had taken a seat in Congress in the United States, when a short time ago the question of whether there should be peace or war came up, became hysterical and could not give her vote. [Miss Rankin's] kindness of heart and her sex undoubtedly prevented her from giving a decision upon a question of peace or war. Already in America the women had decided that they did not wish their sons or relations to run the risk of being killed, and that action was confirmed by Miss Rankin ... It might not have been considered so important in 1912 or 1913, when this House rejected on those two occasions a Woman Franchise Bill, but it is certainly very important now, when all our views as to war and the possibility of war have changed, when we know that human nature now is the same as it was a thousand years ago, at any rate in certain parts of Europe, and that we have to face a, hostile and cruel enemy and may have to do it again before many years are over. If that is so, we do not want to put the power into the hands of women, who naturally feel so very intensely and who will be averse from taking very strong action. ... Who was it that prevented Mr. Hughes, I think a year ago, getting conscription? It was the women in Australia. They did exactly the same thing there, and I find on looking at 'Whitaker's Almanack' where Finland is described as having women voters that this is the description: 'There is universal suffrage for both sexes. Women are likewise eligible for election to the Chamber.' The Finnish troops exist only in name.

Before I sit down I should like to say one word, and one word only, upon the very far-reaching results of this change. As the Bill stands, 6,000,000 electors will be added to the register—that is, women. Roughly speaking, somewhere about seven-and-a-half to eight million male electors are now on the register, and about 2,000,000 more will be added, making 10,000,000; while about 6,000,000 women will be added, making a total electorate of 16.000,000, instead of something under 8,000,000 at the present time. That is to say, it will be double, and a very large proportion of the increase will be women. But once you admit that sex is no disqualification, why are you going to stop at six millions of women? You will be obliged ... to admit other women on the same terms as you admit the men. ... you will have added to your present electorate some 14,000,000 people. The electorate, instead of being 8,000,000 will be 22,000,000; of these 22,000,000, 12,000,000 will be women, and they will, therefore, have a majority of one-and-a-half millions of women. These calculations have been made very carefully on the basis of the population before the War. They are not really accurate now, because we have, unfortunately, lost a large number of men in the War, and, consequently, the majority of women would be greater than the figures which I have given indicate. ... It must not be forgotten that if you give women a majority you put the entire destinies of this country into their hands. It may be said quite truly that women and men will not all vote separately. That is quite true, but on the other hand when you come to have a question which is supposed—probably wrongly—to affect the interests of women, the nature of women being, as I said, hysterical and sentimental, the nature of women being —and I believe every man in this Committee will agree with me—that when a woman has once made up her mind you cannot move her, and arguments are of no avail; somebody has told her something, and she has come to a conclusion without investigating it thoroughly, but, having come to that conclusion, nothing can move her—something of that sort will occur, and I think we shall regret the day if the Committee does not accept my Amendment.

Sir F Banbury was supported by Sir C Hobhouse, who quoted and refuted Asquith's reasons for supporting the Bill (as several people mention, he was not in the House at that point, but he is listed among the 'Yes' votes):

Sir C. HOBHOUSE ... [Mr Asquith] has told us ... that while he was going to vote differently from what he has done before, his convictions and opinions remain the same... He grouped his arguments under five heads, the first of which was what he called public expediency. He said, indeed, that his opposition always and solely had been based on political expediency.

... He said that women had worked out their own salvation in this War ... [other members] have poured great scorn upon this argument, because they have said in this House and elsewhere that the courage and tenacity displayed by women during the War have not added a single argument to those which already existed for the grant of women's suffrage. ... The most shallow acquaintance with ancient and modern history will tell us all that there has been no time in the military struggles of this or any other country when women have not displayed great and exceptional qualities on special occasions. ... One [Member] was represented as saying that it was impossible to wage war on a great scale even to repel, not only to defeat, the enemy, without the services which had been rendered by munitioneers, motor car drivers, and Red Cross and Army nurses. Not only do we not wish to deny such a statement as that, but there is no female who has taken her part in France or Italy or Russia who is not able to show some examples, small though they may be, of fortitude and courage. It is said that this is the basis upon which some have changed their opinions. See what the Bill does for these people who have exhibited this courage and endurance and fortitude. The bulk of the people are unquestionably under thirty years of age; therefore if you want to reward them at this particular time in this particular way you ought to alter the Bill fundamentally before you can grant the reward which is fit and proper reward for their endurance. The present Prime Minister, in a statement on this subject before the Bill was introduced, told us that it was an injustice which was ungrateful, and it would be an outrage if the munitioneers were not included in the draft of women's suffrage, and the Home Secretary, who unfortunately is not here now, in supporting him, said that it would be monstrous if the nurses were not brought in. But neither the munitioneers, the Red Cross nurses, or the Army nurses have been brought in. They are suffering what was described as a monstrous outrage, and the whole ground of my right hon. Friend has been cut away by the action of the Bill itself.

There has been no statement on the part of anyone, either inside or outside the House, to show that the women want this reward for services they are doing in the country. They have not asked for any political reward and still less do they ask for this privilege. From what I know of the. methods of my hon. and my right hon. Friends who conducted the suffrage campaign for the last four years, they would not have been remiss in showing and advertising to the public the fact that there was a genuine concensus of opinion demanding the vote, and that that and that alone would satisfy them for rendering services to the country, and that this had animated them in giving that service to the country. There has been no attempt to show that, it would not be possible to show it, if the attempt were made. So the attempt has not been made and you are asked to make a complete change in the constitution of the country, not in accordance with the wish or desires of the people affected by this proposed change.

There is yet another argument we have to deal with. It is proposed to make this reward for past services to the country, but future generations are going to exist when this War is over, and in these new and changed conditions women are to have a vote and, of course, office. Now as to whether all these great changes which are prophesied are going to take place when the War is over, whether all these practices, duties and customs all over the world are to be thrown out and reset in another place. We must also consider the position as regards trades, industry and commerce, which is going after the War to take a new aspect. Surely the consideration is forced upon us to some extent that we are the trustees of the future in this matter, and should consider before we force upon women, before we permit them to accept the new place in industry and commerce. We are forcing upon them a double obligation of motherhood and an artificial complication of industry and politics. Just consider whether they are physically capable of bearing all these burdens, greater burdens than have been put on the strongest man in the country. I have had an opportunity of talking with many different women on the subject, educated, thoughtful women who are giving great care and attention to it. So far as I can ascertain, they are clearly of opinion that it is not possible during the period when women are capable of bearing certain burdens that they should have the additional burden of taking part in Imperial politics or of taking service, and a large part, in the industrial and commercial life of this country. If it were possible that this House could be addressed on a subject of this sort by a non-member, I cannot conceive that there is any subject on which it could be better addressed than by a woman on this particular point. The pains and sufferings which are entailed upon some of them are beyond the imagination of any man to understand and comprehend. I believe in talking plainly on this subject, because it is important. They are subject to the strain of bearing children when men are devoting their years to the study and formation of character and ideals. It will put upon women a physical and mental strain which she is incapable of carrying. That is not only my view, but the considered opinions of others.

I do not wish, on a subject which has been raised during the course of many Debates, to detain the House at undue length, but there is one consideration which it seems to me that has not yet been advanced to the House, and which I think it important should be advanced. You have at the present moment certain statistics which show that both the birth and marriage rate are decreasing. Can you adopt at this time a policy which might mean an immense destruction of the population of the country which it is essential should not only be retained, but increased. ... I ask the House, before they do this, under what I believe to be a totally false conception of what women should be asked to do, that they should ask themselves what will be the effect in the future of greater burdens than they can possibly carry being put upon women.

I am not influenced by the argument I have often heard that women are coming to the point when they will be more numerous than men and will out-vote men, and that men are perhaps depriving them of their full power. That seems to be a fantastical idea which I will not discuss. But there is no social, or physical, or labour question on which you might not be faced with the possibility that the majority of women, combined with a minority of men, will force legislation to which there may be serious and strong objection. Whether that will want a solution I do not know. I see some representatives of the Treasury here at this moment. At the present, for the purposes of taxation, you combine the income of man and wife. The moment that women come in, that particular form of legislation will be swept away. That will be, in our judgment, a most unfortunate proceeding. Go a little further, and deal with labour administration. There are a great number of people who are supporting the change, but they must remember that you will enable women's labour to be utilised by employers against the present existing rule of trade union. I know quite a considerable number of persons who are in favour of the grant of votes to women upon that ground alone. Will that be accepted with equanimity by the great trade unions? The proposal may be quite fair and quite reasonable, but it would be in direct antagonism to the existing rules and regulations of labour. That is one of the difficulties which you will have to face the moment this grant of women suffrage is made.

I have only one other word to say. Those who think with me on this point would much have preferred to put this issue to the House not as a direct negative, as was done in former days. We recognise that there has been a change of opinion in this House, and we recognise that there has been a change of opinion outside this House. Those who are in favour of women suffrage are convinced that the change is so great as to justify them in reversing the verdict which this House gave four years ago. We, on the contrary, believe that this House is much more sensitive upon this point than is opinion outside, that the barometer of public opinion here changes and shifts more quickly than it does outside, and that the change of feeling here has gone far beyond the change of feeling outside. We should have liked to take this question over the heads of a House which is moribund and which renews, not its youth, but its age, and which on the last occasion that it renewed its age—on the very day that it prolonged its existence—brought this stupendous change as a serious proposal before the House. We should have liked to carry the verdict beyond the walls of the House to the people of this country. I should like even, if we are successful in rejecting this Amendment, to carry it from this House to the people of this country, because if a real change has taken place the verdict of the people of the country ought to be recorded upon it. Whether that verdict is in accordance with my views or adverse to them, I should be content to accept their verdict as a final pronouncement on the justice of the case which we have endeavoured to state to the House.'

Lord Cecil, after refuting some of these points, was the first to speak of changes brought about by the war:

'Let us look at it from what, I venture to submit, is the reasonable and businesslike point of view, the aspect of how far the vote will make for the legitimate interests of women and their legitimate claims on public attention. Here, again, I think it reasonable, without pressing the argument ... from the experience of the War too far, to point out in support of the case for women's suffrage that the War has brought into existence great classes of women who, after the War, will have interests affected by legislation independently of their husbands or fathers or other male relations. There have been other classes, and very important classes, of women, even before the War, who were in that sense independent citizens, who were not merely affected through some man; but after the War there will be great numbers of working women who will have a real interest in the industrial and economic policy of the country which they are entitled, not in the right of their sex, which has nothing to do with it, but in right of their interest as being citizens of the country, to have properly represented in Parliament. And while the individual voter has very little authority, and the person considered as an individual can exercise very little influence, classes of voters have, of course, very considerable influence, and classes of working women will undoubtedly have very great influence and very legitimate influence in getting their industrial and economic interests defended.

If you do not give women suffrage, then in Parliamentary discussions in the future on industrial and other questions, with which great bodies of women are concerned, every Member of Parliament would be subject to the bias, which operates sometimes consciously and sometimes unconsciously on the mind of a Member of Parliament, that if he treats badly the female workers who are not his constituents he will not suffer, while if he treats the men badly, or they think he treats them badly, he will suffer a great deal. We want to have the ordinary security given to women engaged in industrial work—the ordinary security that the vote gives, that they shall not be neglected or oppressed by Parliament. Surely that is a reasonable argument. It has nothing really to do with their sex. It has only to do with their occupation and position in life. The vote will only give them influence in this respect. It will not produce any of the fantastic effects that are imagined, but will give them that legitimate political influence that is necessary. I am convinced from that point of view that women's suffrage is a reasonable act of justice. I am convinced that it is an act of policy, because it will satisfy them and remove a very formidable body of discontent. I am convinced that it can have no possible harm. I am encouraged by the simplicity and ease with which the municipal vote has been used by women without any evil effects. Viewing the whole subject together, it seems to me that to give women suffrage—I do not know how many are going to be enfranchised; I will not go into that question now; it will arise later on—is to adopt a conservative measure which is likely to allay discontent, to promote justice, and to maintain the efficiency of representative institutions in Parliament.'

Sir J Simon was also looking beyond the end of the war:

Here are two obvious facts about the industry of this country. On the one hand, whatever may be said as to the necessity of the War or the economy with which it has been conducted, all war creates an immense void which has to be filled up by the effort of industry when the War is over. There never has been such an immense void, such an enormous hole, created which must be filled up by industry as has been created by this tremendous War. Therefore the moment the War is over the whole thought and energy of the community has got to be addressed towards filling up this enormous gap. That is one thing.

The other fact is that having to do that as an additional piece of industrial work, the industrial army, by means of which it has to be done, will, on the one hand, have lost immense numbers of those who would otherwise have been working as men, and, on the other hand, have gained immense numbers of women who have learnt the ways of industry. Consequently, the moment the War is over the industrial problem is going to be, in a greater degree than before, an immediate problem. ... I do not share the newspaper view that merely because a man becomes a Member of Parliament, therefore in every vote he gives and in every choice he makes he is making some wretched calculation as to how it is going to affect him. I do not believe there is any community in the world where more constantly and obviously people deliberately take a line which they know is going to incur some inconvenience to themselves. But whilst that is true, while a man is really conscious that he is under that influence, it is not true in the much commoner case, that a Member of Parliament, in a time of stress—many times every year —whilst persuading himself as honestly as possible that the vote he is giving is in fact based upon a sound reason, is less conscious that there lies at the back of his action, at any rate, a certain spring or influence of conduct which may in reality be the opinions of his constituents. He believes that he is acting from pure logic when he is, in fact, very much influenced—and I do not think altogether wrongly influenced — by considering, 'What are my constituents thinking?' If we are going at the end of the War to have to solve facts, tendencies, and contradictions which are bound to arise in industry, you cannot expect justice to be done to that part of the industrial army which consists of women if you provide every Member of Parliament with an exclusively male electorate. It is asking of human nature something that human nature cannot possibly provide. To my mind these are the two real arguments which even in the midst of this War it is right that we should recognise.

There is this great change in public opinion, and we should make due provision in this Bill for the representation of women in the Parliament which will come after us. Here let me point out—and it is the only other observation I wish to make—for I do not wish to argue the abstract merits of the case—the fact of this change of opinion cannot possibly be gainsaid. We know examples of it in this House of Commons. ... If you examine the great newspapers of the country, with hardly an exception, you see indications of the change. There is no subject on which, undoubtedly, there have been so many conversions, whether willing or unwilling, whether grudgingly or whether accompanied by all the new-found enthusiasm of the proselyte. There is no subject on which so many conversions have been announced in the course of recent history.

...I venture to say that we are not doing wrong in taking the responsibility of this matter—and it is a great responsibility— at the end of this Parliament. ... it is necessary to do this in order that the new Parliament may be constituted on a wider franchise. Further. I do not myself believe that the argument is at all conclusive, or indeed at all powerful, which suggests there is some body of women who are content to leave things as they are. Let me assume that in a given class of voters some are content to leave things as they are, and some are not. You do not, by pointing to that fact, justify your refusal to deal with the grievance of those who are not willing to leave things as they are. The argument involved in this criticism is as old as the hills, and was refuted long ago by Mr. Gladstone. 'It is no use telling me,' he said, 'that there is a great body of agricultural labourers who do not want the vote. It is no use telling me that if you polled the agricultural labourers, some would say they did not care whether they had the vote or not. If it is in the real interests of a community that you should get a means of expression, and cultivate the expression, of the opinion of a section of the community, it is not an argument against it that you can produce some people who are content with things as they are,' It is a complete falsification of the real principle of representative government to say that the only persons whose opinion should ever be asked, the only persons whose representations should ever be focussed, are those who show themselves resigned to things as they are.

The argument for women's suffrage is that you find a very large body of women who feel most keenly on this subject. Ought you not to satisfy, as far as you can, the claim which they make? Certainly you ought to satisfy it, unless it can be shown that to satisfy their claim is to do an injury to the whole body politic. That argument is one which has been advanced time and again in women's suffrage debates in the past before the War, and it has prevailed much more than I think it is likely to prevail to-night. If the true position now is that public opinion has made this great change, then I invite members of the Committee when we vote to-night to follow the example of the Attorney-General and take their courage in both hands about this. ... Whatever the reasons may be, women's suffrage, as we believe, is bound to come, and I am very glad to have the opportunity tonight of a straight vote on that issue.

Ramsay Macdonald gave a long speech in favour of the Bill; Sir J Walton cited the example of Australia, New Zealand and America:

Sir J. WALTON: To get the truly representative system of government in this country which I desire to see established it would be necessary to have adult suffrage, women enjoying votes on the same terms as men. I recently visited Australia and New Zealand, and in both those democratic communities they have adult suffrage. I discussed the question of the result of having given equal rights to women with men to vote in those great communities, and I do not think I met with one single citizen who did not say that the system had worked well. Those of them who had previously opposed the granting of the franchise to women, after the experience they had had of its working, became convinced that there was no longer any ground upon which to raise objection to women having a voice in the government of their country equally with men. This Bill has my support, even though it does not go as far as I should like, because at any rate it is a great step in the right direction. A Bill which will give to 6,000,000 women for the first time a right to have a voice in the making of the laws which they have to obey equally with men and a right to have a voice in the levying of taxation which they have to pay equally with men, is a great constitutional change, a great national act of justice, which I believe is the forerunner eventually of equal political rights for women with men. The right hon. Baronet (Sir F. Banbury) tried to make the Committee believe that the legislative measures passed by men had treated women justly and generously, and afforded them all the protection that they could possibly need. I wonder if he has forgotten that according to the law of this country to-day a man, no matter how much wealth he is possessed of, has the power to leave his widow and children penniless and to will away the whole of his property elsewhere. That is quite contrary to the law of France, where legally a reasonable provision for the family is compulsory.

I do not wish to enter further into details as to the injustices and inequalities which by man-made legislation have for generations been inflicted upon women, because they are too well known. For how long a period did we deny women the right to practise as doctors in this country? What is the position of women to-day in regard to their right to practise as lawyers in this country? America has shown us that women can be most successful in the profession of solicitors. Go through America, and in every city you will find successful women solicitors. I contend that men have not done justice to women in the legislation they have passed in this country. They have not given women equal rights with men; very far from it. It is as a great measure of justice that I support this Bill embodying the whole of the proposals of the Speaker's Conference, even though I disagree with some of the points. I believe that this time of all other times, when we are in the midst of this great War, struggling to maintain the existence of our country and of our Empire, is a unique opportunity for men of all parties to meet together and come to largely agreed proposals to effect great electoral reforms such as those embodied in this Bill. If anyone had told us a few years ago that we should have a Bill of this revolutionary character brought forward as a practically agreed measure, supported by men of all parties, we should have thought it was a vain dream. But it seems to me that without any doubt this Bill will be passed, including this great proposal for the enfranchisement of women.

It has been said that it is an insult to women to say that they are to have the vote as a reward for self-sacrificing service and splendid assistance in this War. I have advocated all my political life equal rights for women with men—political, social, industrial, and otherwise. Some speakers have threatened us with the great danger that in the reconstruction after the War the men workers of the country and the women workers of the country will fall foul of each other, and will be antagonistic. I do not believe that that will happen. I believe we are going to see after the War such an economic reconstruction, such an adjustment between Capital and Labour as we have never seen before. I believe that with wisdom we shall have a more prosperous country as a whole, that we shall have a higher standard of living and comfort amongst the great masses of the people, and I believe that will be brought about not by men and women workers fighting each other politically to get certain industrial rights, one class over the heads of the other, but by co-operation between both men and women workers in order that they may have, not superiority over one another but equal rights and equal payment for the same work, which has not been true where we have had sweated industries. I support this Clause and this Bill believing that it is one of the greatest measures ever brought into this House to stimulate and promote a higher and better standard of life and living throughout the country.'

When the division was taken, 385 MPs voted in favour of the clause enfranchising women, and only 55 against; John Cathcart Wason was, at last, among those in favour.

There was more lobbying as the Bill took its place in the programme of the House of Lords, on 10 January 1918. There, the Earl of Kintore was in the chair, and the first qualification was expanded to:

A woman shall be entitled to be registered as a parliamentary elector for a constituency (other than a university constituency) if she—

    1. (a) has attained the age of thirty years; and

    2. (b) is not subject to any legal incapacity; and

    3. (c) is entitled to be registered as a local government elector in respect of the occupation of land or premises in that constituency, or is the wife of a husband entitled to be so registered.

As in the Commons, the debate was over whether to leave out clauses 1 and 2, retaining only 3.

The debate was opened by the Lord Chancellor (Lord Finlay) giving his view that the clause was

'a mere compromise. There is no principle of any sort or kind underlying it ... the recommendation is not one of a settlement, but that something should be done which will necessarily be but a prelude to further agitation for further change. ...

I wish to make one further observation about this conclusion arrived at by the Conference—namely, that this matter of woman suffrage is quite separate from the rest of the Bill. You may remove it and yet leave a Bill which is complete in itself, and, in my opinion, a very admirable Bill, dealing with the subject of the franchise as it has hitherto always existed in this country. But it is said that though on the framework of the Bill it is clearly separable, you cannot separate it because it would be an insult to women to reject it. ... If Parliament should ultimately say, 'We do not think that the time has arrived for making a change of this kind,' it is only leaving matters as they are. What insult is there? I fail to see it... If the result of the proposed alteration should be disastrous what figure would this Parliament cut at the bar of history if all that it could plead was that it had obeyed the recommendation of the Speaker's Conference arrived at by a narrow majority, on a thin attendance, and in the circumstances to which I have already alluded?

Then he went on to familiar ground:

The first question which naturally occurs to one in approaching this subject is, Do women want the vote? Some of them undoubtedly want it very much indeed. But do the majority of women want it? I confess that I am not at all satisfied that they do. It is impossible, of course, to feel confident, on a point of this kind, as to the opinions of all the women in the United Kingdom, whether there is a majority one way or the other; but the inclination of my opinion would be to say that most women do not want the vote.

... Does the nation want this great change to be made? There is the same paucity of evidence upon that. The nation has not been consulted upon this matter. ... it [is] extremely dangerous to suppose that from resolutions of this kind passed here and there, memorials, and so on, you could get at a genuine knowledge of what is the real feeling of the country upon the subject. ... We do know that the present House of Commons—as has been pointed out in the course of this debate—twice rejected a much more moderate proposal for the enfranchisement of women than that which is embodied in this Bill. So far as the feeling of the country is concerned, judging for oneself, I should say that if there is any strong feeling about it in the minds of the population, it is rather one of being tired of the whole subject.

... It is said, 'Oh, the war has changed everything. Look at women's war work.' My Lords, I admit—no one admits it more ungrudgingly than I do—the splendid work which women have done in this war. That is no new thing. The women of England [sic] have always done their duty in war time. They always will. They have done it in the past, and they will do it in the future, and I cannot see how any one can say that his eyes have at last been opened to the fact that his fellow country-women are patriotic, and will do all they can in times of difficulty. Of course, they will do so. They will do so to the end of time, in any circumstances and under any Constitution. The workers do not ask for the vote as a reward, and I venture to think that the argument should never have been used that the work that has been done entails the consequence that the vote should be conferred upon women.

Then there is this consideration, and it is really a little whimsical. All the hardest part of the work that has been done for the war has been done by women under thirty. The immense majority of munition workers are women who would not be enfranchised by this Bill. It is upon women over thirty and they alone that the Bill proposes to confer the franchise. The proposal is one for a gigantic experiment. It is to put upon the Register six millions of persons who are absolutely new to politics, and whose avocations and manner of life have hitherto precluded them from taking that active share in the discussion of political questions which all men, whatever their avocations, have more or less done. There has been nothing like it before in the history of this country. There is nothing to compare with it in what took place in 1832, in 1867, or in 1885, and indeed I may say there has been nothing like it in the history of the world. Is it not a leap in the dark? Some supporters of the proposal tell us that it will make very little difference. Possibly it may be so in very many cases, but will it be so in all cases? Is this the time, at this crisis in the history of the country, to take a leap in the dark? I think that when dealing with the franchise was first mooted it was contemplated that the General Election on the new Register would be after the war was over; but it is now possible that we may have a General Election before the war is over, but after this Bill has altered the Register so profoundly.

Now, my Lords, what would be the effect of the admission of these six million voters to the Register if that contingency happened? Would not there be a vast amount of material for agitation, by those who are called pacifists, who are in favour of a hurried peace, among the millions of women who without political experience it is proposed to enfranchise by this Bill? They would be suddenly called upon to decide an issue of the most momentous character in the whole history of this country. What effect upon these inexperienced voters might not war weariness produce. By the manner in which this proposal is framed you eliminate the younger and more buoyant elements of womanhood from the function of voting; and in dealing with women over thirty, who alone are to have the vote, is it not necessary to bear in mind what might be on them the possible effect of war weariness—loss of sons, husbands, brothers, and it might be scarcity and privation—I do not speak of privation for themselves, because women are indifferent to privations, but for the children whom they love more than they do their own souls. If so, under the influence of such feelings in which all the better parts of their nature are enlisted, is it not possible that they might be ensnared by pleas for peace, by specious terms which seemed to give something but really gave nothing, by proposals for a peace which really would be no peace at all, a peace which would leave Prussian militarism really unbroken, a peace which, for some temporary ease, would throw away all the advantages for which we have fought and struggled so hard and to obtain which we have made sacrifices so tremendous both in men and in money? My Lords, would these new voters be proof against such appeals in all cases? I hope that the great majority of them would. I think they would be. I have that much faith in my fellow country-women. But can any one say that it is not a tremendous experiment which you are making? It may turn out all right. I hope it will. But if the result of the woman's vote should be a hasty and inconclusive peace, there will be an end of the greatness of this country, and in the near future, I believe, to the continued existence of the British Empire.

... My Lords, women cannot become men. They are something better, and in their own sphere they are supreme. My own belief is that women as voters for the Imperial Parliament are as much out of their sphere as they would be sitting as members of either Chamber of the Legislature. These are the reasons, my Lords, which have led me to the conclusion on this subject which I have indicated to the House.'

The Earl of Selborne pointed out that

'it is a pure delusion to suppose that there is any chance whatever of the House of Commons passing this Bill if votes for women are cut out, any more than they would pass it if the votes for seamen and soldiers were cut out. I suggest to you that if you pass this Amendment, it will be rejected by the House of Commons almost unanimously. ... The cost is this, that in the climax of this war you will split the nation from top to bottom.'

The Additional Parliamentary Secretary of the Admiralty (the Earl of Lytton, brother of Lady Constance) focused on the feelings of his fellow suffragists:

'the feelings ... of those women who, now for a great many years, have been waiting and working—patiently at first, but with ever-increasing impatience in recent years, and I am afraid also even with ever-increasing bitterness—for their admission to the rights of the franchise for the Imperial Parliament. When the Lord Chancellor just now expressed the fear that the women of this country might be more inclined than the men to be influenced by a spirit of war-weariness, I could not help feeling how little he really knows them. It is, perhaps, the case that there is no one in this House who really can express the feeling of those who have agitated for years for this reform, but as I have been privileged for many years to work with them, to enjoy their confidence, to share their hopes, their anxieties, and their many disappointments, I would like to say a very few words from that point of view before we go to a Division.

I would remind your Lordships that this is no new question. It may be new to many of your Lordships, but it is one of the oldest of the political controversies in this country. I myself have taken an active part in the political agitation for the obtaining of the suffrage for women for ten years, and even that has only been the very last phase

288

of the movement. In the past history of the agitation there have been many incidents which have given cause for a sense of soreness, or grievance a feeling that women have not received, fair play; and I think your Lordships can hardly realise the effect which would be produced, upon top of these many disappointments in the past, if the Amendment of the noble Earl were accepted, and at this moment and in these circumstances this clause was struck out of the Bill.

Let me try and explain to your Lordships, if I can, the sort of reasons which give rise to this particular feeling of soreness and bitterness. First of all, at the present moment there are only four classes which are specifically, as distinct classes, excluded from our franchise—paupers, lunatics, children, and women. Now the fact alone that women have been up to the moment condemned to remain in that category has in itself created a great feeling of resentment; and I would remind your Lordships that the last of these classes, women, are in a worse position than any of the others. You are going to remove the pauper disqualification in this Bill; of the three classes that remain, there is a hope that lunatics may one day cease to be lunatics; children certainly will cease to be children—provided that they are of the male sex; and it is only in the case of women that, as a class, at all times, in all circumstances, and at all ages, they are definitely excluded, together with paupers and lunatics, from exercising the rights of citizenship and voting for Members of Parliament.

There is another reason why, especially in more recent years, this feeling of resentment has been increased, and that is because the women have found that in their agitation a different standard of evidence, a different standard of opinion, a different standard of action is applied to their agitation from that which is applied in all other political controversies. ... What is the kind of evidence we require, in discussing political matters, before we can make up our mind which way the weight of opinion lies? When so many people have expressed their opinion, and so many have been silent, we take the expression of opinion from organised bodies and compare the expressed organised opinion on the one side with the expressed organised opinion on the other. ... If you take the two parties, composed of men and women who are engaged in this agitation, those in favour and those against, there is no comparison whatever in the number of meetings addressed, and in all the features of political agitation, between the various woman suffrage societies throughout the country and the one National League for Opposing Woman Suffrage.

I wonder whether your Lordships are aware, wherever the opinion of women is organised for any purpose whatever, that without exception these women's organisations have, at one time or another, expressed an opinion and passed a resolution in favour of the enfranchisement of women. Women doctors, women nurses, women teachers, women trade unionists and workers of all kinds, wherever they have been organised have passed resolutions and petitioned Parliament in favour of the suffrage. Can any one produce a single resolution or an expression of opinion from an organised body of women, except that of the National League for Opposing Woman Suffrage (which is composed of men and women), which can compare with that fact? Women do feel, therefore, a certain resentment that, in spite of all this evidence of meetings and resolutions passed in favour of the franchise, and after having adopted every possible known means of political agitation, at the end of it they are told that it does not matter and that there is no evidence before us on which we can form an opinion. That is really adopting a totally different standard from that which is adopted on every other question. There has not been a single political question before Parliament in the last ten years in support of which you could adduce, according to the recognised standard, a greater measure of public support than the question of woman suffrage.

... I want to go a little more into detail as to what actually was done by this Parliament on this question. I was at that time intimately associated with members of the House of Commons who were promoting various Bills on the subject. I worked with them on a Committee, and I remember exactly what was done in respect of these Bills. This Parliament was elected in December, 1910, and ... there came to that Parliament 419 Members pledged to support the cause of woman suffrage. In May, 1911, a Bill was passed by a majority of 310 to 143, but it went no further; just as a previous Bill, in the previous session, was passed by a majority of 324 to 215, and again got no further. It is just the fact that the House of Commons continually passes Resolutions, or passes the Second Reading of Bills, and that they get no further which was an additional grievance to those who thought that they had a right to expect something from the pledges given to them by their Members. It was because the private Bill could in the circumstances get on further that Mr. Asquith gave a pledge that in the next session he would introduce a Reform Bill to which a private Member could move a woman suffrage Amendment. When that Bill came before the House of Commons an Amendment in favour of woman suffrage was ruled out of order by the Speaker, and it was because that Amendment was ruled out of order that the Bill had to be withdrawn, and it was withdrawn because the Government at that time knew that they could not proceed with a Reform Bill unless the House of Commons had an opportunity of expressing its opinion on this matter.

Instead of an opportunity of voting for an Amendment to a Government Bill, the House of Commons was given a further opportunity of discussing a private Member's Bill. I remember very well what the feeling of suffragists at that time was. They were not content with the private Member's Bill which was offered to them as an alternative. They had no interest in the Bill. They actively opposed it outside, and that was the main cause for the aggravated form of militancy which was agitating the country at that time. With suffragists outside against the Bill, with Members inside prejudiced by militancy, it is quite true that the House of Commons rejected the measure. Those were the conditions under which it was done; and I think it is only right that the House should remember, if you are going to base any argument on the fact that the Bill was rejected by the House of Commons before, the circumstances which brought it about.

Let me come to this Bill. Let me remind your Lordships of the Divisions upon it. The House of Commons passed a Resolution calling upon the Government to introduce it by a majority of 341 to 62. When it was introduced, its Second Reading was carried by 329 to 40. This clause, when under discussion in Committee, was carried by 385 to 55; and finally, when the Motion was put 'That Clause 4 stand part of the Bill' only seventeen Members were found to vote against it; and the Third Reading of the Bill was carried without a Division. Is it possible to produce a single Government measure of great importance in recent times which could claim so overwhelming a support of the House of Commons as that? At last, my Lords, those who advocated this measure were beginning to believe that the question was going to be treated seriously, and it is inconceivable that, after Divisions of that magnitude in the House of Commons, this clause should be struck out of the Bill by the action of your Lordships' House, and another disappointment added to the total of those which women have already had to endure.

The moment in which it is suggested that this should be done is in itself an added aggravation of the grievance which has been created, because you will be doing this in connection with a Bill the object of which is to make the representation of the people more adequate, more perfect, more complete, than it has ever yet been; and it will be at a moment when you are extending manhood suffrage to its furthest limit, at a moment when you are saying emphatically that the only qualification which you are going to impose upon anybody for a vote in Parliament will be a residence of six months in a particular district. Is it to be in connection with the discussion of such a Bill that you are to say again that women must remain in the category of lunatics and children? That is what would be the effect of accepting this Amendment. You will be saying that for all time they are to be disqualified. Those who would like to raise the question of the age limit, those who would like to express an opinion on the Amendment to be proposed by Lord Balfour of Burleigh, will all be shut out. This question will be decided finally if this Amendment is carried.

On the last occasion when this subject was before your Lordships' House it was refused by a large majority, but the wonder was, I think, considering the prejudice which was created at that time, that it received so large a measure of support as it did. At that time the women whom you are asked to enfranchise for the first time were represented to you as engaged in a campaign of organised violence. What is the position to-day? The strongest reason, not for giving women the vote, but for giving it to them now, and giving it to them by this Bill, is the fact that they are engaged in national service so widely diffused, so important in character, as has been admitted by many speakers, that you could not hope successfully to carry on this war without them. It is that, my Lords, which has caused this tremendous change of opinion on the question.

The noble Marquess, Lord Lansdowne, said last night, quite truly, that if you make a mistake now by enfranchising women your mistake will be irreparable, but that if you make the mistake of refusing it your mistake may be repaired. Yes, my Lords, but this is the moment for repairing it. That mistake has been constantly made in the past. It was made in this House in May, 1914. I say that this is the moment and that this is the opportunity offered to your Lordships for restoring it, and it is for that reason that we are asking you now to join with the House of Commons in making reparation for the numerous occasions in the past when the mistake to which the noble Marquess referred has been made.'

The debate must have lasted several hours. The division question was whether the words 'a woman' should stand, and this was voted with 134 Content to 71 Not-Content. The Marquis of Zetland was, I'm sorry to say, among the 'Not-Content'.

The final step, the Royal Assent, was given on 6 February 1918. The NUWSS held a public meeting of celebration in London, and the WFL and Glasgow WSS held a joint one in Glasgow. The *Common Cause* of 13 March 1918 had several pages of rejoicing messages from long-standing suffrage workers, including Millicent Fawcett, Miss S E S Mair of the Edinburgh WSS, and Emily Davies.

Dr Inglis had not lived to use the vote she had campaigned for. She became ill with stomach cancer during the war. She and her Field Hospital Unit remained with the 1st Serbian Army until they were re-assigned to Crete on the outbreak of the Russian Revolution, when she embarked for Britain with her nurses. She died on 26 November 1917, the day after her arrival in Newcastle. Her funeral service and burial were in Edinburgh, followed by a memorial service in Westminster Abbey. She was the first woman to receive, posthumously, Serbia's highest medal, the White Eagle with Swords.

The Shetland WSS held their last General Meeting only two days after the Royal Assent, on Saturday 8 February, 1918, in the Rechabite Hall, with Mrs Leisk in the chair. There was a jubilant note in the first item:

'... contributions were being asked from Societies by the NU for the new fund being opened to commemorate this year in which the vote was accorded to women, to be known as the Mrs Fawcett Victory Thanksgiving Fund.'

The Society agreed to donate £3, a third of their remaining funds.

'The future of the Society was the discussed, but as the attendance was small, no decision was come to, beyond that members be asked to continue their subscriptions in order to keep the society together until the NU decided on a definite course of action.' [SWSS Minute Book 8 February 1918]

Not everyone was satisfied, or even clear as to who could now vote. On March 1918, Chrystal Macmillan, the speaker who'd kicked off the second Shetland campaign, wrote a 15-page pamphlet entitled

And Shall **I** Have a Parliamentary Vote?

Being a description of the Qualifications for the Women's Parliamentary and Local Government vote in England and Wales, Ireland and Scotland, with particulars as to how to get on the Register.

The pamphlet cost 3d, and was published by the NUWSS, Evelyn House, 52 Oxford St. In it, the qualified people were set out: male servicemen over 19, male civilians over 21, married women of 30 whose husbands had the vote, unmarried women and widows over 30 who fulfilled the property / tenancy qualification, and lodgers over £5.

There were some anomalies, particularly in the case of unmarried women who lived (as was still frequently the case) with their family. In the Shetland WSS, the older married women would all have qualified through their husbands, as would Alice Leisk, now Mrs MacMichael; she was 32. Neither Daisy Campbell, now Mrs Sandison, nor Ethel Allison, now Mrs Garriock, was yet thirty, so they did not qualify. Both had lost their husbands in the war. Emily Sandison, now Mrs Grant, was also too young.

Christina Jamieson, Jessie Mitchell, Margaret Morrison and Dolly Harrison would only have qualified if living out of the family home, which Jamieson at least was not, or as the owner of property. However, lodgers renting unfurnished rooms for which they provided the furniture did qualify, and some women achieved the vote by buying furniture for their rooms in their parents' house – one suffragist commented, 'A woman has to have a husband or some other piece of furniture to vote.' Harrison was the only one not on the 1919 Voter's Roll; her mother Jessie was listed. Jamieson (voter no 2540) qualified as the tenant of Twagios House, value £30 per annum; neither her mother nor sister had a vote, and her nephew Bertie had only the Parliamentary vote, not the Municipal one. Margaret Morrison of 1 Mounthooly Street was voter no 2624; her sister-in-law Mary, Donald's wife, was voter no 2015. Jessie Mitchell, of Southness, was voter 2615, sandwiched between her brother Alex and her older sister Mary.

The new Act increased Shetland voters by a third, from 4013 to 6091; that was still less than a third of the population.

A number of Women's Suffrage Societies on the mainland did keep going, but the Shetland WSS was disbanded soon afterwards. In the margin at the bottom of the page below the account of the last General Meeting is squeezed in:

Last Meeting Present Mrs J Leisk, Miss J Mitchell, Miss C Jamieson:

£6 - 13 9

Given subsequently to Elsie Inglis Memorial Fund   £3

In my hands £3 -13 - 9 (signed] Christina Jamieson

Overleaf is the last message from the Society's founding spirit:

'The £3-13-9 left in my hands was invested in War Bonds 'till we saw'. I thought it might be spent in placing some memorial of Mrs John Leisk, as an active and public-spirited philanthropic and social worker during all the years she lived in Lerwick. An alternative is to give it to Child Welfare. I believe I added money to make it an even sum - £5 - when investing it.

Christina Jamieson'

REGISTER OF VOTERS FOR THE COUNTY OF ZETLAND 1919   45

Division XXV.			Parish of Lerwick.
Number.	Christian Name, Surname and Address of Elector.	Number.	Christian Name, Surname and Address of Elector.
2505	Henry, Colin M., Water Lane.	2545	Jamieson, Laurence, 20 Church Lane.
2506	Henry, Jemima, Beverley Villa.	2546	Jamieson, Margaret, Raven's Court.
2507	Henry, John, 103 Commercial Street.	2547	Jamieson, Peter, Gardie Court.
2508	Henry, Mary, Heddell's Court.	2548	Johnson, Agnes, 4 Navy Lane.
2509	Herculeson, James, Annslea.	2549	Johnson, Andrew P., 22 Commercial Street.
2510	Herculeson, Margaret A., Annslea.	2550	Johnson, Charles, 16 Chromate Lane.
2511	Hill, Helen, Crooked Lane.	2551	Johnson, David N., 2 Queen's Place.
2512	Hughson, Andrew B., Ross Court.	2552	Johnson, Elizabeth, 10 Chromate Lane.
2513	Hughson, Mary, 14a Commercial Street.	2553	Johnson, Grace, 40 Commercial Street.
2514	Hughson, Mary, Ross Court.	2554	Johnson, Helen, Widows' Homes.
2515	Hunter, Adelaide B. C., Edinburgh.	2555	Johnson, James, 3 Bain's Court.
2516	Hunter, Laurence, 16 Church Lane.	2556	Johnson, James A., 37 Commercial Street.
2517	Hunter, Jane, 5 Stout's Court.	2557	Johnson, Jane, 14 Church Lane.
2518	Hunter, Margaret, 1 Bain's Court.	2558	Johnson, Jessie G., 5 Chromate Lane.
2519	Hunter, Margaret, 16 Church Lane.	2559	Johnson, Joan, Seafield Court.
2520	Hunter, Margaret, 11 Commercial Street.	2560	Johnson, John, 8 Commercial Street.
2521	Hunter, Margaret E., Edinburgh.	2561	Johnson, John, 30 Mounthooly Street.
2522	Hutchison, Andrina, 10 Church Lane.	2562	Johnson, Laurence, Newcastle-on-Tyne.
2523	Hyslop, Jane, Twagios.	2563	Johnson, Martha, 22 Commercial Street.
2524	Hyslop, Simon, Twagios.	2564	Johnston, Jessie R., Lower Leog.
2525	Inkster, Barbara G., 39 Commercial Street.	2565	Johnston, Joan, 2 Queen's Place.
2526	Inkster, Margaret M., 11 Commercial Street.	2566	Johnston, Margaret J., 8 Commercial Street.
2527	Inkster, Walter, 39 Commercial Street.	2567	Johnston, Thomas, Lower Leog.
2528	Irvine, Andrew, Knowe of Leog.	2568	Johnstone, Annie, 37a Commercial Street.
2529	Irvine, Barbara J. M., Glenfarquhar.	2569	Jones, Charles R., 2 Navy Lane.
2530	Irvine, Charles, 4 Navy Lane.	2570	Kay, Lilias, 8 Church Lane.
2531	Irvine, Charles, 29 Hangcliff Lane.	2571	Kirton, Joseph D., Lerwick.
2532	Irvine, Elizabeth, 14a Commercial Street.	2572	Kirton, Mary A. S., Anderson Institute.
2533	Irvine, Helen, 4 Navy Lane.	2573	Kippie, Eliza A., Glenfarquhar.
2534	Irvine, James W., Glenfarquhar.	2574	Laing, Arthur L., King Harald Street.
2535	Isbister, Margaret, 37 Commercial Street.	2575	Laing, Christina, Norna's Court.
2536	Jamieson, Ann, 56 Commercial Street.	2576	Laing, James, 20 Commercial Street.
2537	Jamieson, Andrew B., jun., 5 Commercial Street.	2577	Laurenson, James, 4 Chromate Lane.
2538	Jamieson, Catherine, 3 Gardie Court.	2578	Laurenson, Jessie D. R., Midgarth.
2539	Jamieson, Catherine, Widows' Homes.	2579	Laurenson, John W., Midgarth.
2540	Jamieson, Christina, Twagios.	2580	Laurenson, Laurence, 1 Annsbrae Place.
2541	Jamieson, Helen, Widows' Homes.	2581	Laurenson, Margaret, 5 Chromate Lane.
2542	Jamieson, Helen B., 3 Commercial Street.	2582	Laurenson, Margaret L., 1 Annsbrae Place.
2543	Jamieson, Jane, 10 Church Lane.	2583	Laurenson, Williamina M., 18 Church Lane.
2544	Jamieson, John, 8 Chromate Lane.	2584	Leask, Elizabeth, Glenfarquhar.

Extract from the Voters' Roll, 1919, showing Jamieson's registration, number 2540.

HER FIRST VOTE

© REINTHAL & NEWMAN, PUBS., N.Y.

Her first vote. Posted in March 1919.

Postcard from author's collection.

The next election was to be held on 14 December 1918. Far from the women voters bringing the Conservatives in – although they were the largest percentage of the vote, with 33.3%, and 332 seats - their percentage of the vote had actually decreased from 46% in 1910. Labour, under Willliam Adamson, jumped from 7.1% to 21.5%, with nearly two and a half million voters; the Coalition Liberals, led by Lloyd George, came in third place with 13.4%. H H Asquith's Liberals were in fourth place, with a loss of 200 seats, including Asquith's own constituency of East Fife seat. A Coalition Government was formed, with Lloyd George as Prime Minister.

The Parlimentary Qualification of Women Act allowing women to stand for Parliament had also been rushed through in 1918, and three women stood for Parliament in the 1918 General Election. The first woman to stand in Scotland was Eunice Murray, for Glasgow Bridgeton, as an Independent. Christabel Pankhurst stood for Smethwick as the Women's Party Candidate, with the backing of the Coalition Government, and lost to the Labour candidate by only 775 votes. The first woman elected to Parliament was Constance Markiewicz (sister of Eva Gore-Booth of the Manchester WSS), for the Sinn Fein party; as a matter of Sinn Fein policy, she did not take her seat. The first woman actually to sit in Parliament was Nancy Astor, elected for Plymouth Sutton in November 1919; the first woman in the cabinet was Margaret Bondfield, Labour MP for Northampton, who was appointed Parliamentary Secretary to the Minister of Labour by Ramsay McDonald in 1924. By then there were eight women MPs in Parliament; one, ironically, was the Duchess of Atholl, that same Marchioness of Tullibardine who had spoken out so strongly against women's suffrage. She was elected in 1923 as the Scottish Unionist Party MP for Kinross and Perthshire, and remained an MP until 1938. From 1924 – 1929, she was the Parliamentary Secretary to the Board of Education, the first woman to serve in a Conservative government.

The NUWSS became the National Union of Women for Equal Citizenship, and continued to campaign for the same voting rights as men, equal pay, fairer divorce laws and an end to discrimination in the professions. The first Sex Discrimination Act was passed in 1919, and this meant women could now become barristers, solicitors and magistrates, and could serve on juries. The first woman Justice of the Peace in England was Mrs Ada Summers, Mayor of Stalybridge; she was sworn in on 31 December 1919. Swiftly following her, on 1 January 1920, were six other women; by 1929, every bench had at least one woman on it. The first woman JP in Scotland was Elizabeth Haldane, sister of Asquith's first Secretary for Scotland, Richard Haldane. She was sworn in in 1920. The Act also gave Oxford and Cambridge the right to admit women students. Many colleges in Oxford took up this right in 1920; Cambridge waited until after World War II.

Women over twenty-one were finally awarded the vote on 2 July 1928. Many of the older suffragists were now dead – Elizabeth Garrett Anderson, Barbara Boudichon, Priscilla Bright McLaren, Constance Lytton and Emmeline Pankhurst – but Millicent Garrett Fawcett attended Parliament to see the vote take place, and wrote in her diary,
'It is almost exactly 61 years ago since I heard John Stuart Mill introduce his suffrage amendment to the Reform Bill on May 20th, 1867. So I have had extraordinary good luck in having seen the struggle from the beginning.'

Christina Jamieson's note on a copy of her pamphlet 'A Sketch of the Votes for Women Movement': 'Since this was written, women have won their rights by their great services to their country and to humanity during the war. 1928'
Photograph courtesy of Peter Jamieson.

The story of the women who were left to reinvent their own lives after World War I is an extraordinary one, but it's a tale for another time.

Here are a few surprisingly late 'firsts':

1929: women became 'persons' in their own right, by order of the Privy Council.

1960: the first female county court judge, Elizabeth Lane.

1965: the first female Secretary of State, Barbara Castle, Minister of Transport.

1970: the Equal Pay Act, and the first female under-writers at Lloyds of London Insurance.

1971: women got the vote in Switzerland.

1973: the first women were allowed onto the floor of the London Stock Exchange.

1975: the first British woman rabbi, Jacqueline Tabbick, and the first female political party leader, Margaret Thatcher.

1976: the Domestic violence and Proceedings Act which enabled a women to obtain a court order against her violent husband or partner.

1979: the UK's first woman Prime Minister, Margaret Thatcher.

1981: the first woman Leader of the House of Lords, Baroness Young.

1983: Corpus Christi College, Cambridge, finally admitted women.

1984: Lichenstein was the last country in Europe to give women the vote.

1986: the Sex Discrimination Act (Amendment) enabled women to retire at the same age as men.

1988: Julie Hayward (a canteen cook at a shipyard in Liverpool) was the first women to win a case under the amended Equal Pay Act

1988: the first woman Law Lord, Elizabeth Butler Sloss, when she was appointed an Appeal Court Judge.

1990: for the first time married women were taxed separately from their husbands.

1991: the first female head of MI5, Stella Rimmington.

1992: the first woman Director of Public Prosecutions, Barbara Mills.

1992: first woman speaker in the House of Commons, Betty Boothroyd.

1994: The Church of England ordained its first women priests. As part of the Criminal Justice Act, marital rape was declared illegal in the UK – a century after Elizabeth Wolstone-Elmy tried to find an MP to sponsor a bill against it.

1997: the proportion of women MPs doubled to 18%

2009: the first woman Poet-Laureate, Carol Ann Duffy.

2010: the first woman director to win a BAFTA award, Kathryn Bigelow.

2015: Lesley Simpson will become Shetland's first female Jarl, at the South Mainland Up Helly A.

On 10 October 2009, in Edinburgh, the Peace and Justice commission sponsored the 'Gude Cause' commemorative walk, a procession recalling the women's suffrage march of a century earlier. It was led by two mounted policewomen, in place of Flora Drummond on her white horse, and the bands included a samba band dressed in white shirts and scarlet kilts. The front of the procession represented 'The Past', with women and men in Edwardian costumes; I was there myself, carrying a banner with the dates of the two Shetland suffrage societies. Around me were women from Women's Aid societies from all over Scotland. The centre of the procession was 'The Present', including graduates in their gowns. Finally, there was 'The Future'; the fight for improving women's lives that began back in 1870 is still not ended. So how is the twenty-first century doing? Here are a few examples:

The vote: Women's suffrage is still denied or conditional in Saudi Arabia, Brunei, the Lebanon, Bhutan, the United Arab Emirates (this is to be remedied in 2010) and the Vatican City. [Wikipedia]

Access to professions: Yes, women can now do any job – although some were slower to accept women. The first woman fire fighter was only in 1976, the first woman train-driver in 1983, and the first woman fighter pilot in 1995. However there is still the 'glass ceiling' problem. For example, the teaching profession is overwhelmingly female, but only 26% of head teachers, 30% of Further Education principals, and 21% of University principals are women. [*The EIS equality bulletin, 2009*]

As regards women in religion, here's a letter from a 2009 copy of *The Tablet*:

' ... orthodox Anglicans, such as myself, insist that the Church has been guided by the Holy Spirit in its understanding of Scripture to hold that it has no authority to ordain women to the presbyterate or the episcopate...' In churches we're still singing modern hymns that talk about 'brothers' when the author means sisters too, or 'man' when the author means people; at least the older hymns had a linguistic excuse.

Municipal leaders and representation in Parliament: 19% of leaders of local authorities in the UK are women. 34% of MSPs are women – better than the UK, with 19% of MPs being women, which makes it rank 70th in the world. Top of the women MPs league is Rwanda, with 49%. The UK ranks below Afghanistan, Iraq and China. The UK women MEP rate is slightly better, at 34% - almost at the average 36% of the other 26 EU Member States. [*Sex and Power, Scotland, 2008; Women in Parliament and Government, 2009*]

Equal pay for equal work: The onus is on a woman to prove that her employer is not paying her equally, not on the employer to prove that the law is being complied with. Over her lifetime, the average woman will earn a quarter less than a man in a comparable job – and this isn't because she's spent time off having children. [*Study by Robert Longley. US Government info*]

An end to domestic violence: In many countries, women are still treated as 'male property' and arranged marriages are common. Female genital mutilation has been outlawed in Senegal, but is still practised in Asia, the Middle East and in large areas of Africa. [bbc news online, 'medical notes' 28 December 1998] In India, a 'bride burning' occurs every two hours. [Kristof, Nicholas D. and WuDunn, Sheryl (August 17, 2009). *The Women's Crusade'. The New York Times*]

In this country, 45% of women have experienced some form of domestic violence, sexual assault or stalking; 750,000 children witness domestic violence every year [NASUWT poster] Refuge, Women's Aid and other charities still find it necessary to run a national network of refuges.

An end to sweated labour: Our desire for cheap clothing means that workers in the developing world still have to suffer the conditions and pay that the suffragists of the cotton mills fought against. Many of these are women and children; they're cheaper for employers, and they argue less. The fashionable glass beads on your bag were probably made by young children in India. Luxury goods, like carnations at any time of year, are grown using pesticides which destroy the hands of the women who pick them. Here, 23 cockle-gatherers died in Morecambe Bay in 2004, all illegal workers exploited by 'gang-masters', and there was a recent case involving children doing sweated work.

An end to sexual exploitation: Human trafficking is becoming a growing problem in the UK. Computers have meant that adults interested in abusing children are able to form communities through the web, and can exchange details of vulnerable children here and 'sex tourism' holidays abroad.

Bibliography:

Newspapers:
Zetland Times / Shetland Times 1872 - 1919, archived in the Shetland Museum and Archives; with kind permission of Robert Wishart
Shetland News 1885 - 1919, archived in the Shetland Museum and Archives
The Common Cause, 1915, in the National Library of Scotland, shelfmark P 62
Votes for Women, 1909-1912, in the National Library of Scotland, shelfmark Q 92
All extracts from these are used with the kind permission of the British Library.

Books and Pamphlets:
Abrams, Lynn *Myth and Materiality in a Woman's World*, Manchester University Press, 2005
Adie, Kate *Corsets to Camouflage*, Coronet Books, 2003. A wonderful account of what women have done in wartime.
Atkinson, Diane *Elsie and Mairi go to War*, Arrow Press, 2010
Atkinson, Diane *The Suffragettes in Pictures*, Sutton Publishing for the Museum of London, 1996
Birkbeck, Ysobel *Russian Diaries*, manuscript; she was chief mechanic with Dr Inglis' Serbian unit.
Butler, E M *Paper Boats, an autobiography*, Collins, 1959; she was one of Dr Inglis' nurses on the Russian Front in 1914
Cahill, Audrey Fawcett *Between the Lines: letters and diaries from Elsie Inglis's Russian Unit*, Pentland Press Ltd, Bishop Auckland, Durham, 1999
Clive, Eric M and **Wilson**, John G *The Law of Husband and Wife in Scotland*, The Scottish Universities Law Institute, 1974.
Couper, Susan *The History of the Lerwick Orchestra*
Crawford, Elizabeth *The Women's Suffrage Movement, A reference guide, 1866-1928* A generally encyclopedic guide to people and events
Crofton, Eileen *The Women of Royaumont*, Tuckwell Press, 1997
Davies, Emily *The Higher Education of Women*, 1866, reissued by the Hambledon Press, 1988.
Eastwood, Martin and Jenny *E B Jamieson, Anatomist and Shetlander*, The Shetland Times Ltd 1999
Fawcett, Dame Millicent Garrett *Women's Suffrage – a short history of a great movement*, written at the end of 1911, and reissued by Elibron Classics, 2005
Graham, John J *A Vehement Thirst after Knowledge*, The Shetland Times Ltd 1998
Irvine, James W *Lerwick*, Lerwick Community Council, 1985: a broader history than Thomas Manson's.
Jamieson, Peter *Letters on Shetland*, Moray Press, 1949, gave some details on socialism in Lerwick
King, Elspeth *The Scottish Women's Suffrage Movement*, People's Palace Museum, Glasgow Green: the pamphlet accompanying their 'Right to Vote' exhibition, 1978.
Lawrence, Margot *Shadow of Swords, a biography of Elsie Inglis*, Michael Joseph Ltd, 1971
Leneman, Leah *Elsie Inglis*, NMS Publishing Ltd, 1998
Leneman, Leah *'A Guid Cause' The Women's Suffrage Movement in Scotland*, Aberdeen University Press, 1991. The text-book for anyone in Scotland who wishes to know more about the Suffrage movement in what was then a front-line battleground.
Leneman, Leah *The Scottish Suffragettes*, Nationl Museums of Scotland Publishing Ltd, 2000
Liddington, Jill and **Norris**, Jill *One hand tied behind us*, Virago, 1978: an account of the northern textile workers fight for the suffrage.
Liddington, Jill *Rebel Girls*, Virago, 2006
McDonald, Ian *Vindication! A Postcard History of the Women's Movement*

Manson, Thomas *Lerwick during the Last Half Century (1867 – 1917)* This book was a wonderful source of information on the personalities and social life of Lerwick then, but I wish Mr Manson had paid as much attention to the wives as he did to their husbands. Perhaps that's a comment on the times; the suffrage movement doesn't even get a mention, even though the *Shetland News*, which he edited, was sympathetic to the suffrage cause.

Manson, Thomas *Manson's Shetland Almanac*, 1892 – 1919, in the Shetland Museum and Archives, gives lists of officials, teachers, school boards, parish councils etc for actoss Shetland

Moore, Lindy *Bajanellas and Semilinas: Aberdeen University and the Education of Women, 1860 – 1920*, Aberdeen University Press, 1991.

Raeburn, Antonia *Militant Suffragettes*, New English Library, 1973: An excellently detailed, though rather rose-tinted, account of the militant movement

Reid, Marion Kirkland *A Plea for Woman*, pub William Tait, Edinburgh, 1843; re-issued by Polygon, 1988: a beautifully lucid rebuttal of the then-current ideas of women's capabilities, and an inspiring manifesto of belief in their possibilities.

Robertson, Margaret Stuart *Sons and Daughters of Shetland 1800-1900*, Shetland Publishing Company, Lerwick, 1991

Scott, Wendy *Gardie: a Shetland house and its people*, The Shetland Times Ltd, 2007, gave more information on Miss Cameron Mouat

Shanley, Mary Lyndon *Feminism, Marriage and the Law in Victorian England*, Princeton University Press, 1989. A very clear and detailed exposition of the 'women's laws'.

Essays and Articles:
Cobbe, Frances Power *Criminals, Idiots, Women and Minors*, 1869 (on the internet)
Cobbe, Frances Power *Why Women desire the Franchise*, 1877 (on the internet)
Cobbe, Frances Power *Wife –torture in England*, 1878 (on the internet)
Ellis, Peter Berresford *Sophie Bryant* a two-part feature on her life and work, in *The Irish Democrat*
Holton, Sandra Stanley *Jessie Craigen 'Silk dresses and lavender kid gloves'* in *Women's History Review*, vol 5, no 1, 1996
Leneman, Leah *Scots Lives: Elsie Inglis*, NMS Publishing, Royal Scottish Museum, 1988.
Mill, Harriet Taylor *The Enfranchisement of Women*, 1851 (on the internet)
Mouat, Lena, MBE *With the W.R.N.S. 1914-1918, New Shetlander,* Voar 1974.
Smith, Brian 'Socialism', a paper

Archive Material:
Centenary of the Anderson Education Institute, Lerwick Booklet, Shetland Archives
Draft Minutes of the Bressay, Burra and Quarff School Board Shetland Archives
Jamieson, J P S *Correspondence from J P S Jamieson, Nelson, NZ* Shetland Archives
Lists of Shetland Clergy – bound volume in Shetland Archives
Reid Tait, E S, President of the Society *The Shetland Litery and Scientific Society, An Historical Sketch*, Lerwick 1946, in the Shetland Archives
Shetland Churches: bound volume in Shetland Archives *including*
        The Parish of Lerwick 1701 - 1901 Jas M Crawford
        150th Anniversary of Lerwick Parish Church E J F Clausen TMY Manson
Shetland Wrens D1/43/4, Shetland Archives. An illustrated account of the WRNs in Lerwick.
Stout, Lady Anna Paterson *MS0257, Lady Anna Stout papers* Hocken Collections, Uare Takoa o Hakena, New Zealand – letters of November 1909 from leading suffragettes to Lady Stout

Film footage:

Almost all of the extant footage is brought together in one documentary about the women's suffrage movement, which can be watched on-line at:

`http://www.britishpathe.com/record.php?id=78523`

Individual film extracts cited in the text can be found using the search engine in the National Film Archives.

Websites:

A huge number of websites helped me write this history.

For Shetland folk, my first act was to check Tony Gott's bayanne website, which gave me details of date of birth, marriages, residence (through where children were born), relationships and often other details as well.

`http://www.bayanne.info/Shetland`

Biographies and photographs of almost all the 'south' people in this history are on-line; the spartacus schoolnet website is particularly good for women's history.

`http://www.spartacus.schoolnet.co.uk/`

It was fascinating reading the original debates in Hansard, the Parliamentary archives:

`http://hansard.millbanksystems.com`

A number of museums have their photograph collections on line; the Museum of London and our own Shetland Museum and Archives were particularly helpful.

`http://www.museumoflondon.org.uk/English/Collections/OnlineResources/`

`http://photos.shetland-museum.org.uk/`

In the 'war' section, I used the National Archives

`http://www.nationalarchives.gov.uk/documentsonline`

Index: